Yoruba Women, Work, and Social Change

Yoruba Women, Work, and Social Change

MARJORIE KENISTON McINTOSH

INDIANA UNIVERSITY PRESS
Bloomington and Indianapolis

This book is a publication of

Indiana University Press
601 North Morton Street
Bloomington, IN 47404-3797 USA

http://iupress.indiana.edu

Telephone orders	800-842-6796
Fax orders	812-855-7931
Orders by e-mail	iuporder@indiana.edu

LIBRARY OF CONGRESS CATALOGING-IN-PUBLICATION DATA

McIntosh, Marjorie Keniston.
  Yoruba women, work, and social change / Marjorie Keniston McIntosh.
    p. cm.
  Includes bibliographical references and index.
    ISBN 978-0-253-35279-8 (cloth : alk. paper) — ISBN 978-0-253-22054-7 (pbk.
  : alk. paper) 1. Women, Yoruba—Nigeria—Social conditions—19th century.
  2. Women, Yoruba—Nigeria—Social conditions—20th century. 3. Women,
  Yoruba—Employment—Nigeria—History—19th century. 4. Women, Yoruba—Employment—Nigeria—History—20th century. 5. Nigeria—History—
  19th century. 6. Nigeria—History—1900–1960. I. Title.
    DT515.45.Y67M35 2009
    305.48'896333—dc22   2008037047

1 2 3 4 5 14 13 12 11 10 09

Contents

Preface and Acknowledgments

AS A RELATIVE LATECOMER to the field of Yoruba history, I am greatly indebted to the many scholars in North America and Nigeria who have
welcomed me into their midst. A decade ago I started a two-pronged research
project on African women whose historical experiences illustrate very different
patterns. The first segment of the project, dealing with women in Uganda during the colonial and post-colonial periods, was done jointly with Professor Grace
Bantebya Kyomuhendo of Makerere University in Kampala. Our research and
co-authored book showed that in that land-locked region, which contained no
real towns and limited trade before the colonial era, most women remained at
home, growing food for their families, until the 1970s.[1] For the second study,
I wanted to identify a society in which women were active participants in the
market economy and played important roles in other aspects of community life
during the pre-colonial and colonial periods. Yoruba women quickly emerged
as ideal candidates. Not only were they essential figures in many public arenas,
but their history is unusually well documented. We are able to draw upon an
exceptional array of primary sources extending back into the 1820s as well as a
rich body of secondary studies written by both Nigerian and foreign scholars.

When I began doing research on Yoruba women, I was assisted by many
scholars of Nigeria working in North America. They gave me invaluable bibliographic advice, offered comments about my early presentations, and shared
their own unpublished drafts with me. I wish to thank in particular Professors Sara Berry, Judith Byfield, Toyin Falola, Lisa Lindsay, and Kristin Mann,
and my former colleagues Chidiebere Nwaubani and Adeleke Adeeko. I owe a

special debt to Dr. LaRay Denzer, who read an early draft of parts of this book with great care, offering her unparalleled knowledge of Yoruba women's history and bibliography, as well as a keen editorial eye. While she caught some inaccuracies, any problems that remain are my responsibility. The anonymous readers of the manuscript for Indiana University Press likewise provided helpful comments. Africanists working in this country rendered further aid by introducing me to their colleagues in Nigeria.

My time in Nigeria was extremely rewarding in both personal and professional terms. Despite the profound changes that marked the country's history between 1960 and the early twenty-first century, many features of earlier Yoruba culture were still clearly present when I was there. Most women earn some income from their own economic activities. People frequently use proverbs to explain attitudes and behaviors, even in academic settings, and they delight in introducing visitors to their social occasions, religious services, and music and dancing. Spending time with family and friends is important, with Saturdays often devoted to social gatherings. Fabrics, clothing, beads, and other kinds of jewelry remain important to Yoruba women: those objects are aesthetically pleasing, sometimes have profound symbolic meanings, and demonstrate one's position and good taste. Members of women's associations commonly go as a group to weddings, religious ceremonies, and civic occasions, wearing similar dresses or head ties. Deeply rooted notions of hospitality to guests and respect for grey-haired elders may have contributed to the warmth and generosity with which I was received.

Nigerian academics went out of their way to make information and opportunities available to a visiting scholar. Faculty members and graduate students provided invaluable feedback at the seminar presentations I gave. I would like to thank especially the following people:

At the University of Ibadan: Deputy Vice-Chancellor (Academic) Prof. A. A. B. Agbaje, Prof. (Mrs.) Bolanle Awe, Prof. Omoniyi Adewoye, Prof. (Mrs.) M. Adebisi Sowunmi, Head of the History Department Assoc. Prof. Olutayo Adesina, Dr. Bola Udegbe, and Mrs. Oluwakemi Adesina

At the University of Lagos: Dean of Arts Prof. Ayodeji Olukoju, Dr. Funke Adeboye, and Dr. Eno Ikpe

At Obafemi Awolowo University, Ile Ife: Deputy Vice-Chancellor (Academic) Prof. A. A. Adediran, Head of the History Department Dr. Akin Alao, and Dr. Olukoya Ogen

At Tai Solarin University of Education (TASUED): Vice-Chancellor Prof. Kayode Oyesiku, Mr. Cornelius Oluwarotimi Onanuga, Dr. Mushay Ogundipe, Dr. A. A. Arigbabu, Dr. T. W. Yoloye, Dr. Oyetunde Awoyele, Mr. Temitope Ekundayo, and Mr. Yomi Okunowo (now at the University of Colorado, Boulder).

Use of the wonderfully rich manuscripts preserved in Nigeria was made easier by many knowledgeable archivists and librarians. These include: at the National Archives in Ibadan, Mr. Abraham Yemi, Mr. Adeniji Adeniran, and Mrs. V. O. Aribusola; at the National Archives in Abeokuta, Mr. Ayodele Adebayo; the librarians at the University of Lagos Library, especially the Gandhi Library; the librarians at the Kenneth Dike Library and Mr. Sina Osunlana, Archivist, University of Ibadan; at Hezekiah Oluwasanmi Library, Obafemi Awolowo University, Ile-Ife, Mr. M. O. Afolabi, Librarian, and the Circulation Department staff.

My warmest thanks go to Mrs. Temitope Oladunjoye Ayodokun for her intelligent and experienced archival research assistance and for her friendship. Mrs. Olabowale Olusanya of TASUED helped me with Yoruba cultural issues and texts, and Joseph Osuolale Ayodokun provided assistance with logistics and translations. I am grateful also to the staff of the History Department Libraries at the Universities of Ibadan and Lagos and at Obafemi Awolowo University in Ile-Ife for their help in using students' long papers and theses. I appreciate the printed materials and tour kindly furnished by Mr. Adebola Lawal, Secretary to the Alake of Egbaland, at Afin Ake, Abeokuta. Thanks go to our exchange son in 1986–1987, Dele Dada, for introducing me to Yoruba culture, and to his uncle, Bisi Fakeye, for introducing me to the beauty of Yoruba carving.

Further help was provided by British archivists and librarians at The National Archives (Public Record Office) in Kew, Rhodes House Library in Oxford, the British Library in London, the newspaper branch of the British Library in Colindale, and the University of Birmingham Library. The interlibrary loan department of the University of Colorado Libraries was consistently good-humored and competent in obtaining works that our library does not hold.

Research in Nigeria was supported financially by a Franklin Research Grant from the American Philosophical Society and by a Grant-in-Aid from the Committee on Research and Creative Work at the University of Colorado at Boulder. Work in England was made possible by several Distinguished Professor Research Grants from the University of Colorado.

Dee Mortensen of Indiana University Press expressed interest in this project when it was just beginning to emerge and has remained a loyal backer and helpful advisor throughout its development. I am grateful to Bankole Olayebi of Bookcraft Press in Ibadan for valuable conversations, and I appreciate greatly the willingness of the two presses to work together in the co-publication of this study.

BOULDER, COLORADO

FEBRUARY 2008

Note on Language and Orthography

YORUBA IS A TONAL LANGUAGE, meaning that a given syllable has different meanings depending upon whether it is spoken at a high, medium, or low pitch. In standard Yoruba orthography, accents are placed over vowels to represent those pitches.[1] The pronunciation of vowels (whether long or short) is indicated by means of dots under the letters. The sound "sh" is normally written as "ṣ," except in personal names, which use a plain "s" in modern Yoruba, and the names of places, which customarily use an "sh."

In this book, Yoruba words that have no direct equivalent in English are printed in italics with standard orthography. The meanings of Yoruba terms are explained in the text; words that appear more than once are defined in the glossary.

Abbreviations, Terms, and Explanations

Action Group	A political party led by Obafemi Awolowo that had strong support in Yoruba areas
Aladura	Independent Christian denominations
Ansar-ur-Deen Society	A progressive Muslim group that promoted education and the advancement of women
Archives, Dike Libr.	Archives, Kenneth Dike Library, University of Ibadan
Archives, Gandhi Libr.	Archives, Gandhi Library, University of Lagos
AWU	Abeokuta Women's Union, active in the 1940s and 1950s
bride price	*See* dowry
calabash	A gourd that has been cut in half and dried, used as a bowl or basket
CivRB	Civil Record Book
CMS	Church Missionary Society, an arm of the (Anglican Protestant) Church of England
CMS CA (in references)	Church Missionary Society Archive, Africa Series, University of Birmingham Library, UK. Used through the Adam Matthew microfilm edition
cowries	A type of shell commonly used as money in precolonial Africa
CrimRB	Criminal Record Book
CustC	Customary Court

dowry	A payment of goods, money, and/or sometimes labor service made by a man or his family to the family and woman whom he was arranged to marry
flogging	Beating someone with a stick or whip, as a punishment
hadj	The pilgrimage made by Muslims to Mecca
JudicCo	Judicial Council
MixC	Mixed Court
NAAb	National Archives, Abeokuta branch
NAI	National Archives, Ibadan
NC	Native Court
NCNC	National Council of Nigeria and the Cameroons, a political party led by Dr. Nnamdi Azikiwe
NLR	*Nigerian Law Reports,* 21 vols. covering 1881–1955 (Lagos, Government Printer: 1915–1957)
NNDP	Nigerian National Democratic Party, active in the mid-colonial period
NUT	Nigerian Union of Teachers
NWP	Nigerian Women's Party
OAU	Obafemi Awolowo University, Hezekiah Olu-wasanmi Library, Ile-Ife
PRO	Public Record Office, Kew, UK (part of The National Archives)
RB	Record Book
RH	Rhodes House Library, part of the Bodleian Library, Oxford University
WORDOC	Women's Research and Documentation Center, University of Ibadan
YWCA	Young Women's Christian Association

Money used in Nigeria during the colonial period was based on the British system:

£	Pound sterling = 20 shillings = 240 pence
s.	Shilling = 12 pence
d.	Penny

Some of the notes contain a second reference preceded by the phrase, "For below, see, . . ." The latter reference provides the source for the sentence immediately following the one to which the note is attached.

PART ONE

Introduction

I | Opening

THIS BOOK EXAMINES the lives of Yoruba women in southwestern Nigeria between 1820 and 1960. During that time span, women had ongoing roles in the family and wider community but also carved out new opportunities for themselves amidst the profound social, economic, and political changes that affected their region. The Yoruba, who compose one of the largest and most influential groups in Nigeria, are noted for the economic activity, confidence, and authority of their women. In addition to their responsibilities within the home and sometimes on the farm, women were involved in the market economy.[1] Because most husbands could not provide full support for their wives and children, nearly all adult women brought in some income of their own. Sellers in local markets were generally women, as were some long-distance traders and many weavers, dyers, and potters. During the colonial period, women took advantage of a Western-style education to enter new occupations. A woman's income was her own, to use as she wished: it was not given to her husband or placed into a common household pool. All women bought food and clothing for themselves and their children and contributed to familial and religious ceremonies. Wealthier women were able to pay for the education of their children, assist other members of their kin group, and buy land. A few accumulated large households of relatives and dependents, sometimes including slaves or other unfree workers.

Women were essential to other aspects of community life as well. Many of these functions stemmed from the fundamental Yoruba belief that all undertakings needed to include and harmonize the qualities associated with such

*leadership roles by women.
Egbe Association.*

pairings as land and water, natural and supernatural forces, and male and female characteristics. Women therefore had to be included alongside men in almost all practical, spiritual, and cultural activities. Although men controlled the governments of the Yoruba states during the nineteenth century and under British colonial rule, some of the kingdoms had specific offices for female members of the extended royal family. Economically successful, respected women could be granted chieftaincy titles, thereby acquiring recognized authority over other women and sometimes participating in decision making for the whole community. Priestesses and prophetesses were necessary to Yoruba religious practices. Women were directly involved in certain cultural activities, such as singing the praise poems that helped to preserve Yoruba traditions, while some of the genres performed by men honored female powers.

Women gained additional influence through their organizations. In many parts of Yorubaland, they formed socio-economic associations (called *egbé* in Yoruba) based on age, occupation, religion, neighborhood or hometown, cultural interests, or simple friendship. Female *egbé* provided experience in group organization and leadership: they elected their own officials, handled their own finances, and planned their own projects. Associations of women traders regulated local markets and commerce, and *egbé* within Muslim mosques and Christian churches performed economic and social functions in their congregations.

Women's roles in many spheres changed over time. During the nineteenth century, they had to adjust to unsettled political and social conditions. There was no single, unified Yoruba state. Until the 1820s, the dominant power in the area was the Oyo Empire, the last in a series of mighty states that had developed in the West African savannah. The disintegration of that empire led to migration of people toward the south and the formation of new Yoruba cities. Jockeying for wealth and power, some of the city-states attempted to extend their control over their neighbors, leading to sporadic warfare for the rest of the century. Mass movement of people and fighting facilitated the capture and trading of slaves to be exported across the Atlantic or used within Yorubaland itself.

Women were likewise confronted by a cluster of powerful outside influences often summarized as "colonialism" that entered Yorubaland beginning in the nineteenth century. Those forces included international commercial capitalism, the arrival of Christianity and Western education, and the establishment of British political rule. Commerce with Europe and the Western Hemisphere, based upon the Atlantic ports, increased greatly after 1800, joining existing trade that linked the Yoruba area to regions lying to the east and west of it and to the lucrative trans-Saharan trade routes to the north. The Atlantic trade focused initially upon slaves, but as trafficking in human beings ended, it was replaced by "legitimate" commerce involving export of palm products, cocoa, and other agricultural goods. In return, the British shipped manufactured items into the country. Participation in this form of international capitalism brought many Yoruba women and men into contact with Western forms of economic activity and new attitudes toward wealth and people.

Traditional religion came under attack as the "world religions" were introduced into Yorubaland. Islam spread down from the north, especially after around 1820, while Christianity moved gradually inland from the Atlantic coast, starting in the western part of Yorubaland in the 1830s and 1840s. The impact of Christianity was magnified because the missionaries quickly set up schools that offered formal education similar to that provided in Europe or North America. Members of the educated, Christian elite that emerged within some of the Yoruba cities possessed a different kind of authority than that enjoyed by traditional kings and chiefs.

The British government became increasingly active in Yorubaland after the mid-nineteenth century. Its involvement was spurred on by British merchants, who wanted greater physical security for their trading activity, and by missionaries, who wanted an end to the slave trade. British political/military intervention started with the bombardment of Lagos, the leading port, in 1851, followed 10 years later by the annexation of Lagos as a British colony. During subsequent decades, the British slowly expanded their control over the various Yoruba states through a combination of military force and political/economic negotiation. The last major treaty was signed in 1893. Lagos remained a Crown Colony, giving its residents the rights of British citizens, while most of Yorubaland was included in the Western Region of the new Protectorate of Southern Nigeria established in 1900. (See Map 1.1.)

The colonial era brought further change to Yorubaland. After Southern and Northern Nigeria were amalgamated into a single unit in 1914, the British implemented a full system of administration and law. Based upon the form of "indirect rule" developed in Northern Nigeria, colonial officials delegated authority to local rulers (kings and chiefs), provided that they complied with British wishes about certain issues. During the twentieth century, the British introduced new courts and unfamiliar laws, affecting economic and social patterns such as slavery and marriage. Colonial officials intensified the production of cash crops for export and the distribution of imported factory-made goods. Christianity and Islam continued to expand, but traditional Yoruba religious and cultural forms maintained much of their vitality. The growth of Western-style education for girls as well as boys created new ways for women to earn money and serve their communities. Women were largely excluded from the colonial administration, and they were not included among the power brokers of the political parties that emerged in Nigeria as the country neared Independence in 1960. Although women devised forceful ways of expressing their opinions about government policies, they could not ensure that their recommendations would be implemented.

This book analyzes how and why women's activities and status changed across the nineteenth century and colonial era. It emphasizes the connections between their duties within the household, their income-generating work, and their responsibilities in religious, cultural, social, and political contexts. Although those roles shifted somewhat over time, women's participation in each aspect of family and community life reinforced their involvement in the others. The study argues further that Yoruba women's adaptability, initiative, and skill at working in groups enabled them to gain substantial public visibility and influence.

We will explore in addition three broader issues that have been debated by scholars within the Yoruba context and in other colonial regions and periods. These analytic or interpretive questions are closely related. The first set concerns gender definitions and the nature and extent of patriarchy, or male dominance. During the pre-colonial period, did the Yoruba see women and men as separate categories with distinctive attributes, and did women face obstacles or constraints that were different from those confronted by men? If male dominance existed, how was it enforced? How did gender definitions and the opportunities available to women change as the result of British attitudes and policies? The

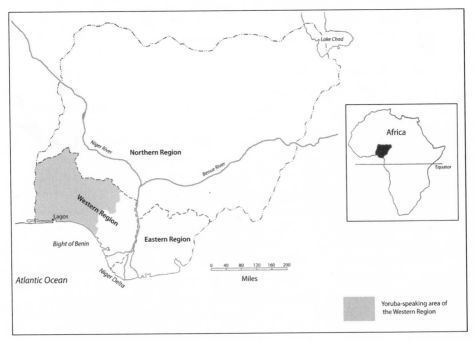

MAP I.I. Colonial Nigeria and Nigeria in Africa

second issue concerns women's place in the interactions between traditional Yoruba patterns and the new ideas and institutions brought by colonialism. In what ways did Yoruba women benefit from colonialism, how were they disadvantaged by it, and where did they subvert or simply ignore unwelcome changes? Most interestingly, how did women combine familiar patterns with new approaches introduced from outside to create novel opportunities for themselves? Lastly, we will look at women's agency (their ability to act independently and exercise control over others) and how it changed over time. Here we focus upon decision making as a rough indicator of agency. In what areas were women able to make decisions about their own lives, either as individuals or as members of groups? Where did they hold positions of authority that gave them the right to make decisions that affected other people's actions?

Before proceeding, we need to delineate the scope of this book: what people, places, and periods will be considered. The Yoruba are defined here as those people who speak any language or dialect within the Yoruba linguistic family.[2] Although most Yoruba people also shared certain religious and cultural practices, economic and social patterns and forms of government varied considerably by region. Even during the colonial period, many Yoruba speakers continued to define themselves primarily as belonging to one of the region's many sub-groups, each of which had its own dialect. (Map 1.2 displays the major Yoruba groupings, plus some of the towns and cities that will be mentioned in subsequent chapters.) A concept of a common Yoruba identity, an umbrella that covered all Yoruba people, evolved only gradually. It was first formulated in the nineteenth century, with the impetus coming from early Christians.[3] A central feature of that identity was the belief that all Yoruba people were descended from Odùduwà, a semi-mythical, semi-historical figure who instituted the Yoruba world. Another common element, found in the oral histories of many states, was that the founder of their community and/or its royal family had come from the town of (Ile-) Ife. A sense of shared Yoruba culture was assisted by the development of a "standard" language that could be understood by all Yoruba speakers, by a method for writing Yoruba, and by the publication of a Yoruba-language Bible and newspapers from 1859 onward.

In geographical terms, Samuel Johnson, an early historian of his own people, defined the Yoruba area rather expansively as lying north of the Atlantic Ocean's Bight of Benin, west of the Niger River below its confluence with the Benue River, south of the western branch of the Niger above the confluence, and east of Dahomey (now the Republic of Benin), Nigeria's western neighbor.[4] This study will be limited to the British Colony of Lagos and the Yoruba-speaking provinces of the colonial Western Region of Nigeria.[5]

Southwestern Nigeria contains four main zones of vegetation, each of which runs roughly west-to-east. (See Map 1.3.) Along the central and eastern

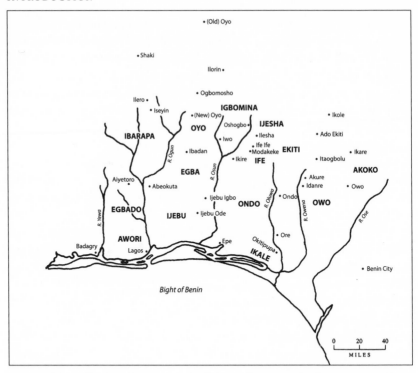

MAP 1.2. Major Yoruba sub-groups in the Western Region with places mentioned in the text

Atlantic coast lies a low area characterized by very high rainfall (70 to 100 inches per year); it is filled with lagoons, salt-water swamps with mangrove trees, and fresh-water swamps. With travel possible only by boat, this area was traditionally used mainly for fishing. The land north of the swamp is wet rainforest whose heavy clay soils were ideally suited to growing palm trees. Farther inland, where the forest is thinner, the land supports agriculture. A third zone, dry rainforest, stretches down to the coast just west of Lagos. A rolling countryside, with some high hills in the east, this zone was conducive to many kinds of agriculture. People and goods could move through both types of rainforest on paths. The fourth zone, which reaches the ocean in the southwestern corner of Yorubaland but lies generally to the north, is savannah. Rainfall gradually decreases as one moves northward, and trees become sparser, replaced eventually by tall grass. The savannah was used for different crops than the forest, and travel through this open country was much easier.

The Yoruba are one of the largest ethnic groups in West Africa. Despite terrible losses to trans-Atlantic slavery (it is estimated that nearly a million Yoruba men, women, and children were carried to the New World between the mid-seventeenth and the mid-nineteenth centuries), the Yoruba at home remained numerous.[6] In 1906, the population of the Colony of Lagos plus the Western

Region, both of which were composed mainly of Yoruba people, was somewhere around three million.[7] In 1952, Lagos plus the Western Region contained just under five million people; in the 1963 census, the Yoruba population of those areas was just over ten million. Smaller groups of Yoruba lived in the Northern Region of Nigeria and in Dahomey. Others had migrated farther afield in West Africa, especially to Ghana, Togo, and the Ivory Coast, and many former Yoruba slaves lived in the western hemisphere, especially Brazil and Cuba.

While it is sometimes convenient to speak about "the Yoruba" as a collective group or about "Yorubaland" as a whole, we must recognize that those terms encompass great contrasts between people and communities. In this study, the various Yoruba sub-groups will be divided into three simple geographic areas.[8] (See Map 1.4.) Central Yorubaland contained the cultural heartland around Ife and Ilesha, forming part of the colonial administrative province of Oyo. Western Yorubaland, which shared many features with the central area, included the colonial provinces of Ibadan, Abeokuta, Ijebu, Colony (Lagos), and the western segment of Oyo. Eastern Yorubaland contained Ondo Province. We will occasionally refer also to Kabba, a mainly Yoruba area that lay just beyond Ondo's northeastern boundary.

Eastern Yorubaland retained many traditional features during the second half of the nineteenth century. With the exception of the numerous and centralized Ekiti people, the eastern Yoruba were divided into small linguistic/ cultural/political communities.[9] The fundamental unit of organization was

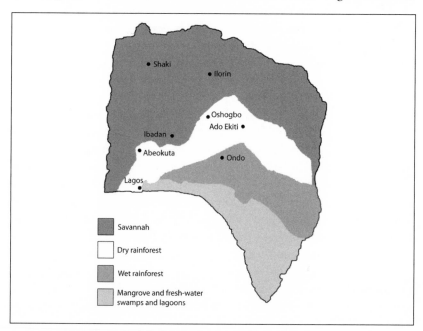

MAP 1.3. Vegetation zones in southwestern Nigeria

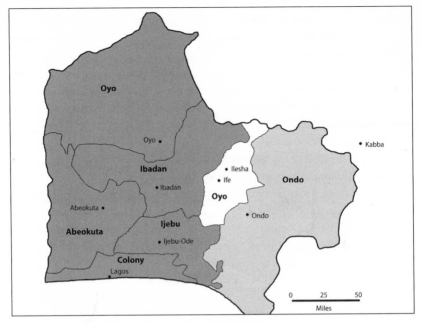

MAP I.4. Western, central, and eastern areas of Yorubaland within the colonial Western Region

the lineage, or extended family; lineages were grouped into villages and small towns. Those were in turn organized into "mini-states," with their own leaders and systems of rule, but kingship was weakly developed and few large cities were present. Agriculture was the main economic activity, with some production of food for the market. Here as in nearly all of Yorubaland, draft animals could not be used, so farming work was done by humans equipped with metal-tipped hoes and knives. Eastern communities engaged in local trade, but relatively few people participated in long-distance commerce, which was made more difficult by the extended area of wet rainforest.

In central and western Yoruba areas, where patterns had probably been similar in earlier periods to those described for the east, massive changes occurred during the course of the nineteenth century. After the collapse of the Oyo Empire, large-scale migration of people, the founding of new city-states, warfare between the larger political units, and active slave raiding led people to move into fortified towns as a protective measure. Western and central Yorubaland was thus much more heavily urbanized than the east from the 1850s onward. It was also more heavily affected by commerce with Europe. The earliest caravan routes going northward from the Atlantic made use of the roads and open paths that led through the savannah and dry rainforest along the western side of Yorubaland. The first Christian missionaries, the schools they founded, and the freed slaves who had accepted Christianity and received Western training before returning to Yorubaland were all concentrated in Lagos, Abeokuta, and Ibadan, cities in the western section. An educated elite therefore arose there first, followed by towns in the central area; comparable developments occurred in eastern communities only during the colonial period. The pioneer Yoruba historians and sociologists who recorded their people's traditions were themselves part of that early elite, and they described patterns found in the western and central region as if they applied to all Yoruba peoples. (When they referred to the eastern Yoruba at all, it was often in derogatory terms, as less civilized.) Because eastern Yorubaland has only recently started to receive detailed attention, largely from historians working in Nigeria itself, modern scholars have similarly tended to over-generalize on the basis of experiences in the better-documented western and central areas.[10] The present study is careful to highlight regional variations in the lives of women.

In chronological terms, our account starts around 1820, when we begin to gain information from narratives by foreign travelers and from retrospective comments by Yoruba people who wrote somewhat later. To demarcate an earlier period when British influence was largely indirect from one marked by formal colonial rule, we will use the convenient though rather arbitrary date of 1893, the treaty with the last of the Yoruba city-states. In practice, however, effective British rule was introduced gradually over time. Lagos and its hinterland felt a colonial presence throughout the second half of the nineteenth century, whereas many parts of the east became aware of British rule only after 1900. The study ends with Nigeria's birth as an independent state in 1960. Because the country moved in new directions during the post-colonial period, marked by civil war, oil production, and periods of military rule, the roles of women after 1960 need to be examined separately, not as a part of this book.

The decision to divide the study into periods defined by British rule is not intended to suggest either that pre-colonial Yoruba society was static, locked into "traditional" patterns prior to 1893, or that it was dominated by foreign influences during the colonial era. Although many Yoruba beliefs and practices were deeply rooted, nineteenth-century Yoruba culture was already familiar with change. During previous centuries the area had been influenced by contacts with its neighbors and by the opening stages of the introduction of Islam, as well as by early dealings with European merchants along the coast. The developments of the nineteenth century and official British colonialism thus constituted only the next steps in a long history of indigenous evolution and interactions with unfamiliar ideas and behaviors.

Nor did outside pressures cause a total transformation of Yoruba society during the later nineteenth century and colonial period. Many aspects of people's cosmology and daily lives continued along pathways that were visible in

[handwritten marginalia: found it difficult b' coz of new long term rel. with customs / profits.]

[handwritten marginalia left margin: change as positive]

1820 and may have existed in similar form well before that time. Although the Yoruba accepted change as a necessary part of life and were open to new beliefs and opportunities, they also had strong religious, cultural, and social values of their own. Their ideology and practices therefore ignored or successfully resisted many foreign influences. Sometimes people accommodated themselves to new demands by conforming externally while maintaining earlier traditions at their core, or they developed alternative patterns that incorporated features of both systems. This book is therefore a study of adaptability and syncretism, not of simple continuity or abrupt change.

The book is organized into four sections. After chapter 2, which talks about the sources that enable us to study Yoruba women's history and the debates that surround our three broader analytic questions, part 2 lays out the context of women's lives. Chapter 3 summarizes major developments in the wider society between 1820 and 1893, and chapter 4 reviews the colonial era. Chapter 5 moves to the domestic context, describing family structures and kin relationships, traditional marriage patterns, and how marriage was affected by Islam, Christianity, colonialism, and divorce.

Part 3 focuses on women's economic activities. Chapter 6 considers the demand for labor and women's roles in providing it (including slaves and pawns), landholding by women, and their contributions to agriculture. Women's income-generating work during the nineteenth century is investigated in chapter 7. The bulk of that chapter looks at trading, particularly the opportunities created by palm products and the careers of some exceptional female merchants; it closes with discussion of women's participation in craftwork and the gendered economic obstacles that confronted women. Chapters 8 and 9 address the colonial period. The first explores how familiar roles (trading, craftwork, and services) developed in new directions, while the second examines how women converted Western skills they had learned at school into money-making ventures and how they entered teaching, nursing, and other educated careers.

Part 4 describes the other arenas in which Yoruba women participated. Chapter 10 looks at their roles within religious practices, forms of cultural expression, and women's *egbé* and similar associations. It shows also how religion and culture could be used to discipline women. Chapter 11 considers women's public authority: as members of royal families and as titled chiefs, in economic organizations, in protests mounted by market traders and elite women, and in the political parties that emerged during the 1940s and 1950s. Chapter 12 returns to the three interpretive issues. It offers a summary assessment of gender, patriarchy, and the restraints faced by women; it highlights the interactions between Yoruba women and the multiple facets of colonialism; and it addresses women's agency as decision makers and authority figures.

2 | Sources and Questions

THE HISTORY OF YORUBA WOMEN is unusually well documented, by both primary sources and secondary studies. Because Yoruba women were so active in their families and communities, researchers have tried to determine what factors contributed to their importance. People concerned with economic development have looked at Yoruba women's past experiences in hopes of identifying strategies that might improve the lives of women in the present and future. The three broader interpretive issues explored in this study have received particular attention. In this chapter we will look first at the primary and secondary materials and then at the debates that surround our central questions.

Primary Sources and Secondary Studies: A Rich Legacy

Scholars interested in Yoruba women are fortunate to have a wide variety of primary sources, defined as those written down or told during the period being studied.[1] The Yoruba have been writing about their society and its traditions since the late nineteenth century, and most Yoruba sub-groups have their own oral histories and chroniclers. Outsiders have also contributed to our knowledge of Yoruba patterns. Travelers and missionaries began recording their observations during the first half of the nineteenth century, joined later by academic researchers. While foreign authors lack the deep understanding of local life and beliefs enjoyed by a member of that society, they have offered different perspectives and raised some new analytical questions.

This book is based upon that rich array of primary sources. For the early and middle nineteenth century, it relies on first-hand accounts by visitors to Yorubaland and freed Yoruba slaves. Some early Yoruba historians, sociologists, and anthropologists who wrote between the 1890s and the 1930s described previous patterns. Newspapers were published in Lagos from the 1860s onward, and the records of the courts founded in Lagos by the British after 1861 provide information about economic and social matters. Oral histories and local chronicles tell us about patterns in eastern Yorubaland, whose histories are less well documented in written form until the twentieth century.

Missionaries working in Yorubaland during the second half of the nineteenth and the early twentieth centuries offered invaluable narratives. The records of the Church Missionary Society (CMS), a wing of the (Anglican Protestant) Church of England, are especially full and well preserved. During the first two generations of conversion, starting in the 1830s and 1840s, many of the CMS missionaries in the western and central parts of Yorubaland were "returnees" (former slaves who had been freed and taken to Sierra Leone, where they converted to Christianity and were given a Western education before coming to Yorubaland to preach the gospel). Returnee missionaries and some local Yoruba missionaries were joined by a few Europeans and North Americans, but until quinine came into regular use as a way of preventing malaria later in the nineteenth century, white people rarely survived in Nigeria. All CMS missionaries were required to submit regular letters and reports to the organization's home office in Britain. Those manuscript materials are augmented by the written and pictorial descriptions they provided for CMS newsletters.

During the colonial period, the primary sources increase in number and variety. British Colonial Office documents in London describe central government policies and debates; abundant information is provided by the archives of colonial administrators on the ground, preserved in Nigerian archives. Newspapers became more numerous in the twentieth century, most still published in Lagos but a few appearing in Ibadan and Abeokuta. Newspapers initially provided insights about issues important to educated and Westernized Yoruba, but the range of social coverage increased from the mid-1940s onward. We also have diaries, letters, and financial accounts of some Yoruba families as well as of British people who worked in Nigeria. Early photographs bring written descriptions to life. Additional material about the twentieth century comes from reports of anthropological and ethnographic fieldwork, some written by Yoruba scholars, most by outsiders. More recent studies based upon oral histories and interviews with elderly people—including some of the Long Essays written by undergraduates doing Honors degrees at Nigerian universities—offer further information.

The native courts had the right to interprete certain Britsh

laws

Particularly valuable for studying the daily lives of ordinary people are the records of the Native Courts set up throughout Nigeria by the British early in the twentieth century. These courts were presided over by local leaders who served as judges, and each had a clerk who made a hand-written record of every case in a bound notebook. Most Native Courts heard both civil cases (private suits between two parties) and criminal cases (where someone had been charged with a public offense by a policeman or other official). The Native Courts had to give precedence to certain British-based laws, and the records prepared by the clerks were written in English, not in Yoruba. Cases heard in them could be appealed to the courts convened by British District Officers or other colonial officials, and from there to the High or Supreme Court that sat in Lagos.

But the Native Courts were founded upon a long indigenous tradition of courts held in the presence of kings and chiefs, and they based most of their decisions upon the customs of their particular community or group. If a case stemmed from a village or town other than the one in which the court met, judgment might be postponed until the chiefs or elders of the other community had been summoned to testify about its traditions. The clerks' notes often include a detailed account of what the parties and witnesses in each case said, what questions were asked by the judges, and what criteria they used in rendering their judgments. Despite the role of the British in overseeing the Native Courts, their records provide glimpses of the lives of unexceptional people who are normally invisible to historians.

In using Native Court materials, we focus upon the narratives presented in the pleadings, not on whatever illegal action brought the matter before the court. Unlike the nominal offense, which may have been atypical, the narratives often tell us about routine aspects of women's experiences that are not recorded elsewhere. Thus, in a case where a man was charged with stealing four large pieces of cloth from a woman selling in Ejinrin market in 1926, her pleading says that she was nursing her baby as darkness fell, but before she had lighted up her stall, when the thief came in.[2] The pleadings in a suit brought by a seamstress in Abeokuta against a female trader in 1907 for possession of a girl who had been pawned to her provide information about the occupations of the two women and the labor and treatment of children.

The abundance of primary materials coupled with the inherent interest of Yoruba patterns and strong pride in Yoruba traditions has led to a huge number of secondary studies. (Secondary studies are written after the time period they describe, based upon primary written and oral sources and/or retrospective interviews.) Yoruba scholars themselves and foreigners working in such fields as history, anthropology, sociology, economics, political science, religion, and cultural studies have contributed to this project. A bibliography of published work about the Yoruba prepared in 1976, which covered all fields of writing but did not claim to be complete, numbered 3,488 items.[3] Hundreds of other books and articles have appeared since then. The Yoruba are one of the most heavily studied ethnic groups in the world.

Though most primary and secondary sources tell us more about men than women, we can nevertheless paint a multi-faceted picture of Yoruba women's lives. Relatively few materials were written by women themselves prior to around 1945, but missionary accounts, local court records, newspaper articles, and secondary studies based upon interviews provide mediated access to them. Female Yoruba scholars in the second half of the twentieth century offered information about the experiences of earlier women in their culture, and some foreigners did careful research about women while living in Nigeria.

Despite the excellent primary materials and the many secondary studies, we have no survey that pulls together information about Yoruba women's lives across the nineteenth century and colonial era. That is the gap filled by this book.[4] In providing an overview, it recognizes the distortions created by the nature of the sources. Most written materials privilege those women who had a Western-style education and participated in the kinds of activities that were documented by literate people. We therefore know more about members of the Christian elite and successful merchants in the major cities than about rural women engaged in domestic tasks and family agriculture, illiterate traders in small towns, and Muslim women. The present study tries to provide more even coverage, thanks in part to material from Native Court pleadings.

Broader Issues and Debates

For scholars, development workers, and Yoruba women seeking to clarify their own identity, knowledge of the historical trajectory is essential. Yet people do not always agree about how the sources should be interpreted or what conclusions the sources suggest about Yoruba women's experiences. Professors and students, members of the public in Nigeria, and Yoruba people now living in other parts of the world are currently debating each of the three broader issues explored in this study: gender and patriarchy, women and colonialism, and female agency. These disputes remind us that history is not just a description of a dead past: it has powerful meanings for people today. In the rest of this chapter we discuss the three clusters of questions that will recur throughout this study, giving the functional definitions to be used, providing some background, and summarizing the views of other scholars. Also introduced here are the arguments that emerge from the detailed evidence that will be presented in subsequent chapters and consolidated in chapter 12.

GENDER AND PATRIARCHY

The first set of analytic questions focuses on gender and patriarchy in Yoruba culture, both before and after colonialism. "Gender" may be defined in simple terms as the differing roles and expectations a given society imposes upon women as opposed to men. "Gender" is contrasted with "sex," which refers to biological or physiological differences. "Patriarchy" or male dominance denotes a system in which men as a group have more power within the society than women, even if some individual women have authority over some men.[5] In this study, we will differentiate between two components of a patriarchal system: (1) an ideology that categorizes women as a distinct (and often inferior) group from men and argues that women should play different and less powerful roles in society; and (2) a set of practices or institutions that serve to limit women's options and create male dominance. Within the Yoruba context, we need to establish first how women and men were perceived and what roles they played during the pre-colonial period. Did the Yoruba have a conception of gender in the nineteenth century, and were women subordinate in their dealings with men? How were those attitudes and practices affected by the introduction of British patriarchal ideology and the practical changes associated with commercial capitalism, Christianity, and the colonial state?

A topic of lively debate at the turn of the twenty-first century, involving both scholars and members of the public, was whether Yoruba ideology perceived two distinct genders, with women seen as secondary to men. Several scholars had raised that question in the 1980s and 1990s, replying in negative terms. Sophie Oluwole stressed that although the Yoruba recognize biological and temperamental differences between men and women, they do not define the sexes as distinct groups with exclusive roles or associate them with moral values (e.g., women are weak or evil).[6] Thus, women are highly regarded as mothers, but a mother may also be respected as a businesswoman and a chief. Jane Guyer commented that "gender in Yoruba culture and history is more a secondary than a primary characteristic. A person is a person first, a member of a kinship-political unit, and thereby a woman is eligible in principle for many activities normally considered male."[7] Niara Sudarkasa concluded an examination of women's position in society, politics, and the economy during the pre-colonial era by saying, "A 'neutral' complementarity, rather than subordindation/superordination, more accurately describes the relationship between certain female and male roles."[8]

The question of gender became the center of attention in 1997 with the publication of Oyeronke Oyewumi's strongly worded book, *The Invention of Women: Making an African Sense of Western Gender Discourses*. Oyewumi, a Yoruba who received her Ph.D. at the University of California at Berkeley in the United States, claimed that Western feminist scholars have incorrectly assumed that all cultures have a category called "woman," based upon a dichotomous biological opposition between male and female, and that women are necessarily subordinate to men. Oyewumi argued that in pre-colonial times, the Oyo Yoruba ranked people primarily according to seniority, based upon age and position within a kinship group. Where people fit within the Yoruba hierarchical system depended upon a series of individual relationships with others, not upon their anatomical differences. In support of this claim, she noted that the Yoruba language is not gender specific (for example, it does not distinguish linguistically between son and daughter or between brother and sister), nor are personal names gender limited. Lists of early Yoruba *Qbas* (paramount rulers), who are normally thought to have been kings, may therefore refer in some cases to queens.[9] After showing that women could participate in all types of activity prior to the colonial presence, Oyewumi traced how the patriarchal assumptions and gendered expectations of the British changed local social and political structures and how those changes removed or lessened the roles formerly played by women.

While many scholars accept Oyewumi's general point that the Yoruba had no fixed gender categories, some aspects of her argument and methodology have been severely criticized.[10] Much of this discussion, which includes other Nigerian-born women, has occurred in on-line journals, sometimes extending into newsgroups devoted to African issues. Bibi Bakare-Yusuf objected in part to what she regarded as Oyewumi's simplistic linguistic emphasis.[11] What happens in everyday practice is not necessarily reflected in the words a given culture uses. Pre-colonial Yoruba society did contain normative female roles, Bakare-Yusuf argued: women were not only responsible for most domestic duties, they were defined as nurturers within the extended family and community too. Likewise, women were at a disadvantage after marriage because they were expected to leave their own family and lineage to live with their husbands. Since status in the kin group depended upon seniority as defined by when one entered the family, women had to start over at the time of their marriage, as opposed to those who were already part of the group. Bakare-Yusuf further questioned Oyewumi's insistence that gender differences were first introduced into Yoruba culture by the British. It is unlikely that colonialism could have relegated women to a subordinate position if existing Yoruba society had not already contained "an unmarked gender ideology." Yoruba culture was sufficiently powerful to maintain many of its features even among slaves carried across the Atlantic, so how could an egalitarian pre-colonial relationship between men and women have been so thoroughly changed by foreign influences operating within Yorubaland itself?[12]

Rejecting Oyewumi's attempt to discover a "pure" Yoruba cultural framework as it existed prior to its contamination by Western ideas about gender, Bakare-Yusuf offered what she felt was a more effective way to think about Yoruba beliefs and approaches both prior to and during colonialism. She argued that Yoruba culture was deeply "polytheistic" in its understanding of all objects, categories, and concepts. Fluid and open to difference, Yoruba beliefs and daily practices contained complex and often competing elements. An absence of clear gender definitions was thus consonant with the multiple positions occupied by individual women as they interacted with others but also with certain forms of male dominance. Bakare-Yusuf's critique of Oyewumi's thesis has in turn been attacked, and the debate will no doubt continue.[13]

This book reinforces the argument that Yoruba did not have a concept of gender similar to that found in Western societies. Sharp boundaries were not drawn between the sexes: conceptions of men and women stressed ambiguity and gender play through synthesizing opposites in creation stories, twinning male and female characters in performances, and having people wear the clothing of the opposite sex in ritual contexts.[14] In Yoruba cosmology, many of the deities lacked a clear identification as male or female. Even the market place, commonly perceived as a female space because women were the dominant sellers, has been described as a representation of the sexual ambivalence and disequilibrium that characterized Yoruba life.[15]

The lack of gender distinctions was implemented in certain aspects of daily practice. Labor roles outside the domestic context were often shared between men and women, and younger men (as well as younger women) were expected to show respect and deference to more senior women within their family and community.[16] In some settings, whether a person was male or female was irrelevant in inheritance of family land and claims to traditional offices. Because a married woman's status was shaped by her own age, occupation, wealth, and the standing of her parental family's descent group, her husband's position was not essential to her position. The husband of a prosperous woman trader who had been granted a female chieftaincy title might be a nonentity in the town.

At the same time, however, the Yoruba did associate certain qualities with women rather than men and assigned certain roles only to women. Women were seen as gentle, patient, cool, and peaceful, as opposed to hot-tempered, confrontational men. While both women and men were expected to marry and become parents, only women were given the jobs of raising children, cooking food for the family, washing clothes, and cleaning the compound. Those gender-specific responsibilities at home limited their ability to pursue other activities, including earning money.[17] Nor were women eligible for all positions in the public community. During the nineteenth century, for example, the rulers of all the kingdoms were male (apart from temporary regencies).

In some periods, women—especially those who had gained an unfamiliar level of wealth and independence—were subject to forms of control that made reference to supernatural powers.[18] Male dominance in practical terms, a form of patriarchy quite different from that found in nineteenth-century Britain, could thus exist even without a gender-based ideology.

Yoruba customs were modified by the Christian, class-based attitudes introduced by the British. During the second half of the nineteenth and the early twentieth centuries, returnee and foreign missionaries, merchants, and colonial officials promoted Victorian ideas about women and the home. In this formulation, one that shaped middle-class patterns in Britain and North America, women were regarded as a category distinct from men.[19] The thinking was that because women were weaker (emotionally as well as physically) and less rational, they needed to be governed by men, both within the family and in the public realm. Women were to remain within the safe confines of their monogamous family homes, supervising domestic tasks, attending to their children, and making the house a pleasant retreat for their husbands at the end of the working day. Men were to be the breadwinners, going out into the harsh and competitive world to earn money to support their families. When the British attempted to impose these gender definitions into Yorubaland, their ideas were viewed with dismay, for they conflicted with a lack of fixed gender definitions and the participation of many Yoruba women in the economy and community. In British eyes, Yoruba women violated appropriate gender expectations, whereas in local eyes, they were merely filling their proper roles.

By the 1930s, and especially after World War II, British gender attitudes in Yorubaland were changing. Men were still viewed as the appropriate decision makers in most economic and political settings. It was male farmers with whom the colonial government expected to work in the production of cash crops, and it was only men who might vote and compete for office in the legislatures. But missionaries and colonial officials were increasingly prepared to accept that many Yoruba women worked outside the home. In some communities women were allowed to sit on local councils. A more flexible definition was due in part to changing ideas about women's roles within Britain itself, and it was affected by British women in the missions and colonial administration who argued on behalf of African women's right to public participation. But the obvious competence of Yoruba women was a powerful factor. The form of male dominance present during the colonial years thus contained elements of traditional Yoruba practices operating alongside evolving British gender expectations and the policies of the colonial state.[20] Though the resulting version of patriarchy restricted women's options in some respects, it also created spaces in which women could create new opportunities for themselves.

WOMEN AND COLONIALISM

Another interpretive issue that runs through this study concerns the inter-actions between Yoruba women and the cluster of outside forces grouped together as colonialism. The main components were inclusion in a system of international commercial capitalism, in which Nigeria was a producer and exporter of raw agricultural goods and a consumer of factory-made imports; Christianity and the social and cultural institutions that accompanied it (which in Yorubaland followed and competed with Islam as well as with traditional religions); Western education; and the political, legal, economic, and social structures of British colonialism itself. Whereas earlier imperial historians commonly explored how colonialism affected the native population, schol-ars increasingly recognize that all exchanges involved two-way and reciprocal negotiations between local people and foreigners. It is not enough to focus simply on how patterns from the "metropole," the center of imperial power, were imposed upon colonial subjects. Patterns of belief and behavior present in indigenous cultures not only responded to but also modified the forces introduced from outside.

Yorubaland offers an especially interesting setting in which to explore such contacts. The Yoruba had a vibrant and deeply rooted set of social, cultural, and religious traditions, many of which continued right through the colonial period, but people were willing to accommodate to change. Yoruba society has never been stable, nor does it expect to be. The Yoruba believe that change is part of life, that the world is always in flux, so social practices must constantly be re-constructed in response to the challenges that confront people.[21] As far back as one can trace, the Yoruba have responded to new forces by altering certain of their own practices while holding on to core values.

An example of the Yoruba ability to synthesize familiar and introduced patterns comes from the reactions of local people to the demand of nine-teenth-century Christian missionaries that men abandon polygamy, a prac-tice widespread in Yorubaland, in favor of monogamous marriages.[22] Some men acceded to this requirement, while others conformed nominally, with a single "church wife" but other wives married in traditional ceremonies. A third group accepted most of the teachings of Christianity but were not persuaded that monogamy was a necessary part of that faith. They therefore created a range of highly popular independent Christian congregations that permitted men to have more than one wife.

A further ingredient of British dealings with the Yoruba was racial assump-tions. In the nineteenth century, racism was relatively muted. Many of the first generation of Christian missionaries were themselves West Africans, and a Yoruba minister was named as Bishop of Western Equatorial Africa by the

CMS in 1864. The educated Lagos elite in the later part of the century included local people and members of other West African families as well as whites. These people might live in the same neighborhoods, and they were members of the same sporting and cultural associations. By the 1930s, however, racist attitudes had intensified. Few British people were now prepared to accept even highly educated, Christian Yoruba men and women as their peers, and segregation in housing and social activities was far more rigid.

Historians are now adding women and gender issues to their analyses of colonialism, trying to overcome the earlier assumption that what mattered in imperial history was how foreign men and their institutions dealt with native men and their concerns. While some studies focus on the role of European women, others are beginning to examine how local women and gendered practices interacted with colonial attitudes and structures.[23] But even the best of the new scholarship has at least implicitly continued to assume that women were *acted upon* as earlier patterns came into contact with outside pressures. Philippa Levine, editor of an important volume of essays on colonialism and gender, commented: "Historians investigating the lives of colonial women thus look simultaneously at the impact of colonization and at customs and laws that predate colonialism, investigating how the former has shaped and changed the latter, and how this might have affected the lives of women."[24]

Within the Yoruba context, although scholars generally agree that women's lives and work were influenced by colonialism, the nature of that impact is hotly disputed. Some analyses have suggested that the changes introduced by the British brought certain economic benefits to women, such as the new opportunities gained through production and sale of palm products and other agricultural export goods.[25] Slavery was gradually ended, and the British terminated the fighting between the Yoruba states, making the movement of people and goods safer. An increasing urban population during the colonial period stimulated market demand for food and other goods, and improved transportation facilitated trade over longer distances. As the popularity of imported manufactured goods increased, foreign firms often relied upon women to act as the bottom layer of the distribution system.

Colonialism had some other positive features too. Looking at the early effects of colonial rule in Lagos, Nina Mba pointed to a few advantages for women, such as the Marriage Ordinance of 1884, which increased women's legal status and improved their rights to marital property in some kinds of marriage.[26] British rules prohibited marriages without the woman's consent. Judith Byfield showed that the unsettled conditions of the late nineteenth and early twentieth centuries enabled some dependent women to challenge their inferior position in Egba society: female as well as male slaves deserted Abeokuta farms, and "significant numbers of women left unsatisfactory marriages."[27] As we shall see, the divorce laws were used by tens of thousands of women who wanted to leave their husbands and marry again. Some women found that a Western education offered new opportunities to gain an income or hold a respected position within colonial schools, hospitals, and later the Civil Service.

But colonialism also brought many problems for Yoruba women. Mba suggested that women had had a stronger sense of gender-based solidarity than men during the nineteenth century, an identity undermined by introduction of colonial divisions based on education, wealth, and in some cases religious affiliation.[28] British policies weakened women's ability to compete in the most lucrative levels of long-distance trade, and women were disadvantaged in gaining access to privately owned land. The new forms of patriarchy were particularly strong in twentieth-century cities, which were permeated with British attitudes, ordinances, and work places. Urban life thus promoted male domination in such areas as altered family and housing patterns, education, and new types of employment. The system of rule imposed by the British limited the consultative role formerly played by people other than kings and male chiefs, thereby excluding women. The colonial legal system, in which British laws operated in parallel to "customary law," expanded the influence of the local men who controlled the Native Courts even though new legislation was in some respects favorable to women's rights.

Oyewumi argued more generally—and with characteristic vigor—against any claim that colonialism conveyed benefits to women. She stated that "The idea that women, or for that matter any category of people among the colonized, benefited from colonial rule does not reflect reality."[29] Insisting that colonialism began to affect the Yoruba with the Atlantic slave trade, not just through political/military conquest in the late nineteenth century, her analysis included multiple considerations: the impact of European patriarchal ideas as embodied within colonial policies; Christianity's denigration of women's roles in traditional Yoruba religious practices; sex discrimination in favor of males in colonial education and waged employment; the commercialization of land and women's exclusion from private ownership; and the legal marginalization of women through the process whereby flexible traditional rules were encoded into legal principles now defined as customary law. She argued that European colonization of Africa featured two intertwined processes: "the racializing and the attendant inferiorization of Africans as the colonized, the natives"; and "the inferiorization of females. These processes were inseparable, and both were embedded in the colonial situation. The process of inferiorizing the native, which was the essence of colonization, was bound up with the process of enthroning male hegemony."[30]

LaRay Denzer's assessment was more balanced, in part because she allowed some agency to women themselves. She noted that "the imposition of colonialism generated complex social interactions—sometimes beneficial, other times diminishing—of women's roles and status."[31] Female leadership proved resilient during the colonial years, with female chiefs, market women, and members of the educated elite joining together to draw attention to women's issues. She concluded, "Yoruba women—versatile, confident, assertive, bold, certain of their rights and abilities—preserved their status in society despite the complex changes set in motion by colonialism."

In this book, although we will discuss the impact of colonialism upon Yoruba women, assessing the areas in which they lost ground as well as some gains, our primary concern is with women as actors: how they themselves responded to the changing world around them, and how they created new opportunities in the interstices between traditional practice and colonial policies. Examples of Yoruba women's initiative abound. In some cases they took advantage of altered structures to improve their own situation. When British demand for palm oil and kernels rose sharply in the nineteenth century, many women who had previously produced those items only to fill their family's needs shifted to production for sale. When the British introduced laws that authorized divorce, women flocked into the courts to end unhappy marriages and legitimize new ones. In other areas, women brought imported patterns into conjunction with indigenous ones to carve out new niches for themselves. Rather than simply accepting or rejecting change, they developed alternative ways of functioning effectively in a modified environment. For instance, women converted the domestic skills they had learned in Western schools, intended to make them better housewives, into methods of earning money for themselves and their families. Women who had been denied the right to hold spiritual offices in their mosque or their Protestant or Catholic church commonly formed religious egbé that gained some say in their congregations; other women joined one of the independent Christian congregations that allowed them to preach. Women used the skills in organization that they had learned through their egbé and associations of market traders to organize mass protests against unpopular economic or political policies of the colonial government. They thus demonstrated in striking ways the adaptability and ability to work within groups that characterized Yoruba society more generally.

WOMEN'S AGENCY AS DECISION MAKERS

Although many observers have characterized Yoruba women as unusually empowered, scholars differ about the nature and extent of that agency and how it changed over time.[32] An emphasis on the exceptional independence enjoyed by Yoruba women was particularly common among Western historians and anthropologists writing during the 1970s and early 1980s. For those authors, eager to identify "liberated" women around the globe, the Yoruba presented a prime example of the ability of women to control their own lives.[33] Many of the accounts that highlighted Yoruba female autonomy stressed the achievements of the exceptionally powerful women who prospered through trade in palm oil, slaves, and imported goods during the middle and later nineteenth century. Some studies extended that positive assessment to a wider geographic and chronological terrain, portraying the later nineteenth and early twentieth centuries as a time of improving opportunities and greater autonomy for women in many parts of the West African coast.[34] With that period as a baseline, the authors then described "the tragedy of African women's economic decline in the twentieth century."

Scholars based in Nigeria similarly contributed to the image of their fellow women as having held considerable authority during the nineteenth century and colonial era. Mba's *Nigerian Women Mobilized: Women's Political Activity in Southern Nigeria, 1900–1965,* published in 1982, suggested that market women and female members of the educated elite wielded considerable influence over colonial political life. Bolanle Awe reinforced the image of independent and highly effective women through the biographies included in her collection, *Nigerian Women in Historical Perspective,* which covered the pre-colonial and colonial periods. Although Awe was well aware that Yoruba women had experienced many disadvantages, her introduction to that 1992 volume did not emphasize that the achievements of the women leaders she described, based upon their "outstanding intellect, courage and industry," were limited to a relatively small number of women.[35]

Some revisionist scholars have suggested that Yoruba women's autonomy and successes have been exaggerated. They objected to the assumption that because most women worked, they enjoyed equal opportunities with men or may legitimately be regarded as "empowered." Stressing instead the constraints found within pre-colonial Yoruba society itself and the patriarchal values institutionalized by the British, they argued that most women were confined to the bottom of the economic system and faced limited options in many other spheres of life. Simi Afonja noted that although men and women shared the tasks involved in physical production (such as working in agriculture), cooperation in the productive sphere did not lead to an equal distribution of benefits (such as the money gained from raising food for sale in the market).[36] Bernard Belasco suggested that apart from a few exceptional nineteenth-century figures, "women were more exploited as traders than exploiting."[37] Customary Yoruba wealth was based on agriculture and war, male pursuits that depended upon the accumulation of dependents to provide labor. Men gained followers by devoting resources to rituals, hospitality, and support of kin and clients, whereas women were themselves normally counted as a form of wealth.

Other work too challenges an unduly rosy picture of Yoruba women's economic opportunities. Kristin Mann's studies of Lagos during the second half of the nineteenth century highlighted the adverse consequences for women of new forms of landholding, the demand for labor, and the changing nature of slavery.[38] Karin Barber showed that the ability of most Yoruba women to develop and retain public status within the community during the pre-colonial and early colonial periods was blocked, due in part to a belief that women, especially older ones, had supernatural powers.[39] Women who gained wealth or authority were suspect: they were perceived as deviant, and their power was seen as destructive. Whereas wealthy and powerful men sought fame, women feared to display their position: "Any reputation was likely to turn into a reputation for witchcraft."

In exploring the nature and extent of Yoruba women's agency, this book will avoid the terms "power" and "empowerment," which lack precise meanings.[40] Instead we will use as a functional measure the ability to make decisions. Our analysis distinguishes between making decisions about one's own life and holding a position of authority that gives one the right to make decisions that affect other people. This study demonstrates that throughout the period under study, decision making was common among Yoruba women who had not been enslaved or pawned. In western and central parts of Yorubaland from the second half of the nineteenth century, most free women were able to exercise individual choice in such matters as how to earn and use their own money and what social and religious organizations to join. Among the eastern Yoruba, women entered more fully into the market economy and began to form egbẹ́ only as the colonial period progressed. Women in all areas were allowed to make decisions concerning younger women and children as they advanced through the system of seniority within families. A few held formal authority through their royal, religious, or cultural positions or their chieftaincies. Although a woman's relatives often played an important role in setting up her marriage, colonial marriage and divorce regulations gave her more voice in creating and dissolving such unions. Women did not gain top leadership positions in the political parties that developed during the 1940s and 1950s, but market women, sometimes joined by members of the educated elite, formed powerful pressure groups around specific issues. Many Yoruba women enjoyed considerable agency, as individuals and members of organizations, during the nineteenth century and colonial era.

PART TWO

The Context of Women's Lives

3 | Yorubaland, 1820–1893

YORUBA WOMEN lived within a practical setting shaped by political, demographic, economic, and social factors and within a cosmological and spiritual setting shaped by strongly held religious and cultural beliefs.[1] Because Yoruba society emphasized family relationships, women's experiences also depended upon the nature of the kin group and household of which they were a part. In this and the next two chapters, we summarize the context of women's lives, looking at general developments in Yorubaland during the nineteenth century and colonial period and at family and marriage.

In many regions of Yorubaland, familiar patterns altered in significant ways between 1820 and the end of the century, due to pressures both from within Yoruba society and from outside. The changes confronted by local people included civil wars between the various Yoruba kingdoms or city-states; migration of people from north to south within Yorubaland; increased urbanization; large-scale slaving, in which people were captured for export across the Atlantic or for use within the region; the beginnings of "legitimate" trade with Europe, particularly in palm products; and the opening stages of British imperial control. Those practical shifts were compounded by the introduction of Islam (from the north) and Christianity/Western education (from the Atlantic coast), both of which challenged familiar Yoruba religious beliefs and many social practices. This chapter presents a general overview of the nineteenth century, tracing indigenous developments and the early stages of contact with the factors that together constituted colonialism. Parts 3 and 4 of this book will discuss how women were affected by those changes and how they devised strategies to function effectively in their altered world.

Any account that stresses the disruptions of the nineteenth century must, however, be qualified in several respects. The strength of Yoruba traditions served to mute or modify some of the forces for change, ensuring considerable continuity in many aspects of life. Our picture is probably distorted by the nature of the sources. Foreign visitors and returnee missionaries—like many modern travelers—noticed and were quick to record behaviors that they found unfamiliar or violent, like warfare and slaving. This problem was magnified because missionaries were committed to demonstrating for an audience of European or North American readers the transformative impact of their faith upon African converts. In addition, the early visitors and Christian workers were concentrated in western and central parts of Yorubaland. They did not recognize that some of the patterns they observed there were recent and perhaps atypical, a response to the specific conditions of that period. For example, they described great Yoruba cities surrounded by defensive walls and the large households of wives accumulated by some of the powerful war chiefs as if they were traditional elements of the culture. Because few nineteenth-century commentators were familiar with eastern Yorubaland, which was far less affected by the pressures felt in other areas, they had no basis for comparison with more stable Yoruba communities. Many Yoruba people's lives were probably troubled only occasionally or to a limited extent by the destabilizing forces that are so well documented in the sources.

Government, War, and Migration

Around 1800, the (Old) Oyo Empire, based in the city of Oyo, governed northern Yorubaland directly and exercised some control over southern areas.[2] (See Map 3.1.) Having been one of the most powerful states in the savannah region of West Africa during the seventeenth and eighteenth centuries, Oyo was at the end of its term, about to disintegrate into civil war. The semi-autonomous local rulers of the groups under Oyo's domination had been required to gather once each year at the capital city of Oyo, bringing tribute and gifts to the king, who was considered semi-divine, and to supply military contingents when demanded. One of the sources of Oyo's power was its location in the open savannah area, which facilitated good communication and trade and made possible the use of cavalry in military expeditions. The city of Oyo itself was "an emporium for the collection of European manufactured goods from the coast, as well as kola, indigo, gourds, calabashes, parrots and other products of the forest belt, and local manufactures which were then exchanged for horses, leather goods, rock salt, and other items from the north."[3]

Early in the nineteenth century, however, the Oyo Empire collapsed. By around 1830, its power was gone. Although the causes are not entirely

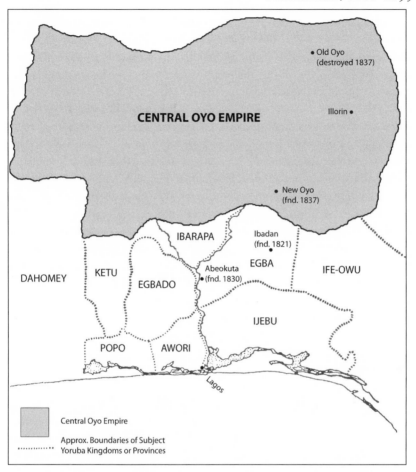

MAP 3.1. Central Oyo Empire and subject Yoruba areas, mid-eighteenth century

understood, they certainly included political and military factors.[4] The increasing power of the war chiefs and other non-royal leaders led to rebellions against the king and to civil wars. The economic potential offered by growing coastal trade with Europeans, including slaving, probably contributed to the difficulty Oyo faced in maintaining its authority over its subject areas. Islam may not have been directly responsible for the empire's collapse, but pressure from the Muslim Fulani armies moving southward into the Oyo area as part of their religious and political war ("the Fulani jihad") weakened its power. The northern Yoruba kingdom of Ilorin had formerly been part of the empire. By 1823, however, Ilorin had been taken over by Muslims and incorporated as an emirate within the new Sokoto Caliphate, whose center lay on the far side of the upper Niger River. Ilorin was henceforth a frontier post for the Islamic state, whose rulers hoped—unsuccessfully, as it turned out—to "dip the Koran into the sea" (i.e., carry the jihad down through Yorubaland to the Atlantic coast).[5]

Because the peace and prosperity of the whole region had depended to a large extent upon Oyo's rule, the empire's implosion had far-reaching consequences.[6] During the rest of the nineteenth century, Yorubaland was divided into a number of independent city-states and smaller "mini-states," each with its own political system. Although most governments included a king and a set of chiefs, the power of the ruler and the importance of hereditary descent among the chiefs varied greatly. Royal authority, the complexity of the palace system, and the inheritability of chieftaincy positions were strongest in the new city of Oyo, built by refugees to the south of the old capital; similar patterns were seen in Ekiti, one of the few large states in the eastern region.[7] A different arrangement obtained in Ijebuland (near the coast) and in much of the eastern part of Yorubaland. In those regions government was less formalized, kings were less powerful, and hereditary restrictions on obtaining a chieftancy title were weaker.[8] Another kind of organization emerged in the young, military states founded in the western region, like Abeokuta and Ibadan. In those places, the government was run initially by various grades of chiefs whose positions were non-hereditary and rested largely on success in warfare. Kings were introduced later, but their authority was never as secure as in the older kingdoms.

Around 1830, the more powerful of the city-states began a long series of wars with each other, trying to acquire some of Oyo's former authority and to gain control over lucrative trade routes. After an initial period of fighting that lasted until 1855, Ibadan emerged as the dominant power.[9] During the next 20 years Ibadan was able to establish its hegemony over much of the previous Oyo Empire. But when it tried in the following decade to defeat the Egba and Ijebu, many of the other Yoruba united against it. Despite a long series of battles, Ibadan failed to take control over the entire region. Peter Lloyd argues that conditions prevailing in Yoruba country inhibited the transformation of what he calls "tribal kingdoms" into highly centralized monarchies.[10] Competition for authority continued to rest upon traditional forms of control over wealth and personal followers: no new systems of government emerged. Those conditions had contributed to the collapse of the Oyo Empire and made it difficult for successor states like Ibadan to establish more extensive rule.

Some parts of western and central Yorubaland were destabilized by the civil wars. Towns were destroyed, agriculture was hindered, and insecurity was heightened by roaming bands of armed men who raided farm hamlets or waylaid travelers in search of people to be sold as slaves. When Yoruba states were at peace, it was not considered appropriate for their citizens to capture one another, "but when war was in the offing, the authorities would announce that the enemy's farms were open for kidnapping."[11] Trade—and the travel upon which it relied—was disrupted by fighting and slave raiding. Because roads through the savannah along the western edge of Yorubaland were sometimes closed by fighting, alternative trade routes were developed, contributing to the growth of commercial centers like Ijebu Ode, Ibadan, and Abeokuta. Some travelers moved to a route that led through more difficult terrain from the eastern end of the Atlantic lagoon northward through Ikaleland to Ondo, Ife, and Ijesha. (See Maps 1.2 and 1.3.)

Yoruba groups living near the coast gained some economic profit from the wars, serving as middlemen between European merchants and local traders farther inland. During periods of fighting, cowries (the principal unit of currency) and salt often became scarce and expensive, which promoted the development of innovative financial and credit methods.[12] In political terms, E. A. Ayandele believed that the wars "exacerbated inter-state bitterness and left behind a legacy of sectional parochialism" that still underlay politics in Yorubaland in the late 1970s.[13] Many eastern Yorubaland kingdoms were brought into more direct contact with the Atlantic and the north as traders shifted to the land route through that region.

To escape the violence of armies and raiders in the northern part of Yorubaland, hundreds of thousands of people moved southward during the first third of the nineteenth century. Prior to 1800, the semi-circle extending 60–70 miles south of the northern Oyo capital was the most densely populated part of Yorubaland, but by 1830 two-thirds of the area had been largely abandoned. As many as a half-million people may have emigrated from the savannah to the forest zones.[14] Many of the refugees joined older Yoruba communities: a chief and his followers would settle a new block of land adjacent to an existing settlement. Other migrants founded entirely new towns. These included (new) Oyo and the militarized cities of Abeokuta (a conglomeration of Egba refugees who had previously lived in 150 dispersed small towns and villages) and Ibadan (which contained people from many different Yoruba sub-groups).[15] That diaspora spread Oyo cultural influence throughout Yorubaland and probably enhanced the growth of a pan-Yoruba consciousness by bringing migrants from diverse areas together. It also helped to spread Islam, through the migration southward of Muslim people.

The generations of chronic warfare and population movement had pronounced—though contradictory—implications for women. When men were away fighting or had been captured, senior women often assumed greater economic and social importance within their families, keeping the household and farm running.[16] They may also have been more influential within the community. Women took some part in the wars, though they rarely fought in battle as did the famous "Amazons" of Dahomey's standing army.[17] In many places,

Yoruba women provided food and water for warriors, made charms for them, and boosted their spirits with inspiring words. The most direct participation occurred in Abeokuta and Ibadan during the 1860s and 1870s. There leading women traders supplied arms and ammunition, provided their own fighting troops (actually leading them into battle on at least one occasion), nursed wounded warriors, and stood by the gates of the city to encourage exhausted men to continue their fight against the enemy.[18] The Ìyálóde (the leading female chief) joined male leaders in formulating policies in those cities.

But women and children usually suffer most severely from the disruptions of civil war and migration, and nineteenth-century Yorubaland was no exception. It was difficult for women to maintain their normal activities and provide for their families. Going to the fields and traveling for trading purposes were dangerous. If a town was defeated, most of its women were commonly taken captive. Female captives might be put on public display and humiliated, and many were sold into slavery. Migrant women were forced to start life anew (though the Yoruba tradition of welcoming dependent strangers and marriage of newly arrived women to local men may have eased this transition). Because many men were killed in battle and military success conveyed high status, some of the war chiefs built up huge households of wives and concubines. Lorand Matory argued that the civil wars contributed to male political, social, and cultural dominance more generally, as displayed in such forms as the cult that venerated Ògún, the deity of iron and war.[19] If a town's military situation stabilized and women's practical support was no longer needed, the influence of the female chiefs generally declined. Likewise, when two of the most prominent Ìyálódes in Abeokuta and Ibadan decided to stop supporting their cities' warlike approach, which they saw as harmful to trade, and instead gave their backing to factions that promoted peace, their authority was weakened.[20]

Towns and Trade

Urbanization within Yorubaland was promoted by physical insecurity and large-scale migration.[21] Already in the eighteenth century and probably earlier still, a town and its surrounding villages had formed the primary unit of organization and administration. Serving as the center of government and the setting for religious festivals, litigation, markets, and craftwork, a town was usually headed by a king, advised by a council of senior chiefs. The larger towns were linked by trade routes that crossed Yorubaland, in north-south and east-west directions. Although we lack solid demographic information, a number of towns probably had populations of 5,000–20,000, with a few, like Old Oyo itself, somewhat larger.

Scholars do not agree about how much that pattern changed during the nineteenth century. William Bascom believed that because large towns existed prior to 1800, they should be considered a traditional and distinctive feature of pre-colonial Yoruba life.[22] J. S. Eades suggested, however, that prior to the nineteenth century, it was only the capitals of the major Yoruba kingdoms that were larger than towns found elsewhere in West Africa.[23] Robin Law proposed an intermediate position: although "urbanism is probably an ancient feature of Yoruba civilization, it is clear that the concentration of the population in large urban settlements was considerably stimulated by the wars of the nineteenth century, which caused people to seek security in large towns."[24] Comparison with eastern Yorubaland—which experienced little fighting during the nineteenth century and where people continued to live in unfortified farm camps, villages, and small towns—suggests that urbanization should not be considered a necessary part of Yoruba society but rather a response to atypical circumstances.[25]

Towns offered obvious benefits during unsettled conditions. The walls of a community, when backed by its military force, provided some degree of security. Even when a town was not actively at war, its residents might be at risk if they moved outside its perimeter. Thus, when Egba migrants settled on the western side of Abeokuta in the early 1830s, bands of raiders from the rival cities of Ibadan and Ijebu overran the newly established farms and kidnapped anyone who ventured beyond the town wall.[26] Archdeacon Graf of the CMS, who visited Ijaye in 1854–1855, described the area's "bloodthirsty" king, who killed his wives and subjects if they were even suspected of any wrongdoing. "Yet thousands prefer being under the protection of such an iron sceptre, to being exposed, as formerly, day by day, at home and abroad, to the marauding kidnappers of former years."[27] Larger towns encouraged the development of powerful urban or regional governments and the trading systems necessary to support them.

Towns were surrounded by close-in and more distant farms. A family whose primary home was in the urban center would send its members out to its farmland to raise crops. Depending on the season, the work to be done, and the distance from the town to the farm, these men and/or women might stay for several days or several weeks at a time. When extra agricultural labor was needed, especially at the harvests, they would be joined by other members of the household. This practice resulted in the development of temporary farming villages scattered outside the periphery of the towns.[28]

By the second half of the nineteenth century, many people in the western and central parts of Yorubaland lived for much of the year in a town of some size.[29] Existing towns were fortified and new ones constructed to meet the need for "security and defence, the organisation of food supply, the succour of refugees, and the establishment of a stable political and economic life."[30]

Archdeacon Graf noted that the countryside might appear utterly deserted for distances of 20–50 miles, but when one came to a town, it was of vast extent. M. R. Delany, an African American who traveled in Yorubaland in 1859–1860, said that he passed through large cities with 70,000 or more residents, as well as villages with 100 to 2,000 inhabitants.[31] The smaller places may have been farming villages, though some towns destroyed their dependent villages during wartime in an attempt to gather the whole population into one defensible place. Akin L. Mabogunje has identified six Yoruba towns, including Ibadan and Abeokuta, that were said by travelers to have had populations of over 40,000 in the second half of the nineteenth century.[32] Another ten had populations of 20,000–40,000, and six more had 10,000–20,000 people. That is an exceptionally high level of urbanization for an African area at the time.

Although towns were founded under a variety of conditions, most had a similar appearance. A British missionary working in Iseyin, a town to the northwest of Ibadan, wrote in the 1850s,

> Great and small, these towns are surrounded by clay walls, about five feet high, and sufficiently thick to be a good defence. At the foot of the wall runs a ditch, three or four feet wide and several feet deep, the wall being perforated with gates at convenient distances. Within the wall are to be seen thousands of low, broad, grass-thatched cottages. The streets, when you enter, are crooked and narrow, with the exception of one broad, although seldom straight, street, running from each gate to the market-place, and commonly shaded with beautiful, wide-spreading trees.[33]

Delany noted that urban houses, built of unburnt clay that had hardened in the sun, were covered with an attractive thatch made of long grass.[34] Irregular and narrow streets were "frequently agreeably relieved by wider ones, or large, open spaces or parks shaded with trees." The gates where roads came into the town were supervised by chiefs who collected tolls on goods being brought into the community and used the income to keep the walls in repair.[35] Most towns had a palace for their king, some of them imposing compounds, as well as a central market place. In new or expanding towns like Ibadan, growth might occur in roughly concentric rings out and around the original settlement.[36]

The town's main market, usually founded or authorized by the king, was normally located across from the royal compound.[37] Because most local traders were women and female officials controlled the market in many Yoruba communities, the physical location of the market place had symbolic importance in gendered terms. As Helen Callaway noted, "If the palace represents the symbolic centre of political authority, primarily a male domain with certain limited positions of authority for women, directly outside the palace stands the main market of the city. It is here that women flourish in independent economic activity. This is an arena both of women's solidarity and of self-achievement. . . . In this sphere of economic exchange, women operate unambiguously as independent women."[38]

The physical appearance of markets was described by several nineteenth-century observers. T. J. Bowen, a missionary who traveled in western Yorubaland between 1849 and 1856, portrayed the market place in Iseyin as follows: "The market . . . is not a building, but a large area, shaded with trees, and surrounded and sometimes sprinkled over with little open sheds, consisting of a very low thatched roof surmounted on rude posts."[39] A drawing of the market in Abeokuta from 1893 shows sheds or stalls with thatching on the roof and upper part of the sides.[40] Poles held up the front of the thatch. Several female sellers were seated on the ground, chatting with buyers who were standing nearby. Another drawing in that set shows a shop in the town.[41] The sellers sat on a mat, with woven baskets of goods to sell in front of them and a smaller bowl or calabash to scoop out items for customers.

Delany confirmed that every town had at least one market place, some of them very large. The general market in Abeokuta covered 12 acres, and that in Ijaye covered 20 acres.[42] "These markets are systematically regulated and orderly arranged, there being parts and places for everything . . . with officially appointed and excellent managing market-masters." Special sections of the markets sold animals, with as many as 800 sheep offered at one time, plus horses, mules, goats, and edible birds. Bowen's listing of the commodities sold in the Yoruba markets included both locally grown items and goods imported "from the four quarters of the globe":

> Various kinds of meat, fowls, sheep, goats, dogs, rats, tortoises, eggs, fish, snails, yams, Indian corn, Guinea corn, sweet potatoes, sugar cane, ground peas, onions, pepper, various vegetables, palm nuts, oil, tree butter, seeds, fruits, fire-wood, cotton in the seed, spun cotton, domestic cloth, imported cloth, as calico, shirting, velvets, etc., gunpowder, guns, flints, knives, swords, paper, raw silk, Turkey-red thread, beads, needles, ready made clothing, as trousers, breeches, caps, shirts without sleeves, baskets, brooms, and no one knows what all.[43]

In many places, a larger market was held every fourth or eighth day, combining local with longer-distance trade.[44] In describing these "fairs," Bowen noted that "the few thousand people who attend daily are increased to a multitude, and the noise and glee are proportionately increased." William Clarke, who traveled in the western region in the mid-1850s, wrote that as many as 12,000–15,000 people might come to buy and sell in the larger markets. "That such immense crowds should meet day after day in perfect harmony and order, and transact their affairs like one great family without fighting and bloodshed is the more wonderful because it stands out in such bold contrast to what is seen in lands boasted for civilization and good government."[45] Markets, which continued to bring together a large number of people in the later nineteenth century, sometimes served as sites for Christian preaching.[46] When Archdeacon Hamilton visited Ojo, an unexceptional place on the southwestern lagoon, in the 1880s, he commented that its market, used by several thousand people from the surrounding area, "will be an admirable centre for evangelization."[47]

Though much of the produce sold in markets was grown locally, other goods were carried over longer distances. Because the Yoruba were rarely able to use pack animals and did not have wheeled vehicles, all goods were either transported in canoes (on the coastal lagoons and rivers) or carried on human heads.[48] (See Figure 3.1.) Head porters were commonly drawn from the traders' own households, including their slaves, but they could also be hired. Bowen was struck by the large number of carriers he saw, each bearing a load of 60–70 lbs.[49] Traders and porters generally traveled in caravans for protection if they were going through areas of active warfare or slave raiding.[50] Caravans moved on a fixed schedule, tied to the market days of important towns. That system enabled the traders to buy and sell along the way, as well as at the end points of the route. Caravans were often protected by local political authorities, who derived trade and tolls from them.

While some caravans operated between smaller communities within Yorubaland, the most important started at a town located at the end of a trade route that connected one of the Yoruba kingdoms with other regions. Such long-distance routes linked the Yoruba with the Akan to the west, with the Bariba, Hausa, and Nupe to the north and thence on to North or Northeast Africa, and with the coastal ports to the south.[51] Caravan travel on these major routes, located usually in dry rainforest or savannah zones, was well organized. Roads were wide, and caravansaries that lodged the travelers were established outside the towns. On one main route, Bowen saw caravans of 2,000–3,000 people passing every 5 days, carrying goods that he estimated would have required a hundred teams of oxen to transport in wagons.[52] Clarke commented that when several caravans joined together for defense, they might "stretch over several miles in length."

Traditional and New Religions and the British Government

Traditional Yoruba cosmology and religious beliefs were complex and tolerant, allowing for different forms of worship in particular communities.[53] All Yoruba envisioned a universe controlled by a supreme being (*Olódùmarè* or

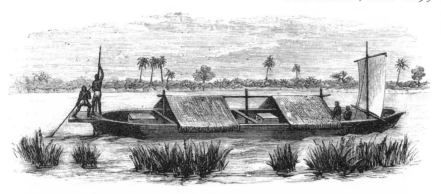

FIGURE 3.1. A large canoe, carved out of a single tree, as used on the lagoons and rivers, c. 1880s. From *The Gleaner Pictorial Album,* Vol. I (London: Church Missionary Society, 1888), p. 13, middle image. By permission of the Church Mission Society, Oxford.

Ọlọ́run, who was without gender) and many lesser deities called *òrìṣà.* The *òrìṣà* used authority derived from *Olódùmarè* "to administer cosmic principles to ensure harmony" between the various forces in the world: spiritual and physical, unseen and visible, heaven and earth, good and bad.[54] Those forces had to operate in complementary ways to ensure life and meaning within the universe and success in people's endeavors on earth. The qualities associated with men and women—some positive, some negative—were among the elements that Yoruba religious practice sought to align. That goal was paralleled by the concern of the Yoruba judicial system with promoting reconciliation and social harmony.

Religious activity fell into two main categories. The *òrìṣà,* who were sometimes associated with rivers, lagoons, hills, or trees, were worshipped at designated shrines. They helped people to cope with the challenges and uncertainties of their natural environment, and they enabled people to approach *Olódùmarè.*[55] The particular *òrìṣà* that were venerated and their number varied by place and occupation. In Ikaleland, for example, people dependent upon fishing worshipped the goddesses of the rivers and the sea, while blacksmiths and hunters celebrated the god of iron and farmers venerated the gods of the land and palm kernels. The Ikale did not, however, develop "an elaborate pantheon of gods" such as was found in many central and western areas.[56] Annual festivals celebrating the leading deities of a given community filled religious, cultural, and social functions: a renewal of the link between the *òrìṣà* and the people; performance of traditional chants, poetry, songs, and dancing; and a chance for extended families to get together for feasting and discussion of practical issues.

Each *òrìṣà* had a cult, headed by its priests and priestesses, that attracted followers who hoped to gain access to the benefits offered by that deity. Andrew Apter described òrìṣà as "a practical religion which 'feeds' deities with offerings, and sacrifices in return for requested services. Individuals propitiate for personal protection and private gain."[57] Women from all kin groups, occupations, and backgrounds were members of cults.[58] Whereas men and women alike appealed for wealth, health, and peace, much òrìṣà activity among women was directed at the goal of conceiving and giving birth to children and keeping them alive. Women could move freely among the different deities as their own needs shifted over the course of their lives.

Ifá, the second main religious form, offered divination (foretelling the future or revealing hidden causes) and protection linked to one's ancestors.[59] Ifá divination poetry contained a large body of oral texts that were regarded as the source of knowledge and the guardian of good behavior for the Yoruba. Although both men and women played essential roles in Ifá, men were generally dominant. This was because Ifá included an emphasis upon one's biological forebearers within the lineage, and most Yoruba communities based lineage primarily upon male lines. Married women thus gained access to Ifá power primarily through their husbands.

The Yoruba believed in the existence of supernatural forces. It was widely accepted that some people and objects could influence what happened to others in ways that were not apparent to the senses. Although foreign missionaries and colonial officials scorned such ideas as superstitious, many local people assumed that strange or unexplained events derived from hidden spiritual agency, which could be either benevolent or malevolent.[60] This belief, closely related to the interconnectedness of the material and the spiritual worlds in Yoruba cosmology, was fed by fear that rivals or enemies might try to harm you, especially if you were successful in such ways as attracting a spouse or lover, producing healthy children, or prospering in trade. The magical charms and medicines (commonly known as "juju") produced by spiritually powerful people were held to have real power, and it was believed that witches (ordinarily women) could harm or kill others. Although Christians were taught to abstain from juju practices and witchcraft, most Yoruba continued to accept that forces that could not been seen—especially evil ones—operated in the world.

In examining the introduction of two of the "world religions," Islam and Christianity, during the nineteenth century, we need to stress the importance of the strong Yoruba attachment to their own religious beliefs but also the deep commitment to polytheism and religious tolerance. Unlike those parts of Africa in which most people accepted one of the new faiths within a generation or two, many Yoruba remained loyal to traditional practices well into the twentieth century. They also created independent, syncretic churches that integrated familiar social practices with Christian beliefs. Although tension occasionally developed between advocates of the new religions and practitioners of traditional ones, the dominant pattern was acceptance of diversity. Many Yoruba families and communities by the late nineteenth century included Muslims and Christians as well as followers of older practices, and those people lived in harmony with each other.

The first contacts of the Yoruba with Islam probably came in the sixteenth century, through interactions between the Oyo Empire and the Songhai Empire to the northwest.[61] By the eighteenth century Hausaland, on the northern side of the Niger River, provided some Muslim influence, due to regular trade between the regions. Even among the Hausas, however, Islam expanded slowly until 1804, when the Muslim scholar and reformist preacher Usman dan Fodio began "the Fulani Jihad." Only then was Islam accepted by most people in what is now northern Nigeria. Islam must have been spreading into adjacent Yoruba areas by the 1810s, when some local Muslims joined the revolt that helped to establish Fulani rule in the Yoruba kingdom of Ilorin. Ilorin subsequently became the main locus of contact between the rest of Yorubaland and the Muslim states to the north, as well as a seat of Islamic learning and a trading center connected with places as distant as Tunis and Constantinople. Once Islam was established among the Oyo Yoruba, it spread southward into the forest belt, appearing in Egba towns, for example, by around 1830. Yoruba converts and non-Yoruba traders and slaves from the north carried Islam to the southern ports. When Christian missionaries began to work in Yorubaland, they found Muslims there before them in many communities. As a Yoruba proverb states, "We met *Ifá* [already present] in the world, we met Islam in the world, but Christianity arrived suddenly."[62]

In his sociology Ph.D. thesis completed at the University of London in 1939, N. A. Fadipe suggested that because Islam reached southwestern Nigeria by way of Hausaland, the agents of diffusion were other Africans with a material culture not far removed from that of the Yoruba.[63] Unlike Christianity, which was too rigid and complex, demanding an excessive amount of self-discipline, Islam could be reconciled with many traditional practices. At the same time, it offered greater scope for individuality than was possible under Yoruba religion and provided an incentive for accumulating wealth. T. G. O. Gbadamosi suggested that the leadership role of the imam in Yoruba Muslim communities was culturally familiar.[64] Holding office for life, the Imam played a religious role in Yoruba towns similar to that performed in social and political terms by the head of a descent group or a leading chief. Islam did, however, introduce certain social and economic changes.[65] It limited polygamy, defined new rules about other aspects of marriage, divorce, and inheritance, and banned the taking of interest on loans.

During the second and third quarters of the nineteenth century, British influence in Yorubaland was spread by three groups of men: missionaries, traders, and military or political officials.[66] While those groups had different specific goals, their activities were complementary: missionaries sought a Christian Yorubaland in which slave trading would be abolished, while merchants hoped that slaving would be replaced by new economic patterns that would enhance British trade. To accomplish those goals, British military and political protection was required.

Christian missionary activity, which moved slowly northward from the Atlantic ports starting in the 1830s and 1840s, grew out of the European religious revival of the late eighteenth century.[67] Both the evangelical movement and the campaign to abolish slavery stemmed from a sense that Christians must proselytize their faith more energetically, carrying its moral as well as its spiritual benefits throughout the world.[68] The first and most influential missionaries in Yorubaland were members of the CMS, an evangelical wing of the Anglican church, founded in Britain in 1799. They were followed by Roman Catholics (especially the Holy Ghost Fathers) and other Protestants, including British Methodists, American Baptists, and the Canadian Sudan Interior Mission.[69] We will focus upon the CMS, because it had the most influence among the Yoruba and is the best documented.

A key feature of early Christian activity in Yorubaland—one seldom found in eastern or southern Africa—was that most of the initial missionaries were themselves West African, often Yoruba, "returnees."[70] After Britain outlawed the slave trade in 1807, its navy patrolled the West African coast, looking for ships that were setting off for the western hemisphere with a cargo of slaves. The people rescued from slave ships were taken to the British colony of Sierra Leone, where many were converted to Christianity, educated, and given British names to add to their African ones. During the later 1830s and 1840s, hundreds of freed slaves of Yoruba descent returned from Sierra Leone to Yorubaland, settling mainly in Lagos and Abeokuta. They were joined over the following decades by several thousand more Sierra Leoneans. The CMS's decision to use Africans as missionaries derived from several causes. The organization was eager to create a self-supporting and self-propagating church in Yorubaland, and that required local leadership. Further, most Europeans who came to Nigeria succumbed with troubling rapidity to malaria and other diseases.[71] Roman Catholicism was likewise introduced into Yorubaland largely by returnees, ex-slaves who left Brazil after the 1835 revolt. (Many of them were originally Muslim Hausa who had converted to Catholicism in Brazil or did so in Lagos.)

Missionary activity expanded during the second half of the nineteenth century. Between 1850 and 1865, the CMS opened missions in other western and central Yoruba towns, translated the Bible into Yoruba, and began publishing a Yoruba-language newspaper. Many of the workers in the field were still returnees, but men who had been converted and educated within Yorubaland itself henceforth carried the faith into new communities. From the 1860s and 1870s onward, they were joined by a growing number of European missionaries, as quinine came into use as a malaria prophylactic. The nature of their congregations likewise shifted. Whereas the early converts had often been marginalized members of local society, some of the second-generation Christians were rising to positions of influence in their communities.[72] By the 1890s, conversion to Christianity was beginning to occur on a larger scale in some areas.

The process was nonetheless slow. Even in Lagos, with its returnees and early mission churches and schools, the population of non-Christians outnumbered Christians seven-to-one during much of the second half of the nineteenth century; Muslims alone outnumbered Christians two-to-one.[73] In Ibadan, where the German missionaries David and Anna Hinderer were active, the CMS had three congregations in 1884, but together those churches had only 133 communicants, joined by about the same number who were "connected" to Christianity.[74] J. D. Y. Peel has calculated that by 1890, after a half century of missionary activity, all the Christian denominations in Yorubaland had together converted only around 20,000 people, constituting just 1 percent of the estimated total population.

A factor that stood in the way of conversion was that religion was so closely bound up with other cultural and social aspects of Yoruba life. For Africans to become fully Christian, it was not enough to accept new religious beliefs and practices. Instead, they were expected to abandon a range of fundamental behaviors in such areas as marriage, inheritance, and burial. Many of the missionaries scorned traditional African culture, even if they were themselves Yoruba by birth, so they demanded that converts also cease such practices as customary drumming and dancing. Because many Yoruba were unwilling to give up their familiar rituals, some local Christians began to found their own independent African churches.[75] These denominations, commonly known as the Aladura churches, were more evangelical in their approach and more expressive in their forms of worship. Usually permitting polygamy, they often allowed women to preach and sometimes to head their own churches. The most popular Aladura churches developed huge followings, some of which continued through the twentieth century.

In the late nineteenth century, tension arose between African missionaries and British members of the CMS.[76] In 1864 Samuel Ajayi Crowther, a Yoruba returnee and early CMS missionary, had been named Bishop of Western Equatorial Africa by the Anglican church. Because Bishop Crowther and many other African clergymen in the Yoruba mission recognized the difficulties facing converts, they were prepared to be flexible, willing to accept compromises with local customs in areas that seemed of secondary importance.

An important figure in this attempt to set up a "native pastorate" and more accommodating practices was Rev. James Johnson, born in Sierra Leone to Yoruba parents, who was active first in Lagos and then around Abeokuta during the 1870s. Others too attempted to create a version of Christianity better suited to their own culture, part of a broader movement described as "Ethiopianism" that flourished between 1875 and 1914.[77] Such practices caused conflict between Yoruba ministers and the increasingly numerous European missionaries. Eventually the CMS ruled against Crowther, criticizing him for lax supervision and for accepting "heathenish" practices among his clergy. In 1890 Crowther was demoted and a British bishop named.

One of the greatest attractions of the Christian missions—and one of the most powerful forces of change introduced by them—was Western education.[78] Because the missionaries wanted to modify many aspects of the children's lives, not just provide training in Christianity, they favored boarding schools. The CMS set up boys' schools in Lagos and Abeokuta in the 1850s, and in 1869 it opened the first school for girls, in Lagos. Parents (especially mothers) were at first hesitant about sending their children to these schools, but gradually they became aware that formal education offered advantages, at least to boys.[79] The new opportunities were not limited to positions within the church itself. Being literate and knowing English enabled people to trade more effectively with European companies and might open possibilities for employment in those firms or lower levels of colonial government.

Girls studied a different curriculum from that offered to boys. From the founding of the first schools, Christians had argued about the purpose and form of education.[80] For boys, returnees generally advocated an academic education of the kind they had themselves received in Sierra Leone; many local and British missionaries, however, stressed the need for vocational training in agriculture or mechanics. But neither of those early groups advocated serious intellectual work for girls. Instead girls' schools stressed "character training," good morals, domestic science, and preparation for marriage. In practice this meant instruction in religion, reading/writing (in Yoruba for younger girls, English for older ones), and a little arithmetic, as well as sewing and other domestic arts. During the 1880s and 1890s, CMS missionaries wrote that their schools stressed Bible reading and sewing (both plain and fancy needlework), with some attention to English, oral recitation, and music.[81] That approach, which was similar to the curriculum of most schools for girls within Britain itself, was welcomed by some members of the educated Yoruba community. In 1883 the *Eagle* newspaper was full of praise for Lagosians' interest in educating their daughters and for the nature of that training: "The subjects taught them are, as far as we know, very suitable; they are directed to make them useful in their homes and generation."[82]

By the 1880s and 1890s, a few wealthy parents—especially returnees and early Christian converts in Lagos and Abeokuta—were sending their children to the Gold Coast (now Ghana), Sierra Leone, or Britain for further schooling.[83] Their sons might train as lawyers or doctors, while their daughters attended "finishing schools." London women advertised in Lagos papers that they were willing to receive young African ladies as boarders to study English, French, and such accomplishments as music and painting.[84] Musical skills were particularly important within the thriving world of elite culture found in Lagos in the decades around 1900, which integrated educated Africans and Europeans. Olayinka Moore, the daughter of powerful Egba and returnee parents, was sent to boarding school in England in the late 1880s, when she was 10 or 11.[85] First at the Young Lady's Academy at Ryford Hall and then at Portway College, Reading, the future Lady Ajasa studied music (including the Spanish guitar), dancing, and housekeeping before returning to Lagos to marry. Stella Davies, whose returnee family had branches in other West African cities, attended Pembroke House School in the mid-1890s.[86] There she memorized the key facts of early modern English history alongside her British classmates. After coming back to Lagos to marry, she corresponded with her dear school friends about their shared interests in music, clothes, horses, and sports.[87]

Children educated in Western schools gained a new kind of authority that stemmed not from the holding of a specific office but rather from their ability to function in a world closely associated with the prestige and power of British missionaries, merchants, and government officials. Christian schooling thus became both a producer and an indicator of status due to the wealth, power, and contacts that it could bring. It created a new, educated elite in Yorubaland that in some cities had begun to challenge the authority of the traditional rulers—the king and chiefs—by the end of the century. Further, because most of the early Nigerian schools were located in Yoruba areas, they gave this ethnic group a competitive advantage within the proto-colonial world.

Missionary concerns also contributed to the gradual expansion of British government influence after the mid-nineteenth century. Christians asked for official help in combating the slave trade, joining pressure from British merchants who wanted physical protection for commerce and who found that they could arouse little interest among African farmers in the "legitimate" forms of trade they were proposing so long as slaving yielded much higher profits. Slowly Britain began to expand its military and political authority. In 1851, the British intervened in a dispute over Lagos's kingship, bombarding the port and deposing a ruler whom the missionaries portrayed as a wicked slaver; 10 years later British officials forced the king whom they supported to cede Lagos to them as a colony, a move intended to promote British commercial interests.[88] British ability to intrude in Yoruba affairs was enhanced by the fact that the towns in the interior were so bitterly divided among themselves. Most kings, chiefs, and cities saw the British as dangerous intruders, but a few regarded them as potential allies in their disputes with other Yoruba states. The most receptive city was Abeokuta, due largely to its 3,000 returnees. During the latter part of the century, the British carried out a series of military expeditions and negotiations with the individual city-states, resulting in treaties that granted the foreigners political control. The final treaties, signed in 1893, completed the establishment of British power throughout Yorubaland, though that authority was implemented fully only over the course of the following generation.

Slavery

Demand for slaves accentuated the political/military and social instability of the nineteenth century. Slavery—and hence slave trading—assumed two main forms in Yorubaland: trans-Atlantic slavery, in which captured people were shipped to the Americas (joined to a lesser extent by provision of slaves to kingdoms north of the Niger); and "indigenous" or "domestic" slavery, in which slaves were used within Yorubaland itself. Slaves might be obtained through warfare, especially when a town was defeated and its inhabitants seized, or they could be captured in raids. The Yoruba had been involved in slaving prior to the nineteenth century. The Oyo Empire participated in the slave trade across the Sahara, some of the Yoruba city-states included slaves within the system of royal administration, and slaves had been exported from the Atlantic ports. But the demand for slaves in plantation economies in the Americas mounted after around 1800, as did the call for slaves in the new types of commercial agriculture emerging in Yorubaland after around 1830. Though eastern Yorubaland and other adjoining areas served as a reservoir of potential slaves for their militarized neighbors, many western and central Yoruba people were enslaved as well.[89]

Trans-Atlantic slavery, in which Africans were taken to the coast and sold to foreign slavers, was the most destructive in social and demographic terms. Slaves had been shipped out from ports in the Bight of Benin, the region of the coast that adjoined Yorubaland, during the second half of the seventeenth and the eighteenth centuries, with French islands in the Caribbean a common destination.[90] Britain's abolition of the slave trade in 1807 had little immediate impact. Demand for African slaves remained high in such areas as Cuba and the Bahia region of Brazil until the 1860s, and some European countries continued to trade in slaves during those decades despite British naval patrols. Early in the century, slaves were exported primarily from the ports of Badagry and Lagos, at the terminus of the main trade routes that served the western

Yoruba area. Badagry became less important during the 1830s as the center of the trade moved eastward, leaving Lagos as the leading Yoruba slave market. Despite vigorous objection from abolitionists in Britain and missionaries in Yorubaland, export of slaves from Lagos continued until 1861, when it was annexed as a British colony.[91]

The role of the Yoruba within the slave trade changed across the nineteenth century.[92] During the later eighteenth and early nineteenth centuries, the Yoruba participated mainly as merchants and brokers. They bought slaves supplied by the Hausa and sold them to Europeans on the coast. Lagos traders also had a secondary supply of slaves in the Ijebu towns located north of the lagoon. But when established trade routes to the north were disrupted by the Muslim Fulani take-over in Ilorin, merchants in Lagos tried to step up production of slaves from within Yorubaland itself. After the collapse of the Oyo Empire, Ilorin became the leading supplier of slaves, joined later by Ibadan.[93] Especially in the 1840s, the movement of displaced people offered a bonanza to slave traders: tens of thousands of refugees were captured. The Yoruba wars and the raiding that accompanied them likewise provided ample slaves. Even in areas where the official policy was opposed to slaving, as among the Egba in Abeokuta in the 1840s (influenced by returnees), chiefs attacked other towns and felt comfortable in stating publicly that their object was to gain slaves for export.[94] Archdeacon Graf explained the devastation of Yoruba towns and villages that he observed in the 1850s as the combined result of slaving raids and warfare.

Recent quantified analyses have provided estimates of how many Yoruba were captured and sent to the New World as slaves. David Eltis suggested that about 968,000 Yoruba-speaking people were sent to the Americas between 1651 and 1867.[95] Whereas relatively few appear to have been enslaved prior to 1776, the number rose after that time. During the first quarter of the nineteenth century, about 211,000 Yoruba slaves were exported; during the peak years, 1826–1850, 257,000 Yoruba were sent. Slaves came from two primary areas during the nineteenth century.[96] A small zone near the coast supplied almost exclusively female and child slaves. Nearly all the slaves captured in the second zone, located 60–100 miles from the coastal ports, were adult Yoruba males, many of them Muslims. Although we do not have figures for the age and sex distribution of Yoruba slaves specifically, adult men and teen-aged boys formed the largest fraction of those exported from ports in the Bight of Benin in several samples between 1800 and 1867, followed by adult women.[97]

Scholars have presented divergent assessments of the economic and political impact of trans-Atlantic slaving upon Yorubaland. Law argued that the Oyo Empire profited in material terms from participation in the Atlantic slave trade during its period of expansion in the seventeenth and eighteenth centuries.[98]

The wealth derived from that trade, gained primarily at the expense of its non-Yoruba neighbors who provided most of the slaves, contributed to Oyo's success. But in the early nineteenth century, civil wars within the disintegrating empire were exacerbated by European demand for slaves. B. W. Hodder agreed that the slave trade contributed to the wars among the Yoruba kingdoms during the nineteenth century, as rival groups or city-states, especially the Egba, Ibadan, and Ijebu, attempted to control the lucrative commercial routes connecting Lagos and the lagoon areas with the hinterlands.[99]

J. F. A. Ajayi, however, has downplayed the role of trans-Atlantic slavery as a causative factor in the Yoruba wars, part of his broader argument that lessens the importance assigned to foreign economic and political influences as opposed to pressures found within Yoruba society itself. Ajayi argued that an expansion of slaving in the 1820s and the resulting growth of Badagry and Lagos as slave ports "were the result, not the cause, of the collapse of the Old Oyo empire."[100] He believed that over-reliance on sources of information produced by the British, who were preoccupied with their own economic and ethical concerns, has led to misunderstanding of the nature of the Yoruba wars. Officials in Lagos, committed to protecting Britain's commercial interests, viewed African events—including the Yoruba wars—in purely economic terms. British abolitionists perceived the wars as the outcome of the slave trade and "the consequent social and moral degeneration of the Africans." Neither group recognized the significance of unresolved political problems among the Yoruba city-states.

A second type of slavery was practiced within Yorubaland itself. Although it is often termed "domestic" slavery, the term "indigenous" slavery will be used here, to avoid any suggestion that slaves were used only within the household context or that it was a purely benign, family institution.[101] Because the Yoruba had no tradition of waged employment whereby one person worked willingly for another in return for pay, free labor could be provided only by members of the household or by other followers or clients within a patronage relationship.[102] During the second half of the nineteenth century, as trans-Atlantic slaving was replaced by commercial production of agricultural goods for export, the demand for labor within Yorubaland grew. If households and their dependents could not provide enough workers, the primary source of additional labor was slaves. These slaves lived within the compound of their master or mistress and did the work assigned to them. In some cases they were allowed to earn money of their own, with which they could trade or purchase their freedom if they wished. Indigenous slaves were obtained in ways similar to those that produced slaves for export, and they were often transported to coastal or inland markets along the same routes.[103] As British naval patrols gradually curtailed the Atlantic slave trade, a surplus of slaves built up in local markets, leading to a drop in prices that made them more affordable for Africans. Unlike trans-Atlantic slaving, however, women and girls were preferred as slaves within Yorubaland.

Slave labor was used in a variety of ways.[104] In (Old) Oyo, the king and leading chiefs had recruited large numbers of slaves into their households—some of them as tribute from subsidiary kingdoms—to perform administrative, economic, and military functions. During the nineteenth century, palace slaves in several of the Yoruba states held important titles and played key roles within royal government. Slaves were assigned to the worship of particular deities, and some were used in warfare. Much more commonly, however, slaves lived in ordinary households, assisting with agricultural work, domestic tasks, the production of food or craft items, and trade. The Ikale people, in the southeastern part of Yorubaland, depended upon slave labor during the second half of the nineteenth century to produce increasing amounts of foodstuffs to be sold to their neighbors, many of whom could no longer feed themselves because they had switched to growing cash crops.[105] Ownership of slaves was essential to the men who were building new political bases, both because slaves provided the labor that sustained their position and because control over people demonstrated their power to others.[106] Mabogunje believed that the ethnic heterogeneity of the urban population of Yorubaland in the nineteenth century was increased by domestic slavery: many Yoruba compounds included some non-Yoruba slaves, mainly Hausas and members of ethnic groups in Nigeria's Middle Belt.[107]

The existence of indigenous slavery in Yorubaland (and in other African regions) has raised difficult moral questions for contemporaries and more recent commentators alike. Discomfort about African participation in this institution as well as in trans-Atlantic slaving has led to what Ajayi has described as "the collective amnesia" about slavery in oral traditions and to a near dearth of scholarly studies.[108] In the nineteenth century, people who opposed the export of slaves struggled with whether it was ethical to accept a different kind of slavery within Africa itself. As A. B. Aderibigbe has noted, the paradox was that "Legitimate commerce [the term used by the British for the new kinds of trade they promoted] would solve the problem posed by the foreign, Atlantic Slave Trade by offering a substitute and thereby made Domestic Slavery difficult of eradication."[109] To meet "the ever-increasing demands of honourable trade," more slaves were required: they were needed to work on farms, process goods to be exported, and carry produce from rural areas to the coast, returning with British manufactured goods. British commerce flourished only on the back of indigenous slave labor. That fact was recognized by Benjamin Campbell, the British consul in Lagos in the 1850s, while promoting cotton production.[110] Noting that the Yoruba already knew how to grow cotton and only needed a stimulus to raise more for export, he admitted that slave labor was used on the cotton farms. He felt that the practice was acceptable, however, because "a domestic slave always had the hope of manumission." By around 1860, however, British official policy began to question indigenous slavery.

The issue was likewise complex for missionaries working in Yorubaland. The official stance of the CMS was to define indigenous slavery as relatively harmless, or at least as substantially better than trans-Atlantic slavery, and hence to tolerate its existence. When Bishop Weeks, newly appointed bishop of Sierra Leone, paid his first visit to Nigeria in 1856, he startled local CMS workers by challenging their acceptance of domestic slavery.[111] To defend local practice, Samuel Crowther, the highly respected returnee missionary and future bishop, wrote, "The slaves and masters in this country live together as a family; they eat out of the same bowl, use the same dress in common and in many instances are intimate companions, so much so that, entering a family circle, a slave can scarcely be distinguished from a free man unless one is told."[112]

But as time passed, missionaries became increasingly unhappy about indigenous slavery. James White, another returnee, commented in 1866 that although "there are a great many of our people who are very indulgent to their slaves. . . yet the recollection that he is a slave fills his breast with gloominess, discontent and murmurs, and he groans as it were under a very heavy load."[113] In the late 1880s, Rev. T. Harding, a missionary in Abeokuta, complained about the ongoing prevalence of slavery. Whereas he and other Christian churchmen exhorted their converts "to do their utmost to set their slaves free and stamp out the inhuman traffic," most people in his own congregation were "indifferent to our appeals, and look upon slavery as a necessity. If a man has money, the only way he can invest it is by buying a slave, or increasing his trade, and to increase his trade means also that a man must increase his slaves."[114]

One way to excuse indigenous slavery was to emphasize its differences from "chattel slavery" as practiced in the Americas.[115] Earlier Yoruba cultural nationalists presented domestic slavery as a benevolent social institution used to recruit labor and assist the needy. While that view is overly positive, it is nevertheless true that indigenous slavery was generally less oppressive than the version found in the western hemisphere. Because the Yoruba did not have a concept of private property, slaves were not "owned," not seen as the possession of their master. Instead they were regarded as quite similar to the other dependents and clients of the household's head. They were generally referred to as *omo*, the word used for a child, not as *erú*, the word for a slave, and it was in the master's best interests to maintain good relationships with the workers on whom his wealth depended.[116] Over time, the distinction between free and slave status tended to blur, and some slaves were gradually absorbed as full family members. If a master formally married a female slave, she would have a lower position in the household than his freeborn wives but would enjoy more privileges than other female slaves.[117] The children of a slave wife had the same standing as the father's other children, and if masters had children by their female slaves without marrying them, those offspring would be recognized by their fathers and sometimes granted limited inheritance rights.

The slaves of traders might be given considerable responsibility by their masters or mistresses and allowed to work for themselves part of the time. In Ibadan, for example, which relied heavily on slaves for its commercial activities as well as its wars, missionary Anna Hinderer noted in 1853 that the slaves of some traders "are so implicitly trusted, that they are sent out on expeditions which involve an absence of several months at a time, and return when their commission has been fulfilled."[118] Some slaves carried and sold their own goods as well as those of their master, keeping a share of the profits.

Despite those moderating factors, one must acknowledge that indigenous slaves were not full members of the household and faced the possibility of physical coercion. The degree of equality was limited. A person who died while still a slave was buried outside the compound, not inside as were other family members.[119] We are told that physical punishment of slaves was considered inappropriate, but CMS documents and legal records make clear that at least a few masters and mistresses maltreated their dependents.[120] In most regions, only a few slaves were sacrificed as part of òrìṣà worship, killed at the funeral of an elite personage, or buried alive with a deceased king, but flogging (beating with a whip or stick) was commonly mentioned as a punishment. Masters or mistresses could always sell their slaves if they were lazy or disobedient or if cash were needed, or abandon them if they were too sick or old to work.

Although slavery remained the leading source of supplemental labor throughout the nineteenth century, the institution gradually weakened, due largely to pressure from missionaries and the British government. When slavery was banned in Lagos after the annexation of 1861, a growing number of slaves of both sexes escaped from the interior and came to the colony in search of liberation and protection by British authorities. As the king and trade chiefs of Abeokuta complained to the British consul in 1872,

> Our slaves, . . . our wives, our children, are all running away to Lagos, and for which we dare institute no enquiry. Our slaves here are used in the same way as children on our own body begotten, . . . to help us in working our farms to obtain the produce needed in the European market. This is the only investment we had here. By taking them from us, [you are] reducing people of importance to abject beggary in a day.[121]

By the 1890s, the termination of slave labor was said to be causing economic and social problems in some areas.[122] Sale of slaves had largely ceased by 1898, when the Native Court in Ibadan began trying to abolish it formally, but the local administration in Egbaland was still regulating slavery and standardizing the process whereby slaves could purchase their freedom early in the twentieth century.[123] Only in 1916 was slavery abolished formally throughout Nigeria, and cases involving the inheritance rights of former slaves continued to come before courts in Abeokuta and Ibadan for several decades more.

Trans-Atlantic and indigenous slavery had many consequences for the Yoruba. For those who were captured and marched to the coast, misery continued with the voyage across "the middle passage." So harsh were conditions aboard the slave ships that about 13 percent of the slaves who embarked from the African coast are thought to have died before they reached the New World.[124] Their lives after being sold in North or South America belong to the histories of those regions, but any study of the Yoruba must acknowledge the terrible human toll taken by the export of nearly a million people from just one ethnic group. Although the birthrate was evidently high enough to prevent a serious drop in the population that remained in Yorubaland, the loss of so many people—especially able-bodied adults and adolescents—from a region that had ample land but limited labor certainly constrained economic growth.[125] In western and central areas of Yorubaland, slave raiding compounded the negative impacts of warfare. Thomas King, a Yoruba returnee missionary who described his recollections of his early life before being taken as a slave, mentioned in passing a 3-year absence of his older brother in the early 1820s. When the young man left home and was not heard of again, "we concluded that he was either killed or sold."[126] In places where a preponderance of males was captured and exported, slaving presumably reinforced polygamy and decreased the pool of men available for leadership positions. Within Yorubaland, many people—especially women and children—were forced to live and work under the control of their masters and mistresses. But it is also true that some rulers and large-scale traders earned sizeable profits from participation in the traffic in human life.[127] Local suppliers gained a lesser income, and many farmers, traders, and craftspeople benefited from the use of slave labor in their own productive activities.

To the dismay of some moralists, slavery was replaced in many parts of Yorubaland by another form of involuntary labor known as "pawnship."[128] In that system, a person who owed a debt or other obligation to someone else assigned his own labor or—more commonly—the labor of another person temporarily to his creditor. The pawn then served as collateral for the debt, while at the same time his or her labor helped to repay the loan. The debtor might pawn himself or herself, a wife, sister, child, or slave. Young pawns and unmarried women usually lived in the household of the creditor until the debt was repaid. Pawnship continued until around 1940.

The Growth of "Legitimate" Commerce

The agricultural and trading economies of West Africa were affected during the nineteenth century by the industrialization of Europe. Industrial activity created a demand for certain agricultural products from tropical regions while expanding the search for new markets for exported manufactured goods. The success of the British abolitionist movement in crushing the opposition of powerful slave-trading interests in Liverpool, Bristol, London, and the British West Indies during the early nineteenth century stemmed in large part from a new conception of the most useful economic role for West Africa.[129] After the Industrial Revolution, obtaining human labor for plantation agriculture was no longer the primary concern. British industry now needed tropical products: primary agricultural commodities that could be grown in Africa but not in Europe. Some economic thinkers around 1800 therefore argued that it was shortsighted for slave traders to be allowed to remove from Africa the labor needed to produce those commodities. Moreover, British industry was increasingly geared toward exports, leading many people to think that "the Negro, left a free man in Africa and given purchasing power through 'legitimate' commerce, was of more value than the Negro, transported as a slave to the West Indies, sullenly working in response to the stimulus of the whip, with no cash income to spend on British goods."[130] Africans thus needed new economic forms whereby they could earn money at home with which to buy imported goods. This attitude was close to that of abolitionists, who believed that the supply of slaves for the trans-Atlantic trade could only be cut off fully at its roots when other types of income became available to African people. Traders and missionaries, supported later by British officials in Lagos, worked together to promote the growth of cash crops as the kind of "legitimate" commerce that would replace the profits from slaving.

The simple vegetable products advocated for commercial agriculture were of several sorts. Some were already present in the area, most importantly the palm trees that grew naturally in wet but not water-logged areas, in Yorubaland's rainforests and farther east, along the Niger River. Many households had traditionally kept a few palm trees on their land for their own use. Palm products were employed in many ways by the Yoruba. The leaf ribs of the tree were used in building, its leaves in thatching, and its leaf fibers in rope making; palm wine, an intoxicating drink, could be made by tapping the tree.[131] Reddish-orange palm oil, derived from the fruit of the tree, was the most important vegetable oil used in Yoruba cooking, and it provided essential vitamins.

A different kind of oil was extracted from the kernel of the palm nut. The Yoruba used it to make soap and by 1860 were burning it in lamps to light their houses.[132] Fiber left from the fruit after the oil had been extracted was used for kindling, and the hull of the palm nut was used to make the charcoal needed by local blacksmiths.

The great expansion of the export trade in palm oil and kernels during the nineteenth century stemmed both from British realization that palm oil production could be an important form of legitimate commerce and from mounting demand for oil in Europe.[133] From an early nineteenth-century commercial perspective, palm products were an ideal export crop for West Africa. Making palm oil required considerable labor, but it could be provided locally and integrated with other domestic tasks. Since the producers were usually women, this activity did not keep men away from other kinds of work.[134] Transportation was not a major cost because palm trees generally grew within a day's journey by canoe or foot from the ocean and larger boats. For missionaries, promotion of palm oil products was a more complex issue in gendered as well as ethical terms. While they supported the development of cash crops as a way to suppress trans-Atlantic slavery, missionaries assumed that commercial agriculture would be controlled by male household heads, thereby contributing to the formation of Christian, patriarchal families.[135] Palm oil, by contrast, left production and trading in women's hands, thereby supporting undesirable female economic independence.

Production and export of palm products in Yorubaland was stimulated by European industrial demand for oil. In the first half of the nineteenth century, when whale oil became less abundant but petroleum products were not yet available, palm oil was vital to the growing productivity of European factories. It was employed in many ways.[136] Around 1800, oil from palm fruits was used primarily to make soap and candles, answering the call for improved cleanliness and nighttime illumination in Europe. Later, oil obtained from palm kernels—which were shipped to Britain and processed there—was an ingredient in margarine and cooking fats, soap, and lubricating greases for a wide range of machinery. When tin-plating of the cans used for food storage became common, demand for palm kernels increased, for their oil was an essential component in the plating process. The residual "cake" left over after the oil had been extracted proved to be a good livestock food.

A small amount of palm oil was already being exported in the 1790s, and by 1830 it had become clear to many European merchants that it was the most valuable commodity that could be obtained from West Africa.[137] During the next few decades, exports shot up, though prices were highly unstable. After 1855, while production continued to rise, the price paid by coastal traders for palm oil began a decline that lasted on an irregular basis through the rest of the century. That decline was due to increased competition from vegetable oils and fats manufactured in other parts of the world, the beginnings of petroleum production, and the European economic depression of the last quarter of the century. It was fortunate for West African producers that new industrial uses were discovered during the second half of the nineteenth century for the oil derived from palm kernels. In 1892 it was estimated that at least 15 million palm trees were in production for the export market in Yoruba country.[138]

The growth of the trade in palm products had major repercussions for the economy of southern Yorubaland during the middle and later nineteenth century. Whereas raising palm trees generally remained in the hands of small farmers, some powerful war chiefs and traders acquired extensive estates that used slaves to produce oil and kernels. In the western forest belt and the Egba and Ijaye areas, travelers in the 1850s and 1860s commented on the large number of people engaged in production of palm oil, either as individuals or in groups of as many as 50 people.[139] Palm oil likewise contributed to the emergence of Lagos's African trading elite.

The British promoted other cash crops too during the later part of the century. Some were familiar to the Yoruba. Forested areas produced kola nuts, which were sold primarily within West Africa, and parts of the savannah were suited to cotton, which had long been grown for local use in cloth making. But traditional kinds of produce were increasingly augmented by new crops. Cocoa had come to West Africa from Brazil, by way of Spanish and Portuguese colonies elsewhere in Africa, and was introduced to coastal and western areas of Yorubaland starting in the 1880s.[140] When African and foreign merchants looked for alternative cash crops when palm products were in recession, cocoa was a common choice. Because cocoa growing offered few economies of scale, it was well suited to production on the small holdings of Yoruba farmers. The British also made some efforts to introduce tobacco into northern areas of Yorubaland. Christian missionaries and their converts were among the most effective advocates for a commercial approach to agriculture and experimentation with new crops.[141] In Egbaland, for example, CMS missionaries successfully promoted production of palm oil and cotton, thereby contributing to a significant rise in exports from the region and the increased prosperity of many of its residents.

Agricultural exports helped to lessen the negative commercial impact of the abolition of trans-Atlantic slavery throughout West Africa. That transition was not sudden or complete. Until around the middle of the nineteenth century, traders in many regions took a cautious approach, sending both slaves and agricultural crops to the coast.[142] But gradually producers and merchants shifted over to the new products. Whereas it has been estimated that at the height of the Atlantic slave trade at the end of the eighteenth century, West

Africa's overseas commerce was worth about £4 million (British pounds) per year, the value of exports of legitimate goods had reached almost that level (at least £3.5 million) by the early 1850s. During the second half of the nineteenth century the value of trade expanded roughly four times, amounting to about £15 million per year by 1901–1905. Though the rate of growth was not even across this period, with fluctuations in price that caused problems for both farmers and merchants, and though that growth was to be dwarfed by the expansion that occurred during the colonial era, it was enough to support the claim that legitimate trade generated a much bigger economy than had slaving.

While it is unclear whether the transition from slaving to cash crop production led to a broader "crisis of adaptation" that affected political as well as economic structures in nineteenth-century West Africa, cash cropping certainly spread the proceeds from trade more widely than had slaving.[143] As A. G. Hopkins noted,

> The capital and labour requirements of slave raiding and trading had encouraged the rise of a relatively small group of large entrepreneurs, many of whom became the rulers or senior officials of great states in the Western Sudan and in the forest. Producing and selling palm oil and groundnuts, on the other hand, were occupations in which there were few barriers to entry. Legitimate commerce therefore enabled small-scale farmers and traders to play an important part in the overseas exchange economy for the first time.[144]

Many Yoruba farmers and traders profited at least to a limited extent from commercial agriculture in the nineteenth century. With even a modest cash income they could acquire more land and the additional household members who both increased their productivity and displayed their status. They were able to buy some of the tempting imported manufactured goods that were now starting to appear in local markets. Innovative and entrepreneurial people in areas like Egbaland and Ijebuland, women as well as men, were finding new ways to take advantage of the changing economic world. By the time the British established control over all of Yorubaland, the region was already moving in many of the religious, social, and economic directions that were to characterize the colonial era.

4 | Colonial Yorubaland, 1893–1960

DURING THE COLONIAL PERIOD, the British introduced policies and institutions that affected many aspects of Yoruba people's lives. They ended internal warfare and slavery while also implementing a system of "indirect" political rule and creating new laws and courts. Christianity and Islam continued to spread, though some Yoruba remained loyal to their traditional religious patterns and new churches emerged that combined elements of different faiths. The Yoruba were also integrated more fully into a global economic system that defined them as producers of agricultural goods for export and consumers of European manufactured goods. The growth of trade was facilitated by improvements in transportation within Yorubaland. Movement of people from rural areas into the cities continued. Western education expanded, initially in schools operated by the missionaries but joined later by the government.

Although colonialism brought profound changes to Yoruba life, the new patterns did not eradicate the core features of Yoruba culture and society or eliminate the decision-making capacity of local people. In some respects, the Yoruba either actively or passively resisted change, continuing along familiar pathways, while in others they embraced the new opportunities colonialism offered. More characteristically, however, they modified British introductions in order to produce outcomes that accorded better with Yoruba wishes and traditions. As LaRay Denzer commented, "More often than the colonial administrators liked to admit, their African subjects transformed European policies and institutions into new syncretic forms in tune with their own values and culture. Possessing a rich material culture, a complex ideology, and a well defined constitution, the Yoruba peoples readily adapted the new culture of the British to their own needs."[1]

This chapter summarizes the major developments of the colonial period. Many of the changes that arose from within Yoruba society itself as well as those triggered by the British had profound implications for women. In most cases, however, we will postpone discussion of how colonial patterns intersected with women's lives until we discuss those particular topics in subsequent chapters. Here we will explore only the consequences of Western education for women, an issue that informs much of our later analysis.

Political, Legal, and Religious Change

Yorubaland's incorporation into a British colony occurred through several steps.[2] After the mainland area became part of the Protectorate of Southern Nigeria in 1900, that unit was merged administratively with the Colony of Lagos and the Protectorate of Northern Nigeria in 1914 to form the Colony and Protectorate of Nigeria.[3] The newly amalgamated unit was governed through a system of indirect rule based upon Lord Lugard's experiences in northern Nigeria. In that pattern, the British divided each region of Nigeria into administrative provinces (six of them for the Yoruba-speaking parts of the Western Region); each province was sub-divided into districts or divisions. Although every unit had a resident British officer, the day-to-day processes of government were assigned to Native Authorities. Those kings and chiefs were nominally chosen by traditional means, but the British exercised supervision over them and could veto or remove men who were unwilling to act in accordance with colonial wishes. The colonial system also appointed new local African officials, such as policemen and later sanitary inspectors and tax collectors. This system lessened the amount of control the British had to exercise themselves, minimizing the cost of running the protectorate and ideally reducing the amount of friction between foreign administrators and local people. While indirect rule had worked reasonably well in areas accustomed to powerful hereditary leaders, in southern Nigeria it conferred extensive and unfamiliar political and legal power on local kings and male chiefs. Many parts of the Eastern Region, beyond the Niger River, did not have a system of kings and chiefs at all, and even in the Yoruba kingdoms, royal authority had generally been limited by the obligation to consult widely with other members of the community, including women.

Law was a conspicuous feature of colonial authority. In 1914 the British began to introduce a uniform system of courts throughout southern Nigeria.[4] At the bottom lay the Native Courts. These were held in villages and small towns as well as larger cities, with male leaders of the community (usually primary chiefs, joined sometimes by the king) serving as conveners and judges. Although no British official was normally present at lesser Native Court sessions, their judgments could be appealed to provincial courts, held by the colonial officers, and from there to the Nigerian High or Supreme Court in Lagos. Following British practice, most Native Courts distinguished between civil cases (private suits between parties) and criminal jurisdiction (charges brought by policemen or other local officials). The courts met frequently, usually every day or two, to deal with problems as they arose, and they had messengers who summoned people to appear and delivered other orders. Local languages were used in the courts, but court proceedings were recorded in English: each court had a clerk who had been at least to primary school and could write notes in the colonial language.

In these new courts, where the flexibility of previous Yoruba legal practices was lessened, women could not serve as judges. Female chiefs or heads of women's organizations might, however, be called upon for information. In a divorce case from Ilero in 1932, when the husband said he did not want his wife back but claimed the child she was then carrying, the judges ordered that the woman be examined by the *Ìyálóde,* the leading female chief, to find out if she was truly pregnant.[5] When an immigrant woman in Itaogbolu in eastern Yorubaland refused to marry a relative of her deceased husband in the late 1950s, claiming that by her own Ado-Benin tradition she was free to marry anyone she wished, a female chief among the Ados living in that area was called as a witness and confirmed the custom.

Michael Atkinson, a colonial official during the 1940s and 1950s, described a case heard by a Native Court over which he presided while on circuit.[6] A well-liked young woman was suing an unpopular old one for defamation of character: the latter had told people that she had seen the younger woman fornicating in a farm hut. The young woman denied the charge and said she was still a virgin. At that point Atkinson ordered that she be examined by the British Medical Officer and said he would adjourn his decision until the next session of the court in 4 to 6 weeks. The 15 local members of the court then "rose in a body," and their president said: "Is the D[istrict] O[fficer] going to disappoint all these people by not giving a decision today? The proper person to do the examination is the head of the Women's Society who is here in court. Behind you is the Court Members' retiring room. It won't take a minute." Atkinson's account continued: "Neither did it. The old lady whisked the girl through the door and returned within a minute to announce in ringing tones the equivalent of 'She's all right'." The decision Atkinson delivered in favor of the plaintiff "was greeted with prolonged acclamation."

The British decreed that "customary law," defined as the body of traditional practices found within a given community, was to form the basis for legal decisions in Native Courts, so long as those traditions were not "repugnant to justice, equity and good conscience." The latter qualification was used to ban such practices as slavery and human sacrifice. Because earlier legal judgments had not been written down, the concept of customary law allowed judges to decide how those traditions should be applied in individual cases. It has been suggested that elsewhere in Africa "custom" was heavily influenced by the wishes and needs of the colonial administration and by the local men who acted on its behalf, many of whom had not held equivalently powerful positions in the past.[7] It has also been suggested that men were able to use the colonial courts to control the behavior of women. Those consequences were less severe in Yoruba-land, due to the ongoing strength of traditional attitudes and practices.

The British also imposed some new laws, which henceforth operated in parallel with customary law. For example, the Marriage Ordinances intro-duced in Lagos in 1863 and 1884 and later extended to the whole protector-ate defined monogamous marriages for those who chose to enter them. The ordinances were shaped by unfamiliar Western ideas about society and gender, posing a challenge to traditional definitions.[8] During the opening decades of the twentieth century, divorce became a legal option for Yoruba people who were dissatisfied with their marriages. In the following decades, tens of thou-sands of women seized upon this opportunity, especially those who had been slave wives or were inherited by their deceased husband's male relatives. The British introduced private ownership of property too.[9] This was a very differ-ent concept from Yoruba practice, in which land was held by kin groups or communities and allocated to individual people based upon their need and the amount of labor they controlled. Although men were generally better posi-tioned to acquire private property, some women began to buy farm land or buildings for their own use.

The cumulative impact of the formalization of customary law, the restric-tions placed upon it, and new legislation was gradual but considerable. As Omoniyi Adewoye commented,

> By the imposition of their own concept of law and justice . . . [the British] set up standards of social behaviour more compatible with the achievement of imperialist objectives than the traditional laws and mores. The objective was, as much as circumstances allowed, to inculcate into colonial people certain basic attitudes, and to establish patterns of inter-personal relationships, con-ducive to economic productivity—whatever lip service might be paid to the desirability or even the necessity of preserving indigenous civilizations.[10]

Adewoye showed that in Ibadan the new legal system not only ended slav-ery but also promoted individual self-confidence, a willingness to insist upon one's rights, and greater equality among the sexes with respect to marriage and property owning.

Opposition to colonial rule mounted gradually within Nigeria.[11] Beginning in the 1890s, Nigerian intellectuals joined their peers elsewhere in West Africa in identifying themselves with people of African descent in the Americas and arguing for self-determination for all Negroes. More specific protests usually focused on practical issues like taxation, land tenure, and lack of representation in colonial administration.[12] Among these acts of resistance was the famous uprising of women, especially market traders, in southeastern Nigeria in 1929, which the British put down with substantial violence.

More specifically nationalist feeling and activity, with the goal of Nigerian independence, began to arise in the 1920s. The early movement included members of the Sierra Leonean/Yoruba intelligentsia in Lagos (journalists, lawyers, and merchants) as well as Nigerian students studying abroad. Herbert Macaulay, a grandson of Bishop Crowther, was the most vigorous and articulate spokesperson for this group. In the late 1930s, several proto-nationalist organizations formed within Nigeria. The Nigerian Youth Movement included both Obafemi Awolowo and Dr. Nnamdi Azikiwe (known as "Zik"). In the following decades Awolowo would become the principal figure within the Action Group, the most popular party within Yorubaland; Zik later became the leader of the National Council for Nigeria and the Cameroons, a party founded by Macaulay that attempted to gain a national membership, though its core support came from Igbos in the Eastern Region. Nationalist feeling was promoted by the Italian invasion of Ethiopia in 1935 and the unwillingness of British officials to engage in dialogue with educated Nigerians about policies that affected their country. Through the 1930s, though the British were increasingly reliant upon Nigerians to fill the lower ranks of the colonial administration, they refused to appoint well-trained and capable Africans to higher positions. The Nigerian soldiers who fought in World War II became aware that not all white people were rich and powerful, creating a realization that class could be more important than race. New constitutions for Nigeria in 1947 and 1952 drew more Africans into the government, but the increasingly militant—and increasingly ethnically identified—political parties were not satisfied. Only with the passage of a constitution in 1954 that accepted Nigerian demands for what was in effect self-government until formal independence in 1960 did the nationalist struggle subside. Attention focused in the next few years on issues related to the effective administration of the soon-to-be independent nation, such as improvements in the economy and education, coupled with intense competition for power among the major political parties and their leaders.

In the religious sphere, many Yoruba remained loyal to older beliefs and practices.[13] *Ifá* divination was still used officially in Abeokuta—an early

Christian stronghold—in the later 1930s concerning important issues like droughts, epidemics, and selection of the king and chiefs.[14] The 1921 Nigerian census reported that in Ondo State in eastern Yorubaland, 84 percent of the people followed the traditional religion; in Lagos Colony and Ijebu Province the levels were 38 percent and 47 percent.[15] As late as 1952, 21 percent of the population of Ondo adhered to traditional religion, a fraction only slightly higher than the average for all Yoruba provinces.

Although the number of converts to Islam and Christianity rose across the colonial period, the pace varied by region. Lagos, other coastal communities, and some towns in the interior developed sizeable Muslim populations, joining those in Ilorin and other northern Yoruba areas. The western and central Yoruba cities in which missionaries had started work during the nineteenth centuries produced large Christian congregations, whereas the process of conversion did not begin until after 1900 in many parts of eastern Yorubaland.[16] In the 1963 census, 49 percent of the people in the Western Region said they were Christian and 43 percent Muslim.[17] Although most ministers in the twentieth century were Yoruba, they were joined by male missionaries from Britain and North America and by a growing number of foreign female missionaries.

Conversion to Islam or Christianity did not necessarily mean giving up all earlier beliefs. Some people who had nominally accepted one of the world religions maintained older practices, a reflection of the Yoruba gift for synthesis and synchrony. In the Oyo area, worshippers of the *òrìṣà Sàngó* and *Yẹmoja* who used spirit possession as part of their devotion were heavily influenced by Muslim ideas and practices.[18] Among Christians, a blending of old and new was seen especially in the Aladura denominations, like the Celestial Church and the Cherubim and Seraphim Society, with their evangelical approach and acceptance of polygamy. Even in the mainstream churches that retained ties with their British or Roman Catholic parents, pressure for stronger Yoruba elements was apparent. Charlotte Olajumoke Obasa was a pillar of St. Paul's Church, Breadfruit Street, a leading Anglican congregation in Lagos.[19] Nevertheless, she waged "an uncompromising battle" during the 1920s and 1930s against the use of English during morning services, repeatedly admonishing the British archdeacon that all important services should be conducted in Yoruba. Herbert Macaulay, though the grandson of a CMS bishop, used his newspaper to advocate polygamy and traditional healing practices.

Economic and Demographic Developments

The Yoruba were affected by the combined impact of an increasingly globalized system of capitalist production and trade and the specific policies of British colonial rule. With the conclusion of the Yoruba wars at the end of the nineteenth century, trade increased.[20] We have no measures of internal trade within Yorubaland before 1900, but the elimination of warfare, kidnapping, and local trade tolls certainly facilitated commerce. After the British assumed control, and especially after the Northern and Southern Provinces were amalgamated in 1914, colonial officials promoted transportation, building railways and roads suitable for motorized vehicles.[21] Construction of rail lines had begun in Lagos in 1896, reaching Ibadan in 1900. From there the line moved up into northern Nigeria, connecting with the separate network there in 1911. Railroads enhanced the movement of goods and people, and the men who worked on them were later to form the center of Nigerian trade unionism and contribute to new definitions of masculinity.[22] Colonial authorities introduced a common portable currency (British coins and paper money), which gradually replaced cowries or iron bars, thereby assisting growth of the internal market.[23] The policies of the colonial government promoted production of unprocessed or lightly processed vegetable products for export and encouraged consumption of British manufactured goods. Following rapid growth after 1900, the economy developed at an uneven pace during the years of global depression and World War II. In the later 1940s and 1950s, however, it surged forward again.

Some economic changes were not introduced directly by the state but came rather at the hands of private capitalists, both foreign and indigenous, who were supported by colonial authorities.[24] European trading firms, joined later at middle levels by Middle Eastern merchants, expanded their activities in the interior. As early as the 1920s, British firms had established an effective cartel over the import/export trade of southern Nigeria as well as a banking monopoly. Foreign companies controlled exports, but they hired African male agents to obtain supplies from local producers.[25] Some of the Yoruba brokers, especially those dealing in cocoa, became very wealthy. For distribution of imported items, European firms sold to African entrepreneurs who established wholesale and retail businesses. Local people handled petty trade in produce and the somewhat more profitable trade in merchandise.

Throughout the colonial period, exports from Yorubaland consisted almost entirely of agricultural crops, especially palm products and cocoa, grown mainly on small farms, not on specialized plantations.[26] In the western forest zone, some palm oil was still prepared, for home consumption or sale within Nigeria or other parts of West Africa, but Ikaleland in southeast Yorubaland had become the major center for commercial production of palm oil for export to Europe.[27] Palm kernels continued to gain importance. Before World War I, most kernels were shipped to Germany, but thereafter Britain required that all Nigerian kernels be sent to it. By 1955–1958, Nigeria completely dominated West African production of palm kernels, and much of that crop came from

Yoruba areas.[28] The price paid for kernels was generally low, and it fluctuated widely from year to year, making it difficult for local producers to predict what their profits might be.[29]

In many parts of Yorubaland, production of palm oil was replaced by cocoa. Although cocoa was not introduced into interior areas like Ife, Ondo, and Ekiti until the 1910s, by the 1930s it had become the most widespread and profitable cash crop in forest areas.[30] In 1940–1941 more than 99 percent of the total tonnage of Nigerian cocoa was produced in Yoruba territory. The colonial government tried to promote cotton for export, but with only limited success, and although tobacco was introduced as a commercial crop and some farmers took it up, Nigeria never became a major producer.[31]

After World War II, colonial officials introduced a new system for handling agricultural exports. Government-run Marketing Boards, created for palm kernels and cocoa, henceforth set a flat scale of prices every year, and all sales had to go through their agents. Those agents were large firms—most of them foreign—to which the board had issued licenses. The companies then hired local representatives who operated in towns and markets, employing sub-buyers to collect smaller quantities directly from farmers. Everyone licensed to act on behalf of the Marketing Board had to give a bond at the beginning of each season.

Money became increasingly important in the Yoruba economy during the colonial years. Mounting demand for cash was caused in part by taxation, a highly unpopular policy introduced by colonial officials with the support of British traders. Both groups wanted to stimulate production of commercial crops by Yoruba farmers, and the government hoped to gain some income to offset the cost of administering the protectorate. Men and women alike resented and resisted "fixed, compulsory, regular payments of cash, which required the objectionable counting of persons, and the benefits of which could not be immediately appreciated."[32] Africans' need for money for taxes was reinforced by a desire for the European goods that were becoming available throughout Yorubaland as well as by the availability of Western education, which required payment.[33]

Markets expanded in number and degree of organization, though their physical layout changed little.[34] (See Figure 4.1.) In towns and cities, some markets opened early in the morning, remaining in session throughout the day, while others were active only in the evenings. Larger markets were normally divided into sections, each selling a particular type of food or a cluster of other items directly to consumers or wholesale. Urban governments owned the land on which most markets were situated, and they were responsible for maintaining the buildings and sheds. In some regions, traders sat alongside the roads and paths that led toward the market site and tried to induce people bringing

FIGURE 4.1. The market place in Ojo (Awjaw), a small town in the vicinity of Lagos, 1927. The man in a uniform, middle left, is probably the market master. Snapshot by I. F. W. Schofield. Rhodes House Library, Bodleian Library, Oxford: GB 0162 MSS. Afr.s.1863 (Schofield Papers), box 6, vol. 1, sheet 8, top left. By permission of the Bodleian Library, University of Oxford.

goods to the market to sell to them.[35] They paid slightly lower prices than could be obtained in the formal marketplace but saved sellers the time and bother of going all the way to the market. People who sold in markets (nearly all of them women) were subject to rules about when, where, and how goods might be offered.[36] These regulations might be imposed by a variety of authorities: the market women's own associations, a woman leader responsible for the market, male officials, or a "market master" appointed by the local government.

Periodic markets were common in villages and rural areas that did not offer sufficient supply and/or demand in their catchment area to support a daily market. Some met every 4 days, others every 8 days. These rural markets expanded as new settlements were built outside the confines of town walls, thanks to the cessation of slaving and civil wars. Some of the periodic markets were heavily attended. The village of Akinyele, located 12 miles north of Ibadan, had a permanent population of only 280 people around 1960, but 3,500 buyers and sellers crowded into the market place every 8 days.[37] The growing availability of motorized transport promoted the growth of "farm markets." Located often at intersections of paths and roads, they functioned primarily as collection sites for agricultural produce, which was then taken to larger markets by truck.[38]

While markets had a clear economic role, they functioned also as social centers. The nature and extent of that conviviality varied with the time of day and setting. A study done at the end of the colonial period found that morning markets focused more narrowly on business.[39] Although some community or family news was exchanged, most of the conversations centered on trade and financial affairs. Evening markets, in both small and large settings, were more sociable. They were places where people celebrating important occasions brought their entourage and drummers, and places where unattached men and women could meet. In Oyo's evening markets, attended by roughly even numbers of men and women, men came mainly for social purposes, while women did most of the trading.[40]

Market places were the setting for a variety of religious, cultural, and later political events. When a procession of more than 300 worshippers of the Ọya cult passed through a market place on their way to a sacrificial grove in 1910, some of the market women left their wares to go meet them: they touched the ground with their foreheads as a sign of respect and joined the worshippers in dancing to drums for a few minutes before returning to their trade.[41] Markets could be closed by religious/cultural confinements or ceremonies. The Orò and Egúngún cults imposed curfews in some parts of Yorubaland, during which women had to remain at home; and markets in Ibadan were closed for a day or two during the annual festival of Òkè Ìbàdàn.[42] That practice, mentioned in 1912, was still present in 1950, when "women who were found in the streets were taunted by the vulgar mob." The massive economic and political protests of the later colonial years were commonly organized by traders who boycotted the markets.

Women and men had different functions in colonial markets. Most of the items handled by female sellers were related to goods that their predecessors had traded in earlier generations.[43] Initially these included food and textiles as well as bags and sacks, imported soap, and occasionally household goods like kerosene and small pieces of hardware. In rural markets around Akinyele in the 1950s, women sold local foodstuffs and some goods imported from other parts of Nigeria or abroad: gaàrí (a coarse flour made from dried cassava and cooked with water to make a thick porridge), ẹ̀gúsí (made of melon seeds), beans, rice, fresh fish, dried stockfish, sugar, salt, mats, cloth from Manchester, matches, and gunpowder.[44] The few male traders were usually concentrated in certain areas of the market, working as butchers or selling meat or wood.[45]

In many communities, market trading was supervised initially by women. Organizations of market women regulated prices and quality for their own types of goods, and a leading female chief or the head of the market resolved commercial disputes.[46] Across the colonial period, however, many urban governments assumed some degree of control over markets. Especially if the land on which the market was located belonged to the town, local authorities might appoint a male market master to rent out stalls and maintain good order on market days. Yet urban officials and market masters always required cooperation from the sellers and their organizations. If the colonial government or individual towns imposed unpopular policies, for instance by setting up price controls and regulating the sale of food as happened during World War II, female traders could simply refuse to sell, thereby closing the market.[47] The problems were magnified if the traders who were boycotting the normal system set up private black markets. Even a threat of shutting down the market might be enough to make government officials reconsider their plans.

By the 1950s, problems related to the location, sanitation, and safety of markets abounded. To meet increased demand from growing urban populations, markets frequently sprawled outside their original confines. In Ife in 1950, a major road leading to the prison had recently been "converted to a market by the market women who spread out their wares right on the road."[48] A few years later, Ibadan tried to forbid market women from selling along the road near Gege bridge, due to repeated motor accidents there. In Abeokuta, Madam Ayisatu Ajile Ain, speaking on behalf of the market women, thanked the Native Authority in 1952 for its interest in their well-being but opposed the government's plan to move the market place outside the town; instead she asked that the current site be modernized.[49] Market masters were often held responsible for general sanitation in the market area, facing at least passive resistance from sellers, and some urban governments attempted to regulate the cleanliness of the foodstuffs being sold. The safety of markets might require help from the police. Women traders in Ibadan in 1953 were said to be relieved that the police had succeeded in removing pickpockets and vagabonds from their markets.[50]

Demographic patterns affected and were affected by these political and economic developments. The total population of Yorubaland grew rapidly, especially during the later colonial years. In the 1931 census, the Lagos area plus the Western Region, most of whose residents were Yoruba, together numbered 3,900,000 people.[51] By 1952–1953, the combined population had risen to 4,900,000, and in 1963 it was 10,900,000. Growth contributed to increasing urbanization, most conspicuously in the western and central areas but extending now to eastern Yorubaland as well. By 1963, 38 percent of the population of the Western Region plus Lagos lived in urban areas.[52] For the western and central Yoruba, the fact that they were town dwellers became a matter of pride, even of self-definition. People who lived in dispersed rural settlements in the early Independence period were derided, called by a term that literally meant "country people" but was translated by English-speaking Yoruba as "bush men."[53]

Colonial levels of urbanization were very high by global standards. Based upon decadal estimates and census figures, William Bascom listed ten Yoruba cities in 1911 with populations of 26,000–80,000, plus Ibadan with 175,000.[54] In 1931, Ibadan had 387,000 residents and Lagos had 126,000; ten other cities had between 22,000 and 87,000. By 1952, Ibadan had a population of 459,000 and Lagos 267,000; four other cities had 100,000–140,000, and six had 41,000–84,000. Using a standard index of urbanization, Bascom showed that the percentage of the Yoruba population living in large communities in 1931 and 1941 was comparable to that found in many Western nations. Yorubaland was more urbanized than Canada, France, and Sweden, though below the United States, Germany, and Great Britain.

Rural-to-urban migration stemmed from many factors. Some immigrants sought better schools for their children or modern amenities such as piped water, tarred roads, hospitals, and sometimes electricity, which were concentrated in the metropolitan town within each division or district.[55] As commercial agriculture expanded, more landholders moved their primary residence to an urban community, using dependent or hired labor on their farms. Young men who would previously have lived with and worked for their fathers in rural communities until they were around 30 years old might now leave home at a younger age, hoping to earn their own income in a city. Village craftspeople who could no longer compete with cheap, imported manufactured goods sometimes moved into towns in search of alternative employment. Improved transport for both passengers and goods, by road or train, contributed to the rapid growth of some towns and cities. Population influx helped to create a large group of under-employed or marginally employed people in the cities.

The resources available to urban authorities for dealing with the consequences of immigration were limited. New housing and roads were needed, new schools and hospitals were demanded, and problems of water supply and sanitation mounted. Colonial officials, however, were eager to "exploit the economic resources of the territory with the minimum possible expenditure for overall development and the maintenance of law and order."[56] Likewise, traditional forms of control within towns and cities had been disrupted by the powers given to the British-defined Native Authorities. Yoruba cities thus continued to expand without planning and without the development of adequate infrastructures.[57] They also became more sharply divided racially, with distinct African and European (white) housing areas and increased segregation of social activities.[58]

Western Education and Its Consequences for Women

Western education expanded during the colonial era, though initially it moved slowly. In 1913 the Western and Eastern Regions of Nigeria together had only 534 schools, all of them run by various missionary societies.[59] After

World War I, the government began to establish schools, as did some private individuals, but mission schools remained the most abundant. By 1937, Nigerian schools had places for 268,000 elementary pupils in a total of around 3,500 schools. Not until the introduction of free primary education by the Western Region government in 1955 did school attendance mushroom. Secondary education, which had started on a very small scale earlier in the century, also grew rapidly after 1955, but there was little government support for technical education. In 1948, the University College at Ibadan was created, preparing students for degrees awarded by the University of London. By 1958–1959 it had over a thousand students. A teaching hospital, linked to the university, opened in Ibadan in 1956, offering training for doctors and nurses.

In examining Western-style education and its implications for women, we encounter each of the three interpretive questions that recur in this book. The availability of places for girls and the content of their curricula were affected by gendered and patriarchal attitudes, both Yoruba values and the changing expectations of the British about women's proper roles. Formal schooling of girls was one of the most influential adjuncts of Christianity, and the colonial government later became the major provider of Westernized training. The agency of many Yoruba girls and women is clearly visible in this area, as they decided how to convert the domestic arts they learned at school into money-making ventures. Women who obtained advanced training and moved into educated careers gained authority over other people as well as the extra status that accompanied participation in British-linked institutions like hospitals, schools, and offices.

Education of girls lagged a little behind that of boys. Early missionaries regarded the instruction of girls as less important, mainly because women could not enter the clergy and few became teachers.[60] Parents too might be reluctant to educate their daughters in ways other than the traditional methods that taught appropriate household skills and good conduct within a family context. Coeducational schools were thought to contribute to immorality, and it was feared that education would make a young woman unwilling to accept a husband's control. Until late in the colonial period, few employment opportunities were open to women in European businesses or the government. Because schooling was expensive, many parents thought that it made better sense to educate boys, who would later become income earners for the family. In some cases, kinship obligations required that a man assist in the education of his younger brothers or nephews in preference to his own daughters.[61]

For these reasons, few girls completed more than primary schooling until the later 1940s, and most did not finish even the elementary grades. Between 1900 and 1920, for example, 882 girls "passed through" the CMS Girls' Seminary in Lagos, but some stayed for only a short time.[62] In 1914, the total number of girls enrolled in missionary and government-assisted schools in southern Nigeria, many of whom were Yoruba, was about 16,000, as compared with nearly 24,000 boys.[63] Actual daily attendance of girls was lower. By 1935, enrollment of girls in southern Nigeria had reached 43,000, as compared with 51,000 boys. In 1960, 39 percent of the children enrolled in primary schools in the Western Region were girls, as were 47 percent in Lagos.[64]

 The content of education for girls was shaped by disputed and changing expectations about what they would do as adults.[65] During the first half of the colonial period, a domestic focus was paramount. Many parents wanted their daughters to obtain access to the social advantages of Western culture while at the same time reinforcing Yoruba traditions concerning women's roles within the family. Missionaries in the opening decades of the century were concerned primarily with training girls to become good Christian wives and mothers. In the dominant British Victorian ideology, a proper middle-class woman did not engage in paid employment or take part in public life. Most early missionaries therefore assumed that the graduates of their schools would devote their full attention to the family. That view coincided well with certain Yoruba concepts: Yoruba women too spent much of their time caring for their husbands and children, cooking, cleaning, washing clothes, and nursing sick relatives. Articles by conservative authors in Lagos newspapers during the 1920s and 1930s stressed that "the right type of Western education" should produce a Christian woman able to speak English who was capable of applying selective modern ideas concerning hygiene and consumption "but who still remained basically African in her attitudes and behavior concerning parents, husband, children, and the home."[66]

In keeping with those attitudes, primary schools for Yoruba girls during the earlier colonial period, nearly all run by Christian church groups, offered a mixture of domestic training and academic work.[67] The balance between them depended upon whether the student was being prepared for marriage or for further education. At the high status CMS Girls' Seminary in Lagos, pupils in the opening years of the twentieth century studied basic subjects like reading and writing in English, religion, and arithmetic, joined by sanitation, dressmaking, and freehand drawing.[68] They were also required to do a considerable amount of "industrial" or domestic labor at the school itself, including cooking and laundry, which was thought to instill habits of discipline and hard work among these generally privileged girls. At the CMS girls' boarding school in Ibadan in 1908, the pupils spent 6 hours each day on coursework (academic and domestic subjects), plus 4 1/4 hours on domestic chores. When prizes were awarded for girls in an annual competition among primary schools in Egbaland (around Abeokuta) in 1926, the fields were English Composition, Hygiene and Sanitation, Plain Needlework, Fancy Needlework, and Darning and Patching.[69] The

CMS and other religious groups provided basic instruction for adult women in such areas as hygiene, nutrition, and domestic arts.[70]

A narrowly domestic emphasis was, however, undermined by the belief among many Yoruba people that married women should earn their own incomes. Even at the start of the colonial period, newspapers were publishing critiques of the British assumption that women would remain at home while supported by their husbands. An article in a local paper in 1899, written by a man, noted "the precariousness and fallaciousness in our women in starting life and continuing it without a definite and independent means of livelihood."[71] Another contemporary writer commented that "there is next to nothing for our girls to do besides teaching and sewing," while a third said that girls should be taught "industries so that they may not be mere logs in the hands of their husbands." The idea that educated women should work outside the home was advocated by Herbert Macaulay in a draft speech or editorial written probably in the early 1930s.[72] In an interesting manifestation of Yoruba adaptability, many women who had received domestic science training at mission or government schools converted that education to their own ends: they used Western skills plus the status gained from attending school to create new kinds of economic opportunities, in some cases obtaining considerable wealth and prestige by doing so.[73]

By the late 1930s and 1940s, British expectations were shifting. A narrowly domestic model had been challenged within Britain itself by early feminists, and as the colonial period advanced, a growing number of missionaries and government education officers in Nigeria—especially women—acknowledged that Yoruba women were expected to earn money of their own.[74] Some schools now accepted that girls would later use Western domestic skills within their own businesses and structured their courses accordingly. They also increased the academic content for talented girls capable of going on for further education and promoted leadership. British administrators, who became concerned about female education in the 1930s, wanted in addition to promote sanitation, orderliness, and an interest in European consumer goods.

A call for practical training for girls was linked to their ability to find work after leaving school. During the 1930s and 1940s, Gladys Plummer, the colonial Superintendent of Girls' Education for the Southern Province, expanded and regularized the teaching of domestic science, leading to formal certificates.[75] She called attention to the serious lack of economic opportunities for young women who had been to school: they had few options other than working as seamstresses or becoming teachers or nurses. She therefore encouraged vocational classes that taught young women how to convert female domestic arts, like cooking, baking, fancy sewing, and embroidery, into commercial enterprises as bakers, caterers, restaurant owners, hoteliers, and skilled dressmakers.[76] Until the end of World War II, however, commercial subjects like bookkeeping, shorthand writing, and typing were generally seen as suitable subjects only for boys. Meanwhile, craftswomen, especially weavers and dyers, continued to provide formal or de facto apprenticeships for girls, sometimes lengthy and rigorous.[77] A Muslim women's group in Ibadan set up adult literacy classes during the 1950s, extending its programs to market women even if they were not members of the association.

Girls had few opportunities to obtain an academically focused secondary education until late in the colonial period. Initially, some daughters of elite families went to boarding schools in Britain. Oyinkan Ajasa was sent to England in 1909 at age 12, having started her education at the Girls' Seminary in Lagos.[78] Enrolled at Ryford Hall, the same school her mother had attended, she studied music, drama, and literature before going on to receive an Academic Diploma in 1919 from the Associated London College of Music after 2 years of study. During the mid-1930s, Ladipo Solanke, the head of the West African Students' Union in Britain and director of its hostel in London, provided assistance to a number of Yoruba girls enrolled in British secondary schools, including the daughter of the king of the Egba.[79] Within Nigeria, secondary training for girls developed slowly. The Girls' Seminary in Lagos started providing some post-primary education early in the century, and a few girls were allowed to sit in on classes in boys' schools elsewhere. In Egbaland in 1926, two schools for boys and three for girls—all run by Christian denominations—offered the equivalent of basic secondary training.[80]

The first government-supported secondary school for girls within Yorubaland was founded in the 1920s as the result of pressure from women's organizations in Lagos. The wives and daughters of some important African professional men and bishops urged the colonial government to set up a secondary school.[81] When officials denied that there was any demand for the post-primary education of girls, the women launched a fund-raising drive that led to the establishment of Queen's College, Lagos, in 1927; subsequently it received government backing. In 1930, Queen's College and the upper division of the Girls' Seminary in Lagos were the only schools in the whole Western Region that offered advanced secondary-level courses for girls; together they enrolled just 47 girls.[82] Although secondary schools prepared girls to take exams for government-defined school certificates as well as entrance exams for British universities, the range of subjects they offered was limited. In 1948, a student complained to a newspaper that Queen's College was not offering courses in the sciences or Latin, hindering young women who wanted to become doctors or lawyers.[83] In Ede, it was only in the late 1950s that a determined female principal introduced chemistry and physics at the girls' secondary school, supplementing courses in general science and biology.

Muslim education was likewise expanding, especially in Lagos and the other leading cities. The early twentieth-century schools for Muslim children, whether focused on Koranic learning or run by the government, had produced relatively few young men who went on for a higher education and virtually no women with advanced training.[84] The Ansar-ur-Deen Society was formed with the aim of preparing Muslim boys and girls to study such Western fields as science, law, and medicine, but within an atmosphere that encouraged them to maintain their religion. A branch of Ansar-ur-Deen began operation in Ibadan in 1937, and other Islamic societies interested in education—including the Ahmadiyya—followed. Although these organizations encouraged the participation of girls, a newspaper article in 1941 blamed the present limitations of Muslim women upon "the appalling neglect of Muslim education."[85] The author argued that "Muslim women must be educated to fill their place in the contemporary history of Nigeria" as doctors, barristers, educators, and religious figures and as the mothers of future leaders. Some Muslim women took the initiative in promoting girls' instruction. When Humuani Alaga, a wealthy but minimally educated businesswoman in Ibadan, tried to enroll her daughter in a grammar school in 1958, she was told that Christian girls had priority. Angered, she rallied the members of her Muslim *ẹgbẹ́* to join her in founding their own secondary school for girls. Although most of the women were illiterate traders, they organized effectively, gained new members, and raised the necessary money.[86]

The increasing readiness of schools to prepare girls for well-paid and respected work as adults or for advanced training contributed to the mounting popularity of female education in the 1940s and 1950s.[87] The Native Court in Ibadan accepted a mother's insistence in 1940 that her daughter should complete her secondary education before being handed over to her father, as required by the divorce of her parents.[88] In a family dispute over the custody of two daughters in Egbaland in 1946, the king ruled that they should be given to the younger sister of their deceased father under the condition that she keep them in school; if not, the king would take them back and send them to school himself.[89] A decade later, a female trader in Ibadan who wanted to educate her daughter devised elaborate stratagems to persuade her conservative husband and mother to agree; the girl herself had likewise to employ a ruse to win entry into one of the few places available.

The later colonial period saw an increase in the number of women who obtained a post-secondary education or professional training.[90] In the early 1930s, 76 young women were studying at one of the three colleges that prepared female teachers (a large joint CMS/Wesleyan Methodist college in Ibadan, a Catholic one in Lagos, and an American Baptist one in Ogbomosho).[91] Other women traveled to Britain to get training. Most of those assisted by

Solanke during the mid-1930s were studying teaching or nursing. A government report prepared in 1948 urged that special scholarships be made available for women who wished to obtain qualifications overseas in such areas as nursing, librarianship, and upper-level secretarial work; they would help to fill demand within the colonial system.[92] When the federal government awarded scholarships for study in the UK or Nigeria in 1955, however, only nine of the 76 positions were awarded to women.[93]

An overseas educational pioneer was Kofoworola Aina Moore, later to become Lady Ademola, who was taken to England in 1924 when she was 10 years old.[94] (See Figure 4.2.) Her grandparents were well educated, and her father had attended a boarding school in England before studying at the Middle Temple in London and returning to Lagos to work as a lawyer. Her mother had likewise gone to England after studying at the CMS Girls' Seminary in Lagos, gaining abroad the accomplishments that her daughter characterized in her autobiography as "the general 'finishing' course available to 'young ladies' in those days."[95] Kofoworola herself spent some years in English boarding schools, those willing to accept members of the West African elite, and then became the first black African woman to enroll at Oxford University. Her father wanted her to study law, but she decided to take up teaching. Although she initially felt out of place and homesick at Oxford, she soon became involved in its intellectual and social life. Like many other West Africans in England in the 1930s, she resented British color prejudice and became deeply interested in political developments at home. After receiving a BA in 1935 (having spent a total of 11 years away), she returned to Nigeria, where she became a teacher at Queen's College, Lagos, and joined a small group of professional women committed to educational and social improvement.[96]

Folayegbe Akintunde had to fight to gain her advanced training. She was the exceptionally intelligent and determined daughter of a successful cocoa farmer and a trading mother, whose aunt was the *Ìyálóde* of her small town, Okeigbo.[97] Thanks to the backing of the headmaster of the CMS school at which she was studying in the mid-1930s, who persuaded her father not to withdraw her from school to become a seamstress, Folayegbe finished her primary education and then competed successfully for a scholarship at Queen's College in Lagos. Entering the school when she was 15, she found it difficult at first to maintain her confidence in an elite school in a big city. Once she settled in, however, she performed at a very high level in all subjects except domestic science, which she loathed, and quickly became a leader in her class. After passing the Cambridge Senior Certificate Examination in 1941 (one of only eight candidates who succeeded), she enrolled in a year-long teacher training course at the United Missionary College in Ibadan. She disliked the college's narrow approach, but she graduated and began teaching at the Methodist Girls' High School in Lagos in

FIGURE 4.2. Kofoworola Moore and her father, early 1920s. Originally published in Margery Perham, ed., *Ten Africans* (London: Faber and Faber, 1936), facing p. 324, with no photographer named; republished by Northwestern University Press, 1963, facing p. 17.

1943. After working in various schools for 6 years and becoming the headmistress of one, she applied for and received a government scholarship for a course leading to a teacher's certificate at the Institute of Education in London. While there she decided to prepare to become an Education Officer in the colonial Civil Service at home, a position that had just been opened to African women. Staying on in London to complete an undergraduate degree in economics, she initially supported herself by working during the daytime and vacations while taking classes at night. Later she received a scholarship from the colonial government. In 1954 she obtained her advanced degree, qualifying her for a senior post in the Civil Service of the Western Region.

Within Nigeria, though more young women were attending teacher training colleges or nursing programs during the 1940s and 1950s, they were slow to take up places at University College in Ibadan. This stemmed largely from insufficient secondary school preparation. Only four women were enrolled at the university in 1948–1949, as compared to 100 men; their number rose to 11 in 1952 and to 31 in 1957. In 1961 women constituted just 11.5 percent of the students, and very few of them studied mathematics or science.[98]

At the time of Independence, though the number of school places for girls was small in comparison to the total population, access to education for both girls and boys was better in Yorubaland than in other parts of Nigeria or in most other parts of the continent, with the exception of South Africa.[99] Urban Christians in the western and central areas had the most opportunities. The presence in Ibadan of the country's only university provided an incentive for further education. Their academic advantages placed the Yoruba in a favorable position in the post-colonial state.

The impact of Western education was profound and multi-faceted. The original mission schools have been credited with preserving the vernacular languages and shouldering much of the responsibility for the "social and moral development of the Nigerian peoples."[100] Critics, however, have objected to the cleavage they created between Christian and traditional patterns and to their inhumane treatment of children, including corporal punishment and poor food. Early graduates of mission schools in Sierra Leone or Nigeria constituted the first Yoruba elite, people who interacted on a surprisingly even basis with the British in Lagos during the middle and later nineteenth century.[101] During the first part of the twentieth century, educated Yoruba continued to dominate Nigerian life. The majority of doctors, lawyers, teachers, and clerks active in southern Nigeria until 1920 were Yoruba who had attended Christian schools, as were many of the first commercial magnates and leaders of the early nationalist movement.

But the position of the initial educated elite was gradually undermined: by expanding educational and economic opportunities for other Nigerians, by mounting economic competition from European companies and Middle Eastern retailers, by an influx of British colonial officials and professional men, and by increased segregation of Africans and whites. Yoruba leaders of the later colonial period were well educated, but they came from more diverse social, cultural, and religious backgrounds, and they were differentiated more rigorously from the British. Many of the characteristic leisure-time activities of the early elite were nonetheless maintained well into the colonial period.[102]

Missionary and government schools transmitted powerful new values that extended far beyond the immediate subjects taught. Some were economic. As N. A. Fadipe noted in the 1930s, "When the educated Christian engages in farming, he does so as a capitalist farmer on however small a scale."[103] Schooling also affected family life and gender attitudes. Fadipe observed that education helped to make family groups smaller and more individualized, weakening their involvement with the extended family. Other changes in family patterns included the selection of spouses, relations between husbands and wives, lower fertility levels, and different ways of rearing children.[104] British patriarchal attitudes and gendered stereotypes formed part of the cultural baggage of many Westernized Yoruba, even if they did not implement those values fully in their own daily lives.[105] Oyeronke Oyewumi suggested that ideas of male superiority were especially strong among the elite because its members were in closer and more extended contact with the new civic/public realm that was defined by the British as a male space.[106]

Nor did Western influence end when one left school. Literate women were subjected to an ongoing barrage of foreign values in the newspapers, through articles, editorials, and advertisements. The way that manufactured goods were portrayed to Nigerian women demonstrates that British merchants were working hard to develop consumerism in the colony. Some ads offered women new ways of filling traditional domestic roles, building upon the instruction in domestic arts and hygiene they had received at school. Notices from 1930 and 1950 show African women cooking over small metal stoves that burned kerosene, not wood or charcoal.[107] Other advertisements suggested that it was not enough for a mother simply to cook traditional foods for her family: to keep her husband and children fit, she now had to supplement their diet with manufactured nutritional products. An advertisement for Ovaltine beverage powder from 1941 showed an African woman offering the drink to her husband and four children. The text read:

> Mothers throughout the world are building up strong healthy families on Ovaltine. They know that with Ovaltine they will see their children grow up fine men and women. They know that for father, Ovaltine is the finest tonic food beverage to build up his nerves, maintain strength and vigour, and help keep illness away. For themselves, mothers know that there is no other beverage to equal Ovaltine for keeping them fit for the many duties they are expected to perform.[108]

Women's responsibility for their own health and that of their family was complicated by the presence of a wide range of patent medicines. In 1920, for example, advertisements offered remedies for babies suffering from diarrhea and pills to keep children's livers healthy.[109] A decade later, women were being offered medicines that would deal with their own constipation (a major concern in many of these ads), cleanse their blood, or invigorate their livers. By 1940, advertisements showed pictures of African women and babies as they promoted such items as "Indian Blood Tonic," said to produce radiant health in women.[110] Women were also being told that infant mortality was a problem that could be avoided, no longer a sad but inevitable part of parenthood.[111] This could be done while pregnant by taking special medicines that addressed malnutrition and anemia, thereby improving the chances of survival for newborns. Some ads implied that use of a company's product was a necessary part of elite culture. One advertisement showed an African man with an African woman holding his arm while leading a toddler. All three were smartly dressed in Western clothes.[112]

By the 1940s and 1950s, newspapers were providing their educated female readers with abundant advice and information about their personal and social lives. Special columns for women, with names like "Milady's Bower," dealt not only with beauty and dress but also with such questions as the age at which a woman should marry and the qualities that a man seeking a wife should emphasize.[113] Most of these columns reflected a Westernized and sometimes elitist perspective, even concerning issues that Yoruba women generally regarded in a different light. In 1960, "Josephine," an African columnist for the *West African Pilot,* titled one of her columns "Madam, Your Home Suffers."[114] In it she warned women that they should not work to earn money unless it was absolutely necessary due to their husband's unfortunate inability to provide for the family. Arguing that a woman's desire to have her own income was not a legitimate reason to work, Josephine laid out the damaging consequences of women's economic activity for their children, husbands, and households, as well as for their own health.

For Yoruba women, Western education thus had divergent consequences. For some, it meant an opportunity to gain basic literacy and practical skills that enabled them to generate more income for themselves and their families.[115] A smaller number went on to further training, preparing to enter respected occupations and to marry men from comparable backgrounds. Through their fluency in English and their Western knowledge, these women acquired the additional cachet associated with British ideas and institutions. But the picture was not uniformly positive. The emphasis on domestic science training in schools impaired the entry of women into upper levels of education, waged employment, and the professions. Western conceptions of gender and consumerism as presented to literate women in newspapers reinforced the gap between them and uneducated women and made it more difficult for the two groups to work together effectively in economic and political arenas.[116] Oyewumi argued that the disadvantages girls faced in the Western educational system, including repeated reminders that they were less capable than boys, was a major determinant of women's inferiority and lack of access to resources during the colonial period and thereafter.[117] However one evaluates its impact, formal education was among the most significant components of colonialism for women.

5 | Family and Marriage

THIS CHAPTER DESCRIBES a more personal aspect of the context of Yoruba women's lives: the families within which they lived and their marriages. It begins by looking at kin relationships and the organization of households. Even prior to European contact the Yoruba had differing expectations for women and men within the domestic setting, an aspect of indigenous patriarchy. We turn then to marriage and motherhood, starting with traditional patterns—including polygamy—and looking next at how marriages were affected by the introductaion of Islam, Christianity, and colonialism. British ordinances insisted that women must consent to their own marriages, and they instituted a new definition of monogamous marriage that gave women increased rights. The last section of the chapter explores how divorce was defined by the Native Courts and how women utilized that legal option to end unhappy marriages. Marriage and divorce were areas in which colonial laws and courts increased women's ability to make independent decisions about their own lives.

Thinking about households requires attention to the various settings in which Yoruba women functioned. A simple distinction between a public sphere controlled by men and a private sphere dominated by women is not a helpful analytic tool. Because many Yoruba women participated in extra-domestic economic and social activities, and some had religious, cultural, or political responsibilities, they were necessary members of both spheres. More useful here is the concept of "domains," referring to the physical and social spaces into which a society is organized. Helen Callaway, for example, examined four settings as relevant to "the particular constraints and the notable independence of women in Yoruba society": the layout of the city; the traditional compound belonging to a lineage segment; the dwelling of a modern "nuclear" family unit; and a woman's reproductive capacities, her own inner space.[1]

The domains in which Yoruba women functioned were affected by economic, social, political, and religious factors, including the gender definitions and forms of patriarchy present at particular times and places. For many African women, it was more difficult to compete in mid-twentieth-century urban domains than in smaller communities or earlier periods.[2] Because men had an advantage in such areas as Western schooling, new types of employment, and the emerging political parties, they assumed the great majority of formal leadership positions. Markets were among the few spaces in which women predominated numerically and where they exerted recognized control. The domain of urban housing likewise acquired new forms, with a shift away from large kin-based compounds that were centers of production and had a communal approach to economic activities and child raising in favor of units that contained a much smaller number of closely related people and served primarily as residences.

Kin Relationships and Households

In Yorubaland as in many other parts of West Africa, men and women belonged to three basic kin groups.[3] In most areas these were qualifiedly patrilineal (i.e., descent was traced primarily through male lines), though some Yoruba—including the eastern Ikale—recognized both male and female lines.[4] The broadest kin units were lineages, or corporate descent groups, which traced their common origin to a named ancestor who had immigrated to the present place at some time in the past. That person's sons founded the constituent "segments" or sub-sets of the lineage, the second category. A segment consisted of male members of an extended family who lived with their wives and children in a shared compound. (Men married exogenously, to women of a different lineage, bringing their wife or wives back to live with them.) A large segment's compound might contain several hundred people. In the towns founded or enlarged during the nineteenth century, influential immigrants who brought a following with them commonly founded compounds of their own; lesser people were accepted into existing compounds as stranger clients and were sometimes absorbed into the family.[5] While segments were usually not important in allocating land, they formed the basis for granting chieftaincy titles in some communities. The final unit was the immediate family, based normally upon one man, his wife/wives, and their offspring. It was within that narrower group that procreation and the raising of children occurred. The family might live in a sub-section of the segment's compound, or—especially in eastern Yorubaland—have its own dwelling close to its fields. In unsettled periods, the heads of households sometimes became clients of powerful chiefs in order to to gain protection for their family.

All members of a lineage were seen to have a family relationship. The group had a sense of shared identity, demonstrated by such features as food taboos, customary personal names, and facial or body markings. The lineage was also a corporate entity, with a legal identity distinct from that of its individual members. It held family property, including a block of farm land, as a group, and traditionally its members were collectively responsible for each other's debts. Lineages and segments did not all have the same status. Some were accepted as particularly powerful, while others were dependent upon larger, more influential groups. Kin units, which could split or merge with others, competed for position in such areas as land, wives, and power (demonstrated by markers like the size of the group and the rank of chieftaincy titles held by its members).

Married women formed part of two lineages. They remained part of the lineage into which they were born, allowed to participate in the ancestral and òrìṣà cults of that group and sometimes entitled to a share in the profits from their fathers' farms.[6] They were eligible for a piece of their family's communally owned land if they controlled the labor to grow crops, and in the event of marital discord, a woman could turn to her natal relatives for protection. Women—like men—were expected to offer material assistance to other members of their kin group. Married women maintained their ties by visiting their natal compounds, taking their children with them and joining the ceremonial activities of the group. A woman's closest emotional ties were often with her own relatives, while her husband and children belonged to a different lineage.

After marriage, however, women became important members of their husbands' lineages and segments, even though they had not been born into them.[7] They were considered to be wives of all members of their husband's extended family, male and female, not just of their own individual husbands. That formulation, which does not imply sexual activity, indicates that married women were expected to provide help and care to everyone in the group. Niara Sudarkasa believed that the tendency of Western scholars to focus only on the immediate husband-wife relationship has led to severe misunderstandings of the nature of Yoruba family ties.

Within a given lineage, each person was ranked in seniority based upon the time of entry into the group: by birth for full members, by marriage for wives. Senior members—both men and women—were shown considerable deference. Other people prostrated themselves when greeting senior relatives (women kneeled, men lay flat on the ground), and they carried loads for them and did not allow them to do any demeaning manual work. Seniority operated both between generations and within them, as, for example, between senior and junior brothers. The oldest man in the descent group was its leader, the *baálẹ̀,* who acted as chairman of the lineage. The *baálẹ̀* was expected to settle disputes within the unit and often played a role in the government of the larger community as well.

Age affected one's position in other ways too. Most Yoruba were members of an "age set," a single-sex group consisting typically of people born within 3 or 4 years of each other.[8] Age groups were formed when young men—and in some communities young women—reached adolescence, and they remained a strong social unit throughout their lives. Leadership in an age set was achieved through merit, unlike descent groups, where it derived from seniority. Young people were thus acculturated to cooperating within associations. Broader age grades, containing men within about 7 years in age, were sometimes organized to provide warriors or for public work in the town. During the twentieth century, age-based authority structures were dislocated by the movement of young men in their twenties away from their family's home and into towns and by new methods of defining "elderhood."[9]

Once married, a woman lived with her husband in his section of the family's compound, usually occupying a few rooms or a small house within a larger space shared by other members of his lineage segment.[10] (See Figure 5.1.) A female witness in a case heard in Abeokuta in 1917 said that she shared a compound with her husband, two of her husband's brothers, and the mother of one of those brothers (who was apparently different from her husband's mother); each of those people had his or her own room or house within the compound. In a polygamous marriage, every wife had a separate room, as did the husband; the husband would take turns spending the night with his various wives, to give them all a chance to become pregnant. Open space in the compound was shared by the families, for such purposes as food preparation, craftwork, and keeping chickens and goats.[11] Children slept either with their mother or on a verandah alongside the building.

Major decisions affecting the family or compound were normally made by senior men, but they were expected to consult with the group's leading women. During the nineteenth century, when many households in the western and central areas were disrupted by warfare, migration, and slaving, older women gained unusual prominence within their families, especially at times when male heads were away. Senior members of a family were held responsible for the behavior of those beneath them: husbands for their wives, fathers for children, older siblings for younger ones. Although beating and other kinds of physical punishment were not encouraged, moderate use of them was accepted

FIGURE 5.1. A Yoruba family compound with a woman carrying a baby on her back at the entrance, c. 1880s. The family's shrine stands just outside, a drummer walks past, and several animals graze in the open central area. From *The Gleaner Pictorial Album*, Vol. I (London: Church Missionary Society, 1888), p. 13, bottom image. By permission of the Church Mission Society, Oxford.

as a legitimate form of correction if relatives, slaves, or other dependents misbehaved.[12] Should quarrels arise within the family group, senior members commonly intervened to restore peace.

Many compounds included people other than members of that lineage segment. Labor for agriculture and other productive activities was provided largely from within the household, so more people meant more workers. Further, one of the best ways for a Yoruba man to demonstrate his economic status and power throughout the nineteenth century and colonial period was to head a large compound, filled with wives, children, slaves, pawns, dependent relatives, and clients. (This has been described as "wealth in people."[13]) Immigrant strangers accepted into the household were likewise a sign of prestige. During the colonial period many urban households became much smaller, consisting of the nuclear family and a few relatives, but as late as the 1940s and 1950s, the compound of a secondary royal household in Ibadan contained over 200 rooms.[14]

Although most households were headed by men, some women were able to set up their own domestic units. They were usually older women, either widows who had chosen not to remarry or wives who had left their husbands. Although women generally found it more difficult than men to acquire private property, they could be granted family land by their natal lineage and sometimes—if they had children—by their husband's lineage. Or a woman might support herself through trading or craftwork. In accumulating people around her, a female household head was disadvantaged mainly by her inability to marry wives who would set up their own sub-units within the compound.[15] The women who gained exceptional power during the mid-nineteenth century had huge households, and some of the more prosperous businesswomen and female chiefs of the colonial period similarly generated labor and displayed their status by having many people in their compounds.

Marriage and Motherhood
TRADITIONAL PATTERNS

For the Yoruba, marriage formed an essential part of adult life for nearly all men and women. Traditionally, the Yoruba sociologist N. A. Fadipe wrote in the 1930s, "no person remained unmarried by choice after passing, say, the age of thirty in the case of men and twenty-five in the case of women."[16] (The exceptions among women were those who became religious priestesses or prophetesses.) Although patterns varied among the Yoruba sub-groups, freeborn people were supposed to marry only with the consent of their parents and often the wider family group. Marriage was a matter of concern for the whole lineage segment, because a woman who was brought into it would affect the health and capacities of its future members and the peace of the social unit.[17] Many of the rituals that together constituted a valid marriage therefore symbolized the union of two lineage groups, not two individuals. Marriage also required payment of dowry (sometimes called "bride price") by the prospective husband to the woman, her parents, and sometimes other relatives. The dowry could include in-kind gifts, the provision of labor, and cash. Marriage of a daughter thus offered material benefits to her family. A dissatisfied wife could leave her husband provided that she or her relatives paid back the dowry to his family. Divorced or deserted wives commonly returned to the household of their father or a brother.

The processes whereby customary marriages were constituted among people of free status were described by several early Yoruba scholars.[18] Samuel Johnson, writing in the 1890s, divided courtship and marriage into three stages: (1) an early intimation; (2) a formal betrothal; and (3) the marriage. These stages, which might extend over several years, began with inquiries on the part of both families about the man or woman their relative might marry and about the quality of that entire family. If the answers to those questions were satisfactory, the man would propose to the woman or her parents, with both parties acting through intermediaries. If the woman or her parents consented, the details of the marriage contract—including the amount and nature of the dowry—would be worked out between the parents or other go-betweens. Once payment of the dowry had begun, the marriage was solemnized, with the bride conducted to her new home by her companions and welcomed into it. Although a marriage might be arranged by the parents while a girl was a child, the ceremony would not take place until she had reached puberty.

Local records and biographies provide some details about the formation of marriages during the colonial years. Girls could be betrothed by their parents while they were just babies, though their consent was supposed to be given later, and daughters were expected to follow the wishes of their parents or other relatives about whom to marry.[19] Women sometimes arranged for the marriage of younger females. In most cases the matchmaker was a relative of the girl's, but she might also be a chief or other respected person in the community.[20] Sometimes an *Ifá* priest set up a marriage, or an *Ifá* divination instructed a man to marry a particular girl.[21] At least occasionally in Ibadan, women were married through a practice known as *àṣàntẹ,* in which a man forcibly abducted a woman and took her to his home; later his family would send emissaries to her relatives to normalize the relationship.[22]

Other forms of marriage were used for slave wives, girls who had been pawned, and women without kin.[23] In those cases, all that was required for the woman to be regarded as the man's lawful wife was her consent and her recognition as a wife by the man's family. Ire of Oke, a slave, explained in 1902 that when her mistress died, the woman's husband took her for his wife.[24] She did not mention a formal agreement or payment of dowry, nor did her marriage make her and her children free, as was supposed to happen in indigenous slavery. Amino, a slave woman in Abeokuta, asked for a divorce from her current husband that same year.[25] She reported that when her first husband died, his sister gave her to a fellow slave in the household, by whom she had a child. When that man died, Akinbami, the son of her first husband, took her as a wife, but the relationship was disliked by her first husband's sister, who took her away from him. Amino then accepted another man as a "concubine" (a term applied to both male and female lovers), whereupon Akinbami began to beat her. In a case involving a female pawn who was sued by her master in 1902 for a debt of £7-6-0, the court ruled that because the man admitted he had had sexual relations with her, the sum was forfeited.[26]

An alternative type of marriage—one that missionaries found repugnant—was practiced by some of the eastern Yoruba. "Woman-to-woman" marriage, motivated by a desire to have children, was widespread among the Yagba people of the northeast and present to a lesser extent among the Ekiti, Okun,

Akoko, and Owo during the early twentieth century.[27] A wealthy woman who had been unable to bear children or wished for more of them would "marry" a younger woman, bringing her into the household. That "wife" was allowed to have sexual intercourse with any man acceptable to her and her "female husband." The children born to her were regarded as belonging to the female husband and, if the latter was currently married to a man, to him and his family.

In conventional marriages, the relationship between husband and wife depended upon the region of Yorubaland, the period, and the individual positions of the two spouses. All wives were expected to greet their husbands by kneeling or curtsying, and they used special terms when addressing him, not his given name. Romantic love did not form the basis for marriage in Yoruba culture, nor did men and women expect that their spouses would be their closest friends. Many husbands and wives developed a close partnership nonetheless, as well as often enjoying sex with each other. Women who had their own incomes generally gained enhanced status within marriage. They could contribute to family events and join discussion of family decisions as individuals, and they could educate their children as they wished. If their husbands maltreated them, they were able to repay the dowry and support themselves after leaving the marriage. Wives might also loan cash to their husbands and could sue them over money matters.[28] In eastern parts of Yorubaland, wives were generally more subordinate to their husbands, especially in the nineteenth century. For example, in Ikaleland, where women provided much of the unpaid agricultural labor for their families and were involved in trade only secondarily, men were dominant within the household.[29] Among the northern Ekiti, a wife was defined primarily in domestic terms, valued for the work she did in the family's fields and compound. Ekiti wives were commonly addressed by their husband and his relatives as *erú* (slave).

Although patterns whereby a prospective husband gave dowry to a woman and her parents varied by community and date, the process always involved a series of payments spread out over several months or even years. In traditional marriage formation, dowry was rendered through in-kind gifts and the provision of labor to the woman's relatives.[30] By the mid-1930s, a man was expected to give some mixture of cash payments and presents like yams, cloth, and jewelry to his future wife's father, mother, and the girl herself. An example comes from an Ibadan case in which the aspiring husband first paid £5 as a consent fee and gave £1 to the girl.[31] He presented her family with the leg of a ram plus 10s. during the *Iléyá* Festival (the Muslim Eid-el-Kabir) and 10s. during the *Awẹ* Festival. Later he gave £1-5-0 to the girl for her preparations for marriage, paid £2-10-0 to her parents as the formal dowry, and gave 10s. to a priest to offer prayers. By the 1940s and 1950s, dowry payments were nearly always made in cash.[32]

The amount of dowry demanded by women's families rose across the colonial era, causing concern among Native Authorities and in the press. It was feared that younger and poorer men would not be able to marry: the ability of senior men with more resources to pay high dowries was driving expectations up to an unreasonable level. Articles and letters to newspapers objected to the size of dowry payments and sometimes asked whether the entire institution of bride price was wrong, amounting in practice to the sale of a woman by her parents. Anxiety about dowry appeared occasionally all through the colonial years, with a surge in the early 1950s.[33] The male author of a letter to the *Nigerian Tribune* complained that dowry used to be less than £10, "but nowadays one cannot get a girl for anything less than £50."[34] J. O. Mingla, writing under the headline "Selling Our Girls" in the Women's Forum of the *Southern Nigerian Defender,* said that parents should not force their daughters into unhappy marriages by demanding high dowries; instead, they should lower the amount of the payment and "give freedom to our young generation." During the first half of 1953, the *Daily Times* featured a series of articles and letters about payment of dowry. A letter sent from Lagos to the *Egbaland Echo* in 1954 was more radical, proposing that dowry be abolished entirely. "Let our young girls act according to their will and so avoid the wasting of heavy sum of money that should have been used for the benefit of the future family of the couple."[35]

By Yoruba custom, men were permitted to have more than one wife.[36] In the nineteenth century, polygamy was integral to the social order and system of rule. Men who held political and economic power were expected to have many wives as well as many followers and clients. The conspicuous polygamy of the war chiefs, who might have dozens of wives, sometimes led to a shortfall of wives for others. It also had implications for age relations among men. Since marriage was a necessary step toward adulthood, polygamy reinforced the power of chiefs and senior men over their juniors by delaying the age of marriage. Nineteenth-century polygamy was commonly accompanied by a considerable gap in age between the partners, with older husbands marrying younger wives. In settings where many young adult men had been killed in warfare or captured as slaves, polygamy helped to maintain a high birthrate, thereby avoiding a sharp population decline.

In less disrupted circumstances too, polygamy offered many advantages to men.[37] Wives were a good economic investment, for they provided labor in the family's compound and fields and often brought in some cash income through their trading or craftwork. They bore children who expanded the family's labor force and increased its claim to a larger share of lineage land. Proponents of polygamy argued that it lessened sexual activity by men outside marriage. A Yoruba husband was not allowed to have sex with his wife while she was menstruating, pregnant, or breastfeeding a baby (which usually continued for 2–3 years). A wife who had an average number of children would therefore have been sexually unavailable for more than half of her fertile married life. Even if a man had two wives, there was a 30 percent chance that at any one time he could not have sex with either one. If a man was not satisfied sexually by his existing wife or wives, the Yoruba thought it better for him to marry an additional woman than to have concubines or girlfriends. Whereas casual relationships often led to abandoned women and children, all wives in a polygamous marriage enjoyed the same legal status, as did all their children.

For women, polygamy had variable consequences. In settings that contained more women than men, polygamy gave women the chance to marry and bear children, roles that were essential to their identities. In economic terms, a man who had several wives was less likely to provide fully for them and their children, intensifying women's need to bring in some money of their own. Beyond that, polygamy's impact depended largely upon a woman's place within the marriage hierarchy. Senior wives sometimes chose younger wives for their husbands, focusing on how the prospective bride would interact with the female members of the household and whether she was a good worker. A senior co-wife was often able to direct more attention to her business or other extra-family activities, because a younger wife could take care of their husband and the domestic chores. A senior wife might also be able to mobilize family labor—that of her junior co-wives and any slaves and pawns—to help with her trading or craft activity.[38] For some senior wives, polygamy thus enhanced their ability to accumulate wealth and acquire greater authority vis-à-vis their husbands and other relatives. But for junior wives, obliged to work for both their husbands and their older co-wives, the load at home was proportionately heavier and the chances to trade in any significant way on their own decreased.[39] As nineteenth-century travelers noted, and as Fadipe said in the early twentieth century, "A great deal of drudgery and heavy work normally falls upon junior wives, whether they like it or not."[40]

Personal relationships among the wives in polygamous marriages ranged from close cooperation and friendship to bitter competition. The daughter of a large polygamous family in Ibadan during the 1940s later described the lack of jealousy between her father's many wives.[41] The younger children were not even sure who their own mothers were, since they were raised collectively. But co-wives could also compete for the attention and favor of their husband and for his interest in their own children. In a dispute from Ado Ekiti in 1922, one of two wives described as "rivals" accused the other of being a sorcerer or witch, demanding that she eat Odo bark to prove she was not.[42] A man described in 1941 how his first wife had fought with the second woman he married; after he married for a third time, "there arose a serious dispute amongst the three wives caused by jealousness."[43] In a divorce case heard in Abeokuta in 1952, Sariyu complained that her husband had forced her out of his house because she fought with her co-wife.

Although the Yoruba liked to think of marriage as lasting, in practice some relationships became strained and might fall apart entirely. If conflict developed between a husband and wife, relatives or neighbors might attempt to restore goodwill between them. More severe problems could be referred to a chief or town ruler. Court records tell us little about successful mediation that reconciled two spouses, for it was only failed marriages that led to suits for divorce. In an unusual example, Salisu took his wife Sidikatu before the Egba Complaints Committee in 1952, demanding that she hand over his five children to him.[44] Sidikatu and a spokesperson for the children explained that Salisu had treated them badly, driving them away from his home. The committee ruled that the four older children should be given to the father, who was warned to be kind to them; the youngest child was to remain with his mother until he was 5 years of age. In the meantime, however, "the families of both parties should settle the misunderstandings between Salisu and Sidikatu at home so that Sidikatu might go back to her husband and children."

Marriages could be disrupted for many reasons. A husband might throw a wife out of his household because she refused to obey him or caused discord with other members of the compound. Adultery was a common cause of tension. In a double standard found in many cultures, the Yoruba defined adultery as sexual activity between a married woman and a man who was not her husband. (A married man who had sex with an unmarried woman was not guilty of adultery.) Especially in eastern Yorubaland, adultery had traditionally been punished severely: by flogging both parties; by selling the woman and perhaps her lover into slavery; or even—in the case of the wife of a king or leading chief—by death.[45] But adultery could also be treated more casually. A British official reported in the 1930s that an adulterer in Idanre was obligated to pay damages to the woman's husband, such as gunpowder, weapons, salt, or clothes; no other punishment was prescribed.[46] If a woman was deserted by her husband, she could remarry without repayment of the dowry. In Abeokuta in 1946, Lolade claimed that her husband, Sore, with whom she had had two children, had disappeared; neither she nor his other relatives knew where he was.[47] The king therefore decided that she "could have any man that she likes since Sore . . . could not be found."

Some marital problems involved physical violence. Yoruba culture did not approve of a husband who ill-treated his wife. A sexual lapse or other serious misbehavior would normally be referred to family elders (women as well as men), the head of the lineage group, or local chiefs. Men were, however, allowed to use some degree of physical force in controlling their wives. In 1860, an Ibadan man who had been called before the CMS missionaries, David and Anna Hinderer, for beating his wife responded indignantly, "I tell you, you no understand the business at all. White people no understand husband and wife palaver [arguments] at all. I tell you, in this country, if man no flog his wife now and then, she no [re]spect him at all, no 'spect him one little bit."[48]

If a husband and wife quarreled severely, she could return to her parents or hometown. Slave wives might simply run away from their husbands. In a case of suspected poisoning heard in Abeokuta in 1917, a man explained that there was "a small palaver" between him and his wife, "which made her go to stay for a short time at her parents house, until the palaver was settled, when she returned to live with me."[49] In 1936 a wife in the small town of Modakeke planned to go to her father's house due to "vexation of fighting" between herself and her husband; a wife in Ibadan who had fought with her husband about her cocoa trading left him to go to her father's house.[50] A woman charged by the local policeman for fighting in the street at Ado [Ekiti] in 1923 said she was a weaver from Ilorin, in northern Yorubaland.[51] She and her husband had been quarreling, "and on the day in question he was fighting with me and beat me greatly. I escaped and was coming along the street with full intention to go to my country, Ilorin." Her husband, a petty trader, explained that "the miff between us" arose because "she would not allow me to cohabit with her [have sexual relations] whenever I have the lust of doing so." On the day they were arrested for fighting, he was beating her with a broom "because she would not allow me to have to do with her."

If attempts at reconciliation failed, a separation could become permanent. Divorce as a formal legal proceeding was unknown in traditional practices.[52] A woman who left her husband might remain with her parents or live on her own, claiming a share of family land or pursuing her own trade, with no official termination of the marriage. But if she wished to remarry, she needed to separate formally from her first husband.[53] (A man, by contrast, could remarry as often as he wished, without any official termination of earlier marriages.) In Egbaland in the mid-1940s, the king authorized a number of what were termed "separations," provided the dowry was repaid.[54] Regardless of who initiated the break-up of the marriage, however, the husband had the right to keep all children he had fathered. As Fadipe noted, the fact that children belonged to the father held many marriages together: "the woman who had given birth to them had provided hostages for the husband's extended-family."[55]

Motherhood formed an essential component of most Yoruba women's lives. The respect in which mothers were held is reflected in some oft-repeated Yoruba proverbs.[56] The maternal role symbolized fertility, fecundity, and fruitfulness, and women often prayed to òrìṣà—and gave them offerings—in hopes of becoming pregnant and having healthy children.[57] (See Figure 5.2.)

The Roles of women in Yoruba restored in terms of social religious, cultural and even in their Communities as well of their fourte

FAMILY AND MARRIAGE   91

FIGURE 5.2. Wood carving of a kneeling mother with a baby in a shawl on her back and a small child beside her. The carving originally had another child on the far side. The mother holds a bowl for kola nuts or other offerings. The sculpture was an offering to the òrìṣà Oko, probably from a woman who hoped to have a child or in thanks for having done so. Yoruba peoples, Nigeria. Early–mid-twentieth century. Wood, indigo pigment. H x W x D: 15 ⁹/₁₆ x 7 ¹/₂ x 9 ¹/₁₆ inches. Museum purchase, 85-1-11. Photograph by Frank Khoury. National Museum of African Art, Smithsonian Institution.

Mothers gained authority over their children as well as status within the family and wider community. Women also wanted to have children to ensure their own and their family's immortality: ancestors were venerated as intermediaries between the òrìṣà and humans. Pregnant women were excused from heavy labor during the first trimester but then returned to normal activity until the baby was born. Babies stayed close to their mothers, carried in shawls on their backs as they moved about the compound or community. Although most Yoruba women hoped to give birth to "as many babies as God gave them," the average number of children was smaller among this group than in many other Nigerian and West African communities. The lower birthrate was probably due to a late age of marriage and sexual abstinence during pregnancy and breastfeeding.

In traditional practice, any child acknowledged by a father was considered legitimate, whether or not the child was born in some kind of accepted matrimony. Children generally remained under the supervision of women until they were around 6–8 years old. Thereafter, boys spent an increasing amount of time being trained in adult skills by their fathers or other men, while girls acquired domestic, agricultural, and trading/craft experience by working alongside their mothers or other women. A woman who wanted to be away from home in connection with her trading or other activities needed either to arrange with another woman in the household to look after her children (perhaps a slave woman or a dependent relative) or send the children away to another family to stay.[58]

The relationship between a mother and her children is often described as the most important bond in Yoruba society, followed by the bond among siblings who shared the same mother. Mothers gave birth to their children, cared for them physically, and in many cases worked to earn the money that helped to support and educate them. Equally importantly, they taught them good ethical values and proper behavior, socializing them into Yoruba patterns.[59] They ensured that children learned the necessary cultural forms, such as proverbs. Fathers were usually more remote figures. The ties between a woman and her children may have been particularly strong in polygamous families, where each wife hoped to see her own offspring receive special favor from their father.

Children raised in polygamous households experienced both benefits and challenges. That complexity was nicely expressed by the biographer of Hannah Dideolu, who became the wife of Obafemi Awolowo, Yorubaland's primary political leader at the time of Independence.[60] In describing Hannah's childhood, Tola Adeniyi first said, "The beauty of coming from a large family, the one provided by a polygamous home, is multiplicity of experience one shares with so many children, wives and perhaps relations under the same roof." The author went on to say, however, that to be successful, a child had to win the father's notice and approval. Children therefore "learn very early in life to be competitive, combative and assertive. Each finding protection in their rivalling mothers." It is striking that a number of the most successful Yoruba women during the colonial period were the only children of their mothers (or of both parents) and therefore received special attention and opportunities.[61]

Childless women constituted a challenge to a system of gender definitions that stressed women's roles as mothers, not just wives.[62] Women who were unable to conceive or whose children had all died might raise the offspring of relatives or friends. Working women could take on female apprentices, and once formal education started, school teachers gained a new kind of nurturing role. In some areas, a "woman-to-woman" marriage might be possible. Childless old women were especially likely to be accused of witchcraft, responsible for impotence, infertility, problems in pregnancy and childbirth, and the death of babies.[63]

In traditional Yoruba society, widows normally remained within the family and compound of their deceased husbands. Customs surrounding widowhood differed between sections of Yorubaland, but in some western and central areas a widow was to mourn for 3 months after the death of her husband.[64] During that time she remained secluded inside her house and was not allowed to bathe, change the clothing she had worn when her husband died, or do up her hair. Thereafter, those women still capable of having children were married by one or more of their former husband's male relatives in a practice known as "widow inheritance" (or "levirate marriage"). This practice ensured that a widow and her children would remain part of their current family group and be supported.

A man who wished to take a widow as his wife first obtained approval from her other relatives and then notified her of his wish to marry her. If she agreed, they married when her period of seclusion had ended. Customarily, younger widows were usually inherited by the deceased man's relatives on his mother's side.[65] If his wives were numerous, his first-born son and other grown sons might also inherit some of the wives (but never their own mother). A woman who was above the age of childbearing would not remarry but normally remained in the compound, with a male relative of her former husband as her protector. Within royal families, an incoming king was obliged to marry all the wives of his deceased predecessor, apart from his mother, as well as any women sent to him as gifts in order to cement relationships with the various lineages over which he ruled.

The practice of "widow inheritance" is sometimes described by the Yoruba as a socially valuable means of protecting widows, raising orphaned children, and enabling younger widows to have additional children. But it could also cause problems. The dead man's relatives might quarrel over the distribution of his wives.[66] Widows were not always willing to accept the man to whom they had been assigned: a young widow hanged herself rather than marrying the family's choice for her, and a man rejected by his deceased brother's widow assaulted her repeatedly after she married another man. Marital conflict and divorce seem to have been especially high in situations where the wife had been inherited, particularly if she had become the wife of several consecutive relatives of her initial husband due to multiple deaths.[67]

Some widows chose not to be inherited and not to remain within the compound of their deceased husband, preferring instead to live on their own, as the head of a separate household. This practice occurred occasionally during the nineteenth century and became increasingly common during the colonial period. Because widows who had their own means of support were able to say whether they wanted to remain with a relative of their deceased husband or to form an independent household, Yoruba women had an extra incentive to develop a business or career while married.

THE IMPACT OF ISLAM, CHRISTIANITY, AND COLONIALISM

Yoruba marriage patterns were modified, in some respects very severely, by Islamic and Christian teachings and by colonialism. Certain Muslim beliefs and practices concerning marriage and family were fairly close to those of the Yoruba. Islam allowed polygamy; it accepted Yoruba concepts of the extended family and lineage; and it authorized some familiar inheritance customs.[68] But Islam introduced new patterns in such areas as the categories of relatives whom a person was allowed to marry, the procedures through which marriage was arranged and carried out, child-naming, and circumcision procedures. (Some but not all Yoruba groups had traditionally practiced circumcision, for both sexes.) Islam also limited the number of wives a man might have to four, and only if he could support them all and treated them equally. It established firm procedures to be followed before a man could reject or divorce his wife, and it laid down rules for how a woman could divorce her husband. Yoruba Muslim women were not expected to live in seclusion either before or during the colonial period.

Christian conceptions of marriage had the potential to serve as more powerful agents for change. The Yoruba pattern of a sequence of events between betrothal and the wife's move to her husband's house was eliminated in favor of a single church ceremony (though some Christians continued to celebrate the betrothal as well as the official marriage).[69] Monogamy was required by the mainstream churches; the children of any subsequent, polygamous marriages were denied baptism.[70] Missionaries taught that marriage should be based upon love and companionship between two individuals and must not be arranged by parents without the daughter's consent.

The impact of those teachings was, however, muted in practice. Not all Yoruba Christians abandoned polygamy. In Lagos around the turn of the century, an educated, Christian elite composed in part of returnees from Sierra Leone and Brazil but augmented increasingly by local Yoruba held considerable influence.[71] Of several hundred male members of that group between 1880 and 1915, only two-fifths were monogamous: the majority had multiple wives. Those men resisted monogamy for several reasons. They said it prevented wives from refraining from sex for several years after the birth of a child, which local culture saw as essential to the health of mothers and babies. Because men could not be asked to forego sex during this period even if women could, husbands would be driven either to have sexual relations with the new mother, damaging her milk, or to fornicate. Monogamy would deprive some women of the chance to marry and have children, their natural calling, and it created a problem about what to do with widows. Western problems like prostitution and female poverty were blamed upon monogamy. When elite men's complaints achieved no relaxation in the Christian demand for monogamy, many of them formed unsanctioned secondary unions, sometimes with lower-status women. A man could thus enjoy both a Christian marriage with an educated woman who sought a Western, conjugal partnership and a series of non-binding—and often unacknowledged—relationships. At least a few educated men and women who opposed monogamy in principle entered into extra-marital liaisons with each other.[72]

Some Christian men set up "outside marriages." A man who had already wedded a first wife officially, at church, could use traditional Yoruba rituals to marry one or more other women. In early colonial Lagos, the impact of outside marriage upon women differed in accordance with their educational and social level.[73] For elite women, the existence of outside unions reinforced their insistence upon a monogamous marriage under new British marriage ordinances, to protect their own interests and the inheritance rights of their children. Should their husbands enter into outside marriages, high-status women would probably not raise any public objection, to avoid losing face or risking a breakup of their marriage.[74] For outside wives, such relationships offered access to resources and opportunities that they might otherwise not have enjoyed, a chance at upward mobility for themselves and their children. At the same time, however, these women were vulnerable in social and economic terms. Men sometimes wanted to keep outside marriages hidden, and they could withdraw from them more easily than from an "ordinance marriage." The legitimacy and inheritance rights of children were questionable, because colonial law did not acknowledge the validity of an outside marriage contracted after a monogamous, Christian one. But usually men recognized and gave some financial support to the children of outside marriages even if they had broken ties with the children's mother.

Christianity also affected marriage by offering an alternative vision of female domesticity. Early missionaries transmitted middle-class British Victorian values about the ideal roles of husbands and wives, portraying husbands as economic providers and wives as mothers and homemakers. Especially for elite women, engaging in trade was considered unsuitable. The wives of ministers, teachers, and catechists were supposed to create model Westernized households. As well as being monogamous and patriarchal, their homes were to demonstrate the domestic virtues of the new faith. These qualities included the household skills that the wife had learned at school, which she put into practice herself and taught to her servants and female children. She was encouraged to help women in the congregation to become better Christians, but she was not supposed to work to earn her own money.

The expectation that Christian women would not have income-generating activities constituted a major break from Yoruba patterns.[75] While educated women generally approved of the *social* components of a Christian marriage (unlike their husbands, who often resisted the demand for genuine monogamy), wives chafed at the *economic* confinement it imposed. From the early days of Christian conversion onward, many women simply ignored the requirement, continuing to engage in their own businesses. The wife of the Sierra Leonean returnee and future bishop Samuel Crowther persisted in her trade around 1860, despite vigorous complaints to the CMS by European missionaries.[76] A missionary wrote disapprovingly in 1879 about Mrs. Allen, the wife of one of Abeokuta's Egba pastors. Rather than living with her husband in his station, she stayed mainly in their house in another town, "where she does her own business . . . and has her own slaves."[77] Abigail Macaulay, daughter of Bishop Crowther and wife of the Rev. Thomas Babington Macaulay, insisted on trading to supplement the small salary received by her husband from the church (they had 11 children to support), though the CMS pressured her to stop. Some Christian women leaders in the early twentieth century, objecting to the unwelcome and unhealthy economic dependence of wives upon their husbands, initiated projects designed to provide elite women with suitable income-generating skills. By the mid-1920s many daughters of the leading families were taking up one of the new careers.[78]

Colonialism too affected marriage. The laws imposed by the British created a new system of marriage that provided an alternative to traditional Yoruba patterns.[79] The Lagos Marriage Ordinances of 1863 and 1884, which were later applied to the rest of the protectorate, were based upon laws current in Britain. Colonial legislation defined a different kind of monogamous marriage, one that created a nuclear family, though it could be contracted under any religion.[80] The spouses were regarded as a single legal entity, with common interests and preferences. If a man who had entered into an "ordinance marriage" took another wife while the first marriage was still in place, the second was defined as bigamous and hence void. If he had children outside of the original marriage, they were deemed illegitimate and unable to inherit, even if recognized by the father. In addition, the marriage ordinances prohibited child betrothal and forced marriages without the woman's consent, they laid out procedures for legal divorce (which could be initiated by either husband or wife), and they defined adultery in a manner that gave women easier access to divorce.[81] While colonial officials may have hoped that these laws would help to promote British "moral and social thinking" and reduce what they considered the inappropriate independence enjoyed by Yoruba women, in practice the legislation had very different effects.[82] It gave women more freedom of choice in entering marriage, enabled them to end unsuccessful marriages, and increased their ability to move between communities.

Several secondary features of colonialism likewise affected marital patterns. Improved transportation and expanding commercial agriculture created a demand for labor, especially for unskilled male workers.[83] As young men seized the chance to earn money, they became less reliant upon their elders. One way to use their earnings and their newfound autonomy was to marry when and whom they wished, rather than going through the traditional betrothal pattern controlled by senior members of the lineage. The age of first marriage for men therefore fell. Young women too began to demand a greater say in picking a husband. A man who had come back from waged employment with money in his pocket might be more attractive than the kind of stable, older man favored by a woman's relatives.

The railway was disruptive of customary marriages. Fadipe noted in the 1930s that problems about betrothing girls and the size of dowries had been intensified by the opening up of the interior to trade.[84] Women sometimes left their homes to come to a railway construction camp, where they might meet men whom they wanted to marry or at least to live with temporarily. Because railway workers were paid in cash, they could often give their female partners a nice sum of money with which to set themselves up in trade. The records of the Railway Commissioners around the turn of the twentieth century show both free and slave women acting with considerable independence, released from the control of male relatives, lineage authorities, and masters. Later some women—whether married or not—moved to towns that adjoined the railway in hopes of better trading opportunities. Women who were married to railway workers gained free travel and transport of goods on the lines, a great advantage for their businesses.

In the later colonial decades, a factor affecting some marriage relationships was the concept of the "breadwinner." In this economic/social formulation, common in Britain at the time, households—especially those of the working class—were to be supported by the wages earned by the male head, who brought home enough money to support his immediate family; women performed the unpaid domestic work that enabled men to sell their labor outside the home.[85] Whereas colonial officials did not expect African workers' households to be identical to those in Britain, Yoruba trade unionists in the late 1930s and 1940s were beginning to push for higher wages on the grounds that they were the breadwinners for their families. An important moment was a massive strike in 1945: 40,000 mainly Yoruba civil servants, railway men, and others stayed off their jobs to protest the government's refusal to raise wages.[86] But while male workers were pressing for a paycheck sufficient to support their families, they were able to survive during the strike only because of the income brought in by their wives, usually through participation in trade.

By the 1950s "breadwinner discourse" was circulating widely among southern Nigerian workers. The argument had now grown to include the idea that "Breadwinners make Good Husbands."[87] Many women regarded wage earners who brought home steady paychecks as ideal mates, and male workers were providing a higher fraction of total household income than had been true previously and than was found in other sectors of the economy. Women rarely worked for wages, and when they did, it was assumed that they did not need to earn enough to support a family. In the Civil Service, however, equal salaries were paid to all employees at a given rank, a benefit to the growing number of women who entered government employment in the 1950s.

Marriage was affected also by Western schooling. Educated men often preferred to have educated wives. This was justified sometimes in terms of companionship but more often because such women could maintain a "modern" home, entertain guests properly, and raise the children well.[88] As early as 1902, elite men had worried about how they could find Western-educated wives. The main item on the agenda of a high-status men's college in Oyo was, "Where shall we get our wives from and how should they be trained?"[89] By the late colonial period, men and women who came from literate homes were likely to intermarry, but because the schooling of Yoruba women lagged behind that of men, some men had to take wives whose educational level was lower than their own. The daughters of educated families had often been raised with different ideas about marriage. They expected a fairly egalitarian relationship, with an emphasis on shared roles and responsibilities, and they typically wanted to develop careers of their own. Expanding secondary and university education increased marriages between ethnic groups. Over two-thirds of female university graduates in 1962 married men from a different ethnic background.[90]

Polygamy remained popular throughout the colonial period. A study of Yoruba marriage patterns in 1950–1951 found that 63 percent of all households were polygamous; the average number of wives per married man was 2.2.[91] Christian missionaries recognized that the requirement for monogamy was an obstacle to the advance of their faith, and it was a factor in the development of the Aladura denominations.[92] The independent churches placed no restrictions on the number of wives their lay members or clergy could have, arguing that the European missions had undermined morality by devaluing polygamy and other African social institutions.[93] Even some of the conventional churches were prepared to look the other way. In the area near Ife, regarded as the cultural center of Yorubaland, the Rev. J. S. Adejumo was assigned by the CMS to Aiyetoro's church in 1925.[94] He was both polygamous and a famous traditional healer, practices opposed officially by the missionary organization. Although Adejumo never became a bishop, probably because of those activities, he is considered the most important figure in the history of the Anglican Church in Ife.

The colonial government, despite its marriage ordinances, did not actively oppose polygamy. A government report in 1922 provided a brief but surprisingly sympathetic account of the reasons for the popularity of "one of the most cherished of their ancestral customs," and at least a few British people working in Yorubaland credited polygamy with some important social benefits.[95] Fadipe thought that polygamy was more widespread in the 1930s than before the establishment of British colonial rule.[96] He attributed its popularity in part to economic factors. Rising prosperity enabled some men to pay dowry for multiple wives, but at the same time, a new class of polygamists was emerging, men who were supported by their wives rather than vice versa. The increasing reliance of male farmers upon the labor of their wives in producing cash crops may similarly have promoted polygamy, and the British may have given legitimacy to the institution by including it among the descriptions of marriage practices that formed part of the Intelligence Reports prepared for each district in the 1930s.[97]

Newspapers and public fora hosted active debate over monogamy vs. polygamy during much of the colonial period. In the 1920s and 1930s, editorials and articles in the Lagos papers argued that neither monogamy nor Westernization was necessary to salvation. Their authors noted that the Bible provided many examples of polygamy and that Jesus said nothing about monogamy; they defended "the beauty of a regulated polygamous home and nation" and criticized foreign churches that did not give their African branches "home rule."[98] The early 1940s saw a burst of interest in forms of marriage. One columnist argued that monogamy could not easily be "grafted into the make-up of the African. It is definitely unsuited to their temperament, character and philosophy of life."[99] That opinion was shared 2 years later by the author of a long essay who claimed that monogamy might be fine in Europe, but it was foreign to Africa.[100] At least a few leading Yoruba intellectuals defended polygamy even at the end of the colonial period.[101]

By 1960, marriage assumed divergent forms in Yorubaland.[102] In more traditional households, patterns were strikingly similar to those found prior to 1900. Marriages were regarded as economic and social units, and husbands and wives spent relatively little time together. Men were the dominant figures within the lineage, but the most senior wife was the head of the family's domestic activities, often wielding considerable authority. At the other extreme were "modern" or "egalitarian" marriages in which couples made family decisions together and went out in the evenings with each other, rather than seeking separate recreation or holding large mixed gatherings at their house. A shared pattern was found most commonly among couples who came from literate homes, especially those of the local Christian elite. In both patterns, however, women remained active in their natal families and kin groups, gaining but also giving social and economic support to a wide network of relatives.

DIVORCE IN THE COLONIAL COURTS

For women, the greatest change in marriage during the colonial period century was probably the opportunity to leave an unsatisfactory marriage and take a new husband. The eagerness with which many thousands of women seized upon this option conflicts with the Yoruba emphasis on marriage as a binding link between lineages, in which any disagreements between spouses would be resolved by other members of the family. The possibility of obtaining a divorce reinforced the importance for a woman of having her own income. In 1950, a long discussion of "why women should be educated" on the women's page of a leading newspaper argued that "women [who are] well trained and having a means of livelihood need not be perpetual slaves to an unhappy marriage. They can within their own rights claim their freedom and maintain themselves and their children without being a burden to anyone."[103]

Options for ending marriages were affected to some extent by the new religions. Though Islam discouraged divorce, allowing it only as the last resort if all efforts to reconcile the husband and wife had failed, Yoruba Muslims did specify legal procedures for how divorces should be handled.[104] A Muslim woman who wished to divorce her husband generally had to go before an Islamic court and substantiate the grounds on which she requested the divorce. If it was granted, she would usually lose her dowry. A man who wished to divorce his wife had to wait 3 months before ejecting her from his house, during which time efforts at peacemaking continued, and he had to leave his dowry with her. Christian missionaries likewise disapproved of divorce, but they were often sympathetic to appeals from women who claimed they had been married without their own consent or were denied freedom to convert to the new religion by their husband or his relatives.

The most important modification of traditional Yoruba practices for separation and remarriage came from colonial marriage laws. The Marriage Ordinance of 1884 enabled women who had entered into the new kind of monogamous union to apply to the courts for a divorce.[105] If a divorce were granted on the grounds of her husband's wrongdoing, the woman had the right to remain in the matrimonial home and be maintained by her husband. The Divorce Law of 1907, which formalized a process for divorce in the Native Courts of most western and central Yoruba areas, had greater impact. (Equivalent

measures were not implemented until 1919–1920 in some eastern regions.[106])
By the new rules, a woman could no longer be sent away at the wish of her
husband: divorce was now a defined legal procedure to which both husband
and wife had recourse. When a divorce was granted, the wife (or her relatives
or new partner) would have to repay the dowry that her first husband had
given when the marriage was being created, and the husband would receive
custody of the children. Over the following years, local authorities—both
native and colonial—attempted to define the reasons for divorce and fine-
tune the legal process for achieving it. During the 1910s and 1920s, the Egba
Council in Abeokuta, where divorce had already become common, listed the
circumstances that could lead to the repayment of dowry, limited the amount
of dowry that could be claimed (depending upon the number of living children the woman had produced), and established procedures whereby the size
of dowry could be proved before local courts.[107]

During the rest of the colonial period, wives and some husbands flocked
into the Native Courts to obtain divorces. The arguments in these cases rarely
concerned whether the divorce should be granted: it almost always was, even
for very slight reasons. Disagreements focused instead on the size of the dowry
that had to be repaid to the husband. (The husband of course claimed that
he had made very large payments, while the wife and her witnesses attempted
to show that he had given much less.) We do not yet have detailed analyses
of changing levels of divorce and the reasons for them in various parts of
Yorubaland.[108] Although everyone who uses these court records is struck by
the large number of cases, quantified assessments are rare. One study found
that in 1939 the Native Court of Ibadan Division heard 7,035 matrimonial and
related suits, in most of which a divorce was requested; all other cases together
numbered only 1,105.[109] In 1947, the court heard 12,176 matrimonial suits, as
compared with 1,437 other kinds of cases. Ibadan and the other major cities
almost certainly saw a higher level of divorce than more isolated rural communities, but Ibadan was only one of many divisions in 1939–1947, and divorce
continued at a high rate during the later colonial years.[110] These figures imply,
therefore, that more than a hundred thousand divorce cases may have been
heard in Yorubaland prior to 1960.

The grounds on which Yoruba people requested divorce varied widely. In
Egbaland, the following were listed as legitimate reasons in 1926–1927: ill-
treatment, female barrenness, male impotence, disease of a permanent nature,
such as leprosy, desertion, habitual laziness and neglect of work, a betrothal
that occurred before the parties were of marriageable age, and adultery.[111] A
colonial official said in 1935 that a husband could get a divorce through the
courts "for such slender reasons as incompatibility of temperament. The wife
is granted divorce if she can prove that her husband has maltreated her, is

impotent, always quarrels with her, or that he has become poor."[112] Some women did indeed allege boredom or dislike of their husband as reasons for divorce. In 1908 a woman from Otta, just north of Lagos, rejected her husband, saying "I am tired of staying with him, I would like to get another husband."[113] Adetoro, who was living in Ilero in 1932 with a man she termed her "concubine," stated that she was willing to repay her husband's dowry and an especially large seduction fee because she was pregnant by her new partner: "I don't want my husband again & have conceived for another man." In a complaint to the king of Egbaland in 1945, Layinka said only that "she dont want Bello Apoola her husband any more."[114]

Just as women in other parts of the British empire "creatively wielded the colonial system to bring neglectful or abusive husbands to heel," Yoruba women too sometimes reported violence or lack of support.[115] A female weaver told the Native Court in Ado Ekiti in 1918 that she had left her husband "because he flogged me too much. That's all."[116] In 1950, an Ibadan woman was granted a divorce from her husband, who was then studying law in Britain, not only because he had committed adultery with another woman before leaving the country but also because "he had consistently flogged her . . . with a whip he used on students while he was a teacher." Some women pointed to their husband's poverty or inadequate financial assistance. In 1902, Madandola told a court in Abeokuta that she had left her husband 5 years before because "he is a lazy husband, I had to get provisions & money from my father to feed him."[117] In 1944, however, the Supreme Court of Nigeria denied a woman's request for a divorce on the grounds that her husband had told her before their marriage that he had a salary of £128 per annum, whereas in fact he earned only £39 each year and was heavily indebted.

A factor in many divorce suits was the wife's adultery. In such an action, the husband brought suit against his wife's "seducer," the man with whom she was currently living, demanding return of his dowry and payment of a seduction fee.[118] Almost never did the wife and her new man deny the charge of adultery, and only rarely did the husband say he wanted the woman to come back to him. The actual dispute concerned the amount of the dowry and fee, who would pay them, and by what date they were due. This process was open to abuse, perhaps especially in eastern Yorubaland. Some Ikale husbands set up their wives to seduce men who were then blackmailed into paying reparations.[119] A colonial official in Idanre commented in 1935 that the fees paid to husbands for the adultery of their wives had risen greatly, and that some married couples were abusing the practice by bringing charges of adultery against innocent men in order to extract money from them.

Although divorce was usually granted, Native Court judges were prepared to listen to opposition if expressed by a married woman's parents. In 1939,

Adeoti of Ibadan appealed to the District Officer for review of a judgment by a local court that specialized in marriage disputes.[120] She claimed that she was the wife of Omotoso, "but when I could not tolerate his ill-treatment towards me any longer," she brought an action for divorce with return of his dowry. Her father, however, insisted that the court should not allow the divorce, because—she said—he did not want to be deprived of the farm that his son-in-law had given him. The court therefore refused to grant the divorce, and her husband pushed her into a car and carried her back to the village where he lived. Later she escaped and began living with another man. When she was told that her new partner would have to pay a seduction fee, she appealed to the District Officer against the initial decision. The D. O. commented that the original court had "adhered to the old native custom of following the father's wishes," but since it appeared that Adeoti might suffer hardship because her father had been influenced by inappropriate considerations, the officer recommended that the case be reviewed.

In a petition for appeal submitted in 1945, Subuola Okuku said that she had previously sued for divorce because she did not like her husband and he owed her money.[121] When her suit was heard, her mother and father told the court that they objected to a divorce. For that reason, the judges refused her request, but rather than insisting that she return to her husband, they handed her over to her parents. To her dismay, her parents were now pushing her to remarry. In her request for an appeal, Subuola ended with a fine rhetorical flourish. After pleading that "I can't remain any longer in my parents house, and my parents have no right to give me to another husband," she ended, "I am not an unmarried girl but a woman who have spent over ten years with my husband. I believe you will be good enough to consider me as one of the British Subjects put in your care and never allow me to remain suffering for years."[122]

Husbands who lost (or discarded) a wife through divorce gained several forms of recompense. The dowry and other payments made in setting up the marriage were repaid to him, though the exact amount depended in part upon whether the woman had borne a child for him.[123] In virtually all divorce cases, husbands gained custody of any children that resulted from the marriage, unless they were still young. (Children usually remained with their mothers until they were 3–5 years old, but the father might be required to pay maintenance at a level determined by the court.[124]) The policy for assigning children stemmed from the traditional view that all children "belonged" to their father. A woman who did not obtain a formal divorce but just left her husband to live with another man was expected to give custody of any children conceived in that new relationship to her legal husband.

Most fathers cared about the right to keep their children, in terms of perpetuating and enlarging the family, if not always from personal affection.

Yesufu Akinpelu of Ibadan brought suit in 1954 to get custody of the baby to which his divorced wife had recently given birth.[125] "What motivates my submitting this petition to you is that this woman went away with my pregnancy of 2 months and 8 days old." Although his ex-wife had not yet returned his dowry, he was not concerned about that, only about "my child in her womb. . . . I beg to state that both legitimately and naturally I am the owner of the new borne babe." Husbands owed more respect to ex-wives who had given them children. In Epe, a quarrel between Oyenaike and her divorced husband, Banjo, blossomed into a public fight in 1926 that led to their arrest for breaking the peace.[126] (She had repaid his dowry and was now living with another man.) Banjo denied Oyenaike's charge that he had sworn at her: "She left me, and I have kept and tended our child since then. I would not swear at her, seeing she has given me the child."

In light of the strong Yoruba emphasis on the mother/child bond, it is quite surprising that so many women were prepared to divorce their husbands when it meant leaving their children behind. In very few cases did women attempt to maintain or regain custody of their children after they had been weaned or even to stipulate conditions for the care of the children. A rare example comes from Ibadan in 1920, when Ejigbere asked the court to overturn an earlier decision that had granted her child to her ex-husband.[127] She wanted to get the child back from her ex-husband's concubine, but since Ejigbere admitted that she had been living with her husband at the time the child was conceived, the court upheld the previous ruling.

Divorce attracted particular attention and concern during the 1930s. By that time, because divorce cases had overwhelmed all other kinds of legal action in the Native Courts of some parts of Yorubaland, new courts had been created to deal specifically with matrimonial issues. Fadipe referred to the "popularisation" of divorce, and the availability of this remedy was publicized by newspaper accounts involving important people or unusual allegations of cruelty.[128] Several requests for divorce submitted by the wives of kings—women who had been inherited from the previous ruler—heightened the sense among many Yoruba that marital problems should be resolved informally, within the family, rather than being brought before public courts.[129] One such solution permitted a woman to live apart from her husband without a divorce, pursuing her own activities and perhaps taking a new partner but returning occasionally to her husband if she wanted to visit her children or conceive a child by him.

Some local leaders worried about the potentially unfair economic consequences of divorce for husbands, especially during the depression of the late 1920s and 1930s, when many Yoruba men went into debt. For a man who had pawned himself to raise the money needed for dowry but had not yet repaid that loan, divorce could be devastating.[130] If his ex-wife failed to refund the dowry quickly, he might remain pawned to the creditor who had advanced him the money but no longer have a wife who could help him to repay that debt. In Abeokuta, the king re-worked an earlier Egba practice known as *dìpòmu* in an effort to force divorced women to repay their dowries promptly and to discourage frivolous suits.[131] He ordered that women who had been granted a divorce should be brought to his palace, where they would be confined until they had cleared their obligation to their former husbands. In the mid-1930s, it was reported that if a divorced woman failed to provide sufficient sureties that she would repay the dowry within a specified time, the husband could obtain "a *dìpòmu* order."[132] That order compelled her to stay in the *dìpòmu* ward at the palace, usually for 30 days, under the supervision of two wardresses or matrons. Even in the mid-1940s, women in Abeokuta who ◆ had initiated divorce cases might be told to remain "in *dìpòmu*" until formal action had been taken by the court.[133]

The authority that Yoruba women gained over their marital situation through the marriage ordinances and the right to sue for divorce conflicts with Sean Hawkins's assessment of the damaging impact upon women of similar legislation in the Gold Coast.[134] Further research is needed to examine what appears to be a disproportionate number of suits in Yorubaland involving unhappy slave wives (early in the century), women who had been pawned (into the 1940s), and widows inherited by their deceased husband's relatives. It is also interesting that women involved in divorce cases had sometimes left their original husband long before their current court action, living informally with one or more other men before coming to the partner named as the adulterer in the formal legal action.

Although Yoruba men commonly blamed the increasing (and in their opinion unfortunate) marital independence of women on the influence of Christianity, Islam, and/or colonial laws, other pressures were also leading women to assert greater control over their own marriages.[135] In some cases a woman seeking a divorce was motivated by economic considerations: she might be trying to gain freedom to move away from a setting with few trading opportunities or hoping to escape from heavy household duties as a junior wife in order to work for her own profit. It is significant that divorce came to be seen as a particularly severe problem by Yoruba men just at the time when the demand for labor as provided by household members was at a premium.[136] Another factor was the ongoing power of natal lineage ties, which gave women an alternative to living with an abusive or disliked husband by returning to their own relatives and qualifying for use of family land. Although British officials probably neither foresaw nor welcomed Yoruba women's enthusiastic use of the new laws, one sees little evidence in this region that colonial officials were attempting to curtail divorce, as has been reported elsewhere in West Africa.[137] British administrators in Yorubaland had no economic reason to oppose divorce: women whose marriages had ended continued to operate as producers or traders as they had before, in some cases engaging even more extensively in the market economy. It is to women's economic activities that we turn in the next part of the book.

PART THREE

Women's Economic Activities

6 | Labor, Property, and Agriculture

YORUBA WOMEN WERE necessary participants within the systems of commerce, production, and service provision that operated in their region. Those roles were entirely consistent with their own culture's gender definitions, so long as they did not impinge upon women's responsibilities at home, but they conflicted with British patriarchal ideas. In western and central communities during the second half of the nineteenth century, many women earned money through trade or craftwork.[1] During the colonial period, women expanded those options—found now in most parts of Yorubaland—by entering new occupations that required Western training or advanced education. Women of all religions tried to generate some income to help support themselves and their children and to raise the economic position of their household. A woman who had her own earnings could contribute to family ceremonies and to cultural and social events as an individual, thereby gaining agency. She also had more say about when and whom she married, could leave an unsuccessful marriage, and had a choice about whether to be "inherited" if left a widow.

Our analysis of women's economic functions begins with a chapter that explores several foundational questions. What types of work did women do within the household and public settings, whether as free members of a family or as slaves or pawns? What access did they have to real estate, using or owning land and buildings in their own right? What roles did women play in agriculture? In answering these questions we observe the impact of traditional Yoruba gendered attitudes and practices (including the different assignments given to women and men within the domestic setting), as well as marked changes during the colonial period. During the second half of the nineteenth and the early twentieth centuries, many women and girls were forced into unfree labor. The ending of these practices was due in large part to opposition from missionaries and the colonial government. The British introduced private property, a concept different from Yoruba ideas about land. Women could now own real estate, though in practice they did so less often than men, and the right of a limited number of women and children to inherit property was increased by the new marriage ordinances. Some women used their private farm land to raise crops for sale, but because colonial administrators assumed that commercial agriculture was the prerogative of men, women were less likely to receive assistance from government extension services or to quality for government-funded loans. While colonialism thus increased male dominance in certain respects, it also brought some improvements to women's economic and social status and provided new spheres in which they could exercise their agency. This discussion serves as a base for the following three chapters, which examine the other—and more common—ways in which women generated an income during the nineteenth century and colonial era.

Labor

When analyzing the allocation of work to men and women, economists commonly speak of "the gender division of labor." Because the Yoruba did not distinguish sharply between the tasks assigned to men and women outside of the domestic setting, that analytic tool is not helpful here.[2] We will look instead at the domains within which Yoruba people worked and at who provided the necessary labor.

Many types of work were performed within a given family's compound and fields in order to sustain that household: maintaining the living space, looking after children, and providing food and shelter. Farming was the primary occupation of most Yoruba households, with crops grown for the family's own consumption and sometimes for sale. As will be discussed below, the distribution of agricultural activities between the sexes varied greatly by region, period, and the type of farming undertaken by the household.[3] Within the compound, routine domestic jobs were handled almost exclusively by women. This was true in the nineteenth as well as the twentieth centuries, in all sections of Yorubaland, and in urban as well as rural settings. Though the Yoruba did not have an ideological conception of two genders, they certainly did distinguish between normal male and female roles at home. Women prepared, cooked, and served food, furnishing the necessary utensils. They kept the compound clean, washed clothes, and refreshed bedding materials. They cared for babies

and toddlers, though men commonly spent time with somewhat older children. Men were responsible for obtaining the family's basic farm land, and
they either built and maintained its compound or—in urban contexts—paid
rent. Traditionally they also fished and hunted.

Most households had to interact with the wider economic world in order to
bring in the money needed for domestic purchases, ceremonies within the family and community, and tax payments. Income-generating activities were commonly carried out by women, with trading the leading pursuit.[4] Some women
merely went once or twice each week to a nearby market, taking extra produce
from their family's fields, or sold some small items from their own homes, but
others were dedicated businesswomen, traveling over longer distances to buy
and sell. During the nineteenth century, women were most heavily involved
in trade in western and central areas, but by the later colonial years they were
active throughout Yorubaland. Other women engaged in craftwork, making
cloth, pottery, soap, beads, mats, or baskets. Processing food supplies offered
additional opportunities. Women did all the hand-grinding of coarse flours
made from dried yams, cassava, and corn until the spread of mechanized milling late in the colonial period. A few women performed services for pay, like
head carrying goods for traders or doing laundry. During the twentieth century, a range of new occupations emerged, most of them requiring a Western
education.[5] These included dressmaking, nursing, and teaching.

Women's involvement in the public economy in western and central Yorubaland during the nineteenth century was probably intensified by the physical
insecurity and increased urbanization of that period.[6] Members of households
based in a town usually had to walk some distance to reach their farms. While
people were working in scattered fields, they were far more vulnerable to attack
from soldiers and slave raiders than when they stayed behind defensible town
walls. It made sense, therefore, for women and young children to spend most
of their time in the family's urban compound while men went to the fields. An
urban woman with limited agricultural responsibilities could focus on income-
generating activities, and the family might need her earnings to compensate
for lowered farming production. Urbanization created niches for women as
producers and traders of processed and cooked food. Polygamy reinforced
these options, allowing senior women to devote much of their time to money-
making activities, while younger wives maintained the compound or went out
to the fields with their husbands.

Male economic dominance was limited in most Yoruba sub-groups by the
fact that women generally kept any income they earned and decided how to
spend it themselves, rather than handing it over to their husbands or putting
it into some kind of shared family pool.[7] Women used their own earnings
to supplement whatever food and clothing were provided by their husbands,

especially in polygamous families where husbands had more difficulty in supporting all their dependents. After formal education became available, if the father was not willing or able to pay for the children's schooling, the mother might do so. The division between the resources of husbands and wives was reinforced by the fact that married women often participated independently in family ceremonies, religious rites, associations, and community events, making their own financial contributions.

By the late colonial period, many urban women provided a considerable fraction of their family's total cash income. In 1948, Alison Izzett, the colonial Welfare Officer for Women, analyzed the financial obligations of 2,000 wives, based on case histories handled by her department.[8] She separated the women into three categories: educated, semi-literate, and illiterate. In each group, she found that the wife was largely responsible for the maintenance of her children, feeding her husband, and providing for her own needs. Even educated women married to men in government service or business usually received such a small household allowance from their husbands that it did not cover the family's food expenses. Although most husbands paid the rent, a man's primary financial obligations were to his parents and siblings, not to his wife/wives or his children. Ideally he paid part of the children's school fees and bought their uniforms, but often the mother covered those expenses as well.

The female labor essential to Yoruba economic activities was provided by several categories of women. In the simplest case, members of the immediate family were able to carry out all the necessary tasks. Wives did the domestic work; women and children joined men in farming; and women brought in money through their trading or craftwork, training their daughters as de facto apprentices. Polygamy therefore offered strong economic incentives for men. The labor of another wife was of greater value than the cost of marrying and maintaining her, and she would probably produce children who would—over time—become family workers. In the traditional pattern, in which women and men alike remained at home with their parents until their marriages, vigorous adolescents and young adults provided an important supplement to the labor of their parents. A married woman who wanted to expand her business and devote less time to the home might ask her husband to take a younger wife who would assume much of the domestic load.[9]

Many households, however, were in a position to utilize more workers than the immediate family could provide. In most parts of Yorubaland, the demand for labor increased during the second half the nineteenth century and the colonial period, due to the spread of cash crops and heightened commercialization of the economy. Land was generally abundant, so a family might be able to get additional farm plots if it had sufficient labor with which to work them. Or a trading or craft operation could expand if it had more hands. Women and girls were especially desirable, for they could be used in agriculture, in business, or in domestic tasks as needed. The Yoruba did not have a tradition of employing people to work for them in return for cash wages (though they might provide free labor for a patron or ruler as part of a clientage relationship). The challenge was therefore how to gain additional labor from outside the immediate family in such a way that it could be employed within the household economy.

Female labor could potentially be obtained through family or patronage ties. A household that needed more workers could take in the daughters of other relatives from the husband's or wife's lineage group. These girls would receive training in adult skills, and their new family might take responsibility for finding a husband for them when the time came. Wealthy and powerful people, known commonly as "big men" or "big women," found it easy to attract dependent people to their households. The patron provided protection, material backing, and a social unit in which to live, while the client provided labor and deference. Women on their own, of whatever age, might decide that the security of a patronage relationship was worth any loss of independence. In Lagos after the British annexation of 1861, female slaves commonly left their masters or mistresses but then set up a new dependency relationship with someone else.[10] Some became clients of important people, while others became concubines or semi-free wives.

Prior to the abolition of indigenous slavery in 1916, forced workers provided substantial amounts of labor throughout Yorubaland.[11] Unlike the trans-Atlantic trade with its primary demand for adult and teen-aged male slaves, women and children were often preferred as indigenous slaves.[12] When the British introduced an ordinance in 1878 that required registration of non-local children in Lagos, 39 prominent female traders complained that it would impede the supply of goods from the interior, for they were commonly carried by domestic slaves, some of them children.[13] In eastern Yorubaland, the strong preference for female slaves (and pawns) stemmed largely from a desire for the children they would produce as wives or concubines.

Women as well as men bought slaves to assist in their work. A missionary in Ondo mentioned in 1876 that a rich, industrious female trader had some ten slaves, and a few years later he noted that another woman bought a male slave whom she sent to another town to trade on her behalf.[14] Five Christian women in Abeokuta in the late 1870s had slaves who helped with their trading enterprises.[15] The Yoruba missionary James Johnson commented in 1879 that a woman who was trying to "buy" the title of Ìyálóde at Ake had no children but did own a number of slaves. In Ibadan, where well-to-do women commonly bought slaves of both sexes, local authorities ordered in 1880 that all the wealthy women in the town were to contribute some of their slaves toward funding the war effort.[16]

Even when a female slave was owned by the male household head, her labor might be utilized by free women in the household. Senior wives, for example, sometimes mobilized the labor of their husbands' slaves, including concubines and wives. In the 1860s, Awa, a female slave who was probably a war captive from Ibadan, was bought by Henry Robbin, a prominent male cotton producer and trader in Abeokuta connected with the CMS.[17] Becoming her master's concubine, Awa spent part of her time transporting cotton for Robbin, but more often she and her seven fellow concubines worked for his senior wife, assisting with her trade.

In the Yoruba form of indigenous slavery, many masters and mistresses—especially those engaged in trade—allowed slaves to work for their own profit some of the time. That practice enabled slaves to accumulate money, which they sometimes used to buy their own freedom and that of their children.[18] A female slave belonging to a chief in southeast Yorubaland was trading on her own in the 1870s. When her canoe loaded with goods collided with a salt trader's boat and overturned it, she had to pay him the considerable sum of £4 in recompense. A male chief from Badagry reported in the later nineteenth century that most of his fathers' slaves had run away, but those who had been given land stayed; the women produced palm oil, keeping a third of what they made as well as half of the kernels that remained as a byproduct.[19]

Female slaves were vulnerable to abuse, including physical violence. Freed slaves in the nineteenth century described the punishments they had received for misbehavior: being put in shackles or chained to a ceiling with an iron ring around the neck, denied food and water, flogged with a whip, or threatened that they would be sold to coastal slave merchants.[20] In sexual terms, N. A. Fadipe presented a positive image, writing that if a master wished to have relations with a female slave, "he made her his wife and thereby automatically gave her her freedom." Forced marriage, however, does not sound like an entirely favorable alternative to slavery. Nor were female slaves always accorded full marital rights, freedom, or even better treatment if their masters had sexual dealings with them.[21] Slaves might be sold or abandoned after the death of their master or mistress, and in some parts of nineteenth-century Yorubaland, unfree women, including slave wives, were offered as human sacrifices, especially at the burials of prominent people.[22]

Court cases from Abeokuta in the early twentieth century allow us to watch slave women dealing with some of the problems they faced. One woman gradually redeemed herself and her children in the years around 1900, earning enough money through her own work to pay the fees demanded by her master to obtain their freedom.[23] Another, named Ire, was the slave of a woman who died, whereupon her deceased mistress's husband married her. Later, when her business failed and she was in debt, Ire's husband pawned her son to repay the obligation. He said he would permit her to redeem herself and her two children from slavery, but she could not afford the amount he demanded. A slave wife sued her husband in 1903, alleging massive beating and other improper treatment; one of the sources of conflict was a load of cotton goods for trade worth over £200 that she had received from another man.[24] The courts in Abeokuta continued to hear occasional cases involving former slaves for several decades after 1916. In the 1930s, for example, a complicated land action revolved around the inheritance rights of the descendants of a slave woman who had been absorbed into the family several generations before.[25]

During the later nineteenth and early twentieth centuries, as slavery died out, many households began to use a different kind of constrained labor. The Yoruba word *iwòfà* is usually translated as "pawn," meaning someone whose labor is temporarily assigned to another person to fulfill some kind of debt or other obligation. Under the *iwòfà* system, sometimes described as debt bondage or peonage, a borrower who needed cash might approach someone with ready money, either directly or through an intermediary.[26] The borrower offered to pay back the loan by providing someone to work for the creditor. Conversely, a person who needed more labor could offer a loan to someone else in return for a pawn. The resulting arrangement was made formally, in the presence of witnesses. While borrowers sometimes pawned themselves, it was more common to hand over the labor (and sometimes the person) of a child, slave, or wife. Married adults who had been pawned usually lived in their own homes, working for the creditor a specified number of days per week but allowed other time to work for themselves. When younger people were pawned, they normally lived in the creditor's household. In some versions of the system, the pawn's labor over time was held to repay the full loan, while in others it constituted only interest on the loan. The *iwòfà* system was a response to the need for cash on the part of the borrower, in settings where money was in short supply, coupled with the demand for household labor on the part of the creditor during a period when waged or slave labor was unavailable.

This type of working arrangement had a long history in West Africa. Pawning had been common during the eighteenth century in various parts of the region, and it was used at least occasionally in Yorubaland during the first half of the nineteenth.[27] Later in the century, many large farmers, producers of prepared foodstuffs, and traders relied heavily upon *iwòfàs*. E. A. Oroge suggested, however, that pawnship was geographically concentrated, found mainly among the Egba and Oyo Yoruba, and was of fairly recent adoption, becoming an important source of labor only in the 1890s.[28]

Women and girls were frequently pawned. Adults like Orayemi of Ife might pawn themselves: she borrowed £15 from Olopo in the early 1930s, promising her own labor and that of her son on Olopo's farm.[29] Girls were usually pawned by other people. The parents, siblings, and other family members who obtained cash by pawning them probably felt that the home household would miss a girl's labor less than that of an adult, and they may have hoped that the creditor would decide to marry the pawn, thereby canceling the debt. The latter possibility might have been attractive to a male creditor as well: if he married a female pawn, he could keep her labor indefinitely.[30]

Many women with cash to spare profited from *iwòfà* labor. Mistresses used female pawns as assistants in their businesses and as household helpers, and competition to obtain them could be fierce. In 1907, Augusta George, a seamstress in Lagos and Abeokuta, received a girl named Ololade from her parents in return for a loan of £15.[31] Ololade worked for her for 6 months, but when Augusta sent her to the farm to get wood, Ololade ran away and was then taken as a pawn by another woman. That same year, a laundress in Abeokuta acquired Asiatu as a pawn after loaning £6-5-6 in cash to the girl's relative; Asiatu stayed with her for 8 months before being carried away by another creditor.[32] Sittu Ibiloye of Epe borrowed £7-10-0 from a woman named Lajo in 1926. He offered to repay the debt by giving Lajo 2s. 6d. in money every month, but she said she would rather have Shittu's young sister as a housemaid. In Abeokuta, female entrepreneurs in the textile dyeing industry used pawns as a source of cheap labor through the 1930s.[33] A married woman could also acquire *iwòfà* labor indirectly, if her husband let her use his pawns.

The Yoruba minister Samuel Johnson described the practice of pawning children in positive terms. He claimed that because there was no method whereby young people could learn adult skills by acting as a servant for wages, parents might put a child into another household as a pawn even when there was no debt to pay, "in order to train him into habits of discipline and industry."[34] But the system had a darker side. As well as their lack of freedom, girls living in the household of an unrelated person were vulnerable to sexual abuse. In theory—but not always in practice—if a master had intercourse with a female pawn, he forfeited his money and might be assessed a fine by town authorities.[35] Girls might also remain as *iwòfàs* for long periods. If the original debt was forgotten or ignored, the pawn would be freed from servitude only if a prospective husband was willing to pay the amount of the debt to her master/ mistress as well as at least a token dowry to her parents.

Pawning was opposed by many missionaries and—increasingly over time—by the British government, though some local colonial officials were reluctant to cut off a supply of labor for export-based agriculture. The legitimacy of pawnship was debated in the early twentieth century, and in the 1920s,

Native Authorities in Oyo Province and Abeokuta prohibited the pawning of children and tried to provide greater protection for adult *iwòfàs*.[36] Ibadan's courts did the same on a case-by-case basis. Pawning was increasingly associated in people's minds with slavery. In a divorce case heard in 1940, Esutoro described her complicated marital history, which began when her father pawned her to cover a debt of his. As recorded by the court's clerk, she ended her statement with an emotional outcry against her father's decision: "Pawning some one at this time? this is more or less *slave trading*."[37] Between 1938 and 1943, the taking of new pawns was banned throughout Southern Nigeria, but in some parts of Yorubaland remnants of the system lingered until the close of the colonial period.[38] Fear that children would be abducted and sold into involuntary labor remained strong. Newspaper articles in the 1930s and 1950s referred to young girls who had been kidnapped while selling on the streets and forced to work for their abductors, and in the 1940s, some women in Ibadan refused to let their children be vaccinated against smallpox lest they be sedated and carried away into slavery.[39]

Property Holding by Women

Yoruba women were allowed to hold and utilize family and private property, though they did so less often than men.[40] Women who had land or buildings of their own were in a position to make decisions within their households and—if they were economically successful—to gain status and authority within the wider community. Traditionally, because the Yoruba believed that land is essential for life, necessary for the very survival of the society, it was not "owned" in the Western sense of private property.[41] Rather, what was termed "family land" was held by a collective group (usually a lineage, sometimes a geographical unit) that included the dead, the living, and those not yet born. The equitable distribution and efficient management of family property rested with the heads of the lineage or community. Use of particular parcels was granted to households or individuals based upon their need and their ability to command the labor needed to make productive use of the land. When land was plentiful, it might also be allotted to newcomers. Family property could not be sold or conveyed on a permanent basis to someone outside the group.

Gendered customs affected women's ability to hold family land. Although patterns varied by region of Yorubaland, male household heads always qualified for land, and a man who held family property could bring his wives to live there with him.[42] In some areas, however, female as well as male members of a lineage had rights of usage to family land. A woman might therefore gain land through her natal family, though she could not let her husband join her there. A woman marrying into a family had no automatic rights to the land of her husband's lineage, but she was not disqualified from receiving it.

Family property could be inherited. Specific practices varied with period and region of Yorubaland, and the details of inheritance rules caused many legal problems.[43] Traditionally, the principal beneficiaries of a deceased man were his mother's other children, male and female. His full siblings thus had first claim, not his own children. By the 1930s, however, although the former custom had not died out entirely, the right of children as the heirs of their father had been recognized in nearly all communities. When women inherited family land from their fathers, Native Courts often allowed them to pass it on to female as well as male heirs.[44] If family property had been "pawned" or rented to someone else—and hence detached somewhat from traditional constraints—women were more likely to be regarded as legitimate heirs. By Yoruba custom, women did not inherit from their husbands, just as men did not inherit from their wives.

When the British introduced the concept of private property, they developed laws to control the ownership and transmission of this kind of real estate. Beginning in Lagos in the mid-nineteenth century and extending gradually throughout Yorubaland, British property laws were based upon simple, absolute ownership of land, including the right to sell it outright to someone else.[45] During the 1850s and 1860s, the colonial government began giving out crown grants of land, which conveyed rights of private property, and the king of Lagos followed suit. Due to the town's booming economy and swelling population, a market for real estate—both residential and commercial—developed. Among the most active participants were Sierra Leonean and Brazilian returnees, whose Western education and values predisposed them to these commercial transactions. They were joined over time by native-born Yoruba. During the twentieth century, British laws and the expansion of cash crops increased the amount and desirability of private property and promoted the growth of a real estate market. "Europeans" (white people), however, were not allowed to purchase land in any part of Nigeria.

Women were legally able to acquire private land and buildings in their own name. In mid-nineteenth century Lagos, however, many fewer women than men received grants of freehold property.[46] During the following decades, some women inherited private real estate, but few bought their own holdings and none amassed the great clusters of land and buildings accumulated by the wealthiest men. (Women were probably held back by lack of education, cultural capital, and actual currency, but they may also have chosen to invest their resources in different ways, such as the education of their children or expansion of their businesses.) Further, while women who held individually owned property were nominally entitled to manage and benefit from it themselves, they often found it difficult to protect their rights against male relatives. Court records show women fighting over property against husbands from whom they had become estranged, husbands' younger brothers, brothers-in-law, and sons. Private property could be transmitted freely by sale or bequest in a will.

Different laws controlled inheritance of property within those marriages contracted under the new ordinances. When fully enforced, this legislation gave much greater security to widows and children. In monogamous marriages, spouses had rights in each other's real and personal property: widows could inherit land and/or houses from their husbands. It then became the woman's property, and when she died, her children inherited it. If a woman already held private real estate when she entered marriage, other rules applied.[47]

Because British inheritance laws contradicted the Yoruba tradition whereby fathers recognized all their wives and children, whether or not the latter were born in formal marriages, some men found ways of sidestepping the new legislation. Among the early educated elite in Lagos during the decades around 1900, the nominally exclusive rights of a Christian wife married in accordance with the new ordinances and of the children of that marriage were not solid.[48] Men could use their wills to disinherit an estranged wife or to transmit property to outside wives and offspring. Of 54 elite men in Lagos who are known to have had both Christian and non-official wives between 1880 and 1915, 11 provided for their outside wives in their wills, and 20 provided for outside children. That problem was largely resolved in the 1950s, when the courts ruled that the offspring of polygamous and/or outside marriages were legitimate, provided that their paternity had been acknowledged, and hence were entitled to share in their fathers' estates equally with descendants of marriages contracted in accordance with the ordinances.

Women who acquired their own real estate—whether family land or privately owned—gained both security and independence.[49] Sometimes they used their property to generate income. As we shall see, some grew foodstuffs that could be taken to market, while others raised cash crops for export. Women might also erect buildings for their own use or to rent out to others. In Modakeke in the 1930s, a married female trader put up a little shop from which she sold her goods.[50] Early in the twentieth century, Mary Peters paid some of the costs of building a house on land granted by a local chief in the village of Ilugun; she and several other people lived in that house until her death in 1921. During the 1930s, when ownership of the house was in dispute, a different woman collected rent of 1s. monthly from each of eight tenants living in single rooms in the building. In 1954, Abigail Aina, a petty trader in Ilesha, re-built and rented out to tenants a house that she had acquired after her mother's death.[51] On a larger scale, some successful traders in Lagos were earning money as landladies by the late 1940s. Four hundred women, most of them middlemen or wholesalers in the city's markets, had used part of their earnings to purchase houses in which they rented out rooms.[52] The properties were owned individually by the women, even if they were married.

The difficulties encountered by owners of urban rental property are illustrated by the experience of Adenike Osin of Lagos.[53] When her husband, a civil servant, was transferred out of Nigeria in the 1940s, she went with him, leaving the job of collecting rents from the tenants of the buildings she owned in Lagos to her daughter. The latter, a 14- or 15-year-old school girl who lived with Adenike's illiterate aunt, failed to insist that the tenants pay Stamp Duties and did not issue proper receipts. (She was described by her mother as inexperienced in rental procedures and uninformed about government regulations.) When Adenike later returned to Lagos and attempted to raise the rents, her tenants formed an association and complained against her to the attorney general, who ordered her to pay £60 in back Stamp Duties.

Women's Roles in Agriculture

In most areas of Yorubaland, agricultural labor had to be provided by humans, for draft and pack animals were killed or weakened by insect-borne parasitic diseases.[54] Farm plots were cleared from the forest or bush by men, using iron axes or cutlasses. A field was then planted, weeded, and harvested for a number of cycles. (Most regions had two to four farming seasons each year.) Once a plot was no longer yielding a good crop, it would be allowed to lie fallow, usually for a longer period than it had been under cultivation. The customary staple food was yams, supplemented by starches that had been introduced from other parts of the world: corn (maize), cassava, and—in some areas—rice. Domestic animals, like fowls and goats, were generally handled by women. In some traditional communities, men had banded together into cooperative groups for major agricultural tasks and house building, but that practice died out over the colonial period.[55]

The assignment of agricultural tasks to men and women varied by region, period, and the type of crop being raised. In western and central Yorubaland during the second half of the nineteenth century and colonial years, men provided much of the labor for growing the food crops consumed or sold by their families. The jobs of building up the mounds into which seeds were placed, thinning, and weeding were done primarily by men. Women helped when extra labor was needed, especially with planting, harvesting, and carrying produce from the fields back to the compound. Because women were commonly engaged in trade, preparing palm products, or craftwork, the family gained more net value from letting them pursue their own income-generating activities the rest of the time. William Clarke, who traveled near Oyo in the 1850s, noted that "the males are the only class on whom this duty [of cultivating the soil] devolves though the females very frequently aid in harvesting and may be seen daily bringing in loads of provisions from the farm."[56] His statement is supported by visitors to western Yorubaland: T. J. Bowen commented in the 1850s that "women never cultivate the soil as they do in Guinea"; M. R. Delany said in 1860 that women helped with the harvest and carried produce but did not do the "hard work" of agriculture; and a British missionary who traveled in the Ibadan area in the mid-1860s stated that at harvest time, the road was lined with men going to their farm labor, while hundreds of women returned to the town carrying produce.[57] Women's limited participation in agriculture may have constituted a change from traditional patterns, a response to the physical instability and urbanization of the period and the increased demand for female labor in trade and in producing palm oil and kernels.[58]

Eastern Yoruba women evidently furnished more of the agricultural labor for their households. We know relatively little about the nineteenth century from written sources, for few travelers or missionaries went to these communities. Charles Young, a Yoruba catechist based at Ode-Ondo in 1875, reported that many of the men and children had gone away to their farms "and a good many of the women too—as their women also cultivate lands as well as the men."[59] A few years later he wrote that in some seasons the women went to the farms to cultivate while the men remained at home. New research based upon interviews makes clear that in other parts of eastern Yorubaland, women provided a substantial fraction of the labor on family farms.[60] Apart from the initial clearing of a new field, women carried out many—in some cases most—of the tasks involved in planting, growing, and harvesting crops. Spending substantial amounts of time in the fields was related to limited participation in trade. Women might take produce to a market near their farm (most local markets were open a half-day out of every four or eight) or buy/sell other items there, but they rarely traded on a larger scale or traveled to more distant markets. Only during the colonial period did eastern Yoruba women begin to engage more fully in trade.

A farming system that was particularly advantageous for men but difficult for their wives was found in some of the Ikale kingdoms.[61] There a woman was required to maintain two farm plots every year. Produce from the first went to the husband, while the second was hers, used in part to feed her daughters. The husband provided food for his male children, but after filling that obligation, he was free to use the proceeds from his farms in whatever ways he wished, including acquiring more land, houses, wives, or chieftaincy titles. Although the system was widely recognized as unjust and exploitative, it continued until the early twentieth century.

During the colonial period, female participation in farming for market sale increased in many regions.[62] Rising urban demand stimulated production of foodstuffs. As early as 1928–1930, a study of the annual net output of some little farms containing 1–2 acres in Ondo Province found that although yams, corn, beans, and cotton were raised in part for home consumption, one-third of the yam harvest and one-half of the maize harvest was sold.[63] On larger farms devoted more actively to market production, most of the foodstuffs (as well as palm kernels, kola nuts, and cocoa) were sold, forming more than two-thirds of the household's total income. During the 1930s, Ondo women were heavily involved in crop production, whereas in Ife men—often pawns—did the clearing, hoeing, planting, weeding, and harvesting with little help from women.[64] But even if women did not grow crops, their labor might be needed in transporting food to market.

Women's ability to profit from increased production of foodstuffs depended on several factors, the first of which was who held the land. When women took produce to market that had been grown on their family's fields, even if it was flour or meal they had processed themselves, the income went to the head of the household, usually a man. If, however, the land belonged to the woman herself (family land that had been granted to her individually, or private property that she had purchased), she could keep whatever she earned from her sales. The amount of time she could devote to her own fields depended in turn on how much work she had to do on the family's land, which took precedence. Even prior to colonialism some women in Ondo were said to have had small farms of their own for raising animals, which they tended during their spare time.[65] Some of the poultry, pigeons, sheep, goats, and pigs were used for religious or social ceremonies, while others were sold in markets. An early female ruler was said to have angered her chiefs and people so strongly by walking out of a meeting to look after her poultry that the Ondo vowed never to allow a woman on the throne again. In most regions, however, women's farming on their own lands did not become common until the 1930s and 1940s.[66]

Women's engagement with commercial food production was affected also by the type of crop. Cassava, popularized in Yorubaland by returnees from Sierra Leone and Brazil beginning around the middle of the nineteenth century, was seen as a woman's crop.[67] Women thereafter developed cassava agriculture as an alternative to yams, which were usually cultivated by men. During the 1930s and 1940s, for instance, Ekiti women introduced onto their own plots of land cassava and the equally new crop of cocoyams, both of which lay outside the economic sphere controlled by senior men.[68] By the end of the colonial period cassava and the coarse flour made from it, known as *gaàrí,* had become major food sources throughout Yorubaland.

Cash crops raised for export required differing amounts of female labor and affected women's economic status in diverse ways.[69] Whereas women commonly *processed* palm oil and kernels, kola nuts, and cocoa beans, they did not usually *grow* those items unless they had land of their own. Raising palm and kola trees, which took little labor, was done by men, and it was men who harvested the fruits and nuts. Cocoa bushes demanded somewhat more care, but in many regions by the later colonial period, migrant workers were available.[70] A study of labor patterns in cocoa farming in western Nigeria during the 1950s showed that male farmers supplied 61 percent of the labor, as opposed to 32 percent from hired male workers and just 6 percent from women.[71] During the course of a year, women spent an average of only 17 days in farming: 10 days on food crops (including during harvests) and 7 days on cocoa production.[72] Their husbands, by comparison, worked a total of 172 days in agriculture, while hired labor provided another 47 days. Fifty percent of the women's time was devoted to food processing, home industries, or trade; 40 percent went to housework, cooking, and domestic duties. Not only were wives of cocoa farmers free to spend much of their time on trading or craftwork, their husbands might be able to set them up more generously in a business thanks to their increased cash earnings. In this type of commercial crop production, women's status was therefore enhanced.

Cash crops could, however, have different consequences. In Ekiti, wives and children helped to plant cocoa seedlings, spray the plants, and harvest and transport the beans.[73] Family members might also be called upon to replace migrant workers at times when husbands lacked resources with which to pay wages. Further, many Ekiti men withdrew from production of food crops during the later colonial period, since cocoa was more lucrative. Women thus found themselves responsible for growing the household's food as well as providing some of the labor for commercial agriculture. The cotton and tobacco grown in savannah areas of northern Yorubaland demanded considerable labor and reliable workers. Farmers generally preferred male migrant employees, but workers might be requisitioned from the household. When a farmer insisted that his wife devote much of her time and energy to the family's cash crop, she would be less able to generate her own income, weakening her independent status.

Some married couples struggled with the question of how a woman should be compensated if working on cash crops controlled by her husband kept her from her own economic activities. In Ekiti, "women realized that the switch to cash crops eroded their traditional rights, and sought compensation from their husbands for the increase in their workload on the farms. This could take the form of cash, cloth, gifts, or taking responsibility for the children's school fees and material welfare."[74] By the 1960s, wives and other female relatives in Ibarapa too were commonly rewarded through various kinds of reciprocal (but often delayed) payments in return for providing additional labor on their husbands' farms.[75] Thus, a woman who head loaded her husband's crops to the market each week might expect him to contribute to her expenditures for ceremonies within her kin group, egbẹ́, or town as well as giving her cloth or money at annual festivals.

Although men generally dominated commercial agriculture, a rising number of women in some regions were using their own land for cash crops by the middle and later colonial decades. Near Abeokuta, one woman had a farm that produced palm nuts in 1921, while another held land planted with palm trees and cocoa in the late 1930s or 1940s.[76] In Ibadan District, a woman who had been allocated a piece of land by a chief in 1929 used it to grow cocoa; sometime before 1947 another woman acquired family land with kola nut trees by redeeming it from the person to whom it had been pawned.[77] An Ife woman who loaned money to a man who wanted to buy iron sheets for building was promised before his death around 1930 that she would inherit one of his six cocoa farms as repayment of the debt.

Independent female participation in cash cropping may have been especially common in Ekiti and Ondo, eastern areas where women had gained experience through working on family land.[78] The first women to start raising export crops on their own account in Ekiti were widows. Starting around 1940, these women—rejecting the earlier pattern of "widow inheritance"— took over the farms formerly owned by their husbands.[79] Often joined by their children, they devoted the land to cash crops, functioning as head not only of the household but also of the farm. Divorced women in some settings began to purchase land for their own use rather than returning to their parents.

Women farmers, like male ones, might want more workers than their households could provide. Especially because they did not gain labor from their own wives, they had to look for other kinds of workers. During earlier periods, some women utilized unfree labor. Madam Tinubu, an economic and political power in Lagos and later Abeokuta, was said in the 1850s to have 2,000 slaves working on the farm land she had acquired.[80] Efunsetan Aniwura, an equivalently important figure in Ibadan, owned three large farms at the time of her death, each worked by at least a hundred slaves. Iye Jigi of the eastern Kabba kingdom was reported to have "hundreds of drudges" (probably pawns) working on her farmland in the early twentieth century.[81] But most female farmers had to hire and pay any extra workers, usually non-Yoruba men. In 1938, for example, Moworare Aje of Ife employed Momoh Gange, a Hausa man, to work on her farm (but then did not pay him the agreed-upon wages).[82] In the early post-colonial years, women who had their own cocoa farms—many of whom lived in towns and had bought their land with profits from trade—normally hired managers to supervise the operations and male laborers to work them.

Female farmers were at a disadvantage when dealing with the colonial government. The British assumed that commercial agriculture would be carried out by men, and that economic development would be most successfully promoted by helping male farmers to become more productive. Due to their own patriarchal biases, the British were uncomfortable when interacting with independent Yoruba women farmers. Women therefore rarely received attention from the agricultural extension specialists sent out by the government or qualified for government-sponsored loans.[83]

Building upon this discussion, we look now at the other ways in which women earned an income for themselves. To highlight changes over time, our analysis considers the nineteenth century and colonial periods in sequence.

7 | Income-Generating Activities in the Nineteenth Century

THIS CHAPTER AND THE next two explore the income-generating activities of Yoruba women other than renting out property and growing crops for sale.[1] In discussing the nineteenth century, we begin with early descriptions of women traders and lay out some general features of their work. The next section traces how women moved into processing and trading palm oil and kernels and describes the careers of some exceptional women who gained great wealth and political authority between around 1840 and the end of the century. After looking at craftwork, we then highlight a series of obstacles that made it difficult for women to compete on an equal basis with men in economic terms. Chapters 8 and 9 describe women's work during the colonial years.

Women's ability to pursue their economic activities was limited by gender-based expectations among the Yoruba concerning their roles within the home and proper behavior outside it. It was fine for women to earn money, but their domestic responsibilities had to take precedence. Male dominance was thus present in practical terms even though the ideological system was not clearly gendered. British patriarchal assumptions and practices imposed additional economic hurdles. But women were by no means passive recipients of the new pressures introduced from outside: in many cases they were able to manipulate those forces to their own advantage. The success of Yoruba women in creating economic opportunities for themselves amidst the changing circumstances of the nineteenth and twentieth centuries demonstrates considerable female agency.

Trading

EARLY ACCOUNTS AND GENERAL CHARACTERISTICS

The first scattered references to women's trading roles come from the 1820s and 1830s, with more information from the 1850s and thereafter. Most of these accounts pertain to western and central Yorubaland, where gendered economic patterns differed from those found in eastern areas and may reflect recent changes due to political/military and demographic developments. Some women were already trading in the markets of their own or nearby communities in the early nineteenth century. Freed slave Joseph Wright, when describing the Egba town where he was living prior to its fall in 1825, commented that before an *Orò* cult's ritual in which women were normally supposed to go into their houses, a special warning was given to the women who were selling in the market: they were instructed "to hide themselves, or bow down their heads beneath their knees, or cover their faces with their handkerchiefs" so they would not witness forbidden sights.[2] Thomas King, a freed slave who had returned from Sierra Leone, explained that when he was captured in the Abeokuta area around 1825, he was at home alone with some younger relatives: his mother and elder sister had gone to a town some 15 miles away for several weeks of trading.[3] Hugh Clapperton, who traveled up the western side of Yorubaland in 1825–1826, mentioned women selling in a market, and when the Lander brothers reached the large market town of Egga in southwestern Yorubaland in 1830, they noted, "Women here are the chief, if not the only traders."[4]

Women engaged in intermediate and long-distance commerce too. Samuel Crowther, later an important CMS missionary and bishop, was bought as a slave in 1821 by a Muslim female trader from Oyo.[5] During rainy seasons, when travel was difficult, she stayed at home, weaving. When weather permitted, however, she went on trading trips far away from her own area, taking Crowther with her. Both Clapperton and the Landers met many male and female traders on the paths between towns. Clapperton commented that women whom he described as wives of the king of (old) Oyo "are to be found in every place trading for him, and, like other women of the common class, carrying large loads on their heads from town to town."[6] He encountered one group of royal women trading about 200 miles south of their home. The Lander brothers similarly met a hundred wives of Oyo's king trading in a southwestern Yoruba town.[7] The women carried loads of carbonate of soda and locally made cloth from the north, which they bartered for salt and European manufactured goods, especially beads. These royal wives profited from their exemption from tribute or tolls and from the requirement that they must be entertained by the chiefs of every town through which they passed.

By the middle of the nineteenth century, the expansion of commerce had created more opportunities for women traders. William Clarke, who traveled widely in the western area during the mid-1850s, commented that women sold all types of goods in the markets, whereas men seldom took part.[8] T. J. Bowen said in that same decade that in market places, "The women sit and chat all day, from early morn till nine o'clock at night, to sell their various merchandize."[9] Noting that the principal marketing hour, and the best time to see the wonders of the market place, was the evening, Bowen continued, "As the shades of evening deepen, if the weather allows the market to continue, and there is no moon, every woman lights her little lamp, and presently the market presents to the distant observer, the beautiful appearance of innumerable bright stars." In 1861, Richard Burton observed that trading in the markets at Abeokuta was the "peculiar privilege" of Yoruba women.[10]

In hopes of gaining group security from slave raiders and kidnappers, women who traded away from their home communities commonly joined the caravans that carried goods between towns and regions of Yorubaland. Some of the male members of caravans were merchants or porters, while others were soldiers who had been hired to guard the group or were traveling to obtain firearms and ammunition. But women apparently constituted the majority of caravan traders by the 1850s. Bowen commented that "a good many men, and still more women, are engaged in traffic. Some are engaged in exchanging commodities of the interior, chiefly ivory and carbonate of soda from the desert, for the productions and imports of the low country, as salt, tobacco, cotton cloth, beads, guns, etc."[11] Samuel Johnson, a Yoruba minister in Oyo who wrote during the 1890s, described Ibadan in the mid-nineteenth century: "The women of those days were as hardy as the men, and often went in a body—as caravans—to Ikire and Apomu [smaller towns 15–20 miles away] for corn and other foodstuffs although the road was unsafe from kidnappers. They supplied the town with food whilst the men were engaged in slave hunting."[12] Women traders might agree to take other people's goods or slaves with them, for sale in the market to which they were headed. A man who bought five slaves in 1866 and wanted to get them to another town for re-sale entrusted them to a woman trader who was going that way.[13]

Women also produced food and drink for market visitors. Bowen noted that "women are always engaged in preparing all sorts of dishes to passers by"; they also "make a beautiful malt, and a passably good beer, of Indian corn and millet," which they sold themselves.[14] (Men, however, dominated the sale of palm wine, since only they were allowed to climb the tree trunks to make the necessary incisions and collect the sap.) An engraving in a CMS publication in 1851 shows a woman in Abeokuta serving hot food to her male customers. (See Figure 7.1.) The description accompanying the image said that the woman

FIGURE 7.1. A woman selling cooked food to her customers, Abeokuta, 1851. From *Church Missionary Gleaner,* New Series, I (1850–1851): 188. By permission of the Church Mission Society, Oxford.

was selling "the ordinary morning meal of the inhabitants—a sort of hot gruel composed of Indian corn meal. . . . She has dipped it out of the earthen pot with a wooden spoon, and is pouring it into a small calabash, the buyer paying a cowry or two in proportion to his wants and means."[15] Archdeacon Graf of the CMS, who was in Ibadan and Abeokuta in 1854–55, commented that during the morning and evening markets, "food of every kind can be purchased for a few cowries, ready cooked and smoking hot, which is a great convenience to the inhabitants, who can thus provide themselves, before and after the day's toil, without the trouble of cooking at home."

Other women benefited from demand for food and drink among the travelers and caravans that moved through their area. In towns and at designated group resting places, women catered to hungry travelers. M. R. Delany observed in 1859–1860, "Cooked food can always be had in great abundance from the women at refreshment stands kept in every town and along the highway every few miles while traveling."[16] Four thousand people were said to have stopped at a large halting place north of Abeokuta for 2 days in 1856, causing food prices to soar. Over time, regular markets grew up at some of those locations, bringing outside merchants together with local producers and consumers.

Women were commonly used as porters, to head load goods. Apart from the northern savannah, all trade items had to be transported either in canoes or on human heads throughout the nineteenth century. Pack and draft animals could not survive, and mechanized transport using roads and railway lines was not yet available. The canoes used for transport on lagoons and rivers were usually owned by men, and it was men who rowed or poled them. (See Figure 3.1.) Head porters, however, were often women: female traders or their slaves, pawns, junior co-wives, or other dependents. Because women carried agricultural produce home from the fields, it seemed natural for them to transport trading goods as well. Clapperton, accustomed to British ideas about proper gender roles, was upset that when his baggage was divided among the Yoruba porters assigned to him, the heaviest pieces were assigned not to young men but rather to women—and to old women at that.[17] He noted also that Hausa merchants coming south into Yorubaland used female slaves as carriers, together with some women who worked as porters for pay. The Landers commented that the slave women they met on the paths "bore burdens on their heads that would tire a mule."[18] Burton wrote that men carried loads of 40–80 lbs. for weeks on end; women could be seen "staggering, as if about to faint" under loads of 112 lbs.

Women served as local porters and hawkers too, moving about with bundles on their heads or backs.[19] In Abeokuta, for example, women transported grass for rebuilding houses into the city from the wharf where it had been landed by canoe men in 1852. In Ijaye, women walked around in the market offering eggs, fowls, and goats, while in Abeokuta in the mid-1870s, some women went from door to door of people's houses, selling cloth and other wares.[20] (Mobile commerce provided a fine opportunity for Christian evangelizing at the same time.)

Scholars have debated whether female trading was a traditional feature of Yoruba society or emerged out of the atypical conditions of the nineteenth century. B. W. Hodder and Gloria Marshall (later Niara Sudarkasa) claimed that the civil wars only intensified an existing pattern in the division of labor whereby women traded and men farmed.[21] Sudarkasa argued that because Yoruba women had always been traders, they differed from many other West African cultures in which women entered the distribution sector of the economy only during the colonial era, having previously been primarily cultivators.[22] Simi Afonja, however, rejected those arguments, claiming that the level of female trading in Yorubaland was substantially higher in the nineteenth century than in previous periods.[23] She suggested that the economic transformations of that century had profound effects on the gender division of labor, especially in the area of agriculture. Because new crops were being introduced and slave labor was more heavily used, both on farms and within homes, the amount of time freeborn women spent on agricultural production and housework was reduced, freeing them to participate more actively in trade.

That controversy did not pay adequate attention to the marked differences between women's involvement in trade in western and central Yorubaland as opposed to eastern areas. Some sources suggest that eastern women did not trade at all, at least not until late in the nineteenth century. When two Yoruba Christian missionaries traveled to Ikaleland in 1880, they spoke disparagingly of the people and lack of social organization there.[24] Among the ways in which the Ikale failed to live like other Yoruba were the limited presence of markets and the fact that women went to the farm to work just like men, instead of trading. A. Oguntuyi proposed that women in Ekiti may have learned trading during the wars of the 1880s, when refugees from Oyo and Egba areas introduced new skills and gender definitions.[25] Newer research, however, indicates that women *did* trade in eastern Yorubaland during the nineteenth century, though with less intensity. Because they bore heavy responsibility for raising crops, women in Ikaleland, the Akoko region, and Ekiti North participated in trade primarily through the local markets held in their own areas every 4 or 8 days.[26] To them women brought produce from their family's fields, foodstuffs they had processed, and sometimes craft items. While they might travel to other nearby communities, trade over longer distances was normally handled by men.

If we focus on the western and central parts of Yorubaland, for which we have fuller information, we may ask what kinds of women traded during the second half of the nineteenth century, how they obtained the resources to begin their businesses, and how they used their earnings. Women of all ages, socio-economic ranks, and marital statuses traded. New brides, younger wives with small children, and very elderly women sold either from home or in local markets, as did poor women who had little capital to invest.[27] Women with older children could devote more time and energy to trading, especially if they had slaves or junior co-wives to carry out necessary domestic work, and they were free to travel outside their own communities to buy and sell.[28] Women who had accumulated money and/or credit from earlier business activity were in a position to deal in more expensive—and hence more profitable—items. The women who excelled in long-distance trade during the nineteenth century rarely fit the conventional pattern of wife and mother. Those who were married usually had adult children or were childless, while some were widows who headed their own households. As Francine Shields observed, these women were often perceived as having masculine qualities.[29] But older women were not necessarily successful traders. The Landers pitied the elderly royal wives from Oyo whom they met in 1830, who had all "passed the bloom of life": the women "possess scarcely the shadow of royalty, much less the substance."[30] Not only were they required "to make long and painful journeys to distant parts of the empire, for the purpose of trading," but they had to provide themselves with food and clothing and give part of their earnings to the king.

Women commonly obtained their initial trading capital from their husbands. It was expected that a man would give or loan his wife some resources with which to start trading, but the income she derived from her labor was her own. N. A. Fadipe, writing in the 1930s, said that 30–50 years before, a woman "trading in foodstuffs such as cassava, yams, and maize, often required not much more than half-a-crown" (2s. 6d.) to begin her work.[31] Women who specialized in manufactured goods, such as imported wares or traditional woven cloth, needed more capital. Some women carried stocks of 20 or more large cloths, requiring a payment of some 300s. to the weavers. Purchase of slaves and the loans granted to obtain pawns were also expensive.

If a woman needed extra resources to expand her trade or for family or kin-related expenses, she might be able to borrow money from her husband or obtain funds from outside the household. Members of egbẹ́ often assisted each other financially, or a woman could join a rotating savings and credit group known as an èsúsú. In the type of èsúsú most commonly used by women, each person paid in a fixed amount every week or month; the full sum was distributed to the members either on a rotational basis or at an agreed-upon date when the èsúsú ended.[32] No interest was charged and there were no operating costs, but members could usually not access cash on demand, only when their turn came around or the group closed. Èsúsús were in use in some parts of Yorubaland by 1860, and perhaps long before then, and they were already associated especially with women.[33] In 1861 some 300 savings clubs operated in Abeokuta alone. Credit mechanisms that offered larger sums were less frequently employed by women, because they had little land of their own and fewer slaves or valuable goods to put forward as collateral. Other forms of credit were the ìwọ̀fà or pawning system and professional moneylenders, who demanded payment of interest in cash at a level at least equal to the principal.[34]

Women used their profits from trade in many ways beyond the basic purpose of helping to provide for themselves and their children. They might spend part of their income to propitiate òrìṣà, obtain information from an Ifá divination, or assist Muslim or Christian institutions.[35] Many spent some of their earnings in joining and contributing to egbẹ́, gaining social, economic, and sometimes religious benefits. Wealthier women commonly invested in people (slaves or pawns), land, luxuries such as handsome clothing and jewelry, and the kinds of public benefactions that might lead to a chieftaincy title.

Female trading probably benefited the wider Yoruba community as well, not just the individual women and their families. T. M. Ilesanmi suggested that the social interactions that occurred through trade helped Yoruba women to become more accepting of people from other ethnic sub-groups and more committed to peace.[36] Women's "sense of accommodation of the opinions of other people and appreciation of their ways of life" produced more harmonious interactions than men generated, thereby helping to maintain some degree of toleration and cooperation within Yorubaland despite warfare and slaving.

PALM PRODUCTS AND SOME EXCEPTIONAL WOMEN TRADERS

Women living in the rainforest belt of western and to a lesser extent central Yorubaland enjoyed atypical economic opportunities during the middle and later decades of the nineteenth century due in part to European demand for palm products: the oil extracted from palm fruits and the kernels prepared for export. Palm oil was produced in a series of stages. Delany and Robert Campbell described the processes they observed between 1850 and 1860 at several manufacturing sites in western Yorubaland.[37] Men tended the trees and climbed them to harvest the palm nuts, but that was their only role. Women separated the fruit from the nut and husk, boiled the fibrous pulp in large clay pots, and crushed it in mortars. The pulp was then placed into large vats filled with water, where women treaded out the semi-liquid oil, which rose to the surface as it separated from the fiber. The oil was collected and boiled once again to get rid of any water that had adhered to it before being placed in clay pots for transport and sale. In preparing kernels, women cracked open the palm nuts that were left after oil had been extracted from the fruit, separated the kernels from other material, and dried them. The kernels were then sent to Europe for processing. Those operations continued right through the colonial period in most areas. In some cases, however, palm oil was produced by gangs of workers, mobilized by wealthy women or men.[38]

Making palm oil and processing kernels was women's work in western and central Yoruba areas. Samuel Johnson described them as exclusively female industries, and in Ijebuland, located northeast of Lagos, a taboo prohibited men from handling palm products: if they did, they might become paralyzed.[39] The great wealth that accrued to Lagos during the nineteenth century thanks to export of oil from the Ijebu area was thus the result of women's labor. But palm production in the western and central regions was gradually overtaken by the Ikale area of southeastern Yorubaland. In Ikaleland, the leading Yoruba producer of palm products as early as the 1860s, preparing oil and kernels for export was done almost entirely by Urhobo immigrants.[40] These tenant farmers had moved from their homes farther east along the coast, bringing a more efficient native technology with them.

During most of the nineteenth century, women not only *produced* palm items in the western and central areas, they were also the primary *traders* in them. If a woman sold oil or kernels from her family's trees, the proceeds normally went to her husband, but if she produced oil from her own land or bought and sold oil made by someone else, she kept the profits. Many women carved out a new economic niche for themselves by buying oil or kernels from local producers, combining them into larger units, and arranging for their transport to market. In 1850, the returnee missionary Thomas King described preaching to "the women in the palm oil market at Oko," and in 1858 the British Consul Benjamin Campbell wrote that "it is the women that trade at the oil markets."[41] Two decades later, John Whitford noted the predominance of women who came into Lagos via the lagoons to trade palm oil and kernels, among other goods.

Production and trade in palm items created a demand for labor. Making these products encouraged the development of larger households. The goods had also to be transported, often on heads to nearby markets and then by canoe to the Atlantic ports, where they were sold to foreign exporters.[42] To obtain more labor, women might accept the children of relatives to raise, welcome other dependents, or take pawns, but the main source of additional workers was slaves. Wealthier women bought female slaves to help with production of oil, and they used both female and male slaves to act as porters or canoe men.[43] In mid-nineteenth-century Lagos, some slaves were allowed to trade palm oil for their own profit on the side, while a few unusually fortunate ones obtained land on which to produce it.

Women who sold palm products earned "money" (initially in the form of cowry shells) for their wares. In 1861, Burton passed a young Yoruba woman who was sobbing and wailing because she had just dropped a pot of black oil (from processed kernels) worth at least 4 heads of cowries, a sum that would allow a person to live for 4 weeks.[44] While that payment was low when compared to the hours of labor required to prepare the oil, it was more than a woman could hope to earn from the scant profit margins of local market trading or the modest yields from making and selling most craft items. Because prices varied considerably between markets, women who had capital and were able to travel could make a good profit. In 1887 it was reported that a pot of oil selling for 5 heads of cowries at Orun market in the interior would fetch 12 heads at Lagos.[45] A woman who made that trip would thus have gained a profit of 140 percent on her investment.

The destabilized conditions of the mid- and later nineteenth century enabled a small number of female traders in Lagos, Abeokuta, Ibadan, and nearby towns to gain exceptional wealth and political influence through large-scale trade in palm items, slaves, military supplies, and other goods. These women took advantage of the combination of expanded commerce with Europe, the Yoruba civil wars (which created a need for imported guns and ammunition while at the same time furnishing captives), and ongoing demand for slaves (initially for export but increasingly for domestic purposes). Through their own wealth, intelligence, and control over military materiel, they acquired authority within some of the governments of western Yorubaland as well. This window of opportunity lasted for only a few generations, from around 1840 until the end of the century. Thereafter, women found it increasingly difficult to compete at the upper levels of commerce. The women discussed below thus illustrate the kind of power that could be achieved by unusually talented, aggressive, and effective women during a period of political and economic transition when new kinds of activity had not yet been clearly gendered.

Efunroye Osuntinubu, commonly known as Madam Tinubu, was an Egba woman who achieved fame because of her trading success and political influence.[46] She was born around 1805, according to legend in a canoe while her mother was returning with her grandmother from a trading trip to the coast. She received her first training in trade in Owu, but following her marriage and the birth of two sons, she moved with her husband to Abeokuta. After his death, she married a prince of Lagos's royal family who was then living in exile in Badagry. Over the next decade she moved back and forth between Badagry and Lagos, depending upon the political fortunes of that husband and her next one, a war chief in Lagos. Her first two sons died, and she bore no children to her later husbands.

In Badagry, Tinubu expanded the scope of her trade to capitalize upon the new opportunities she observed on the coast. She traded in arms, ammunition, tobacco, and salt and acted as a middleman between providers of slaves in the interior and foreign traders in the ports who were supplying slaves for Brazil. When she encountered particularly healthy and strong slaves, she kept them for herself. This allowed her to broaden her trading, using slaves to carry such goods as palm oil, elephant tusks, and cotton from the interior and deliver them to the warehouses of foreign merchants. She gained great wealth and by 1846 had become a prominent member of the commercial elite of Badagry.

The political component of Tinubu's career began when she attached herself to Akitoye, the exiled king of Lagos. Taking advantage of her powerful economic position, she built up a faction devoted to securing his restoration to the throne of Lagos. In 1851, when Akitoye returned to Lagos, Tinubu followed him. There she became the power behind the throne, wielding influence that increased substantially after 1853 when Akitoye's weak son, Dosumu, succeeded his father. Tinubu was an outspoken critic of both the British government in Lagos and foreign merchants, whom she saw as monopolists who deprived local people of their economic rights.

At the same time she continued to expand her own trading, buying more slaves and extensive holdings of land on Lagos island and the nearby mainland to use for palm groves and food production for her household's consumption. It was said that she owned "some 2,000 slaves in her farms alone, exclusive of those at home."[47] She also trained her male slaves to serve as a fighting force to defend her enterprises and threaten business competitors. Perhaps not coincidentally, she was the only important trader in Lagos who had not come under the influence of the missionaries. By 1855, Tinubu was the leading intermediary between the interior, especially Egbaland, and Lagos-based merchants, including European and Brazilian slavers.

Tinubu's economic and political power caused jealousy. In trade she competed with the returnees from Sierra Leone and Brazil who were trying to gain control over regional commerce. In political terms, her influence over the king was resented by some of the leading chiefs. Benjamin Campbell, the British Consul, disliked her importance in the government and what he perceived as her promotion of slavery; she must have violated his gender assumptions as well. In 1856, Campbell and Tinubu's African enemies, who termed her "the terror of Lagos," agreed that she could no longer be tolerated.[48] When she was forcibly expelled from Lagos, Campbell announced proudly that he had broken up a great middleman monopoly, to the delight of the many traders who had been cheated by it.

But her expulsion was protested by hundreds of Tinubu's supporters and by her creditors, who had attempted to shelter her from disfavor. The trading system of that period was based upon credit and trust, and she owed over £5,000 to the merchants who had advanced her money with which to buy palm oil for them. Her own cash position was weak. She had previously been forced to mortgage part of her property at Tinubu Square in Lagos to settle some of her debts. In justifying her removal from the city, Campbell wrote that "her largest creditors have long given up all hope of obtaining any portion of their claims from her."[49]

Far from defeated, Tinubu moved to Abeokuta, where in a short time she re-established herself as a commercial intermediary, again focusing on weapons, ammunition, and ivory as well as palm oil. Delany, an African American, had several meetings with Madam (or, as he called her, "Princess") Tinubu in 1859–1860 and was impressed by her prosperity and business acumen.[50] About 60 people were attached to her immediate household in Abeokuta, Delany reported, and she kept in constant employment another 360 who supplied her with palm oil and ivory. When she met with Delany, she brought a retinue of six or seven people, including an educated African male secretary, a male servant, and several maid servants. After their final conversation, she sent her secretary to Delany's house to convey written confirmation in English of the topics they had discussed.

Because the kingdoms of Egbaland and Dahomey were at war when Tinubu returned to Abeokuta, she was able to place herself in an extremely strategic position by controlling the supply of arms. Her success in manipulating that control brought her to the front of Egba life. When the Dahomeans attacked in 1864, she was a key figure in organizing the defense of Egbaland and securing the enemy's defeat. S. O. Biobaku wrote:

> Her compound was converted into a veritable arsenal from which arms and ammunitions were issued to the Egba forces on their way to the front. Then she took up a position at Aro Gate, nearer the front, at which the wounded were nursed by her and her female associates, where soldiers whose powder had exhausted in battle replenished their store and from which any would-be deserters were sent back with a renewed determination to fight the Dahomey and save the Egba metropolis from destruction.[51]

After their victory in the war, the Egba recognized her services by awarding her the new title of *Ìyálóde* of all the Egba, the highest female chieftaincy.

Tinubu remained politically active in Abeokuta. She continued her opposition to British authorities in Lagos, fomenting dissent between them and the Ebga and working closely with traditional rulers and returnees in promoting African interests. She made her house "a salon where disgruntled Lagosians congregated and planned to avenge themselves on the interfering Consul at Lagos."[52] Later she became the leader of a "peace party" that demanded an end to the Ijaye war so that commercial routes could be opened up. While that opinion may well have been seconded by most of the town's traders, the war chiefs rejected peace. Her stance probably impeded her efforts to get her choice onto the throne of the Egba, starting in 1869. When her candidate finally became king in 1878, it was in part because Tinubu, "a good friend of his, highly respected by the community for her imposing personality and abundant wealth," had given him the financial resources needed for the position.[53] Henceforth, until her death in 1887, she again held indirect political power, using her influence to challenge British expansion. Due to her activities in Lagos and Abeokuta, Tinubu has been identified as "the first woman to play a part in resistance to British rule."[54]

A slightly younger woman whose great trading wealth similarly led to political power was Efunsetan Aniwura (i.e., "owner of gold"), Ibadan's second *Ìyálóde*.[55] An Egba woman from Abeokuta, she was born in the mid- or late 1820s. Growing up in a period already beset by local wars, she observed the importance of imported weapons and ammunition as articles of commerce.

She began trading as a young woman, gradually expanding her range from Abeokuta to other towns, including Ibadan and the ports of Badagry, Lagos, and Porto Novo. The fact that her marriage was childless (or that her only child died young) gave her more time and energy for trade. Sometime around 1860, Efunsetan and several friends decided that Ibadan offered more economic opportunities and moved to that city. There she lived in the compound of a maternal relative, an important warrior trader who supplied his fellow soldiers with guns and gunpowder on credit at the start of each war, receiving war captives as payment when the fighters returned home. From her new base in Ibadan, Efunsetan widened the scope of her trading, moving from retailing to wholesaling. Her activity within Yorubaland focused on foodstuffs, livestock, woven cloth, mats, kola nuts, and slaves for domestic use.

More profitable were her transactions between Yoruba country and foreign traders along the coast. The European merchants who were flocking into Lagos built warehouses for temporary storage of slaves, palm oil and kernels, ivory, and the cloth that would be used by slaves in South America. In return they provided manufactured goods that Efunsetan and other traders carried back into the interior for sale: textiles, beads, liquor, casks for bottling palm wine, metal boxes, knives, and—most valuable—guns and gunpowder. Efunsetan was also heavily involved in the tobacco trade. When there was a glut, she bought up most of the tobacco available in the ports, thereby gaining a virtual monopoly, and released it gradually as it became scarce.

By the mid-1860s Efunsetan's trading empire had made her one of the wealthiest people in Ibadan. Some of her many slaves produced goods for sale: cloth, mats, and eagerly desired cosmetics. Others manned her canoes on the rivers or head carried goods. In addition, by the time of her death in 1874, Efunsetan owned three large farms outside Ibadan, each of which was worked by at least a hundred slaves. The produce from those farms and the cattle she brought down from the north were sold not only in Ibadan's and Abeokuta's markets but also in the coastal towns. Although she was illiterate, Efunsetan had a good memory for accounts and maintained firm control over all her business operations. (For her operations in Lagos, she probably hired literate clerks.) Her actual capital was limited, but she had a good reputation for creditworthiness.

Efunsetan's success in trade attracted respect in Ibadan, for she had invested some of her earnings in accepted symbols of wealth and influence. In addition to her farms, she had two grazing fields within the town where Hausa slaves tended her cattle. Within her household she supported more than 200 slaves plus various dependents and followers who performed services for her. Her jewelry was lavish, and she had a large wardrobe of local and imported textiles. Thanks to her growing wealth and visible status, honors started to come her way. The first was being chosen by her kinship unit in Ibadan as head of the compound, a rare honor for a woman. Probably around 1867 she was named as *Ìyálóde* of the town, despite the fact that she was an Egba woman.[56] For the next few years, she played a military role as well, granting liberal credit to warriors for weapons, ammunition, and other supplies with the expectation of receiving captured slaves in return. She also fielded her own soldiers: in 1872, her head slave led a hundred warriors from her retinue (both slaves and other dependents) into battle, armed with equipment supplied by Efunsetan.

The respect in which she was held as a trader and as *Ìyálóde* is reflected in the *oríkì* or praise poem that is still sung about her:

Efunsetan, Iyalode
One who has horses and rides them not,
The child who walks in a graceful fashion.
Adekemi Ogunrin!
The great hefty woman who adorns her legs with beads
Whose possessions surpass those of the Ààre
Owner of several puny slaves in the farm.
Owner of many giant slaves in the market.
One who has bullets and gunpowder,
Who has gunpowder as well as guns,
And spends money like a conjurer,
The Iyalode who instills fear into her equals.
The rich never give their money to the poor;
The Iyalode never gives her wrappers to the lazy.[57]

In the early 1870s, Efunsetan became increasingly unhappy with Ibadan's warlike policies. Like Tinubu, she realized that the condition of almost continuous warfare disrupted her own and other people's trading. Further, some of the chiefs involved in the war to whom she had granted credit failed to pay their debts. She therefore became the spokesperson for a group of chiefs who were opposed to the aggressive policy of the leading war captain. For the expedition launched in 1874, she refused to field any soldiers, give ammunition on credit, or demonstrate her solidarity by meeting with the chiefs at the town gate. The war chiefs and those heavily indebted to her forced her deposition as *Ìyálóde*. At that point, custom required that she should either commit suicide or flee the town. Instead, she remained in Ibadan, defying the chiefs and trying to win support for her position.

In May 1874, Efunsetan died. Samuel Johnson, who wrote a contemporary account of her life, said that she was assassinated by the opposing faction in Ibadan.[58] The official reasons for this murder stemmed from her political influence and wealth: a male leader of the town charged her with insubordination and arrogance. Johnson noted that she was also perceived as acting in a cruel and unwomanly manner: "She was accused of being too severe with her slaves, and many acts of inhumanity were said to be perpetrated by her, which could hardly be denied from her masculine nature. She is very determined, . . . which made the matter worse for her." Because the Egba and some of the chiefs in Ibadan demanded retribution for her death, it almost led to civil war. Finally Ibadan's officials deflected the criticism by executing the slaves who had carried out the assassination. Nina Mba assigned special significance to Efunsetan, claiming that "she was one of the few women in Southern Nigeria before 1900 to have engaged in open political opposition to the indigenous government."[59]

Another powerful trader and civic leader was Madam Omosa, the daughter of an important chief in Ibadan.[60] Omosa built herself up economically through trade, which enabled her to acquire male slaves and followers. She armed them all with guns she had purchased as part of her trading, including a more effective kind of rifle that she was the first trader in Ibadan to supply. During the Kiriji War (1878–1893), she organized caravans to supply food, arms, and ammunition to Ibadan's army on the battlefield. At one point, while the army was fighting in Ekiti country, the Ijebu took advantage of its absence to launch an attack on Ibadan. Omosa immediately took charge of the situation. Putting on her father's battle clothes, she assembled her own household and all the other men left in the town. "After infusing courage into the flagging spirit of these men, she distributed ammunition from her armory and told them to prepare for battle."[61] Mounting her horse, she led the makeshift Ibadan force out into the field, whereupon the Ijebu invaders fled. When the Ijebu attacked again in the coming months, Omosa and her followers camped outside the city, successfully repelling all their attempts.

Other trading women too gained considerable wealth and political importance in western Yorubaland during the middle and later nineteenth century. The *Ìyálóde* title had been introduced into Ibadan in the 1850s to recognize the contributions of Subuola, a successful trader who fielded her own soldiers and extended credit to the war chiefs to enable them to buy guns and ammunition.[62] (When Subuola lost her wealth, she was deposed from office and replaced by Efunsetan Aniwura.) In Gbongan, east of Ibadan, Madam Feedge, who was appointed *Ìyálóde* in 1897, was described as a wealthy woman with many followers.[63] So powerful among other women that no one except the king could challenge her authority, she was also the leader of a group of chiefs who opposed the aggressive foreign policy advocated by the war captains. Tinubu's successor as *Ìyálóde* in Abeokuta, Madam Jojolola, employed male and female slaves as well as freeborn people in her large cloth-dyeing establishment and trading empire.[64] Gaining additional power by advancing credit to male farmers, Jojolola presented women's complaints to the Egba government during protests in the 1920s.

After 1900, though some women still succeeded as large-scale traders, they were unlikely to wield the degree of political power enjoyed by the exceptional women of the unsettled earlier generations. It is significant that while some of the remarkable female figures of the middle and later nineteenth century profited initially from warfare, most of them eventually advocated peace as more valuable to the economic and social lives of their communities.

Craftwork

During the nineteenth century, Yoruba women made and sold a range of craft goods. The most important activities were weaving and dyeing cotton cloth and making clay pottery and soap, followed by manufacture of such items as beads, mats, and baskets.[65] Textiles, used for clothing, domestic furnishings, and as ceremonial objects, had profound cultural and religious meanings. Different patterns and types of weaving were used for particular rituals or by people at particular stages in their lives; the most symbolically important kinds of weaving could be done only by certain women.[66] Clothing could also represent a group identity: women's associations commonly appeared in public wearing similar dresses or head ties. (For a later example, see the cover photo.) Young women learned craft skills from their mothers or other adult women, as formal or informal apprentices.

Manufacturing cotton cloth was the primary craft for Yoruba women. At least by the late eighteenth century and probably long before that time, cotton—a native plant—was grown and woven into cloth in many parts of West Africa, including Yorubaland. Cotton had traditionally been grown in small batches by individual families for their own use or local sale. After the bolls were picked, cleaned, and spun, the thread was woven into cloth. If the cloth was to be colored, either the thread or the woven cloth would be dyed with indigenous materials, chiefly indigo, which produced various shades of blue. In 1800, despite three centuries of European cloth imports into West Africa, the Yoruba still produced most of the cloth used in their area.[67] Much of it was made within individual households, but specialized cloth centers produced and exported high-quality goods over long distances within West Africa and in some cases to South America. In some of the newly founded Yoruba towns, cloth was manufactured on an extensive scale. Ibadan, for instance, became known for production of the famous "Yoruba blues."

The earliest references concern cloth woven and dyed by Ijebu women. Captain John Adams, who voyaged to the Yoruba section of the Gulf of Guinea in 1803, wrote that the "industrious" Ijebu "manufacture for sale an immense number of common Guinea cloths," with most of the work done by women.[68] Osifekunde, a freed slave, described for an interviewer around 1840 what life had been like when he was a lad, in the 1810s:

> The Ijebu dress themselves, by and large, in textiles which they make themselves. These are cotton cloths whose raw material is furnished by the soil. In each family, the harvest, spinning, weaving, and dyeing are the customary occupations of the women, and it is known that a considerable quantity of textiles is manufactured and exported, not merely to nearby countries but even to Brazil, whence ships come to Lagos in search of this merchandise so highly esteemed by the people of African origin transplanted to those distant lands.[69]

A foreign traveler confirmed in 1819 that Portuguese traders were exporting Ijebu cloth, which was said by another visitor to be 12–14 inches wide and usually colored white and blue.[70] Clapperton, who found Ijebu textiles for sale on the northern edge of Yorubaland in 1825–1826, said that they were commonly used as clothing for slaves and the poorer classes.

Women were generally responsible for preparing the thread from which cloth was woven.[71] Men grew the plants, but removing the seeds from the bolls, washing the cotton, and spinning it into thread were tasks assigned often to older women who were no longer able to do other kinds of work. The thread was then wound onto reels and sold to dyers or weavers. Samuel Johnson, writing from Oyo in the central area, observed that of the compounds in which weaving was done, about two-thirds contained female spinners who produced for the looms of their male relatives.[72]

Women's role in weaving varied by region. In describing his travels in Egbaland, Robert Campbell emphasized the industrious nature of women. "Rise as early as you please and enter a native compound, and you will there find the women engaged at their various occupations. Go at night as late as you please, and there by the feeble light of her lamp she is seen in the act of labor, spinning, weaving or preparing food for the ensuing day."[73] In the Akoko area of northeastern Yorubaland, weaving was likewise handled mainly by women, who sold their distinctive local cloth to traders from other regions.[74] In some places, however, weaving was done by both men and women, using different types of equipment and making different types of cloth. Looms employed by men in the southwestern corner of Yorubaland early in the century produced cloth that was only 4–5 inches wide but of indefinite length, while women's looms and cloths were broader.[75] Campbell said that the cloth produced by women was as wide as English manufacture (probably around 48–54 inches) and about 90 inches long.[76] Samuel Johnson later commented that men wove strips about 5.5 inches wide, which were then cut to the required lengths.

Dyers were normally women. Clapperton noted that large-scale weaving in southwestern Yorubaland required an equally extensive dyeing industry, the latter in the hands of women.[77] On visits to three dye houses, he observed a minimum of 20 large earthenware dyeing vats in each, using blue indigo to produce "a most beautiful and durable dye." Other travelers and British officials noted similar types of production, with indigo the favorite color.[78] Robert Campbell described the process more fully:

> The beautiful blue, almost purple dye of their cloths is not from the common indigo-plant of the East and West-Indies, but from a large climbing plant. The leaves and shoots are gathered while young and tender. They are then crushed in wooden mortars, and the pulp made up in balls and dried. For dyeing, a few of these balls are placed in a strong lye made from ashes, and suffered to remain until the water becomes offensive from the decomposition of vegetable matter. The cloths are then put in, and moved about until sufficiently colored. There are dyeing establishments in all the towns from Lagos to Ilorin.[79]

Textile production and trading yielded a good income. In 1891, the average wage of weavers was around 16 strings of cowries per day, and women's cloths brought larger earnings than men's.[80] Women who were dealers in cloth had a chance to gain handsome profits. Large hand-woven cloths of a good quality could be purchased for 20 heads of cowries at Orun in 1887, but they sold for 40 heads in Lagos.[81] By around 1900, Yoruba women were trading textiles all along the West African coast.

From the mid-nineteenth century, however, international commercial pressures began to change the nature of cloth production and consumption in Yorubaland. Because British textile mills were looking for sources of inexpensive raw cotton, it was promoted as a cash crop by colonial officials, merchants, and missionaries. In practice, however, relatively little cotton was exported from Yorubaland: most of what was grown there was used by local spinners and weavers. Trade in the other direction, involving cheap cloth imported from British factories, was starting to have an impact by the 1860s, at least in towns like Abeokuta that had regular contact with the coast and a population of Sierra Leonean returnees.[82] But in most regions local cloth retained its popularity for a longer time. Africans did not like the patterns and colors used by the British cotton mills, and the imported cloth was of much lower quality than the hand-made local product.[83] As late as 1890 an observer commented that 95 percent of the cloth used in Yorubaland was home produced.

Making and caring for clothing provided work for a few urban women. For the simple clothing traditionally worn by men, male tailors stitched together lengths of narrow cloth.[84] Women's clothing required little if any sewing. Most women wore one large cloth wrapped around the waist and lower body like a skirt, sometimes joined by a second cloth wrapped around the upper part of the body. If necessary, several breadths could be tacked together. By the end of the century, as elite women in the cities began to adopt new and more elaborate forms of dress, seamstresses who had learned Western sewing skills at school were starting to set up businesses that catered to their needs. Urban women who lived in smaller family units and were busy with their own income-generating activities might be willing to pay to have their clothes and bedding washed and ironed. In 1881, 583 laundresses and seamstresses (mainly the former) were at work in Lagos.[85] These occupations were to expand greatly during the colonial years.

Pottery was made by both women and men. Earthenware pots of many types were needed for domestic purposes, including vessels for cooking food and specialized items like water coolers.[86] Pottery had commercial uses as well: early travelers mentioned clay pots of various sizes and shapes used in the manufacture of palm oil, while dyers needed large, open-necked pots that facilitated the insertion and removal of wet, heavy cloths.[87]

Economic Obstacles Faced by Women

Although the nineteenth century offered unusual opportunities for Yoruba women to participate in production and trade, most of them remained at lower levels of the economic system. Many male farmers, craftsmen, and traders were of course poor too, but women faced some gendered handicaps that made it more difficult for them to compete, especially in middle and upper economic strata. As we have seen, those challenges could be surmounted, but doing so required exceptional intelligence, determination, and energy, together with a willingness to ignore certain conventions about desirable female behavior. Most nineteenth-century women were handicapped by six obstacles that stood in the way of their equal participation in the economy. These problems were found even in western areas of Yorubaland, where male dominance was less pronounced than in the east, and they continued into the colonial era.

(1) Expectations concerning motherhood and domestic roles. Although this handicap had a biological component, its impact was increased by Yoruba assumptions about women's exclusive duties in child raising and within the household. Nearly all women married, and all who were able to bear children did so. Wives were expected to continue all their domestic work (either in person or by finding another woman to fill their place), regardless of any income-

generating activities they might be pursuing. The amount of time and energy a woman could devote to work that brought in some earnings was therefore limited, and she always had to juggle the conflicting demands of her multiple responsibilities.

(2) Problems in traveling, which took two forms. (a) It was often hard for a woman to leave home for extended periods. Young children who were being breastfed could not be left behind, but carrying a baby or toddler on one's back while head loading one's trading goods was difficult. Further, because men were not accustomed to looking after themselves, a woman who needed to be out of town in connection with her business had to line up substitutes to attend to her husband and children. This handicap was less severe for senior wives in polygamous marriages. (b) Traveling could be physically dangerous, especially during times of civil warfare and slave raiding. But even in stable periods, women who were away from home on their own were more vulnerable than men to assault and theft of their goods.

(3) Unequal ability to control or own landed property. As we have seen, family land was normally controlled by men, and although women in some sub-groups had the right to use land belonging to their own lineages, they were less likely than men to have the workers needed to receive an allocation. As the British system of private land ownership spread, women were allowed to buy property but often found it impossible to produce the cash or credit needed to do so. Women who lacked land of their own were at a disadvantage in commercial agriculture, and without a house it was hard to build up the large residential following that provided labor and demonstrated one's status and socio-economic power.

(4) Difficulty in gaining capital and credit. Most women were able to access only modest amounts of money, through their own savings, contributions from relatives, friends, or members of *ẹgbẹ́*, or participation in an *èsúsú*. Moneylenders and banks commonly asked for land or slaves as collateral, which women were less likely than men to have.

(5) Problems in accessing and deploying labor. Labor, in the form of people, provided the productive capacity needed to accumulate wealth, but it was provided almost entirely from within the household. Because women were less likely than men to be household heads, did not marry wives for their labor, and controlled fewer children, other relatives, and unfree workers, they were disadvantaged.

(6) Impaired ability to display wealth and power through the normal cultural markers. Prominent Yoruba men made their position known in part by having big compounds filled with family members, dependents, and clients. They gained additional backers by using their economic resources, influence, and sometimes access to supernatural powers on behalf of other people. When women tried to use similar signifiers to make their status manifest, they might be

accused of improper behavior or witchcraft. Being well known was a benefit for men, but it could be a risk for women.[88]

These gendered handicaps reinforce the argument that women could be disadvantaged in their daily lives even if their culture's ideology did not define them as a separate category or label them as inferior in physical, emotional, or moral terms. The obstacles did not prevent women from taking part in trade or craftwork, and some female entrepreneurs were able to overcome them, but they confined most women to less profitable sectors of the economy. By limiting working women's wealth and control over people, these hindrances curtailed their agency and authority.

8 | New Approaches to Familiar Roles during the Colonial Period

DESPITE THE PATRIARCHAL assumptions of the British and the embodiment of many of those ideas in education and government policies, Yoruba women were essential players in the colonial economic system.[1] Regional variations became less pronounced as commerce expanded in eastern Yorubaland and women moved into the kinds of income-generating activities already pursued in western and central areas. While some women remained in familiar kinds of work, others realized that they could generate new opportunities for earning money and sometimes for serving their communities within the altered colonial world. Displaying imagination and determination, they adapted customary roles within the family and public economy to capitalize upon the options now available to them. As LaRay Denzer has noted, colonial women, "whatever their occupation, made calculated choices about their careers based on their perceptions of what new opportunities offered in terms of their needs and objectives as well as future prospects. Many changed their line of work or extended it into new areas, taking into account cultural codes of acceptable behavior, their family responsibilities, their skills and education, their finances, and new techniques."[2] Women who successfully expanded their economic options enhanced their own agency and sometimes gained formal authority.

Many women modified types of activity present in the nineteenth century to take advantage of the niches created by the developing colonial economy. Some female traders still sold on a small scale in local markets, but a growing number of entrepreneurs with access to cash or credit enlarged their businesses or identified new items to buy and sell. Craftswomen, when confronted by competition with foreign-made wares, experimented with alternative methods of production and protested vigorously when the government prohibited those techniques. Women also earned money by offering services for pay that had formerly been handled within the household or that emerged as opportunities in urban settings. Whereas all those kinds of work might appear to be "traditional," what is important is how women re-fashioned them within the colonial context. Trading, craftwork, and provision of services are described in this chapter.

Other women drew upon their schooling or higher education to move into novel occupations. Some converted training in Western domestic arts, including fancy sewing and cooking, into money-making ventures. Others used their ability to read and write English and their basic mathematical skills to gain employment in offices or shops. Women who had received further education commonly entered work that benefited the community as well as themselves. As teachers and nurses, they were sometimes employed in schools or hospitals but often preferred to set up their own private training institutes or clinics. A much smaller number acquired professional expertise, entering fields like law or medicine. Occupations that required a Western education have sometimes been labeled as "modern," but that term is misleading. In making decisions about how to utilize their training, Yoruba women displayed a strong preference for running their own businesses, as their mothers and grandmothers had done, rather than working for wages. The new careers will be considered in chapter 9.

Trading

In all regions of Yorubaland by the middle of the colonial period, most local market sellers and many shopkeepers and wholesalers were women. In Ekiti North, where it was thought that "a male trader is either a stingy man or lazy," trading was conducted almost entirely by women, and the market was seen as their abode.[3] But the twentieth century brought profound changes to the range of opportunities available to female traders. The ending of warfare and slavery, improved transportation, and expansion of commerce, both within Nigeria and between it and Europe, provided new possibilities for some women, as did ongoing urbanization. Their ability to work outside the home was not restricted by the continuing spread of Islam and Christianity. At the same time, however, the policies and practices of the colonial government made it more difficult for women to compete at higher levels of the increasingly complex system whereby goods were bought and sold, especially those that were prepared for export. When European firms and later the Marketing Boards hired local agents, they were usually male. In this section we will look first at how women participated in trade and the items they handled. We can then describe some features of female traders' lives.

TYPES OF TRADING ACTIVITY

During the colonial period, Yoruba women traded in multiple ways and at various levels. The following outline summarizes information from many local studies, including an important survey of working women in Lagos in the late 1940s.[4] Although the types of involvement are laid out here as separate categories, we need to remember that many women engaged in multiple activities, either at the same time or sequentially, moving from one to another depending on the season, their age and family situation, and the amount of capital available to them.

1. The type of trading that involved the largest number of women consisted of selling within a given market or local area. Simple market selling, which required little capital, was available to women of all ages and economic levels, and it was found throughout Yorubaland.

   a. Some women sat in the market place, selling farm produce, processed foodstuffs, or small manufactured goods. The official estimated number of market women in Lagos's 15 main markets in 1948 was about 8,000, but that figure is probably much too low. (It was derived from the number of shops and stalls, many of which were sub-rented to more than one person, and it did not include the female assistants who helped with market sales.)

   b. Female hawkers sold while moving through the streets. They typically carried food or a variety of smaller items on their heads, in baskets or trays. In Lagos, some hawkers worked on their own, while others were relatives or servants of a larger trader who fed and clothed them and gave them a little gift now and then. Hawkers could also be employed by a shop, paid either by the month or working on commission. The large European firms preferred to hire male hawkers.

   c. Women also sold from their homes, offering small items such as matches, cosmetics, and tobacco to people who could not attend the market or found it inconvenient to do so. Lagos women often had one or two showcases where they displayed objects for sale, placing them out in the street during the daytime and taking them into the house at night.

   d. Other women cooked and sold food, either at a market or as hawkers.

   e. Those women who could afford the rent and furnishings sold from shops, which offered greater comfort and security for their goods and customers than did a market stall. Shopkeepers were the wealthiest of Lagos's local traders (it took capital of at least £50 to open a shop). A woman who started a shop had usually gained previous experience through market selling, hawking, or working for other shopkeepers.

f. Some women sold but also bought items within a cluster or ring of rural markets, generally ones to which they could walk in a day from their homes. Their profits stemmed from price differentials between the various markets, due to the greater availability or scarcity of certain goods in particular markets on particular days.

2. Women frequently operated as intermediaries, middlemen, or wholesalers within a given region of Yorubaland.

a. In urban settings, women traders bought and re-distributed goods. Some focused on agricultural goods that had been brought in from the countryside, which they either distributed to local retailers or bulked into larger units for transport to the cities. Others dealt in manufactured goods, especially textiles, preparing locally made craft products for transmission to larger markets and breaking down bulked units of imported items for distribution to sellers.

b. In rural areas, some women collected and transmitted agricultural produce. Going around to a series of farms or small markets, they bought up whatever produce was available. When they had a sufficient amount, they bulked it by type in preparation for transport to a seller or wholesaler in a nearby town.

3. The third category of activity involved buying and selling over longer distances.

a. Most of these female traders gathered up bulked units of locally produced items (food, craft items, and occasionally cash crops) and carried them to markets in the cities or to ports for export. They returned with imported manufactured goods that they distributed to middlemen and retailers. Trading at this level required enough capital to handle large volumes of sometimes expensive goods and freedom to be away from home. It was therefore open to fewer women than local wholesaling.[5] In Lagos, the traders who bought produce or other items in bulk and brought them into the city for sale were often on the road much of the time.[6]

b. Those women who had significant amounts of capital or credit and were able to travel farther traded textiles, kola nuts, and sometimes other goods along the West African coast. Hundreds of Lagos women regularly did business of that kind, but none took part in import/export transactions with Europe or America. That level of commerce was controlled by foreign trading companies, joined occasionally by African men.

In looking at the types of items that women handled, we begin with agricultural produce. In some areas during the 1930s and 1940s, the control women exercised over trade in farm products enabled them to compete successfully with male buyers, even outdoing them "in acquiring wealth and in tying others to them as debtors and clients."[7] In the Egba and Ijebu regions, most food crops were traded by women into the 1950s, resulting in fairly good profits.[8] These female traders gained new types of economic control within the increasingly sophisticated marketing system that emerged across the colonial period.[9] Instead of bringing their family's own crops to market, they functioned as intermediary traders or brokers for farmers not related to them. During the earlier colonial years, female traders picked up the crops, took them to market, and sold them on the farmer's behalf, acting in effect as his agent. Gradually, however, women moved into "own account" trading, buying from the farmer and selling in their own right. After purchase, they bulked the produce and either carried it to market or sold it to someone with better means of transport. Because that pattern was often linked with an extension of money or credit to the farmer, successful female traders gained considerable economic power over male producers.

Women also processed and traded some cash crops during the colonial period. Production of palm items and the role of women in preparing them varied by region. In many parts of Yorubaland, the importance of palm oil as an export item declined across the colonial years, though women still produced oil for their own households and local sale.[10] They also continued to crack palm nuts to extract the kernels desired by European factories. Alan Pim, writing in the late 1930s, commented that the export trade in Nigerian *kernels* was less severely threatened by competition from Southeast Asia than was palm *oil* because kernels were "a women's industry" and hence had lower labor costs.[11] The household output of an average family farm in Owo in 1928–1930 included about 6 gallons of oil, worth 9s., which the women made and used themselves; they produced palm kernels worth 30s. for sale. When oil was extracted for domestic consumption in Ondo, the entire family participated.[12] During the earlier decades of the twentieth century, women also traded in palm products, including the wine they were not allowed to prepare themselves.[13] In 1916, Osinwete of Abeokuta sent 6 large tins of oil and 14 bags of kernels to Lagos by canoe, adding her shipment to that of her brother.[14] Fiyan of Ibonwon sold a tin of palm oil at a market near Epe, along the lagoon, for 8s. in 1926: the buyer paid 7s. at the time and agreed to pay the balance of 1s. and return the empty container later.

By 1945, however, output of palm oil for export from western and central Yorubaland was so low that the government did not bother to set up a Marketing Board for it, though it did establish such boards for palm kernels and cocoa. In Okitipupa, in the southeast, which remained the leading Yoruba source of palm oil during the colonial years, commercial production was still done by Urhobo men. Immigrants were involved in palm oil production in other eastern areas too. Daryll Forde reported in the mid-1940s that in parts of Owo division, Sobo men, "who are well known for their enterprise, had established oil producing camps with the consent of the local chiefs."[15]

Women were heavily involved in preparing and trading kola nuts. When dried and chewed, these mildly invigorating nuts were used for social and ceremonial purposes in most regions of Nigeria. Because kola was the only stimulant permitted to Muslims, it was especially popular in the north. Producers of nuts in Yorubaland might sell them to visiting Hausa traders or carry them north themselves to cities where higher prices could be obtained.[16] In Ekiti, kola trees were usually raised by men, but because men regarded the laborious task of processing the nuts as women's work, they sold the raw nuts to female traders at a relatively low price. The latter hired porters—usually women—to transport the nuts to bulking centers, where they fermented them, removed the inedible parts, and prepared them for dry storage. Commodity-based women's *egbe* in Ekiti sent the nuts to Lagos, where they were typically retailed by women from the Ekiti area who had moved to the city.[17] Trade in kola could be coupled with other kinds of sales. For example, a woman from Ibadan who traveled north to sell kola nuts in 1940 was dealing also in a wide range of textiles.[18]

Cocoa offered limited opportunities for women. Although processing was generally done by men, in some areas women helped to break open the pods after they had been harvested, removed the beans, and carried them home to ferment and dry.[19] Women traded in cocoa too, but only at the bottom levels of the system and mainly before 1945. The normal pattern in the 1930s was that women would buy up cocoa from local producers and sell the beans to male dealers or brokers, who had often advanced them money to make those purchases. The dealers, many of whom worked for large foreign firms, then bulked the beans and sent them to the coast for export. In Ibadan, for example, a male cocoa dealer gave his wife cash to use in buying cocoa for him.[20] Several Ife women who borrowed money, apparently for buying cocoa, agreed to pay interest in the form of a certain number of hundredweights of dried cocoa beans each year. When an Ife broker was accused of buying cocoa in units measured by his own baskets instead of the official market scales, witnesses on his behalf claimed that it was not uncommon for dealers buying cocoa from female traders to use private measures.[21]

After Marketing Boards were introduced for palm kernels and cocoa at the end of World War II, women were seldom hired as buyers or sub-buyers by the firms that held government licenses. In part this stemmed from the difficulties they faced in providing the surety required of buyers at the start of each season, which usually took the form of land or cash. But British discomfort at dealing with women in economic contexts and the determination of Yoruba men to acquire the income and status associated with working for a Marketing Board contributed to the exclusion of women.

While cash crops thus offered scant opportunities for women, female traders found many other ways of profiting from the expanding commercial economy. Some converted raw food crops into forms ready for cooking. These activities required little capital but were labor intensive. Cassava tubers, for instance, were dried and ground into *gàrí* (a coarse flour or meal used to cook a thick porridge), while corn was ground and fermented to make a popular food, usually served cold, called *àgìdí*.[22] Some women extracted seeds from melons for *ègúsí*, a favorite item in the Yoruba diet.[23]

Many traders sold foodstuffs in markets or hawked them on the streets. The colonial period brought increased demand for food vendors, both because urbanization expanded and because more people were now away from home during the day. School children, teachers, government employees, other men, and market traders might all need to buy their breakfast and/or lunch. In 1926, an Epe woman named Raliatu delivered 8 bags of *gàrí* to a canoe man to take to an agent at Ejinrin market, while a year later Musitura sold corn flour at the police barracks there.[24] Aralole of Ibadan brought balls of *àgìdí* to sell at the railroad station in Ibadan in 1905; two of the people who bought from her were smaller-scale female *àgìdí* sellers who lived next to the line. Osenatu of Epe traded in farina in 1926, buying 40 bags of the meal that she stored in her farm village.[25] Cooked beans were a common item.[26] A woman who had just sold palm oil near Epe in 1926 used some of her proceeds to buy *ègúsí* seeds from one of four women sitting in a market stall. In the late 1940s, many Lagos women cooked food that they took to the market to sell, hawked around the streets, or delivered to people's houses.[27] On a larger scale, Osenatu Taiwo of Ibadan held lucrative government contracts between 1914 and 1940 to provide food for prisons.

Whereas relatively few women offered meat, many dealt in fish. In 1921, Memuna, a fish seller of Oremedu near the lagoon, traveled to Ejinrin market in a commercial transport canoe with her fish. The fish had been wrapped in bundles, one of which was stolen by another woman riding in the boat.[28] Four years later, a bag of fish stored temporarily in a shed at the market in Ejinrin was stolen from a female trader.[29] When Adetutu of Ibadan, senior wife of Busari, asked her husband for assistance in starting to trade in the early 1930s, he bought her two bags of fish worth £5-10-0. In an essay written probably around 1931–1932, Herbert Macaulay pointed out that dealing in fish in the Lagos area had recently become easier thanks to replacement of the uncomfortable and unreliable canoes that had previously plied the lagoon by steam launches.[30] The wives of Lagos fishermen in the late 1940s smoked more fish than needed for their own households in order to have some for sale.

Trading in the textiles used for clothing and domestic purposes provided opportunities for many women. Some sellers took only a small number of cloths from a local wholesaler, while women with more capital and the ability to travel went farther from home to acquire a more diverse array of fabrics. An observer in 1960 commented that some of the wealthiest women in Nigeria were cloth merchants.[31] Interestingly, she noted that many of them were well educated, a reflection of the Yoruba pattern whereby women transferred the skills and contacts they made through their formal schooling into a business context. Most cloth traders, however, operated on a much smaller scale. In 1925, Asimowu of Epe rode by canoe from Lagos to Ejinrin with her load of cloths, done up as a bundle in a bag.[32] Asimowu Adelola had an enclosed shop in Ife in 1938, from which six large pieces of cloth were stolen. Tomori Aisatu of Ibadan claimed that while she was out of town in 1940, a creditor and bailiff came into her house and impounded the trading goods she had left there.[33] The items taken included 34 pieces of cloth worth £17-9-3: various kinds of locally made fabrics as well as imported textiles (black and white velvets, silk, brocade, lace, and woolen and flannel wrappers). Cloths were also offered by mobile sellers. In 1933, two girls were hawking cloths in Lagos when an old woman called them into her house to make some selections.[34] Saratu Ajike, hawking textiles in Shaki in 1957, was accompanied by a female servant who carried the load of goods.

Women sold smaller wares too. If they manufactured as well as sold the item, they usually specialized in one particular product, whereas "petty traders" commonly sold a variety of things. The female plaintiff in a marital dispute in Ado Ekiti in 1917 was a salt seller, while Sabrina of Modakeke sold laundry soap in 1935 to a "wash-man" named Good Luck.[35] Bintu Balogun, born in 1891 and later a principal spokesperson for Lagos market women, began her career as a small seller of pots and charcoal. Although thousands of women were described as "petty traders" in local records, not all of them merely sold a few items at their local market. An elderly petty trader who lived in Lagos traveled to Ilorin in 1933, leaving in a locked cupboard the savings she had accumulated through a lifetime of work.[36] Her savings included £600 in coins and notes plus some "trinkets" (probably jewelry) worth £309.

Canny female traders quickly recognized the potential of new products as they became available during the colonial years. Early in the twentieth century, they realized that the gunny sacks used to ship imported goods formed an ideal container for bulking palm kernels and other produce for local transport.[37] A lively market in the sacks ensued. In Aiyetoro in the 1940s and 1950s, women sold cigarettes, kerosene, and sewing machine needles. Benedina Banjo of Ibadan described herself as "a trader in cigarettes, beer and whatnots" in 1952.[38] Some traders profited from women's desire for beauty products. The wife of a successful cocoa merchant in Ibadan in the 1940s traded both wholesale and retail in facial creams and toilet soaps as well as provisions.[39] In Ekiti North, a few rich women in the late colonial period began to sell imported European household goods, like metal and plastic wares and baby toys. Such items cost more to acquire but offered higher profit margins.

THE LIVES OF FEMALE TRADERS

We may now explore some questions that shed light on the lives of colonial traders, starting with what fraction of women engaged in business. When Suzanne Comhaire-Sylvain posed that question to Lagos people in 1947–1948, she always received the same response: "All women who are neither sick nor infirm work."[40] Niara Sudarkasa, whose research on Yoruba women's work was done in the region bordered by Ibadan, Oyo, Ogbomosho, and Iwo during the early 1960s, likewise found that virtually all women were engaged in some type of trading activity. Female traders were not defined as a distinct group. "No special code of ethics is referable to, no special prerogatives afforded, no special status accorded women traders as distinct from other women."[41] In eastern Yorubaland as well, women were pulled increasingly into trade starting in the 1920s and 1930s.

Further information comes from a study of 207 mothers in Lagos in 1948, all of whom had daughters aged 12–18 years who were in the final year of primary school or in secondary school.[42] This was not a representative sample: because education was expensive, the women had a special incentive to earn money for their daughters' schooling. Nevertheless, only 18 percent of the mothers were totally occupied with their households and families; the rest had some kind of income-generating activities that took them away from home for at least several hours most days. Of the Yoruba women, 88 percent were in trade, which was seen as an honorable occupation. That fraction was larger than among other Nigerian or immigrant women. Those findings are buttressed by the Lagos Census of 1950, which reported that more than 80 percent of the city's 39,000 traders and sales workers were women.[43]

Female traders came from various economic backgrounds and types of marriage. Among Lagos women in the late 1940s, work of some kind, normally trading, was nearly uniform among the poor, regardless of the nature of their marriage.[44] It was the rule also in well-to-do polygamous families and was found even in the majority of wealthy monogamous families. When the mothers in the 1948 study were classified by socio-economic rank based on the occupation of the male head of the family, 93 percent in the lowest group worked, as compared to 82 percent in the middle group and 62 percent in the highest group.[45] As was true in the pre-colonial period, polygamy may have contributed both to a woman's need to trade (because it was harder for her husband to support multiple wives and sets of children) and to her ability to do so in a focused manner (because her co-wives could look after the husband some of the time). Among 103 polygamously married mothers of school girls in Lagos in 1948, 97 percent worked; among 104 monogamously married women, however, only 67 percent worked.

Traders were likewise diverse in terms of their age and stage within marriage. In Lagos, some young wives stayed at home initially, devoting themselves to their husbands and households, but when the additional mouths of their children began to strain the family budget, they returned to work to provide for the children.[46] A. L. Mabogunje noted in the early 1960s that if a Yoruba woman was not trading, it was usually for one of two reasons: either her marital status made it impractical for her to be away from home for the long hours needed (perhaps because she was the only wife of her husband or his most junior wife, who was expected to be available to him); or she was a relative beginner whose financial resources did not yet permit her to rent a stall.[47] In the latter case, she sold from home, "a typical petty-trader, selling single items of various articles— one cigarette, one biscuit, one toffee, four cubes of sugar, or one beer-bottle size of kerosene." Female sellers may have displayed some degree of specialization based upon age, with younger women selling low-value items and older women focusing on expensive imported goods.[48]

Another question is why women traded, what benefits they received from their work. The most immediate and important reward was the cash income it yielded. Even limited earnings helped women to provide for themselves and their children, supplementing or replacing assistance from their husbands. At the end of the colonial period, nearly one-fifth of the Yoruba women in one sample received no financial help at all from their husbands, and another 48 percent received some food but nothing else.[49] It is therefore not surprising that 94 percent of those women were self-employed. But men were not placing onto their wives' shoulders expenses that they could themselves have covered had they so chosen. The cash income of many men was lower than that of their wives, because most males were farmers who devoted at least part of their time to growing crops for their own family's consumption.[50]

Women's need for money—and the contrast between Yoruba and British expectations concerning economic roles within marriage—was nicely expressed in a petition submitted in 1938 to Ibadan's king and council by the Union of Women Traders in Cotton Goods.[51] (They asked the authorities to curtail the competition being offered by male "Syrians" who were using motorized trucks to sell textiles at lower prices than the Yoruba female traders could offer.) Their statement said, "Although we are women, we have responsibilities, same as our menfolk; we feed our children, send them to school, and support our old mothers and fathers; and pay taxes for our old or unemployed menfolk. It is not the practice in this country as it may be elsewhere, that husbands support wives; here wives must work, and maintain not only themselves but their children and other dependents."

Another claim on women's earnings was obligations within their kinship groups. As Sudarkasa observed, "Because of their independent incomes, women are expected to make separate contributions to the ceremonies undertaken by members of the lineages and compounds to which they belong. They are often called upon to render material assistance to their kinsmen in times of exigency, and the kin groups, in turn, provide structural support for the continued participation of women in trade."[52] Trading and appropriate behavior as a member of a kin group were thus mutually reinforcing. A similar pattern was observed in Ilesha, where many traders used some of their earnings to fulfill family obligations: helping to support their parents, or contributing to special events among their kin like naming ceremonies or funerals.[53] As Mabogunje commented, christenings, marriages, and burials within their own or their husbands' lineages "demand some expenditure of money on the part of every adult member of the extended family. To be found financially wanting when such occasions arise is perhaps the greatest disaster a woman can think of."[54]

For women trading above a subsistence level, profits could be used for social advancement. Obtaining a formal education for one's children, seen as an investment that would yield a good reward in the future, was common.[55] In polygamous marriages, rival wives sometimes competed to obtain educational advantages for their own children. A successful woman could make her achievements visible, though she had to be careful not to create any suspicion of witchcraft.[56] She could build up a following of her own ("wealth in people"), build a nice house, and acquire clothes, jewelry, horses, or cars. Within the community she was in a position to supply cash or credit to friends and clients, to assist them with educating their children and finding a job, and to engage in conspicuous charity—both secular and religious. All those activities made it more likely that she would be selected for a chieftaincy title, adding another component to her status and authority.[57]

Trading offered sociability as well. In the late 1950s, B. W. Hodder commented that the rewards of trade for Yoruba women "lie as much in the social life offered by the markets as in their cash profits."[58] He continued, "Petty trading in Yorubaland is a skill, a pleasure and a necessity, and to walk through almost any market is to appreciate that 'trading is the essence of social life, from childhood upwards'." Further, the market was an important place for the reinforcement of lineage and kinship ties. Because Yoruba women moved to their husband's household after marriage, they normally had to travel to see their natal relatives. But in the market, a woman could get news about her family and sometimes see relatives without creating a "role conflict" in herself or making her husband uneasy.[59]

Economically based social interactions occurred though diverse relationships. Within the market place itself, "Good neighbourliness is the first rule. . . . The market-woman is always her neighbour's keeper. She helps her if she hasn't the correct change, looks over her wares if she happens to be away for a short time or is asleep, and never seduces her customers."[60] The *egbé* or guilds of market women provided further companionship. In Ibadan, "a sense of belonging is fostered by periodic outings of such social groups with members all dressed alike in costly apparel."[61] Sellers commonly had long-established ties with regular customers, with whom they bargained on friendly terms. Women engaged in intermediary trade interacted vertically with their suppliers and retail customers.[62]

Trading provided other benefits too. Petty traders and successful businesswomen alike gained an occupational identity through their work. Native Court records commonly described local people—women as well as men—in terms of their primary economic activity: as farmers, petty or specialized traders, or the various types of craft workers. The "Social and Personal" section of the *Nigerian Daily Times* in 1940 noted that "Mrs. Petronilla Olumuyiwa of the Ikosi Industries, Epe," who had arrived in Lagos the previous Friday for the funeral of her late brother, "returns to her station this morning."[63] The term "station" was commonly used for the postings of missionaries and colonial officials, suggesting that Mrs. Olumuyiwa's job was seen as creating an occupational identity in some sense parallel to theirs. Toyin Falola suggested that women gained valuable practical skills from their control over and management of the market place, a site important to politics, communication, and social networking.[64] Trading offered opportunities for illegal activities as well. This could range from simple theft to an elaborate plot that was organized in 1960 by a wealthy female trader in Lagos to defraud two foreign insurance companies by falsely reporting that her shop had been burgled.[65]

Western observers sometimes asked how female traders coordinated their working lives with their family obligations. In Yoruba society, no inherent tension existed between a woman's role as a trader and her functions as a wife. As Sudarkasa observed in the early 1960s, adult women regarded employment in trade or other money-making occupations as "a necessary component of their role as women. To be a 'complete' woman in Yoruba society is, first of all, to be married and to have children. Most women work *because* by so doing they fulfill their roles within the family."[66] The need to earn money to feed and clothe one's children was compounded during the colonial years by a desire to send them to school. Primary schools required a tuition payment and fees until the 1950s, and even after state-supported education was introduced, parents had to pay for supplies and uniforms. Secondary education, often at a boarding school, remained expensive throughout the colonial era.

Husbands were expected to encourage their wives' work, and it was apparently rare for a man to regard his wife's trading as a threat. Mabogunje commented, perhaps in slightly idealized terms, "Security in her marriage is at once the cause and the effect of her essay into trading. . . . The more successful she becomes, the more her standing with her husband improves until after some time she attains to the position of her husband's counsellor."[67] Nor were women's financial freedom and the travel they did in connection with their trading associated with sexual immorality. Only if a woman remained away from home for an extended period might she be suspected of involvement with a man other than her husband.[68]

Traders nevertheless faced a challenge in managing their domestic lives so they could be away from home nearly every day, and for long hours. In Ibadan around 1960, most market women rose at 5:00 or 5:30 to organize the household and get their older children off to school. They then went to the market, arriving at around 7:00 or 8:00 and remaining there for 12 hours. They might take a nap in their stall at mid-day but would still be available to customers. While they were selling, domestic tasks at home could be assigned to their children, "house girls" (young servants who lived with the family for whom they worked), or female relatives. If a woman was deeply involved in her trade but had no one to help at home, or if she needed to travel for an extended period, she might send her children to live temporarily in other households.[69]

To be a successful trader, a woman needed a number of skills. She had to be alert and imaginative in figuring out how to profit from new commercially available goods and the needs of her customers.[70] She required "immense mental capacity" as well, in order to keep track of her earnings. Although most market sellers were illiterate, each evening they calculated the value of the transactions they had made that day. In some cases that involved goods valued at £200–300 that had been received on credit from European firms. A market woman also needed effective sales techniques, enabling her to woo customers and haggle over prices in such a way that both parties ended up "satisfied not only that an exchange has been made but also that a social intercourse has been gone through."

How did women acquire those skills? Though there were no formal apprenticeships for girls interested in trade, many learned by working with or for their mothers. Leo Frobenius, describing his travels in Yorubaland in 1910–1912, said that girls began to acquire necessary market techniques by accompanying their mothers. "When mother goes to market, the little maid goes with her, sits next to her at the stall and learns the value of cowrie-money and the quantitative and qualitative worth of goods from listening to what her mother and the passers-by say and what the latter want to buy."[71] During the 1920s and early 1930s, Folayegbe Akintunde, the oldest daughter of a leading Christian family in Okeigbo, helped her mother to sell produce from their farm, hawking it on the streets even after she started going to school.[72] A female trader leaving Ejinrin market near Epe in 1925 told her 7-year-old daughter to go on ahead to the canoe, carrying a bundle containing £40 in cash tied up in a straw bag. When the girl reached the boat, two men helped her unload the bundle but told her to go sit in a different part of the canoe. When the mother arrived, she found that the bag had been cut open and the money stolen. Sulia Adedeji, daughter of a wealthy Ibadan royal household, was taken out of her kindergarten during a smallpox epidemic in 1947.[73] While she was at home, she went with her grandmother to buy yams at the market and helped to pound them for sale in small batches. As a somewhat older child, she hawked pounded yam and other items that her grandmother had prepared; while in secondary school, she sold oranges to school children in the daytime and kerosene at night. The mother of Hannah Dideolu, later to become the wife of Obafemi Awolowo, was an itinerant trader in textiles and clothing based in the little town of Ikenne Remo, near Lagos.[74] When Hannah came home from her boarding primary school in Lagos, she traveled with her mother to markets in nearby communities, gathering items to take back to Ikenne.

Girls could also be hired as servants or hawkers by adult traders. The lines between training, pawning, and exploitation were often ill defined. Near Ibadan around 1950, the guardian of a young girl whose father had died "attached" her to a woman in Pabiekun village, supposedly "just to acquire knowledge of tradings" but apparently to get rid of the girl to someone who was glad to have her labor.[75] Socially concerned women worried about the many girl hawkers in cities, vulnerable to economic and sexual abuse. In Lagos, the Women's Welfare Council drew attention in 1942 to the "terrible state of degradation" to which many such hawkers had been reduced.[76] Supporting a plan of the Lagos Town Council to prohibit employment of young girls on the streets, the council asked all government officials, teachers, and churches and mosques to urge parents to stop the practice of sending girls under age 14 to Lagos as work as hawkers. But educated women also recognized that slightly older girls might profit from such work if they were under responsible supervision. In 1946 a combined committee of the Women's Party, the Women's League, and the Women's Welfare Council sent a petition to the government protesting against a new ordinance that kept all children and young people off the streets.[77] They argued that girls aged 14–16 commonly participated in the trade of their parents or guardians, thereby "getting the formal training for marriage and doing their bit to contribute their quota to their marriage expenses."

The amount of trading capital a woman could access determined the scale of her activity and to some extent the types of commodities she could handle. Women obtained their capital from various sources. N. A. Fadipe, writing in the 1930s, said that traditionally many women had begun trading when their farmer husbands furnished them with cash or produce that could be sold.[78] Those resources reflected "sentiments of kinship and social solidarity." Mabogunje explained that the expectation that a woman would receive from her husband the wherewithal to trade was "meant to shield her from the temptations attendant on idleness and at the same time to equip her to shoulder some of the monetary responsibilities of both her immediate and her extended family."[79] During the later colonial period, sums of £1 to £10 were frequently mentioned in divorce cases as the amount that had been given by husbands to their wives as starting capital.[80] In the small town of Itaogbolu in the 1950s, a husband initially gave his wife £1-5-0 for trading. When she then said she wanted to deal in salt, he gave her 11s. 6d. Finally he gave her 15s. so she could try trading in rice. The husband in a divorce case in Ibadan in 1945 said that he had taken his wife to the coast, where he and his sister had each given her £5 for trading.[81]

As the colonial period progressed, although it was still felt that husbands ideally ought to give each wife a sum of money to help her begin trading, such contributions became less common. Among women who were setting up shops in Lagos during the 1940s, capital was usually furnished by husbands only if they were civil service workers who were not allowed to trade themselves.[82] Women were more likely to use their own earnings from previous trading ventures, or they might get an inheritance or gift from their mothers or other relatives. Newly married women sometimes had capital in the form of presents made to them during and shortly after the marriage process. Only a few of the women traders studied in Awe in the early 1960s had received even part of their initial trading capital from their husbands, though the man might have helped to build a stall or shop for his wife's business.[83] Most women had started independent trading with money saved while working with their mothers or another female trader before marriage. Others purchased their initial stock on credit.

If women were faced by an unexpected demand for cash, they tried to avoid dipping into what was often a limited pool of working capital for trade.[84] Perhaps they could obtain a gift or loan from their husband or members of their kin group egbẹ́, or trading organization. Some women joined èsúsú savings groups as a financial buffer against hard times.[85] In the worst case, a woman whose business was failing because her expenses outweighed her income could shift to a different occupation, usually one that relied more heavily on her labor than on cash outlays.

Where did women get the goods they traded? Unless they were selling food-stuffs or processed agricultural items from their family's farm or their own private land, they normally bought their supplies from producers or wholesalers. Dealers might be foreign-owned firms or local men and women. In the years around 1900, Ibilola, a female trader and butcher (an unusual occupation for a woman) in Abeokuta, obtained her supplies from the firm C. B. Moore and Sons.[86] The firm kept an account book that recorded her receipts of goods and the payments she made, and she had a similar passbook. Awanotu Abake, a girl of 17 or 18 years, acquired goods from a merchant in Lagos in 1922, which she used in her own trading though she was still living with her parents.[87] When a female trading customer of Chief Akinpelu Obisesan, an important merchant in Ibadan, fell behind on her account in 1930, her husband wrote to say that he would pay her debt in 8 weeks time. On occasion, women dealt in stolen goods. In 1933 women were said to be among the "expert distributors of the booty" stolen by gangs in Shagamu and sold in nearby towns like Iperu and (Ijebu) Ode.[88] Two female petty traders in the latter town were invited to buy salt in 1943 by a man who—they learned later—had stolen six 90-lb. bags of it from a storehouse of the leading firm Messrs. John Holt & Co.

Because many market traders were geographically mobile, traveling within a local region or going farther afield to buy and sell, changes in the forms of transportation across the colonial period had a big impact. In areas where goods still had to be head loaded over paths, the scale of individual market-ing operations was curtailed. Female traders could either transport their own items or hire other people—including other women—to work as porters.[89] As roads and motorized vehicles became more common, however, some women began to hire trucks to transport the agricultural goods they had assembled at staging points or to carry items between towns. But because women rarely drove trucks and nearly all transport firms were owned by men, some female intermediaries were displaced by men able to take better advantage of motor-ized vehicles.

In areas within easy reach of a railway line, women traders profited in several respects. Workers on the railroads and their passengers created demand, especially for food. Even at the very start of the twentieth century, female petty traders had settled next to the railroad station in Ibadan, where they offered ready-to-eat food and poultry.[90] Railways also allowed women to move quickly over longer distances with their goods. Although some women paid for rail transport, the wives of railway employees were often able to get free transport for themselves and their trading wares. Chief Ester Bisoye Tejuoso of Lagos, born in 1916, was particularly successful.[91] She started business with modest capital, dealing in textiles and provisions, but later she became the United Africa Company's agent in Lagos, not a common position for a woman. Astutely deploying the free travel she gained through her husband's employment with the railway, she expanded her trade in imported goods and hardware and used her husband's network of fellow workers to consolidate her business. She later became Nigeria's first woman industrialist and a multi-millionaire as well as *Ìyálóde* of the Egba.

Other women too demonstrated their entrepreneurial skills in recognizing and seizing upon emerging opportunities. Several examples illustrate how such women progressed from generally modest beginnings. In Okuku, a woman called Ayantayo, born around the turn of the century, began by producing and preparing palm oil and kola nuts between 1917 and 1922.[92] From that base she moved into other kinds of trade, selling meat and new items like European alcoholic drinks. Employing a growing number of women from the surrounding area, she outlived two husbands and then remained a widow. Her household was expanded by some of her children and grandchildren, who provided labor but also received her assistance in such areas as education. Quick to recognize the potential of the railway, she built a house and shop next to the train station. She further displayed her wealth by putting an iron roof on her house and riding on red and white horses. As Karin Barber commented, "It was precisely the newness of the trade in European imports—because it had no prior gender associations—which gave Ayantayo an opening. Indeed, since women already controlled the local market and had well-established trading networks, it gave her an advantage."

Comfort Oguntubi of Ado Ekiti, born around 1910, learned weaving and trading from her parents as a young girl.[93] In the 1920s, she began work as an itinerant trader, traveling between Ado Ekiti and Ife. She had accumulated enough capital by the mid-1930s to start specializing in imported cloth, and by 1960 she owned the largest textile shop in Ado Ekiti. From 1945 through 1980 she and another woman of similar background controlled the textile and palm oil trades in their region. Oguntubi played a leading role in the town's political crisis of 1940–1942 and went on to found an *egbę* of wealthy women in the town, devoted to modernization as well as fashion.

Abigasi Bolajoke Ladejobi of Oshogbo entered business as a petty trader dealing in cotton goods, crockery, and enamelware after her marriage in 1936.[94] In 1942, when her husband was transferred to Zaria in northern Nigeria, she moved her business there, setting up a shop stocked with cotton goods obtained from two foreign-owned firms. Her husband died in 1946, whereupon she returned to Oshogbo, continuing to trade in textiles but now also milling corn and baking bread, the latter a novelty for most Yoruba people. Six years later, she applied for a loan of £1,000 from the Western Region's Production Development Board with which to purchase three motorized corn mills and to erect a building to house them. Although she said she wanted to help solve the local shortage of foodstuffs by buying large quantities of corn, guinea corn, yams, pepper, and other items and grinding them for public use, she received a loan for only one mill. As the government began plans to extend public utilities to Oshogbo, Ladejobi quickly realized the potential for her business. In 1955 she applied for a second loan, this time for £3,000 to buy electrically run equipment for an enlarged, modern bakery that would serve the entire area around the town.

Madam Humuani Alaga, described in 1953 as "a fearless fighter for Ibadan women traders," started trading with her mother in Ibadan "at a very tender age."[95] She and her two sisters accompanied their parents, both prominent textile dealers, as they went on trading expeditions throughout Yorubaland. In 1923, when she was 16, Alaga began to trade independently. Nine years later, as foreign firms established branches in Ibadan, she was one of their first registered customers. She specialized in textiles, not only buying and selling them but also advising European firms on the designs and texture of goods intended for West African markets. By 1953, she had accounts with a number of well-known firms and more than 500 credit customers of her own. Alaga organized courses for girls who wished to take up trading as a vocation, helped to construct a maternity clinic, and led a protest of women against conditional sales by "undesirable speculators." The chosen leader of Ibadan's women traders, she held a series of titled positions that culminated in her appointment as *Ìyálájé* of the city in the 1970s.[96] She was also deeply involved in political organizations, such as the Ibadan Progressive Union, the National Council of Women's Societies, and the women's wing of the Action Group. Trading might be a "traditional" activity for Yoruba women, but it was often pursued in very "modern" ways.

Craftwork and Services

During the colonial period, indigenous handicrafts faced increasing competition from factory-made goods. Industrial wares were at first imported from Britain but later produced also in Nigerian factories. In some cases craftswomen responded by experimenting with new techniques that enabled them to produce their wares more quickly and efficiently, but those changes were not enough. Many craftswomen became less able to hold their own as the colonial years passed. Thus, the growing availability of scented white soaps put most traditional soap makers out of business, while potters faced equivalent problems as containers made of enamelware, metal, and plastic became available in local markets.[97]

Textiles remained the most important craft for women. In Abeokuta, a major center, production was affected by several shifts in weaving and dyeing practices.[98] Some weavers began to use imported European threads, which were already colored, rather than employing local dyers; conversely, some dyers bought white European cloth to color. Craftswomen at first profited from their ability to access thread, cloth, and credit from foreign trading firms, becoming independent producers of the tie-dyed cloth called àdìrẹ, popular throughout Nigeria and along the West African coast. A survey of Abeokuta in 1926 listed 1,064 àdìrẹ makers and 1,094 dyers. But from the late 1920s onward, the àdìrẹ industry suffered a steep decline due to falling commodity prices, the cycles of recession/depression that marked the years between the two world wars, and the development of textile industries in other parts of West Africa. Export prices for Nigerian cloth in 1932 were only one-third of their value in 1920. Whereas European traders and local men were able to use privileges based on class, gender, and the authority of the colonial state to protect their own economic positions, African women were vulnerable. In an attempt to remain solvent, Abeokuta's female dyers began to try out new techniques, using caustic soda and synthetic dyes. When the government prohibited those methods, the dyers organized mass protests.[99]

Weaving suffered as well. The Ekiti area of eastern Yorubaland was actively engaged in cloth manufacture earlier in the century. During a 3-month period in 1917, five female spinners and 15 female weavers appeared as parties or witnesses before the Native Court of Ado Ekiti alone.[100] In 1922–1923, four female weavers were parties in cases, two more were involved in fights, and two were witnesses.[101] Probably due in part to demand from weavers, some local women specialized in making laundry soap in the years around 1920. But between 1930 and 1945, cloth producers in Ekiti North faced severe and unwelcome competition from imported goods.[102] By the 1950s, crop production produced more income in Ekiti than weaving or other crafts.

Dyeing and hand weaving did not, however, cease entirely. In Abeokuta, Ibadan, and some towns in central and eastern Yorubaland, traditional dyeing continued at a reduced level.[103] In Lagos, a new and highly successful technology emerged in the 1940s: female merchants bought factory-produced cloth, used stencils to imprint a design, and then delivered the cloth to one of the city's many female dyers, who produced the desired colors. Hand weavers still worked in some regions right through the colonial period, specializing in certain kinds of religiously or culturally significant cloths.[104] In some communities both men and women wove, using different kinds of looms, but in parts of eastern Yorubaland, women were the primary weavers. Among the Bunu in northeastern Yorubaland, female weavers profited from improved transportation. Whereas early in the century they had to head load their cloth to Lokoja market for sale, a trip that required 5–7 days, with the introduction of motorized vehicles in the early 1930s, they could travel to Lokoja and return in a single day, taking with them larger quantities of cloth.[105] In Ondo during the 1950s, the profits from "home industry" (primarily cloth products that had been spun, woven, or dyed) constituted 34 percent of the total income of women, more than they earned from either farming and sale of agricultural goods or from trade.

Service work offered gradually increasing opportunities for women. During the nineteenth and early twentieth centuries, domestic services were normally performed by female relatives, slaves, or pawns. Paid services emerged slowly across the colonial period, used especially by the smaller households that were increasingly common in urban environments. Busy urban residents might be willing to pay laundry women and dry cleaners to attend to their clothing and bedding instead of doing it themselves. In Ekiti North, care of clothing was affected in the later colonial years not only by the increasing number of women who worked outside the home but also by Western-style clothing, including women's dresses and children's school uniforms, which had to be ironed to look neat.[106] Laundresses were common in Lagos in the late 1940s.

After World War II, a small number of urban households began to hire residential female servants. Few European families employed African women (they preferred male servants, often a cook and one or more "boys"), and most African households did all the domestic work themselves. A study of 230 Yoruba households in Lagos in the late 1940s found that two-thirds had no domestic servants at all.[107] Female family members did the housework, shopping, and cooking. But Yoruba households that did have servants were more likely to employ women or girls than males. The most common type was a young maid or child minder who came from the provinces. Such girls were often sent by their parents to a wealthier household in Lagos with whom they had family or business connections. In such cases, where the servant was learning how to manage a household more complicated than that of her parents, she was not paid, though the mistress of the household might give her presents, as she did her own daughters. High-status families sometimes hired an adult female cook, maid, or housekeeper.

By the 1950s, one finds more references to domestic maids, at least in Lagos. One newspaper advertisement announced openings for "4 small house-maids," who were to receive a little salary as well as free food and lodging; another recruited both house girls and a house boy.[108] Some girls began domestic work at an early age. In 1950 a Lagos woman was fined for inflicting grave injuries while punishing her 6-year-old maid, who had stolen some sweets from the local market while on an errand for her mistress.[109] When the magistrate passed sentence, he complained that "the accused should not have sent so young a girl alone to the market to purchase food," but he did not object to the girl's employment within the home. A potential problem was that adolescent servants might become bored with their confining domestic work. In 1960, the 15-year-old baby nurse to a Lagos family ran away from her position to live with the family's 18-year-old former cook.[110]

Personal services were also offered by women. As female hair styles became more elaborate and new equipment came into use, some women set themselves up as hairdressers in Lagos and elsewhere.[111] An advertisement for toilet soap in 1960 showed a photo of "lovely Elizabeth Gayon," who had studied hair and beauty care in the UK and now worked in the Ladies' Hairdressing Department of a large store in Lagos.[112] A few women earned money piercing ears or putting customary ethnic tattoos on young children. (Only immigrants from rural areas utilized the latter service, not Lagos-born parents.) Others were herbalists, traditional medical practitioners, circumcisers, or diviners who were consulted about illnesses.

Provision of sexual services by Yoruba women as a way to earn money is largely absent from the records of the colonial period.[113] That absence may reflect some degree of social reality. Men found it relatively easy to marry an additional acknowledged or hidden woman or to make arrangements with a concubine (an exclusive lover who received ongoing financial support). But the Yoruba ethical system did not permit a man to have casual sex with women for pay. In a case of attempted rape heard in Epe in 1926, the man said that he had asked Musitura to be his concubine, for which she demanded £2 in cash.[114] When he gave her only £1-15-0, she refused to come to him, whereupon he assaulted her. When the term "prostitute" was used at all, it was generally a term of generic abuse designed to weaken a woman's credibility. In a complex and bitter divorce case between Moriamo of Ibadan and her second husband in 1939, an adverse petition described her to the king and leading chiefs as "a prostitute woman" whose account was filled with lies.[115]

But at least a few women apparently did sell sex.[116] A man accused of raping a woman at Ejinrin in 1925 claimed that she was a prostitute whom he visited every market day, giving her 1s. each time.[117] On the day in question, she had another customer with her when he first came to her room. As new types of female employment emerged during the late colonial period, in business and the government, it is possible that some women used their sexuality to gain a position or promotion, a pattern described in the late twentieth century as "bottom power."[118]

In the area of business services, some women worked as agents in Lagos in the later 1940s. They helped to make connections between traders who wished to venture into a new type of business, change supplier, or get rid of part of their stock, and persons who could assist in the desired transaction.[119] When the deal was concluded, the agent took a commission. A few women were pawnbrokers, though that activity was normally handled by men. One of the most profitable services to emerge during the colonial period, providing mechanized transport, was closed to women unless they had family resources that allowed them to make the large investments that such businesses required. Mrs. Charlotte Olajumoke Obasa, who died in 1953, was an educated woman active in civic events in Lagos.[120] She was also a pioneer in motor transport, founding the Anifani Bus Service in 1913 and running it for many years. Her father, Richard Blaize, from a returnee background, was a successful business-man in Lagos in the late nineteenth and early twentieth centuries. (In 1896, he was said to be the wealthiest man in Nigeria.) His backing may have helped Charlotte to start her transport firm. Mrs. Morenike Adigun owned a Lagos taxicab that knocked down and killed a man riding a bicycle in 1958.[121] Her husband, a minister in the Western Region government, was a probable source of financial assistance and contacts for her taxi business.

Although most of the types of work considered in this chapter were familiar from the nineteenth century, they were extended into new areas during the colonial period. Many women remained at the bottom of the trading system, but some energetic and imaginative women, especially those with access to cash or credit, were able to gain larger profits, often by moving into novel kinds of business. Violating British but not Yoruba gender expectations, all traders, craftswomen, and service providers made decisions about their own lives. The more successful ones controlled their workers and gained enhanced authority within their families and communities.

9 | Western Skills and Service Careers

WHEREAS THE KINDS of work examined in the previous chapter all had roots in the nineteenth century, Yoruba women also defined and entered some unfamiliar occupations made possible by the colonial system. Through these careers, many of which offered valuable services to the community, women expanded their options as decision makers and often gained new kinds of authority through association with British institutions and people. Women who had studied sewing or cooking at school set up businesses that made use of their ability to prepare fashionable dresses or desirable foods, while proficiency in English and numeracy enabled a smaller number to find employment in offices or shops. The first section of this chapter examines how women converted Western skills into money-making activities. Women who had been trained as teachers and nurses usually worked initially in church- or government-run schools or hospitals, but some then decided to set up their own institutes or private clinics. A few women acquired the advanced education needed to move into the higher professions or the government's Civil Service. The second part of the chapter looks at teaching, nursing, and careers that required further training.

The entry of Yoruba women into occupations that demanded a Western education was slow, due in part to patriarchal attitudes. The early Christian missionaries who founded many of the influential schools for girls emphasized domestic training that would prepare them for lives as wives and mothers. In accordance with middle-class British Victorian attitudes, they assumed that Christian women would remain at home after marriage, sewing, cooking, raising their children, and supervising their households but not attempting to earn their own money.[1] British colonial administrators likewise felt that husbands were the natural wage earners for their entire family and that women should not compete with men in public spheres. They were therefore reluctant to hire women within government-run services like the railroad, to license them as agents in the Marketing Boards that handled export crops, or to employ them within the Civil Service until after World War II. Those policies accorded with Yoruba men's sense that although it was fine for women to be traders, men should dominate the new types of employment for Africans created by colonialism.

Women themselves were often reluctant to move into wage- or salary-paying jobs, preferring instead to run their own businesses. Although occupations like teaching and nursing were respected for the services they provided, and although they conveyed high status because they were British-linked and "modern," the pay offered by schools and hospitals was often considerably less than what a woman could earn on her own. Many women disliked working under the constant supervision of another person. Moreover, employment at a formal institution kept women away from home for long and fixed hours, and babies could not be taken there. Women who had their own enterprises gained more independence and greater flexibility in coordinating the demands of work with their roles as wives and mothers. Businesswomen could continue their activity throughout their lives, whereas most colonial schools and government positions required that women leave employment when they married and certainly when they became pregnant. All these factors contributed to Yoruba women's experimentation with how to gain at least some of the benefits of new types of work while at the same time pursuing more traditional goals of earning a good income, working for themselves, and filling their family responsibilities.

Occupations Requiring Western Skills

Many Yoruba women who had been to schools that taught Western skills found ways to convert their training into a source of income. That pattern was already visible early in the twentieth century in the area of domestic science. The missionaries were desperate for teachers for their expanding girls' schools, and they needed women with further qualifications and experience to work in the training colleges that prepared teachers. They therefore encouraged some young women to acquire a higher education, which might mean going to Britain. A woman who had studied abroad was expected to become a teacher after returning, placing "at the service of her country women what she has been taught and has learned in England."[2] But even between 1900 and 1915, some well-educated women from elite Yoruba families refused to become teachers. Instead they set up their own companies or managed their families' cash-crop farms on a more businesslike basis.

As the colonial period progressed, a growing number of women found other ways of using their domestic skills to earn money. Knowledge of Western cooking, for example, enabled one to enter business as a baker, confectioner, or caterer; as the operator of a cafe, restaurant, or hotel; or as the founder and head of a private training institute that taught other young women new culinary arts. But the earliest and always the most popular type of work among women who had learned Western domestic arts was to be a seamstress or dressmaker. Supported by Yoruba women's love of fabrics and fine clothes, this occupation combined ability at fancy sewing, including the use of a sewing machine, with knowledge of the latest styles of African and European dress for women and information about the uniforms needed by school children.[3]

Clothes and how they were made changed considerably across the colonial years. At the start of the century, male tailors produced customary clothing for men, and they soon began to make European-style shirts, shorts, and trousers for foreigners and some African men. Throughout the colonial period, tailors of men's clothing continued to be male.[4] Women's clothing had a different history. The one or two simple wraps that formed traditional attire required little if any sewing. Early in the colonial years, female members of the African elite who wore Western clothing as well as the few white women in Nigeria purchased much of their clothing in Britain.[5] By the 1920s and 1930s, however, African-style clothing was becoming more elaborate, and more urban women were wearing European attire in some contexts. These developments created a demand for locally produced clothing that followed chic African or foreign fashions. Because making such clothing required training and expertise, women who had learned sewing skills at school were able to set up lucrative businesses of their own.[6] Many seamstresses also sold cloth, sewing supplies, and sometimes ready-made imported clothing. In 1933, a West Indian woman who had trained in Canada, the United States, and Britain organized the first fashion show in Lagos, based upon her establishment, "where dresses are made to order for Ladies, Misses, and Children."[7] By the late 1940s, buyers of European-style clothing, school uniforms, and infants' wear in Lagos normally went to a private seamstress. Most dressmakers worked alone, but a few had workshops that hired up to six employees.

Although elite parents, missionaries, and colonial administrators at first looked down on dressmaking, which lacked the social status of teaching or nursing, they gradually realized that women could earn more money by sewing than in the highly educated careers.[8] Folayegbe Akintunde's father wanted to remove her from school when she was partway through her elementary education in the mid-1930s, intending to have her trained as a seamstress, an occupation he saw as compatible with familiar gender patterns.[9] Only after Fola's headmaster intervened did her father agree to let her complete her primary education and later to accept a scholarship to Queen's College in Lagos, the leading girls' secondary school. In Ekiti North, where few girls attended school until the 1940s, one of the subjects they learned was needlework, in hopes that "it would eventually produce seamstresses and housewives who would sew for their living."[10]

Girls who wanted to become a seamstress or dressmaker needed not only some formal schooling but also hands-on practical training. In the early colonial decades, girls were usually trained by a parent or another working seamstress, sometimes completing what amounted to an apprenticeship. The daughter of a Christian family in Ijebu Ode in the 1920s was taught how to use a sewing machine by her father, one of the first tailors in the town to have such equipment.[11] With his backing, she attended secondary school but then decided to become a seamstress. When her father refused to buy her a machine of her own, she ran off to Lagos and worked with a seamstress for 3 years before marrying a teacher from Abeokuta. In Ife in 1934, a seamstress charged £3 to train a young woman how to make clothing with a sewing machine; at the end of her training, her pupil was ready to enter business on her own.[12] The government also began to offer training programs, part of the new policy of promoting practical education for girls in the schools.[13] In 1949 the government considered building a Women's Trade Centre outside Abeokuta that would offer courses in dressmaking, needlework, and embroidery as well as cake and bread making, housecraft, English, arithmetic, and clerical work to 150 boarders.

Some enterprising women began to set up their own private training institutes. Initially they were run mainly by locally trained teachers of domestic science subjects who were obliged to resign their posts when they married or became pregnant. In 1930, a well-born woman in Lagos operated a sewing institute on Breadfruit Street that offered training for girls as well as a "perfect fit and stylish sewing" for its customers.[14] An Ibadan woman estimated that her institute had turned out 600 seamstresses between 1930 and 1950, plus many bakers and caterers. During the 1940s and 1950s, some women from prosperous families began going to Britain for advanced training in domestic arts. Rather than intending to work in schools upon their return, they wanted to set up their own institutes. Mrs. Bank-Anthony, from an important Lagos family, went to England in 1945 to study fashion design, having formerly been a teacher. When she returned 4 years later, she founded a dressmaking institute that offered a higher level of training than had previously been available locally.[15]

During the late colonial period, the number of seamstresses and the status of such work increased. Those changes resulted from growing demand for

Western fashions, more elaborate styles of traditional attire, and improved train-ing facilities.[16] By 1950, 2,161 seamstresses worked in Lagos alone. Although many dressmakers did not earn large incomes, some women rose to promi-nence. One of the contestants for seats on the Lagos Town Council in 1950 was an unmarried woman described as a seamstress and confectioner.[17] That same year, "many prominent Muslims attended the grand marriage ceremony" held at an Islamic school in Lagos between Isbat Olayiwola Durosinmi, a successful seamstress, and a man employed by the colonial Audit Department in Lagos. Modupe Adumoso, daughter of a barrister, received a diploma in dressmak-ing and embroidery, completed a specialized course at a technical college in London, and worked at a fashion center in the West End before returning to Lagos in 1953 to set up her own dressmaking business.[18] The following year, a daughter of the king of Ado-Ekiti who had been educated at St. Anne's School, Ibadan, left for Britain to study dressmaking and domestic science.

Another occupation considered suitable for educated women was mak-ing and/or selling Western-style ladies' hats. In 1935, Ladipo Solanke, who was living in London, wrote to his niece in Lagos, encouraging her to learn some technical trade like hat making as well as to prepare either as a teacher or nurse.[19] In an undated essay titled "Encouraging Native Industry, Part I," Solanke praised a young woman in Ijebu Ode who was making exquisite hats for ladies and children in European styles but using African materials and African workmanship. While Hannah Awolowo's husband, Obafemi, was in England studying law in the mid-1940s, she supported herself and her four children by importing foodstuffs from northern Nigeria and selling them in Ibadan.[20] When Obafemi returned to the country, he insisted that she stop trading, but he was willing to let her import and sell hats and make clothing, assisted by apprentices.

A cluster of new occupations that required proficiency in written English plus some technical skills or basic numeracy arose over the course of the colonial period. These included being a typist, secretary, or office clerk. A few girls were beginning to find work as typists in the 1920s, and in 1938 an 18-month training course in shorthand-typing was said to be open to either sex.[21] But opportunities for African women in all those positions were gen-erally restricted by an ongoing preference among business and government employers for African male workers or European females. Thus, a govern-ment report from 1934 refers to clerical workers as men; the clerk hired by a British woman in Lagos to take shorthand notes and type her diary in 1947 was a man; an article about the need for shorthand writers from 1953 describes them as male; and advertisements in 1960 depict male office work-ers.[22] Although an editorial in the *Lagos Daily News* in 1931 had encouraged women to undertake training as clerks, preparing themselves for jobs in the modern world, it was only around 1950 that private employers began hiring women regularly as office workers.[23]

During the 1950s, the government started to accept African women as secretaries or clerks. Although this was part of a deliberate colonial policy of readying government workers to run an independent Nigeria, the base was low: in 1955, only four Nigerians were among the 80 secretary-typists employed by the federal government, and it is not clear how many of those were women.[24] For an African woman to become the primary secretary to a senior British official was sufficiently uncommon in 1955 that it attracted comment from another colonial administrator. M. C. Atkinson noted in his diary that Mrs. Coker, an Egba lady who was secretary to the acting British Permanent Secretary to the Ministry of Home Affairs in Ibadan, was "not only efficient and hardworking but also very attractive."[25] As Independence approached, the new Nigerian political leaders decided that hiring female clerical workers was appropriate for the new nation. When, however, the government of the Western Region announced in 1960 that it would no longer recruit men into "the secretarial and stenographic class," a letter to the local paper complained that the new policy was unfair to the young men who had already spent several years of study to prepare for such work.[26]

From the 1930s onward, women—usually younger ones—began to find employment as sales girls or cashiers in the shops of larger towns. These jobs required the ability to speak English plus some degree of literacy and numeracy. When Miss Mary Abu was taken on as a sales girl by the "fancy goods department" of a foreign-owned "canteen" in Abeokuta in 1930, the *Nigerian Daily Times* hailed this as "a step in the right direction" and hoped that "other firms will follow the lead."[27] In Lagos, 50 young ladies were employed as sales girls or cashiers in the large European stores on the marina in the late 1940s. Women were at first concentrated in areas that related to appearance or domestic concerns, but by 1960 female sales clerks were sought by a company that sold electrical and technical goods.[28] Other women worked in sales promotion and advertising.

During the second half of the colonial era, local and regional governments employed increasing numbers of semi-skilled female workers. Women were hired as bookbinders from the 1920s, later as customs clerks and cooks for the army, and as police constables from the 1930s.[29] Because policewomen could not be married, the government made a special effort to persuade young widows to enlist in 1936. Hiring women in the police force was controversial, and letters to newspapers were still objecting to their presence in the 1950s. Authors complained that "women are temperamentally unsuited to be in the constabulary because of their strong avarice for money," that they were not endowed by nature with the "toughness of habit and a forceful approach" required in police work, and that their personality could not command the confidence of the public.[30] But when a man wrote to a column called "Love and Marriage Problems" in 1958, asking if he should stay with the girl he loved, who had just joined the police force, the response was yes: "I can assure you that behind the immaculate and stern uniform of a Policewoman lies a gentle, affectionate and understanding heart."

After 1945, women used proficiency in English or other Western skills to move into a range of additional occupations. Female telephone or telegraph operators and supervisors were employed by private businesses and the government.[31] Radio broadcasting offered new possibilities. A trader and caterer who had moved to Lagos from Ijesha in 1953 began her own radio program, telling Yoruba folk stories and proverbs.[32] The theatre was a tempting—if potentially immoral—venue for women's work. In 1933, Beatrice Oluhinun Oluwole, formerly an actress and playwright, was praised for having left the stage to become "a devout Christian leader" who was already attracting a considerable flock of spiritual followers.[33] When Hubert Ogunde, a well-known Nigerian actor and playwright, left for a tour of France and Italy in 1947, he was accompanied by Clementina Onabule, his leading actress. She planned to study stage management, costumes, makeup, and dancing while abroad. By the mid-1950s, adventurous women were invading fields formerly reserved for men, becoming technicians, draftsmen, surveyors, and photographers.[34] The early but burgeoning oil business was creating other new positions. BP-Shell advertised in 1960 for women or men who had passed their advanced secondary school exams in mathematics, physics, or chemistry to be trained as future specialists.

A small number of women in Lagos and a few other cities earned money through factory work in the late colonial years. Although this employment did not normally require formal education, it did force women to conform to Western ideas about time and reliability. Most industrial jobs were related to women's domestic roles. Several thousand Lagos women worked in factories that processed food in the late 1940s.[35] Some dealt in dried or smoked meat or fish, while others prepared flour or meal. A few mechanized textile workshops offered waged employment to women as well as men. Lagos women were also hired by factories that made mattresses and pillows, brooms, sponges, and whips (every household was said to have one for punishing children and recalcitrant servants).

Teaching, Nursing, and Other Careers

Teaching and nursing were the only professional careers open to more than a handful of educated women during the early and middle colonial years. Suzanne Comhaire-Sylvain observed in the late 1940s that Lagos women whose roots lay in the Sierra Leonean returnee tradition were unusual in their preference for these "intellectual" occupations, but in the following decade the popularity of such work increased among many Yoruba women.[36] Organizations of educated women now argued that women should be allowed to move into types of employment previously reserved for men, should receive the same pay, and should not have to resign from their jobs when they married or became pregnant.

Teachers, at whatever level, gained authority over their students and sometimes the students' parents, while those in administrative positions were able to make decisions for other instructors. But women moved into teaching only gradually. During the early colonial period, missionary schools were torn between their sense that girls should be taught to become good wives and mothers and their need for teachers. Many schools started training "pupil teachers," generally their own graduates who worked first at the mother school under the supervision of foreign missionaries before going out to teach on their own until they wed. A British teacher at the CMS Girls' Seminary in Lagos reported with pleasure in 1912 that 17 of their girls over the past 4 years had gone on to teach in Lagos or the interior of the country; seven girls were currently in training as pupil teachers.[37] The seminary began to offer more formal preparation of teachers in 1919. After 2 years of training at the school, young women could try for the government's Third Class Teachers' Certificate. The following year a newspaper reported approvingly that the seminary encouraged parents to keep their daughters in school and have them trained as qualified teachers, "instead of leaving school and just wasting their time at home as so many of them do in 'Sewing' as they call it."[38]

During the mid-colonial years, women's entry into teaching was slow. In mission schools, teachers were assumed to be male in 1932, and the few female teachers were concentrated almost entirely within domestic science fields.[39] All the students in a training college for elementary school teachers in Ibadan in the 1930s were male, and in 1936, only 100 semi-private and government-run schools employed even a single woman on their teaching staff.[40] We know something about the female teachers employed in Lagos's primary schools in the late 1940s. Catholic schools hired 50 women, and the Catholic teacher training college had 24 female pupil teachers. The schools run by the various Protestant missions had some 125 female primary school teachers or teachers-in-training. Another 60 teachers were employed in other primary schools, but not all on a full-time basis. That yielded a total of about 260 female primary school teachers. No schools had a female head.

More openings for women as teachers and headmistresses of primary schools were created in the later 1940s and 1950s. Among the factors that contributed to this change were the partial Nigerianization of the Civil Service, permission for married women and mothers to continue teaching, and a dramatic expansion of girls' education after 1955, the result of the Western Region government's decision to provide free primary schooling for all children.[41] Demand for female teachers now exceeded the supply of potential recruits graduating from teacher training colleges. Women were named as head teachers/mistresses of girls' schools in various parts of Yorubaland, and one of the candidates for the Lagos Town Council in 1950 was the principal of a school.[42] By 1960, nearly all advertisements for teachers, including from Muslim schools, invited applications from both men and women in most subjects (though only "lady teachers" were sought for positions in domestic science and needlework).

After World War II, the improvement in female education enabled a few young women to obtain the qualifications needed to teach in secondary schools. Two Nigerian teachers were employed in the late 1940s at Queen's College in Lagos.[43] One taught the Bible and Yoruba, while the other—who had studied at Teachers' College, Columbia University in New York—taught history. The position of principal of Queen's College was reserved for British women.[44] Having a foreign head could result in conflict with African teachers due to the outsider's lack of cultural sensitivity.[45] At the few other secondary schools for girls in Lagos and a center for domestic training, no more than a dozen women were employed as instructors in 1948.

Some women worked as school teachers for a few years before turning in a different direction. As we have seen, experienced teachers of domestic science subjects often decided to set up their own training institutes. Other women went abroad for advanced education in an unrelated field. Mrs. Kuforiji-Olubi trained as a teacher and served as the headmistress of a school for 3 years during the mid-1950s.[46] She then went to England, where she studied the social sciences and gained professional training in accountancy. Later she became the first Nigerian female chartered accountant and an influential banker and company director.

Within the government's Civil Service, only British women were hired in the senior positions of Education Officers and Lady Superintendents of Education until shortly before Independence.[47] The first female African educational specialist to be employed in the upper ranks of the government was Folayegbe Akintunde-Ighodalo, who returned from her studies in England in 1955.[48] At that time colonial officials were being pushed by the emerging political parties to accept Nigerians into upper as well as lower levels of government service, as part of the transition to an independent nation. When the government approved in 1955 the appointment of 15 Nigerians into the highest rank of the Civil Service, Mrs. Akintunde-Ighodalo was the only woman among them. Assigned initially to the Ministry of Development in the Western Region, she was transferred to the Ministry of Finance in 1957 and then to the Treasury after a series of disputes with her British superior officers, whom she considered both racist and sexist. In 1959, she was appointed as senior assistant secretary in charge of secondary schools within the Ministry of Education, where she was responsible for the entire Western Region. After Independence she served two terms as permanent secretary in the Ministry of Education.

The first medical occupation entered by women was midwifery. Because Yoruba culture did not permit a man to be present when a woman gave birth, any assistance had to be provided by other women, whether a member of the family, a neighbor, or someone trained in traditional or Western skills. As early as 1920, the Conference of Africans of British West Africa held in Accra, Gold Coast (later Ghana), called for better education for women about the causes of infant mortality and the need for professional health care.[49] To implement the latter, the conference advocated the building of maternity hospitals with up-to-date equipment and the provision of maternity scholarships for African women. As a temporary measure, suitable candidates should be trained locally in elementary midwifery, but that should be supplemented and gradually replaced by advanced training in England.

The process whereby midwives were trained in Yorubaland became more formal over time. By 1930, the Massey Street Maternity Home in Lagos was preparing candidates for the midwifery certificates offered by the Director of Medical and Sanitary Service.[50] The colonial government in London accepted the recommendation of Nigerian authorities that midwives should be registered and regulated. In 1946, the press called for new maternity homes for the Lagos area, because the one at Massey Street was no longer sufficient, but it was not until 1960 that the older unit was closed entirely.[51] A second, more modern maternity hospital in Lagos had a professional staff of 58 qualified midwives and three midwife tutors, as well as several British women in the supervisory position known as "nursing sister." The new hospital's training scheme hoped to produce 60 nurse midwives each year. One of the first Yoruba women to obtain full professional qualifications in England was Hilda Omolola Coker of Lagos, member of one of the old returnee families and sister to G. B. A. Coker, a barrister in Lagos.[52] After training as a midwife at Massey Street, she left for England in 1947 to do an advanced course in midwifery; in 1950, she began specialized post-graduate training.

Most of the early teachers of midwives were Europeans. One of the first—and certainly the fiercest—was Jane McCotter, an Irish nursing sister who founded the Infant Welfare Centre in Abeokuta around 1915 and ran it until her death in 1955, when she was 85 years old.[53] (Throughout the colonial period most services that provided prenatal care functioned also as centers for infants and new mothers.) An early trainer of African midwives, Miss McCotter

FIGURE 9.1. An unidentified midwife employed by the Native Authority Clinic in Ife, Nov. 1937, with some of the mothers and babies she had assisted. Wearing a white uniform and head tie, she is seated beside a European woman in a hat (probably Mrs. I. F. W. Schofield). Photographer unknown. Rhodes House Library, Bodleian Library, Oxford: GB 0162 MSS.Afr.s.1863 (Schofield Papers), box 6, vol. 2, sheet 11. By permission of the Bodleian Library, University of Oxford.

believed passionately that babies should be born at home and fought energetically with British officials or anyone else who disagreed. She was hired initially by the colonial nursing service in Nigeria, but after violent conflicts with British administrators, she welcomed an appointment from the Egba Native Authority. Although she was awarded several high honors by the British governor, she was much more gratified to be awarded the special chieftaincy title of *Ìyá Ìbíyè* (mother of safe childbirth deliveries) by the king of Egbaland shortly before her death. An obituary in the *Egba Bulletin* said that "the full-fledged midwives whom she trained can be seen in all towns and villages in Nigeria."[54]

African midwives were indeed spreading rapidly. In many cases they were employed by local authorities. (See Figure 9.1 for an example from Ife.) But some of the more highly qualified midwives realized that they could earn more money and have more control over their working lives if they set up their own private maternity clinics. As early as 1933, the Director of Medical and Sanitary Service wrote in a memo about employment of midwives, "Women of higher educational standard who have been trained in England and who do not wish to enter Government service upon a comparatively low scale of pay, can be registered in Nigeria as Midwives and can then undertake private practice in

Midwifery."[55] In Lagos in the late 1940s, 30 young women had British diplomas in midwifery, with roughly equal numbers working in government hospitals and private clinics. Midwives who had been trained in Lagos itself were usually employed by the government. A final group of midwives consisted of women with no formal training who were not allowed to work in hospitals even though some had extensive experience in traditional practices.

Western-trained midwives were appreciated and respected by their communities. Hundreds of mothers and pregnant women joined the baálè and chiefs of Okeigbo in gathering at the Native Administration Dispensary in 1941.[56] They hoped to meet with the colonial Medical Officer for Ondo Province to entreat him to replace the midwife whom he had transferred away from Okeigbo, because women were "suffering bitterly" without her. At a grand party put on in 1946 by an unmarried senior midwife in Akure in connection with the funeral of her mother, speeches were made "paying high tribute to the qualities of the hostess and her work in the African Hospital."[57] When "Mrs. J. E. Falodun, the Midwife," hosted a party in Ibadan to mark the first birthday of her daughter in 1950, she was described as "doing yeoman service among the expectant mothers and babies here."

Regular nursing, often regarded as a typically female occupation, actually opened up to women only in the later colonial era. Starting in 1867, the government employed one or two female African nurses in its hospitals, presumably to deal with problems involving women that men were not allowed to handle, but those positions were atypical.[58] The normal pattern until the 1940s and 1950s was that hospitals were run by a few British doctors and nursing sisters, assisted by male African nurses (described usually as nursing assistants or medical assistants). In 1931, for example, 61 European nursing sisters and matrons were employed in hospitals and clinics run by the colonial Health Department in Nigeria, joined by 333 Africans, including female midwives and male nurses.[59] By 1944, however, 167 women worked as government nurses, joining 695 men.[60] This imbalance stemmed only in part from government hiring preferences. Educated women from good families were initially reluctant to enter nursing due to their dislike of the manual labor required and their resentment of the treatment of African nurses in hospitals (e.g., they were paid less than foreigners for doing the same work and were at first not allowed to wear shoes).[61]

When African women began to move into nursing, those who worked in hospitals were used as assistants to the better-trained male nurses.[62] As late as 1950, the governor of Nigeria argued to the colonial secretary that Nigerians would not accept "a comparatively young African female Nurse being placed in a position of authority over African male Nurses where she will be required not only to control but to teach them."[63] By the 1950s, however, many colonial administrators and Nigerian leaders alike felt that women's participation in the nursing profession was a sign of progress and development. Means were therefore sought to promote their entry into the field. A long newspaper article about nursing in 1956 described it as "a hard but noble job" for women, and advertisements portrayed nurses in a favorable light (though usually working with mothers and children).[64] One showed an African nurse administering medicine to fight malnutrition and anemia as part of prenatal care, while another featured a cute little girl dressed in a nurse's uniform and holding a can of milk powder on her head. By the late colonial years in Ekiti North, "nursing had become the most loved job by women," and local people "saw nurses as saviours."[65] Hospital nurses, dressed in their distinctive uniforms, wielded considerable authority over their patients and those people's families.

Because nurses could gain only basic qualifications within Nigeria until the 1950s, some women went to Britain for further training. In the mid-1930s, several Yoruba women were studying nursing there under the general supervision of Ladipo Solanke.[66] Kofoworola Abeni Pratt, whose parents lived in Lagos, passed the final exam to become a State Registered Nurse at St. Thomas's Hospital in London in 1950.[67] She had previously trained as a secondary teacher and taught at the CMS girls' school in Lagos, at her father's insistence: he was upset that she was interested in what he regarded as the low-status field of nursing. With her husband's backing, however, she went to England, where after obtaining her Registered Nurse certification she gained midwifery qualifications and practical experience in a hospital. Upon her return to Nigeria, she was hired by the newly founded nurses' training school at University College Hospital in Ibadan. There even this highly qualified and self-assured woman experienced racial and sexual discrimination from her British superiors. Later Mrs. Pratt's administrative skills led to appointments as the first Nigerian matron of the University Hospital and the first head of nursing. LaRay Denzer commented, "More than any other person, she was responsible for creating high standards of nursing and improving its status among women in the country."[68]

As with midwives, some nurses decided to set up private clinics rather than continuing with hospital work, which was tedious, poorly paid, and under constant supervision by often arrogant and officious British nursing sisters.[69] The medical section of the colonial *Annual Report* for Nigeria in 1948 included a significant comment: "The most serious brake on all the activities of the Department is the lack of trained staff. The recruitment of senior officers and nursing sisters from the United Kingdom has not come up to expectation, and the position has been further aggravated by the frequent retirement of Yaba graduates [those trained at the government's nursing school outside Lagos], some of whom have preferred to seek their fortune in private practice rather than remain in public service."[70] In the following years, many nurses left hospital employment in order to run their own clinics. One of the most successful was Sulia Adedeji, who trained and at first worked as a nurse but eventually became an extremely wealthy businesswoman.[71]

A few specialized jobs related to nursing began to appear in the 1920s. Health visitors and visiting nurses were almost always female, probably because it seemed less intrusive to have a woman going around into people's homes. In 1924, the Lagos Women's League suggested to the government that a few women be employed as health visitors "for the purposes of ensuring hygienic cleanliness both of premises and inhabitants, particularly in the densely populated areas of the town."[72] The Lagos Town Council approved the idea the following year, hiring and training four female health visitors. The king of Egbaland told the (British) Lady Medical Officer in Abeokuta in 1928 that he had interviewed Mrs. Juliana Badejoko and approved her appointment as a health visitor in connection with the Child Welfare Scheme.[73] In Lagos in 1948, several African visiting nurses were employed at two Infant Welfare Centres, and four others were preparing for that work in England. Barbara Akinyemi, a Scottish nurse working in Lagos at that time, said that the health visitors were distinctive in their blue print dresses and very white "topis" (Indian-style sun hat usually worn by colonial men).[74] Tuberculosis visitors too were generally female. Akinyemi described them cycling around Lagos, wearing green dresses with a red cross on the sleeve as well as white topis.

Women's involvement in higher professions and the government's Civil Service was very limited until the late colonial years. Only an occasional woman became a doctor, in part because so few jobs were open to them. Most doctors were employed by government hospitals, which by the 1930s began hiring African men and British women (instead of just British males), but not African women.[75] Dahlia Whitburne, a Jamaican, was appointed by the Lagos Town Council in 1928 as one of the first Lady Medical Officers.[76] In the following decade, a few Yoruba women went abroad and qualified as doctors, and Abimbola Akerele was appointed as a Lady Medical Officer in 1938. Two female doctors, both graduates of Dublin University, were working in Lagos in the late 1940s, employed by the Massey Street maternity hospital.[77] One was African, and she had a private practice on the side, while the other was apparently British. But despite some local government encouragement of young women to study medicine, it remained an overwhelmingly male field.[78]

The emerging field of social work was somewhat more welcoming to women, probably for the same reasons that they were preferred as health visitors. But Herbert Macaulay, in a draft editorial written probably in the early 1930s, complained that educated Nigerian women made poor social workers.[79] Especially those who had studied in England were separated from their uneducated brethren and sisters by "an impassable class barrier," creating a condescending, patronizing attitude while on the job. A social worker "should be able to identify herself with the people among whom she is to work, understand them thoroughly, not look down on them in her heart." In 1948, two Nigerian women (one a Yoruba), both of whom had studied social work in England, were employed to develop social service programs in Lagos.[80] Six other women, former teachers or nurses who had received practical training from Alison Izzett, an English social worker responsible for the women's section of Lagos's Social Services, were hired that year as social work assistants.

Beginning in the 1930s, women became involved in the print media: as editors, journalists, and production workers for newspapers. The first woman editor was E. Ronke Ajayi, who published the *Nigerian Daily Herald* in 1931–1932.[81] In 1933, the *Nigerian Daily Telegraph* printed a lengthy appeal for more educated young women to write for papers. After describing women's recent achievements as speakers and actresses in Lagos, the author called upon them to move into journalism as well. "Men-writers cannot sufficiently champion your cause as you yourselves can do." If women were too modest to have their real names in print, they could use pen names. A few weeks later, in its special Christmas issue, the *Telegraph* initiated a column by "Rosetta."[82] In her first two-page presentation, Rosetta discussed "African Women and the Home." During the rest of the 1930s, several papers offered columns by and for women. These generally spoke to educated African readers, as did "Milady's Bower" in the *West African Pilot,* but Eve, the columnist of "The Woman's Corner" in the *Nigerian Daily Times,* was clearly a foreigner writing for other expatriate readers.[83] In 1935, for example, she wrote about how hard it was to entertain and be a proper hostess "out here."

Women's participation in journalism gradually expanded beyond women's columns. In 1939, Henrietta Millicent Douglas, a West Indian who had recently come to Lagos from London, was named as society editor for the *West African Pilot;* in 1940 she was appointed editor in chief of the *African Mirror.*[84] By the late 1940s, two or three young women regularly wrote articles for Lagos newspapers, and in 1953, the *Daily Times* inaugurated a new series called "Women Who Matter" by Theresa Ogunbiyi.[85] Each week thereafter Ogunbiyi, who had been the women's editor of the paper since 1951, presented a biography of one of "the leading women of Nigeria who have played and are continuing to play an important role in the progress of Nigeria."

Only after 1945 were African women accepted into positions within the government's Civil Service. The decision of colonial officials to start hiring them at that time was probably influenced by the stellar work done in a range of departments by African and European female volunteers during World War II, when they replaced men called for wartime duty elsewhere.[86] Women were now willing to consider Civil Service jobs because the government was coming to accept that Nigerian women would continue working after marriage and often after motherhood.[87] Circulars sent out by the Civil Service Commissioners between 1948 and 1950 said that African women already employed by the government could continue in their positions after marriage; they ordered that henceforth men and women at a similar rank should receive equal pay; and they laid out rules for pregnancy leaves.[88] During the 1950s maternity leaves were authorized for at least certain categories of government employees.

By the late colonial years, women were starting to enter a few other professional fields. Although an occasional woman gained the necessary qualifications to practice law starting in the mid-1930s, this field offered scant opportunities.[89] Only one female barrister was working in Lagos in 1948, employed as a judge in the Children's Court.[90] Several young Nigerian women were studying law in England at that time, and one of the five women who contested for seats on the Lagos Town Council in 1950 was a barrister. The first Yoruba woman librarian was Rita Akaje-Macaulay, an educator and mainstay of Lagos high society, who started work in 1931.[91] Librarians were among the professional fields in which "a larger number of skilled Nigerian women officers is urgently required," according to a government report in 1948.

Yoruba women who received a Western education thus utilized their training in a variety of ways. Although many of the occupations and careers they entered might be defined as "modern," associated with the new economic, social, and political structures introduced by colonialism, women—even those who had been trained as teachers and nurses—displayed a strong preference for setting up their own businesses, as was customary in Yoruba culture. Working for a school or hospital might bring status through association with British institutions and practices, but having one's own institute or clinic offered a larger income, more independence from unwanted supervision, and greater flexibility in dealing with domestic responsibilities, while still filling an important community need. The careers of these educated and entrepreneurial women provide an excellent example of how Yoruba women seized upon the knowledge and opportunities offered by colonialism but then integrated them with familiar values from their own culture to create novel opportunities for themselves.

The chapters describing women's economic activities have helped to answer the three analytic questions that permeate this study. Expectations about women's domestic duties and proper roles limited their ability to devote their attention and resources to their own income-generating activities even in the nineteenth century. Functional male dominance could exist in the absence of a gendered ideology. During the colonial period, although women were allowed to own private property, they did so less commonly than men, and they were less likely to engage in commercial agriculture or be assisted by the government in their farming. Innovative female traders expanded their activities into new areas, but many craftswomen were unable to hold their own against unwelcome competition from imported manufactured goods, despite attempts to modify their techniques. Some women who had received Western-style training displayed great adaptability in converting their skills into money-making ventures, while others moved into professions that conferred new kinds of authority. Even well-educated women, however, often preferred to run their own businesses rather than working for an institution. A contrast between traditional and modern is therefore not useful here. Nor can one conclude simply that Yoruba women were disempowered by colonialism. Women carved out new spaces in which to earn money, make decisions for themselves, and in some cases acquire authority over those who worked under them. Some Yoruba women were thus able to improve their own prosperity and agency through effective manipulation of the British system. In the next two chapters we look at other ways in which women contributed to the public lives of their communities.

PART FOUR

Other Public Roles and Broader Issues

10 | Religion, Cultural Forms, and Associations

JUST AS WOMEN PLAYED vital roles in the economic sphere, so were they important to many aspects of Yoruba religious, cultural, social, and political life. Those relationships were reciprocal. Having their own money and independent economic status enhanced women's ability to participate as individuals in other areas; their necessary involvement in many public activities and their extensive involvement in organized groups solidified their need and right to participate in the economy as well. In this chapter we look first at women's involvement in traditional religious beliefs and practices, including the supernatural, and then at their place within Islam and Christianity. Women's cultural roles are discussed next. In some oral forms, including *oríkì* praise poems and ritualized criticism, women were themselves performers; other genres, including carving and masquerades, served as vehicles through which men sometimes acknowledged female power. We consider then how certain religious and cultural practices that referred to the supernatural were sometimes used to control women during periods of rapid economic and social change. A final section considers women's *egbẹ́* (associations for mutual support) and other organizations of similar nature. In each of these areas we observe women holding positions in traditional practices that conveyed both decision-making ability and authority over others. Islam, Christianity, and colonialism eliminated or weakened some of those roles, but women were often able to use their *egbẹ́* and other alternative means to retain some influence. Chapter 11 will turn to women's roles as queens and chiefs and their place in economic organizations and politics.

Religion and the Supernatural

Traditional Yoruba religion required the participation of women as well as men: as priestesses, prophetesses, or spirit mediums at the shrines devoted to the various *òrìṣà,* and as worshippers in cults and festivals. Since the goal of religious ceremonies was to restore balance and harmony between the various components of the physical and spiritual worlds, any rituals that did not include women would be pointless. Although the particular *òrìṣà* venerated differed between communities, women's involvement was essential in all parts of Yorubaland throughout the nineteenth century and colonial periods. In Ikaleland, for example, where women were traditionally less likely to earn money of their own and experienced greater subordination within the family, priestesses and spirit mediums nevertheless held authority over both men and women.[1] Among the Ekiti, women who were possessed by the spirit were central figures in the festival devoted to *Oko,* the *òrìṣà* of the farm and agriculture.

Women's spiritual importance stemmed in part from their ability to create life as mothers and—at least potentially—to end it through supernatural means. Women's bodily fertility was associated with the fertility of the earth and good harvests. Thus, the *Olúà* Festival in Osi Ekiti celebrated the harvest of new yams, but it was also popular among women who wanted to have children but had been unable to do so.[2] Because women were the natural procreators, they were also prominent figures in Yoruba myths and accounts of the origins and migrations of particular sub-groups.[3] *Odùduwà,* the reputed progenitor of the Yoruba and a leading *òrìṣà,* was sometimes described as a woman (though Christians and colonial commentators usually presented him as male).

Even those religious activities that were normally carried out by men, such as *Ifá* divination, were not reserved exclusively for them. In the 1920s a woman in Okuku learned the system of divination from her father and husband. After mastering the many poetic texts, some of which celebrated women, and passing an examination, she qualified as a full-fledged practicing diviner.[4] Because divination was used for medical diagnosis and healing as well as by people facing a difficult decision or troubling personal problem, both women and men made the necessary offerings to *Ifá* priests to obtain their services.

Women were more fully involved in the activities of the cults devoted to the individual *òrìṣà.* Some women became priestesses, refraining from marriage and trained to carry out sacrifices and other rituals and collect donations from worshippers. (See Figure 10.1.) Samuel Johnson, a Yoruba missionary with the CMS in Ibadan during the 1870s, described the elaborate 3-month process though which future priestesses were "consecrated to their office."[5] In

FIGURE 10.1. Carved wooden stool (21 inches high × 18 inches wide) showing a priest-ess with a sacrificial knife in her right hand. The stool was probably used at the ini-tiation of novitiates into the cult of an *òrìṣà* who made peace when *Èṣù,* the trickster and troublemaker, had caused a fight. The priestess holds the hand of a novitiate, standing on the right; a drummer is seated at the left. Above, two pythons sup-port the seat. Made around 1950 by Duga (c. 1880–1960), in Meko. Courtesy of the Phoebe Apperson Hearst Museum of Anthropology and the Regents of the Univer-sity of California. Cat. No. 5-14085.

the royal palace at Oyo, where women joined men in the task of appeasing the spirits and reinforcing the spiritual powers of the king, his more experi-enced wives were named as chief priestesses of the principal *òrìṣà.* Prophetesses and spirit mediums claimed other-worldly contacts that suggest a shamanic background.[6] Many other women prayed to the *òrìṣà* for assistance. In the nineteenth century, two-thirds of the references in Christian sources to *òrìṣà* worship mentioned women.[7] Wives usually contributed to the *òrìṣà* indepen-dently from their husbands, an incentive for earning their own income.

One reason that women had to be involved in *òrìṣà* worship was that many of the deities themselves did not have a clearly defined gender identity. The important *òrìṣà* Ọya (also the name of the Niger River in the Yoruba language) was described as a wife of *Sàngó* (an early mythical ruler and later an *òrìṣà* asso-ciated with thunder and lightning).[8] Yet *Ọya* was symbolized by two naked swords and two buffalo horns, and tornados and violent storms were seen as

FIGURE 10.2. A shrine of the òrìṣà Yẹmọja, with clay water pots around the sides. Abeokuta, probably 1920s. Originally published in Stephen S. Farrow, *Faith, Fancies and Fetich or Yoruba Paganism,* which terms the òrìṣà "Yemaja" (London: Society for Promoting Christian Knowledge, 1926), facing p. 46, with no photographer named; reprinted New York: Negro Universities Press (a subsidiary of Greenwood Press), 1969.

signs of *Ọya*'s displeasure. Men who were in the final stage of becoming the priest of an òrìṣà cult sometimes donned women's clothing, presumably to ensure that they could speak to all aspects of the òrìṣà's identity and represent all worshippers in their future work.[9]

Some òrìṣà were nevertheless seen as having predominantly female qualities, and many of their worshippers were women. Rivers had traditionally been associated with motherhood and women's desire to bear children. *Yẹmọja* was the òrìṣà of rivers and streams and mother of many other òrìṣà; her shrines contained sacred water thought to bring fertility and abundant yields. (See Figure 10.2.) Three òrìṣà venerated by women hoping to become pregnant (*Ọṣun, Ọbà,* and *Ọtìn*) were deities of the rivers that bore their names.[10] Women were reluctant to abandon their worship of these òrìṣà. In northeastern Yorubaland, special cults for women were still active in the 1940s and 1950s though attacked by Christians.[11]

Even those òrìṣà with strongly male characteristics had priestesses. The most prominent positions in the cult that venerated *Sàngó* in the town of Ede were held by women during the first half of the twentieth century; one of them was responsible for executing any *Sàngó* worshippers condemned to death for crimes.[12] Efunpeyin of Abeokuta, the plaintiff in a case heard in 1917, described herself (in the clerk's English translation) as "a fetish woman," meaning a priestess or devotee, in this case of *Sàngó*. Derby, the man she accused of stealing cloth, money, jewelry, and gold beads, was the son of one of her *òrìṣà* worshippers. Efunpeyin said that one night she heard a noise, lit a lamp, and discovered that the cloths wrapped round her fetish (presumably a statue of *Sàngó*) had disappeared. She found the accused man outside her door, in the compound's central area, holding "a juju" (an object for working magic), which she displayed in court. When she looked closely, she found that £5-4-6 that had been left beside the fetish and some of her own possessions were also gone. Derby denied the theft, though he admitted that he had previously stolen 1s. from the fetish but had returned it for fear of *Sàngó*.

Some *òrìṣà* changed their form or acquired different meanings during the late nineteenth and twentieth centuries. Some of the redefined *òrìṣà* were thought to offer benefits beyond simple fertility.[13] That transition is seen in the case of river deities. During the colonial period, several of the minor water *òrìṣà* were converted into Mammywata (an Africanization of "water mother").[14] Endowed with many European qualities, Mammywata was portrayed as a beautiful and wealthy but childless woman to whom devotees prayed for prosperity and well-being, as well as health and peace. This transition may have grown out of women's need for a powerful goddess able to assist them in the new economic and political climate of the colonial period and in their interactions with British authorities.

Commerce and the market place gained new religious significance. Trade became ritualized and personified as the *òrìṣà Ajé*, described in female terms, whose personal symbol was cowries. In the Ondo region, a vibrant festival was devoted to *Ajé*.[15] Though the ceremonies still stressed biological fecundity, new songs idealized the profit made through trade and business. *Yemọja* became strongly associated with the market. Toyin Falola suggested that because *Yemọja* had power to give wealth as well as life itself, she was seen as a suitable provider of protection for a commercial setting and its productivity.[16] *Èṣù* the trickster, previously defined as a homeless, wandering spirit who inhabited crossroads and the thresholds of houses and was sometimes linked to witchcraft or the devil, was now confined increasingly to market places.[17] At *Èṣù*'s shrine at every market, daily offerings of palm oil were thought to lessen the chances that he would disrupt the peaceful trading desired by women. In the Oyo kingdom, palace women were in charge of the annual *Èṣù Ọjà* Festival, held in the market and intended to bring prosperity, wealth, and abundance to the area.[18]

Women were also involved in juju or magic, related to religion by the Yoruba belief in the supernatural.[19] Juju charms and medicines, which were generally prepared by men believed to have special powers, could be used for either constructive or harmful purposes. An Abeokuta man accused of exhuming a dead body to get the skull for use in a juju ritual in 1917 said that he participated "in quest of pregnancy for my daughter who is sterile."[20] That same year a woman living in Abore Ikopa village obtained some juju soap and powders from a man who said they would help her to become pregnant. An Abeokuta woman got two kinds of juju from a former slave of her husband's uncle.[21] One was "to assist her to sell her wares" and provide protection against "rogues at the markets," but the other was allegedly used to poison her husband after they had a serious quarrel.

Women were frequently accused during the early twentieth century of having used juju to harm men. Many cases were heard in Abeokuta in 1902–1903 in which a husband said that his wife had poisoned him or employed "bad medicine," a juju fetish, or magic against him.[22] In 1917 a woman in Ado Ekiti obtained from her lover some medicine to injure her husband, and 5 years later an Ibadan woman was beaten by a man who accused her of using juju against him. But women could also be victims. An Abeokuta man bought some juju medicine in 1916 that he placed in his wife's food, which led her to miscarry her pregnancy.[23] (He said he did so because she was unfaithful.) A divorced woman in Ibadan was given juju by her new man in 1922, causing her to become ill.

The Yoruba believed in witchcraft, a supernatural power strongly associated with women.[24] All women, but especially older ones with rich experience and extensive knowledge, had the potential to use witchcraft, for good or evil. Indeed, witchcraft was said in *Ifá* legends to have been a gift to women from *Olódùmarè*, the supreme being, to compensate for their exclusion by men from decision making. Witches, who were generally referred to indirectly as "our mothers," could either bring fertility, health, and wealth to the land and its people, or they could unleash the forces of darkness. Using their powers in positive ways, they might help to curb male abuses of authority or place their talents at the service of political or military leaders.[25] In the oral poetry that accompanied *Ifá* divinations, women were praised for their bravery and the contributions they made to the standing of their husbands and children. When they were called witches in such contexts, their supernatural strength was respected as beneficial to their communities and families.

More commonly, however, people feared that witches would employ their abilities in destructive ways. Elderly women and those who had no children were thought to be most likely to cause impotence, infertility, problems during pregnancy and childbirth, and the death of babies. At a broader level, they could bring about epidemics, floods, drought, or sterility of the soil. It has been suggested that Yoruba women subscribed to witchcraft beliefs in part because it gave them such a mighty weapon with which to challenge their subordination and vent their antagonism to men, and some powerful women

FIGURE 10.3. A high priestess of the *Yẹmọja* cult carrying on her head the sacred cala-bash containing the water that will regenerate the king for another year, but with red feathers on top. Ayede, Ekiti region, c. 1990. From Andrew Apter, *Black Critics and Kings* (Chicago: University of Chicago Press, 1992), Plate 5, after p. 94. By permission of University of Chicago Press.

probably believed that supernatural powers had contributed to their own suc-cess.[26] Yet accused witches were subject to torture, humiliation, and sometimes execution.

Women's control over reproduction underlay much of the anxiety about witchcraft. Andrew Apter analyzed the ambivalence concerning female fertil-ity and the potential power of witches expressed in the *Yẹmọja* festival held annually in Ayede, an Ekiti community in northeast Yorubaland.[27] In one stage of this ritual, *Yẹmọja*'s high priestess, led by drummers, proceeded into the town and through the market place to the king's palace. On her head she carried a sacred calabash containing water from the *òrìṣà*'s rural shrine. (See Figure 10.3.) On top of the calabash were red feathers, a symbol of women's supernatural powers and witchcraft. When the king placed his hands upon the priestess, his body absorbed *Yẹmọja*'s power from the calabash, reconstituting and empowering him for another year of royal rule. The prayer for a successful festival invoked women's ability to regulate the violence of men, praising them as cool, subdued, peaceful, and soft, but the calabash ritual offered a reminder that while *Yẹmọja* and her priestesses could create and sustain life, women also had the potential to cause death and dearth.

The religious roles of women were profoundly affected by the introduction of the "world religions." Oyeronke Olajubu concluded that although patriarchy existed in Yorubaland before the coming of Islam and Christianity, the new religions had a momentous and generally deleterious effect upon women.[28] They modified certain aspects of existing Yoruba family patterns and intensified male dominance within the home and in some public areas. But the strength of Yoruba culture and the determination of women to maintain their traditional rights resulted in considerable compromise between older and newer religious practices.

Islam brought both benefits and disadvantages to women. Yoruba Muslims rejected the custom by which women were confined indoors during secret *Orò* ceremonies; the number of wives a man might marry was reduced to four; and rules for divorce were defined and extended to women as well as men.[29] Factors like those reinforced the sense among Muslim women that their faith was better than traditional Yoruba beliefs. In the lagoon town of Epe in 1925, Akanke, a 15-year-old girl whose lover was charged with abducting her, claimed that she had run away from home voluntarily: she was unwilling to marry the *Ifá* priest her mother had chosen for her because she was herself "a Mohammedan."[30] Yet Islam also eliminated most of the roles previously played by women in Yoruba religious practices. In its efforts to enforce monotheism, it prohibited veneration of *òrìṣà*. Women could not lead Muslim congregations, and they played only a secondary part in collective worship. If they were allowed to pray in the mosque, they were normally seated in separate areas where they could not be seen by men. Women's presence was further diminished by requirements for ritual cleanliness.[31] But Islam did not impede women's independent economic activities: the majority of Yoruba market traders in many communities and some wealthy businesswomen were Muslim throughout the colonial period.[32]

Although women did not perform spiritual functions in mosques, they played other religious roles. Starting in the nineteenth century they formed their own *ẹgbẹ́*, which served as social centers for women, addressed problems within their religious community, and brought women's concerns to the attention of male leaders. In the town of Oshogbo, the first Muslim women's groups were set up in the 1870s.[33] The *Ẹgbẹ́ Alásàláátù*, open to married women, widows, and divorcees, had neighborhood chapters. Its elected executive council was headed by two *ìyás* (mothers), who supervised the religious life of its members and circulated information to them. The *ẹgbẹ́* also maintained a chorus of female singers and dancers to perform a special kind of religious lyrics and rhythm known as "Waka." As the *Ẹgbẹ́ Alásàláátù* gained power, its members built spaces for themselves to sit in mosques. This was opposed by many male leaders, but they were overcome by the argument that women should be allowed to join in the services since they too might perform the hadj (the pilgrimage to Mecca). In practice, however, far fewer women went on the hadj, for even if they had the financial resources, it was more difficult for them to leave their families and trading activities for a long period of time.[34] Those rare women who had made the hadj were not allowed by most mosques to participate in the society of male alhajis who advised the imam.

During the middle and later colonial period, Muslim women became more active within their local congregations.[35] Mosques used women's associations and honorific titles modeled upon secular chieftaincies to promote gender-based solidarity and acknowledge the contributions of female leaders. Women important within the congregation might, for example, be given the title of *Ìyá Àdínnì* (mother, or senior woman, of the faith). By the 1940s, some women in Lagos were beginning to participate in the practical administration of their mosques.[36] Those who had large incomes could gain influence in other ways. When Madam Humu Alake Thompson of Lagos died in 1943 at age 70, she was said to have dealt "extensively in Native cloth by which she amassed some amount of wealth," enabling her to build a mosque at an estimated cost of £3,000.[37] Progressive associations like the Ansar-ur-Deen Society (adherents or helpers of the faith) set up branches for women and encouraged influential women to take up leadership positions in them. A newspaper article in 1953 advocated the formation of more clubs for girls and women as a means of remedying the backwardness that stemmed from illiteracy or semi-literacy among this faith.[38]

Humuani Alaga, the first woman textile trader to have her own shop alongside European-owned businesses in Ibadan, illustrates how energetic Muslim women utilized their *ẹgbẹ́* for religious and community purposes at the end of the colonial era.[39] The association led by Alaga danced at Muslim festivals, organized a credit system, and distributed alms to the needy. When Alaga decided to found a school for Muslim girls in the late 1950s, 12 women from her *ẹgbẹ́* formed a new group that helped to raise money for the institution. Later she set up two additional *ẹgbẹ́*, one to aid young Muslim women who were petty traders, the other composed of women of all religious faiths to work toward reducing overcrowding at the maternity clinics in Ibadan. Alaga built a new mosque in her neighborhood ("to please God and be remembered by") and eventually went on the hadj.

Christianity had a more powerful impact upon Yoruba gender roles. When it was first introduced, it demanded a set of social practices that led many men, especially those living in the militarized culture of some nineteenth-century Yoruba towns, to conclude that it was a "womanly" religion. Christian insistence on monogamy was another problem.[40] The most eminent convert in the first generation of Christian missionary work in Ibadan, later regarded as the "father" of his congregation, was David Kukomi, a wealthy man with 17 wives. He was said in his family's tradition to have resisted Christianity in part because he thought the stories taught by the missionary in his area "were fit only for women and girls," but he was also unwilling to set aside his wives. Although he converted in 1859, he was not officially baptized until 1867, when he finally parted from all but one of his wives.

Many nineteenth-century missionaries felt that women were more resistant to the Christian message than men. J. D. Y. Peel explained that pattern by noting that a desire to bear and rear healthy children was a major factor in Yoruba women's search for spiritual agency.[41] While this might lead them to a Christian mission, it could also lock them tightly into familiar òrìṣà cults. Further, because young women had little authority within the family, they were subject to pressure and even persecution from their relatives if they became interested in Christianity. Senior women had more freedom to make religious choices, but conversion could still lead to disruptive conflict with their husbands, children, or other relatives. Because converts were often obliged to sever themselves partially or completely from their existing social community, Christianity was less attractive to people who were well integrated or of high status. That probably explains why slaves and wives unhappy in their marriages were among the first female converts.

The mainstream Christian denominations, including the Anglicans (Church of England), Roman Catholics, and Baptists, terminated most of the traditional forms of religious participation by women. Òrìṣà worship was forbidden, and until the later twentieth century, women could not officiate in services. In the Protestant churches they were excluded from the clergy; Catholic women had the option of becoming a nun, but to do so meant abandoning the vital Yoruba roles of marriage and motherhood.[42] During the 1940s and 1950s, the Anglican church made some effort to pull women more fully into the practical affairs of the parishes. Even here, however, progress was very limited. When St. Saviour's Church in Ijebu Ode elected officers in 1950, the eight positions that carried real responsibilities were all awarded to men; of the 12-person Parochial Committee, two were women.[43]

To increase their influence within their congregations, Christian women too set up ẹgbẹ́. Starting in the 1850s, Baptist women formed ẹgbẹ́ based upon age and marital status.[44] In 1915–1916 the Baptist church in Ogbomosho and the one in Lagos each had five women's *ẹgbẹ́*. Women's groups in all the Baptist churches decided in 1919 to join together in the Baptist Women's Missionary Union of Nigeria. By 1957 the WMU had 417 branches. The Anglican Mothers' Union and equivalent organizations in other denominations offered training in domestic skills as well as sociability. Associations like these provided women with experience in group organization and decision making and gave them control over certain economic and social activities, though they did not confer spiritual authority.

Women were more important in the independent Aladura churches that broke off from the initial Christian denominations. Women founded some of these churches, and they might be allowed to conduct services in them.[45] The Sacred Cherubim and Seraphim Society in Ibadan, for example, created jointly by a woman and man in the 1920s, recognized women as prophetesses and visionaries. The Aladura churches were popular among women, including those of high social status, in part because they incorporated African traditions into their worship services.[46] They also catered to their female members' needs by providing counseling about such issues as fertility and childbirth, and they had no objection to women's economic activities outside the home.

Some Christian churches—both mainstream and Aladura—created new female titles and developed ceremonies for investing women into leadership positions. Title holders (sometimes termed *Ìyá Ìjọ*, mother or matron of the congregation) and their assistants oversaw women's activities and advised the minister to help achieve smooth operation of the church.[47] At Emmanuel Church in Ado Ekiti, six women vied in 1952 for the post of *Ìyá Ẹgbẹ́* (mother of the association). The winner, who had 105 votes, was "led to the altar for installation and blessing," followed by "a general thanksgiving."[48] In an Aladura church in Ekiti North, a special title was assigned to the midwife for the congregation. A woman who held a religious title gained authority, even if her sphere of influence was fairly limited.

Unlike traditional Yoruba religion and Islam, Christianity as taught by the first few generations of CMS missionaries, including the returnees educated in British-style schools, took a dim view of women's economic independence. Had the missionaries succeeded in transmitting to the Yoruba the Victorian model whereby women were to devote their full attention to their homes and families, they would have introduced an enormous change in the economic and social relations of local families. In practice, however, only a small number of elite Christian women in the cities accepted that approach. Most Yoruba women continued to pursue their own activities and generate their own incomes. Laywomen gained alternative role models from the 1920s onward, as more Nigerian and European women came into local communities as missionaries. By the mid-colonial years, the mainstream Christian churches had largely abandoned their opposition to women's work outside the home.

Forms of Cultural Expression

Women's participation in—or celebration by—cultural forms buttressed their activities in other areas. In the Yoruba belief system, cultural expression was closely intertwined with religion. Genres that are considered "the arts" in Western societies were among the ways in which Yoruba religious beliefs were expressed and taught. Both religion and culture had the goal of inculcating a code for good character and moral behavior.[49] By examining cultural patterns as a distinct category, we are therefore isolating activities that were in practice often inseparable from religion. Further, whereas the specifically religious beliefs of many Yoruba people had been displaced or at least modified by Islam or Christianity by the end of the colonial period, some cultural practices retained their power. Many of the studies describing such activities as *oríkì* chants and *Gèlèdé* performances date from the 1980s and 1990s and were based on observation of current practice. Even women who considered themselves Muslims or Christians could enjoy cultural rituals that perpetuated traditional beliefs and practices.

Women were important as performers of some types of oral expression. In addition to transmitting traditional myths and proverbs, they were key figures in reciting and teaching the praise poetry known as *oríkì*.[50] Some *oríkì* chants were religious, consisting of a series of phrases that described the characteristics of an *òrìsà*. Accumulated over time, these *oríkì* were regarded by the Yoruba as "sacred texts that have been carefully preserved down the ages."[51] As Karin Barber suggested, reciting an *oríkì* expressed the reciprocal bond between an *òrìsà* and its devotee: performing an *oríkì* is a gift to the *òrìsà*, while in return the devotee asks for a favor from the deity. Secular *oríkì*, presenting a string of desirable attributes, might compliment a distinguished but deceased human being (man or woman), a kin group, the husband and wife being joined at a wedding, a new child born into an important family, or a former master teacher and chanter of *oríkì*. In many Yoruba towns, responsibility for the *oríkì* tradition rested mainly with women. The wives and daughters who had learned *oríkì* and were recognized as experts were paid to chant at household and town ceremonies, and they passed on their knowledge to younger women.

Another oral genre consisted of public criticism, insult, or abuse. Yoruba women and men alike made skillful use of spoken attacks upon their opponents. Sometimes these verbal assaults made physical violence unnecessary, but they could also trigger a fight. Insults impugned the virtue or appearance of recipients, while curses threatened them. In nineteenth-century Ibadan,

FIGURE 10.4. A priestess of the *òrìṣà Ìyágbà* singing abusive songs to the king of Ayede and priestesses of the *Yẹmọja* cult. Ekiti region, c. 1990. From Andrew Apter, *Black Critics and Kings* (Chicago: University of Chicago Press, 1992), Plate 13, after p. 94. By permission of University of Chicago Press.

women taunted a leader reluctant to go to war with provocative songs accusing him of cowardice.[52] A man in Modekeke insulted a woman in 1936 by saying publicly that "she was like a dried roasted plantain," while a woman angry with a market official in Aiyetoro in 1942 "abused" or cursed him by saying that all his children would die that year.[53] The market women of Abeokuta who protested against the Egba king in the later 1940s featured sexual insults in their songs.

Verbal criticism was sometimes institutionalized, giving women a recognized platform from which to draw attention to people or policies that were harming the community. During an annual festival in the Ekiti town of Ayede, priestesses of the *Oròyèye* (mother of *Orò*) cult were authorized to express their objections to actions of the king and members of the royally backed *Yẹmọja* cult.[54] "Their task as social critics is to expose, abuse, and in the most serious cases curse malefactors, mobilising the force of public censure and condemnation to bear upon their misdeed and reputations." The consequences of the women's critiques ranged from "payment of a small fine to save face in response to mild teasing to full-fledged ostracism, exile, and death resulting from the most serious abuses and curses." (For another example, see Figure 10.4.) Among the northeastern Kabba, the haughty women from aristocratic families who sang and played instruments in the long-standing "Woro Musical Ensemble" were treated with great respect at the king's court in the late 1950s: "their musical compositions with political innuendoes can sway very easily public opinions on issues relating to peace and stability in Kabba kingdom."[55]

Music was a vital component of Yoruba culture. Traditional music, usually associated with drumming and dancing, remained popular throughout the colonial years. Yoruba drumming was complex.[56] Not only were multiple rhythms present at the same time, but also the pitch of many drums could be quickly changed by tightening or loosing the strings that controlled the tension of the skin over the head of the drum. That flexibility of pitch enabled drummers to mimic the tonal quality of Yoruba speech, producing "talking drums." Jazz and other kinds of Western popular music, spread by the radio and concerts especially after 1945, were welcomed and adapted by young African performers. Dancing, which offered great pleasure to both women and men, was an integral part of many Muslim and Christian ceremonies, civic rituals, family events, and purely social gatherings.

During the early colonial period, the Westernized elite in Lagos loved to study and perform classical European music. Their concerts might include both African and white singers and instrumentalists, and sometimes they incorporated Yoruba elements. In 1910, the Lagos Glee Singers, including men and women from Sierra Leonean returnee families, performed Gilbert and Sullivan's *Mikado*.[57] Dr. Orishadipe Obasa and his wife, Charlotte, directed the operetta, and Ko-Ko sang one verse in Yoruba. In 1917–1918, Mrs. Obasa, who had organized the Ladies Musical Club and was herself a fine pianist, directed several performances of *HMS Pinafore*, with an African cast of singers and musicians, as a benefit for the King's War Charity.[58] A few years later an interracial entertainment organized by Miss Oyinkan Ajasa and patronized by the British governor and his wife raised money for a hospital in London. After the death in 1920 of Mrs. Emma Savage, daughter of an important returnee family, an appreciation highlighted her lovely singing voice, recalling her performance as Josephine in *HMS Pinafore* and her solo in Mendelssohn's *Hymn of Praise*.[59] A newspaper article in 1933 on "African Women and the Home," written by a Yoruba woman who used the pen name of Rosetta, talked about the importance of music within the family and encouraged wives to practice the piano at least 15 minutes daily, no matter how busy they were with other matters; a photo showed Rosetta herself "caught unawares" while playing her piano.[60]

Other cultural forms could be used to honor or propitiate women even when the artists or performers were male. Traditional Yoruba visual art was three-dimensional: sculpture rather than flat painting. Religious objects, carved usually of wood or ivory, carried deep symbolic meanings (see Figure 10.1), as did the thrones and staffs of kings and the gates to royal compounds. But even everyday household equipment and tools might be decorated, appreciated for their beauty and interest as well as their functionality. Early in the twentieth century, women were commonly represented by male carvers as kneeling, a position signifying respect and one adopted by women in childbirth.[61] Sometimes they were shown holding a bowl, evoking women's role in feeding their families and guests, and usually they were displayed in close association with children. Statues might be presented to shrines of the òrìṣà by people requesting benefits or giving thanks for them. (See Figure 5.2.) In the early 1920s Yoruba artists stimulated by the influence of French painting started exploring two-dimensional possibilities, and after the opening of art departments in Nigerian colleges and universities beginning around 1950, artists used a wide range of media. Women continued to be shown mainly in traditional ways, though the positive attributes of femininity (protection, calm, benevolence, and peace) could also be represented symbolically.

Masquerades were performances in which costumed men wearing elaborately carved and painted masks and carrying ritualized paraphernalia moved or danced through the streets, accompanied by drummers. Women did not participate in masquerades, and they were not even allowed to witness certain ones. Egúngún appearances, for example, normally occurred during annual festivals or at the death of important personages. The masqueraders, members of a male secret society, represented the potentially dangerous ancestral spirits who needed to be celebrated and appeased.[62]

Gèlèdé spectacles, providing entertainment and evoking a sense of sacred awe, sometimes honored the power of women.[63] Found mainly in western Yorubaland, these masquerades were intended to placate and win the goodwill of female figures, living and dead, who could enhance fertility or cause harm. Dancers belonging to the Gèlèdé cult dressed up as—and offered praise to—Ìyánlá (the Great Mother, our female ancestor, or owner of the earth), other female òrìṣà, and ancestors, priestesses, and living women. (See Figure 10.5.) Although Gèlèdé performances varied between communities, and scholars disagree about their exact origins, meanings, and relation to other kinds of masquerades, certain dances rested upon the belief that women, particularly old women, could employ witchcraft.[64] Hence they had to be given public

Figure 10.5. A *Gèlèdé* dancer dressed as a woman, Lagos, 1978. The mask displays an elaborate woman's hair style; the dancer has used padding around his buttocks to create an exaggeratedly female shape. The mask was carved by Kilani Olaniyan of Ota (Awori). From Henry J. Drewal and Margaret T. Drewal, *Gelede: Art and Female Power among the Yoruba* (Bloomington: Indiana University Press, 1983), Plate 88, p. 167. By permission of Henry J. Drewal and Margaret T. Drewal.

respect. *Gèlèdé* dances were often performed before large crowds in the market place, a metaphor for the world but also a setting dominated on normal days by female traders. (See Figure 10.6.)

Controlling Women through Religious and Cultural Practices

Religion and culture were occasionally called upon to help control women through reference to the supernatural. Men always had disciplinary authority over their wives, as did the male heads of compounds and lineages and those chiefs who held judicial rights. Extra-normal procedures, drawing upon a belief in the powers of the *òrìṣà* or ancestors, could be used to curtail women's economic or social activities. Or women could be accused of being destructive witches, of using supernatural powers to harm others. These forms of male dominance usually appeared in contexts where women had recently gained unfamiliar economic prominence and/or were violating accepted reproductive and social standards within their households. While men too could be punished through such methods, women were the primary targets.

During the mid- and later nineteenth century, as women in some parts of Yorubaland gained new income from palm products and began to benefit from British laws about slavery, marriage, and property, men worried about increased female independence. Lagos men, for example, believed that women's new freedoms had made them less obedient.[65] Simi Afonja noted that "the increasing prosperity of women in the pre-colonial era threatened the position of the husband. It was incumbent on prosperous women to perform special rites to evade pre-existing taboos against women's economic control through wealth. Ife women recall the songs chanted at such ceremonies which rich women had to perform to remove societal taboos."

The secret societies or cults that helped to maintain order and enforce the law in some western Yoruba communities were actively deployed in the mid-nineteenth century, with particularly negative consequences for women. *Orò* societies used the authority of that powerful *òrìṣà* to announce and administer judicial proceedings.[66] Ceremonies were initiated by "the voice of *Orò*," an eerie set of sounds produced by whirling through the air a flat stick (or "bullroarer") tied to a string. When *Orò*'s voice was heard, all women and children—but not men—were expected to go indoors and remain there. These curfews, which could last anywhere from a few hours to several days, closed the markets and stopped caravans from moving. Women dared not disobey, for a woman caught outside her house during an *Orò* curfew, regardless of her rank, was subject to death. During some *Egúngún* events, especially if convicted criminals were being executed, women were likewise required to remain

FIGURE 10.6. A *Gẹ̀lẹ̀dẹ́* dancer performing in the market place, Ilaro, 1977, with drummers seated in the foreground. At the top of his mask is a folded-up eating/sleeping mat; the women's head ties hanging from his waist fly outward as he spins around. The mask was carved in Meko, Ketu. From Henry J. Drewal and Margaret T. Drewal, *Gelede: Art and Female Power among the Yoruba* (Bloomington: Indiana University Press, 1983), Color Plate 4, following p. 8. By permission of Henry J. Drewal and Margaret T. Drewal.

inside.[67] If a woman said or even heard that the *Egúngún* were actually masked and costumed local men, she could be killed.

In some communities, *Orò* curfews and *Egúngún* appearances evidently increased greatly in the mid-nineteenth century. In 1850, Thomas King, a returnee CMS missionary in Abeokuta, commented that "there has been a general confinement of the females these 5 or 6 days by Oro."[68] Women were allowed out of their homes only for an hour or 2 at a time, an exemption that King thought was intended to permit essential provision of daily needs, sparing men from what they regarded as the demeaning work of buying and selling. Two years later King referred to *Orò* worship as "the females' destroyer."[69] An appearance of *Egúngún* in the streets had a similar effect. A foreign visitor in Abeokuta in 1851 said that one *Egúngún* was dressed as a tall and bony masked man with a sword in his hands, "fantastically clad from face to foot," who spoke "in a hoarse sepulchral voice."[70] Curfews were being called so frequently that several observers thought that the dread that accompanied them was gradually wearing away: women grumbled at being confined to their homes, though they could not object openly.[71] Contemporary travelers and missionaries noted that suspension of business was especially damaging for market women and those engaged in the palm oil trade.[72]

That opinion has been seconded by some modern scholars, who suggested that vigorous use of *Orò* and *Egúngún* in the mid-nineteenth century was an attempt to curtail women's increased economic autonomy. Robin Law observed that the profits reaped by women through "legitimate" trade created tensions within Yoruba society, leading men to use their societies and rituals to dominate women.[73] Francine Shields likewise believed that *Orò* curfews stemmed from male resentment of the increased wealth and greater social independence enjoyed by women.

The secret societies could regulate female behavior more directly as well. If a man had a wife whom he could not control, he was allowed to call upon *Egúngún* to warn her and, if necessary, give her a whipping or beating. This practice was used at least occasionally well into the colonial period. In 1935, a woman named Jolade died as the result of her punishment.[74] Her husband, Gbadamosi, had asked Ladele, an *Egúngún* man, to "come along to his house and assist him to drive Jolade his wife away from the house by flogging." (Gbadamosi described Jolade as lazy, unable to prepare food, sweep the house, or draw water; he said she was crazy and kept giving him trouble.) Two days later Ladele donned his *Egúngún* costume and special headdress, picked up two whips, and came to Gbadamosi's house. When he began beating Jolade, she ran from the house in the direction of her father's cornfield, but she fell down and later died. While the neighbors who witnessed the punishment and the newspaper that reported it all thought it excessive, the decision to call in

Egúngún may have been a reflection of what many men saw as women's inappropriate independence within marriage due to British ordinances and the availability of divorce.

Accusations of witchcraft were another vehicle whereby women might be disciplined. In the mid-nineteenth century, the same factors that led to frequent curfews probably contributed to a rise in witchcraft charges. The *Orò* and—less often—*Egúngún* cults located and "arrested" suspected female witches, who commonly had to face some kind of ordeal, such as taking poison. Shields explained that development as the conjunction of several demographic, social, and economic factors.[75] One was tension among the women in polygamous households. Senior wives were in a position to acquire wealth by exploiting the labor of junior co-wives, causing resentment on the part of the younger women that intensified normal competition between wives for the attention of their husband. Husbands, other male relatives, and local authorities likewise disliked the independence of powerful trading women, leading to charges that they were disobedient wives who ignored their domestic duties and obligations to their families. Bernard Belasco suggested that accusations of witchcraft activity were most common in those pre-colonial regions that were "fattened and traversed by trade routes," places lying often in boundary areas between different sub-groups.[76] There charges were brought especially against newly wealthy women who participated in worship of *Èṣù*.

Worry about possible witchcraft seems to have risen again in the 1910s and 1920s. Women's growing ability to acquire their own land, when added to British marriage and divorce laws, may well have heightened concern about overly independent women. Barber's analysis of "big women" (successful producers and traders) in early twentieth-century Okuku highlighted the issue of reputation.[77] Women were not prohibited from struggling for self-aggrandizement, but when wealthy women attempted to convert their economic power into visible form so as to acquire community status, they encountered problems. For men, "wealth spent on display enhanced reputation, reputation attracted more people and this led to greater wealth. Reputation was thus the medium through which male power was constituted." But when women tried to build up households full of dependent people or publicize their wealth, they ran a serious risk. "Reputation in a woman almost automatically turned inside out and became an accusation of witchcraft. Successful women were almost always branded as witches." Similarly, men who could command juju fetishes or charms were admired, seen as valued protectors, but any suggestion that women used magic evoked fear and condemnation. When a female trader in Okuku named Ayantayo prospered, her achievements were not celebrated in *oríkì:* far from it. Rather, people murmured evasively that "she had great powers", but "we don't know how she did it". In other words, Ayantayo was thought to have been a witch. This response to her supposed supernatural powers was very different from the admiring and celebratory accounts of male control of medicine and spiritual forces, which are described in elaborate narratives and evoked over and over again in *oríkì.*[78]

Witchcraft accusations in the mid-twentieth century assumed more organized form and were part of a wider movement. The Atinga anti-witchcraft cult spread into western Yorubaland from the southern Gold Coast (Ghana) and Dahomey in 1950–1951. In Atinga, male witch-finders identified and led the persecution of thousands of women whom they charged with harming others through witchcraft.[79] An accused woman had to sit on the ground in a designated public place for hours without moving, waiting to see if her innocence was proved. The test was whether a hen whose throat had been slashed died while lying on its back. Women who failed the ordeal or confessed were flogged and occasionally killed. Atinga cult members also attacked the shrines and female worshippers of those *òrìṣà* particularly associated with women's power. In Ijebu Province, however, some women supported Atinga activities, believing that if witches were exposed, barren women would be able to conceive and infant mortality would be reduced.[80]

It is not clear how Atinga was related to women's economic and social situation at the time. Marc Schiltz proposed that the appearance of the Atinga movement was tied to the intensification of female traders' control over agricultural produce and the resulting dependency of male farmers.[81] Apter suggested that the immediate context for Atinga was the sudden increase but fluctuating level of cocoa prices on the world market between 1945 and 1950, because women were heavily involved as petty traders in the crop. But, he continued, the underlying issue was that women's participation in the commercial economy conflicted with their domestic obligations, subverting the ideology of household labor and reproduction. While any successful woman could threaten male authority, a wealthy wife who had gained strength and independence through her own economic activities could precipitate disputes within the kin group and household, involving lineage identities, co-wives, and inheritance. Lorand Matory noted that that posture to be assumed by the dying hen, the least mobile of all positions, "suggests a reversal of the excessive female mobility that many Yoruba blamed on the liberal divorce laws instituted by the British and on the lapse of earlier royal controls over women and witches."[82]

Those arguments do not, however, accord fully with a colonial officer's description of the women in Iseyin who confessed to having killed someone by witchcraft after being accused by Atinga.[83] Most of them were old, poor, and living without husbands. The deaths, usually by poison, had occurred many years before. The majority of those said to have been killed were children, with the most common motives being jealousy between wives and inheritance disputes. While Atinga thus remains a puzzling movement, Yoruba men clearly drew upon a belief in supernatural forces to ensure their own dominance at certain times during the nineteenth century and colonial years. Patriarchy was not merely a foreign imposition.

Women's Associations

Yoruba women—like men—frequently formed associations called *ẹgbẹ́* that provided social and economic support to their members.[84] These organizations furnished an outlet for the Yoruba love of sociability, eagerness to gain group identities, and pleasure in wearing fine clothing on special occasions. In western and central areas, women's *ẹgbẹ́* were already part of life during the nineteenth century, and they maintained their vibrancy and public visibility right through the colonial period.[85] N. A. Fadipe commented that although membership in an *ẹgbẹ́* was not compulsory in traditional society, "it was the rule and not the exception to belong to one. A person who had no *Egbẹ́* was not a properly adjusted and socialised being."[86] In the nineteenth century many *ẹgbẹ́* included both women and men, with separate officers for each, but during the colonial period some became single-sex associations. Early market women's organizations and craft groups may also be seen as a type of *ẹgbẹ́*.[87] In many eastern Yoruba communities, women's *ẹgbẹ́* were later and generally less important institutions. They emerged only after 1900 in Ikaleland, usually under the auspices of the Christian churches; in Aiyede in the Ekiti area, female *ẹgbẹ́* merely organized dances at festivals in the 1930s.[88] By the late colonial era, however, women's associations were found throughout Yorubaland.

In nineteenth-century practice, *ẹgbẹ́* based upon women's age and marital/reproductive status gathered for important family events and at religious festivals. If a family made a sacrifice to an *òrìṣà* or was holding a religious feast, the *ẹgbẹ́* to which its members belonged might be invited.[89] During courtship, a young man would often be accompanied by his *ẹgbẹ́* when he paid formal visits or provided labor to his prospective parents-in-law. When a woman married, it was "members of her *egbe*, childhood friends who join her in chanting the *ekun iyawo* (bridal chants) . . . and who accompany her to the house of the groom."[90] After marriage, she might join a new group of women at a similar stage in the life cycle. When a family member died, a woman would be "helped by the rest of the *Egbẹ́*. They helped her perform tasks that needed to be done as well as to make the occasion grand with dancing, singing and feasting."[91]

Ẹgbẹ́ continued to provide women with social and practical benefits during the colonial period. Many held regular meetings (often every 9th or 17th day) to discuss matters of concern to the group and announce forthcoming events. They elected their own officers, including a president or chairman.[92] When a new head was chosen, she usually hosted a feast for all the membership, with drumming and dancing. Husbands might help their wives pay for such events, which were an honor for the family.[93] Members commonly attended public ceremonies together. Memunatu Seriki, from an important Egba chieftancy family, held office in, or served as patroness to, multiple *ẹgbẹ́* prior to her death in 1941; her funeral attracted "a gargantuan attendance of different societies."[94] When an *ẹgbẹ́* went out as a group, its members generally wore distinctive attire—the same fabric or color of clothing, the same style of dress, or at least a similar head tie—to demonstrate the size and standing of their association. (See the cover illustration for a recent example.) Members were expected to contribute to unexpected costs of their fellows, such as a family wedding or burial, thereby offering a financial cushion, and many *ẹgbẹ́* operated their own *èsúsús,* or rotating credit systems.[95]

The *ẹgbẹ́* and other women's associations of the colonial period were based upon various sorts of common interests.[96] Though they sometimes termed themselves "clubs," "societies," or "unions," they combined sociable activities with other functions, and they had a basic *ẹgbẹ́* organizational structure.[97] Some associations were formed by women engaged in a particular type of commerce or craftwork. Women who collected food crops from farmers and sold them to local and long-distance traders had *ẹgbẹ́*.[98] Craftswomen in such areas as weaving, dyeing, and pottery had their own *ẹgbẹ́* or guilds to protect the interests of producers and sellers. The market women of the leading cities formed powerful associations able to affect political events during the later colonial period.[99] But even organizations whose functions were primarily economic remained important in social terms too. In 1956, Mabel Aduke Williams of Lagos was delighted when her fellow Obalende market women turned up for the party she threw for her 50th birthday, complete with several live bands.[100] The women were all dressed in "'raki raki'—a type of purple woollen wrapper and headties. . . . And how impressive they looked while dancing!"

By the 1940s, some women were members of organizations based upon waged employment. When Mrs. Bolaji Odunsi was buried at Holy Trinity Church in Lagos in 1946, "a long and solemn procession, led by members of the Lady Workers' Union," went from her residence to the church.[101] Some nurses joined unions, while in Ekiti North, midwives and nurses had local "councils" that protected their interests. The group that attained the greatest visibility and political influence as pressure for independence mounted was the Nigerian Union of Teachers, founded by the Rev. Isaac Ransome-Kuti in the 1940s. Women played at best a secondary role within the NUT. A photograph of the union's conference in 1949 shows no African women as regular teacher delegates and just a few as the wives of dignitaries.[102] By the time of the NUT's meeting in 1960, women formed about a quarter of the delegates.

Ẹgbẹ́ might also be based upon age. Some communities had traditionally organized "age grades," groups of men and/or women born within 4–10 years of each other that provided "companionship and mutual help."[103] In some of the Yoruba kingdoms during the nineteenth century, including Ekiti and Ijebu, women's age-based ẹgbẹ́ were incorporated into certain levels of government and administration, though they were apparently less active in public affairs than men's ẹgbẹ́. Patterns varied in other parts of Yorubaland. Ikaleland had no age grades for women without titles in the pre-colonial period, because women were expected to marry young; villages in Idanre District, Ondo Province, had only two female societies, for older and younger women.[104] By the later 1930s, age-based associations were being replaced by other kinds of social and religious groups.

Extended families often constituted themselves as associations equivalent to ẹgbẹ́, and in them women played leading roles. In 1909 the Supreme Court of the Colony ruled that the eldest surviving grandchild of the founder of a Lagos family could become the head of that unit, regardless of sex.[105] The following year, less than a month before her death, the extremely elderly Egba princess Grace Lalotan Efundimeji "decided an important case for her family." Later in the colonial period, families whose members had been dispersed among various communities sometimes elected officers and held annual reunions.[106] Older women were frequently named as heads of those groups.

Another type of organization was formed by people from a particular town or ethnic group who had moved away to a larger city. "Hometown" associations reinforced their members' original identity as part of a local community or lineage group while living within new, socially complex settings.[107] Most of these groups also tried to help solve problems in their home area and raised funds for special needs. Some were highly organized, with formal meetings, elected leaders, a constitution, and an elaborate program of events.[108] Many urban women joined two such organizations so as to maintain a connection with both their own and their husbands' communities. Ethnically based ẹgbẹ́ might do charitable work on behalf of their own members or people in their home area.[109] When, for example, the Egba Society of Lagos held a concert and dance in 1932, its goal was to raise funds for the Girls' Education Scheme in Egbaland. Most hometown or ethnic associations included both men and women, with a distinct wing for the latter. Women generally had little say in formulating and running activities: they spent much of their time preparing and serving food at convivial activities and helping to raise money.[110]

Ijesha women, however, had their own organizations, with separate leaders and agendas.

In urban settings, some associations formed during the colonial period focused on recreation or culture. On New Year's Day 1932, "the Jolly Jenkins Friendly Society" of Lagos sponsored a day of informal athletic events for women and men.[111] These included sack races, thread and needle races, cigar and umbrella races, and a tug-of-war. Over 200 people watched the events from the grandstand at Balogun Square, joined by another 4,500 spectators standing around the square. The occasion was chaired by Herbert Macaulay, "who is now being popularly called 'The Gandhi of West Africa'," supported by four traditional chiefs. In the later 1940s and 1950s, cultural associations gave increased attention to the Yoruba's own traditions. The Choral Society of the Cathedral Church of Christ in Lagos offered a program in 1947 that included not only a religious cantata by a British composer but also an organ solo on Yoruba airs; 3 years later the Lagos Musical Society sponsored a talk on "Yoruba Music—Whence and Whither."[112] Cultural organizations were spreading to smaller communities as well, as seen in Ilaro's Literary Circle. Secondary schools in Abeokuta and Ibadan had for some time given dramatic performances, and in the 1950s University College, Ibadan, became a major center for the arts. The college put on its own musical and theatrical productions and hosted the annual Festival of the Arts, attended by performers from schools and associations throughout the Western Region.[113]

Other associations were for young people. An overtly pedagogic (and ostensibly domestically focused) group was the British West African Educated Girls' Club, formed in 1920. At its first meeting, held at Government House in Lagos, its founders emphasized that educated young women must not be idle. "The more highly educated the girl the more she will realise how essential to the health of her family is cleanliness and also good cooking, and she will certainly not distain to cook or to clean, any more than to sew or to embroider her own clothes, and later on those of her children, whether they wear native or European dress. She will be honored in proportion to her usefulness."[114] The Christian women who were organizing girls' clubs in 1950 likewise hoped that while the girls were enjoying games and other activities, they would also learn to be "good housewives in the future, so that their homes will be happy ones." But youth groups engaged in purely social activities too. In 1946, the Muslim Youth League went on a picnic to Victoria Beach, hosted by the girls' sections within the 14 sub-societies of the association.[115]

Some clubs were organized around sports. Although girls played games at school, adult women acted initially only as sponsors and promoters of sporting events. In the late 1940s and 1950s, however, women who had been introduced to sports when young began to found groups that would allow them ongoing participation. Lagos had a Ladies Sports Club, and the Women's Amateur Athletic Association held annual championships, with one competition for secondary schools and another for girls' clubs and women's groups.[116] Mabel Segun was active in sports at the CMS girls' school in Lagos and at University College, Ibadan, before becoming a professional ping pong player and backer of the Western Nigeria Table Tennis Association.[117]

Another type of organization, led generally by educated, urban women, devoted its efforts to the welfare of women and girls. Charlotte Olajumoke Obasa, for example, was active in the Lagos Ladies' League, established in 1901.[118] Under her leadership, the association functioned as a pressure group: it advocated the creation of a secondary school for girls, promoted medical awareness among women, especially concerning child health, and encouraged its participants to learn new skills. The league lost favor around 1908 but was reactivated under the name of the Lagos Women's League in the early 1920s. The latter addressed a wider range of concerns, including uncontrolled prostitution and traffic in liquor, unsafe and unhealthy conditions in the markets, and the government's failure to provide adequate housing and medical care for Africans in the Civil Service. It also promoted formation of government technical schools and employment of women in the colonial administration. Another key figure was (Lady) Oyinkan Abayomi, who—after returning from England in 1920 and taking a teaching position in Lagos at the CMS girls' school in Lagos—began to develop the Girl Guides movement in Nigeria.[119]

Other groups devoted to women's issues emerged later in the colonial period. The Young Women's Christian Association (YWCA) brought together educated members of various denominations to help women working in urban settings.[120] Lady Alakija, who had studied music in Britain and taught at Queen's College when she was younger, was by the early 1950s deeply involved in the YWCA as well as the Red Cross and prison visiting. The Women's Welfare Council in Lagos tackled such issues as the vulnerability of young girls who hawked on the streets in the early 1940s.[121] During the 1950s, organizations founded by women like Folayegbe Akintunde-Ighodalo campaigned for improved employment opportunities for women, including by the government. Important among those groups were the National Council of Women's Societies and the Nigerian Association of University Women. Despite their claim to speak about matters of concern to all women, however, some elite women's organizations were criticized for their social exclusiveness and their failure to tackle the gritty practical problems confronted by ordinary women.[122]

This chapter has provided mixed evidence about the impact of Western forces on Yoruba women. Comparison of women's roles in traditional religious practices with their position in Islam and mainstream Christianity indicates that they lost important functions through the introduction of the world religions. Only by establishing *egbẹ́* within a religious context or joining Aladura churches were they able to retain some influence. Because Yoruba culture remained vibrant throughout the colonial period, women continued to play a part in such activities as praise chants, ritualized criticism, music, and dancing. Their potential powers were recognized in other genres. Yet Yoruba men could also could utilize a belief in the supernatural to control unfamiliar and unwanted female autonomy. *Egbẹ́* and similar associations provided practical support and taught women how to function effectively in groups. Because most organizations cut across family and kinship ties, they offered a group identity beyond those determined by birth or marriage and brought women into a wider community of people who shared their interests. Some religious *egbẹ́* and many of the later quasi-political organizations gave women experience in organizing and presenting their concerns effectively in public settings, laying the foundation for massive protests against unpopular colonial policies.[123] Through their associations, women made collective decisions about their own activities, and their elected officers gained recognized authority. These groups illustrate how Yoruba women modified familiar practices to fill new roles within the altered colonial context.

II | Regents and Chiefs, Economic Organizations, and Politics

SOME YORUBA WOMEN PLAYED a part in institutions of public authority. Through these roles they augmented the status acquired through their economic activities and involvement in religious, cultural, and social spheres. In pre-colonial Yorubaland, women were necessary to the operation of many of the kingdoms and city-states. With certain specific duties assigned to them, "women participated fully in the political affairs of their communities by right rather than by sufferance."[1] Further, in both the nineteenth and the twentieth centuries, respected women could be named as chiefs. Some chieftaincy titles were limited to the most distinguished woman within a given lineage, but others were open to anyone. In some places, the primary female chief (often termed the *Ìyálóde*, meaning "the mother or senior woman in the public sphere") served as the representative of all women in official discussions and activities.

Nina Mba summarized women's political roles in traditional Yoruba society in positive terms: they "effectively controlled their own affairs and were also involved in executive responsibilities covering the whole society. Though women did not have representation and authority in the Yoruba political system equal to that of men, there was no sex segregation in politics as such, and sex was not used as the basis of political role differentiation."[2] Mba's assessment needs some qualification, however. Women's political position in the nineteenth century was far less prominent and stable than men's, and they did not hold the top offices in government on more than a temporary basis.[3]

Although a few *Ìyálódes* enjoyed exceptional power, royal women and female chiefs generally had authority within more limited spheres.

Women also formed economic organizations, based upon the type of trading or craftwork they did or the particular market in which they worked. During the colonial period the leaders of some of these groups learned how to use their associations for wider economic and political ends, mobilizing mass meetings and shutting down all the markets in their city to object to government policies. Such protests provide graphic examples of how Yoruba women converted their experience within *ẹgbẹ́* into new forms of economic and political power, coming together to wield substantial collective agency. Within the colonial system of government, women took almost no part until the 1940s and 1950s, when they began to be represented on some local councils. As Western-style political parties developed in the decades prior to Nigerian Independence in 1960, women were active in separate wings of the organizations but were rarely included in the inner circles of power. Because the parties devoted to women's issues were weak, women were unable to insist that male leaders listen to and respond to their concerns.

Royal Women and Titled Chiefs

Prior to the nineteenth century, some royal women had held direct authority as rulers in their own names, though the lack of gender specificity of Yoruba names makes it impossible to determine how common this was.[4] A few towns claimed that their founders were women, and oral traditions in many Yoruba kingdoms recall female rulers in the past.[5] In the Ijesha area, for instance, five or six of 38 earlier rulers were said to have been women. That pattern had died out by 1800.

During the nineteenth century, and in some areas during the twentieth, women participated in multiple ways in the system of sacred kingship found in many Yoruba states. Women sometimes ruled as regents between the death of one king and the installation of the next. Indeed, the requirement for an interim period of female governance was "written into the political constitution" of some of the kingdoms.[6] The regent, often the oldest daughter of the dead king, commonly held power for about six months, spanning the period of mourning and final funeral rites. If appointment of a new king was delayed, she might remain in office for a longer period. A female regent wore the regalia of the monarch and was accorded all the respect due to a king.[7] During her tenure, she "holds the ultimate authority on all issues in her domain as the ruler. She oversees the governing council and amicably settles whatever crises may arise in the town." Described as "the husband of all royal wives," she was in charge of the extended royal family and administered family properties. But at the same time, because she was a woman she was subject to certain ritual and cultural taboos. For instance, she could not wear the official royal cloak while menstruating. Oyeronke Olajubu suggested that this ban resulted both from the belief that menstrual blood "defiles and depletes energy forces, especially in sacred settings" and from recognition that such blood was "a vehicle of power, because embedded in it is potential life." If it came into contact with the force of royal authority, the result might be explosive.

Women were often key figures in the rituals that accompanied the installation of kings, such as placing the crown upon the next ruler's head.[8] Although practices varied considerably between the different Yoruba regions, women were also commonly involved in ceremonies that marked particular stages of kingship or that reaffirmed—but in some cases limited—royal power. These roles, which made female authority visible, rested upon the close integration between a ruler's political and religious functions and upon the conviction that successful governance must draw upon both sides of potentially oppositional pairs, including the qualities commonly associated with women as well as with men.

In Ondo, an eastern Yoruba area, the main figure in the ceremonies that conferred power upon a new king was the *Lóbùn,* the paramount female chief. The *Lóbùn's* office was "surrounded by mysteries and taboos," related to a tradition of female rule in Ondo.[9] In Jacob Olupona's narration, the last ceremony in the rites of installation of a new *Ọbà* began as follows:

> The Lobun takes the right hand of the Oba (an act that signifies the transfer of the sacred power), lifts up his hand, and circumambulates the sacred *akoko* tree, the axis mundi. Amidst the acclaim and shouts of *abaye o* (a shout of homage and acceptance) the Lobun proclaims him king three times. The final rite is performed when the Lobun again takes the king's hand and leads him up the primeval mound.[10]

During a ruler's reign in some kingdoms, female members of the extended royal family had prescribed public duties. Some helped to administer the area, while others held appointments as priestesses or "mothers" of royally supported cults.[11] Royal mothers or wives might play drums at religious ceremonies and participate in official festivals.[12] The senior wife of a king often had considerable personal influence over him.

The most extensive participation of royal women in the operation of a palace system was found in (new) Oyo, founded by immigrants from the northern capital.[13] Oyo women helped to select the next king from members of the extended royal family. Eight of the king's wives held designated positions, among them his "official mother," who arranged festivals and communal labor. She also attended consultations with the prime minister and placed the crown on the king's head at his coronation. The mother of the crown prince ruled over part of the capital city, while the influential wife who kept the royal treasures was able to sabotage the king's public appearances by refusing him use of the official garments and paraphernalia. Another palace lady guarded the graves of deceased kings and functioned as an intermediary between the living king and the spirits of his dead predecessors. She was the only person the king addressed as "father" and greeted on his knees. Oyo's royal women also carried out administrative duties in the compound, town, and dependent territories (one, for example, was in charge of the king's markets and the festivals held there). The obverse of the authority of women at Oyo palace was weakly gendered roles for men. Some of the king's male officials, including messengers, diplomatic observers, toll collectors, and royal guards, termed themselves "wives of the king" and might dress in women's clothing.[14] Ambiguous gender definitions thus created a corps of male wives who moved about the country on the king's behalf.

In some settings, rituals surrounding kingship could be used by women to protest the Ọbà's actions. In most Yoruba kingdoms, a ruler could be deposed through pressure from his people, men and women together, as represented by the chiefs. In Ondo, an annual festival that propitiated a culture-hero and savior god provided a safety valve whereby complaints could be made before opposition to the Ọbà became severe. During its core ceremony, which was still being celebrated in the post-Independence years, women, men, and children danced and sang throughout the town all night, following a sacred drum.[15] The words of the songs expressed complaints, ranging from issues of personal and domestic morality to politics. Most of the songs were performed by women, stating their own concerns or those of the broader community. Abusive in tone, they were directed at the king, high chiefs, and other "big men" in the town. They might, for example, complain that the king could only be approached by educated people or that he had inappropriately pocketed money posted by a candidate for an office.

Other public roles for women derived from chieftaincy titles. All Yoruba communities had a hierarchy of chiefs, both male and female, each of whom held a particular honorific title. Female chiefs were respected women who had received a title that gave them some authority in the public sphere.[16] A woman's appointment as a chief usually stemmed from her personal wealth and following, seniority and experience in other public settings, good judgment, and contributions to the community. In some settings, titles were limited to the members of certain lineages, while others were based entirely on personal merit and achievement. Holding a chieftaincy position, and moving up through the progression from lower to higher titles, was an honor eagerly sought by most women. Female chiefs represented and sometimes exercised control over the women of their community, and they articulated their concerns in civic discussions. While the specific functions of women chiefs varied considerably between the various Yoruba states and over time, they normally had some mixture of economic, political, judicial, social, and religious duties.

During the pre-colonial period, both male and female chiefs had been named in the highly centralized kingdoms of Oyo and Ife. The authority of women chiefs was limited, however, by strong palace control, the rights of royal mothers and priestesses, and the economic position of royal wives.[17] Chiefs of both sexes had greater executive and administrative power in the new cities founded in western Yorubaland during the nineteenth century. In the recently formed—and militarily focused—states of Abeokuta and Ibadan, women "operated in a political environment that valued ability and therefore allowed them to translate economic power into political power."[18] In thanks for their service to the state, a number of wealthy female traders were awarded new chieftaincy titles that conveyed real authority. In the system of traditional administration in Lagos, however, which continued into the colonial period, the *Erelú* was the sole high-ranking female chief.[19]

Detailed reports prepared by British officials in the 1930s reveal considerable diversity in the actual roles played by female chiefs.[20] Although women generally did not participate in judicial affairs and sat on the governing council in only a few areas, they were consulted by male chiefs in nearly all settings concerning matters of importance to women. Hence they were likely to be involved in discussions of "trade, markets, female support for community projects, marriage, divorce, their use of land, their rights of inheritance, and religious rites." In many parts of eastern Yorubaland, women chiefs had additional public duties. These might include participating in royal rituals and festivals, forming their own councils, sending representatives to town or royal bodies to speak on behalf of women's concerns, keeping the markets clean, settling market disputes, performing ceremonies to prevent quarrels, and disciplining unruly women.[21]

Ondo had an unusually vibrant system of female chiefs. The most senior, the *Lóbùn,* was assisted by the *Lísà Lóbùn* and the *Jomu Lóbùn.*[22] Those positions were hereditary within extended families, but the particular individuals were chosen by the male chiefs. The principal duties of the senior *Lóbùn* were economic, religious, and socio-political. She officiated at the opening of any new market, in her capacity as priestess of *Ajé,* the *òrìsà* of money and trade. She resolved quarrels between the male chiefs. If a new king was to be selected, all women chiefs attended the meetings of the male chiefs, and the senior *Lóbùn* presided. The lesser chiefs assisted the senior *Lóbùn,* who was paid for her maintenance because she was not allowed to farm or do any other physical work. In 1940, a ceremony at the Native Court Hall in Ondo honoring two churchmen was performed by a male chief and the *Lísà Lóbùn*.[23]

In those parts of Yorubaland that had *Ògbóni* or *Òṣùgbó* societies, female chiefs were commonly members. These secret organizations, sometimes described as councils or cults and associated with worship of *Orò*, were composed of senior people in the community who exercised authority within the state alongside the king.[24] In the nineteenth century they often performed legislative and executive functions as well as presiding over criminal cases, executing people who were convicted, and maintaining a prison for the state. In most settings, at least one person and usually around a fifth of the membership of the *Ògbóni* society were women, selected by senior *Ògbóni* figures on the same grounds as male chiefs. Although the concerns of men were generally dominant in the *Ògbóni*, female members were supposed to safeguard the interests of the town's women.

Women's actual roles within *Ògbóni* societies depended upon the place and time. In the Oyo kingdom—where, atypically, membership in *Ògbóni* was hereditary—a designated woman represented the monarch in the society.[25] Although she only listened during the deliberations without speaking, she warned the king of potential trouble and had access to him at all times. In Oshogbo, *Ògbóni* was initially composed only of male elders, but over time some women were admitted.[26] In many Ijebu areas, the powerful *Òṣùgbó* councils that had traditionally run their communities allowed women holding the chieftaincy title of *Erelú* to join.[27] The *Erelús* "were consulted in all matters that concerned the female community," though they did not participate in judicial judgments. In Ijebu Ode, one section of the *Òṣùgbó* society was reserved for *Erelús*, but by the early 1940s, almost no women wanted to take up that title.[28] Doing so cost £100, and previous *Erelús* had found that they were allowed to take little part in the society other than cooking for meetings.

At the top of the system of women chiefs was a position usually termed *Ìyálóde*. Appointed by the king or senior male chiefs, the *Ìyálóde* and her assistants supervised the market system and its traders and resolved disputes between women. The title of *Ìyálóde* was used in the (Old) Oyo Empire for provincial chiefs who determined trade policy, ran the markets, and served as intermediaries between the women of local communities and the royal administration.[29] That chieftaincy designation then spread to many of Oyo's successor states during the nineteenth century, now carrying greater authority. The office was particularly important in Egbaland (including Abeokuta) and Ibadan.[30] In those city-states, as LaRay Denzer observed, "astute and enterprising female leaders . . . redefined the prerogatives of the Iyalode, making the office more powerful than before."

The leading nineteenth-century *Ìyálódes* wielded considerable political influence. In some cases they sat on the ruling council of their states, taking part
in decisions about the economy and wartime strategy.[31] In Egbaland, where
the title was adopted sometime after 1830, each township had its own local
Ìyálóde, with provincial *Ìyálódes* above them. The new designation of "*Ìyálóde*
of all the Egba" was first awarded in thanks for Madam Tinubu's contributions to the military efforts of Abeokuta in the 1860s.[32] In Ondo, the *Lísà
Lóbùn* participated in peace negotiations with the British in the late nineteenth century.

The authority of *Ìyálódes* was especially marked in nineteenth-century Ibadan. The title was introduced in the early 1850s to recognize the support of the
city's armies provided by Subuola, a wealthy trader.[33] In the political arena,
the *Ìyálóde* was a member of the ruling council, serving as an intermediary
between the leading male chiefs and the town's women. In the economic realm,
the *Ìyálóde* oversaw the operation of the city's market system and was responsible for women's welfare. Judicially, the *Ìyálóde* held a court to which disputes
concerning traders and commodity groups in the markets were referred. She
arbitrated disagreements between women and between husbands and wives
and was the custodian of women imprisoned for theft, malpractices in trade,
and marital offenses. The *Ìyálóde* took part in all the main religious and cultural
festivals. While she was performing those duties, her deputy carried out her
day-to-day police functions and supervised her household and farms.

When Anna Hinderer visited Ibadan's *Ìyálóde* in 1854, she found "a most
respectable motherly looking person, surrounded by her attendants and people, in great order, and some measure of state."[34] Hinderer described her as
"mother of the town, to whom all the women's palavers [disputes] are brought
before they are taken to the king. She is, in fact, a sort of queen, a person of
much influence, and looked up to with much respect." Efunsetan Aniwura
was the most notable of Ibadan's nineteenth-century *Ìyálódes,* but Lanlatu, one
of her successors, played a vital role in negotiations between the Ibadan chiefs
and British colonial officers to end the stalemate of the Yoruba wars.[35] She was
then a witness to the 1893 accord by which Britain gained control over Ibadan,
one of the few examples of colonial treaties signed by women.

During the early and middle colonial period, though the political authority of female chiefs generally declined, *Ìyálódes* and their assistants continued
to carry out important functions in some Yoruba communities. *Ìyálódes* of
the towns and villages in Aiyede District, Ekiti Division, led deputations of
women to local council meetings in the 1930s to speak about matters that
troubled them.[36] In Gbongan—where twentieth-century *Ìyálódes* "kept open
house" for their large followings and survived because of their "strength of
character and considerable political acumen"—the *Ìyálóde* deliberated with

her male counterparts on the king's council and articulated women's concerns as well as controlling the markets and women traders. Because *Ìyálódes* in Gbongan, as in most communities, did not work for the colonial administration, they were able to protest against unpopular government policies without fear of losing their jobs. When market women in Abeokuta had complaints to bring to the Egba Native Authority Council during the 1920s, it was usually the senior *Ìyálóde,* Madam Jojolola, who presented their grievances.[37] The *Ìyálóde* of the Egbas and the three provincial *Ìyálódes* under her were said in 1920 to be "the recognized heads of all Egba women"; Madam Jojolola was described as our "Grand Old Woman" and one of her assistants as "a very distinguished and an influential member of the community."[38] The *Nigerian Daily Times* commented in 1935 that "Among us in this part of Africa, a community without an Iyalode is only a settlement of rabble."

In Ibadan, *Ìyálódes* maintained their status throughout the colonial years. They participated in the installation of the king, watched over the market system, and took unofficial part in council deliberations, where they spoke about women's issues.[39] The *Ìyálóde*'s compound was used for the temporary imprisonment of women whose cases were being heard by local courts. The wife in a divorce case in 1920 was placed in *Ìyálóde*'s custody for 7 days, and in the mid-1930s, a woman who refused to appear when her husband sued her for debt was arrested at the order of the court and "sent to Iyalode's house," where she remained for 15 days.[40] A dispute over property in 1921 was resolved by sending the *Ìyálóde* to the land in question, accompanied by a police constable, to apportion it between the parties.

In Ijebu Ode beginning in the early 1930s, the colonial government made what proved to be a counterproductive attempt to create and use *Ìyálódes* to persuade women to pay taxes.[41] The areas in and around Ijebu Ode and Abeokuta were the only places in Yorubaland where taxes were levied on women as well as men. (Colonial officials argued that because so many women in those settings had cash incomes from trade or craftwork, they could afford to help pay for the services they utilized.) These taxes were imposed on a flat basis rather than reflecting individual wealth. After Ijebu Ode women protested against the taxes, local British administrators and the king of Ijebu Ode decided in 1933 that it would be expedient to appoint three women as *Ìyálódes,* one for each section of the town, in hopes of lessening female resistance.[42] *Ìyálódes* were thus being inserted into a system where they had not previously existed in an effort to appropriate the prestige of their title on behalf of the government. Further, the new chiefs were each to receive a salary of £9 per year from the district Native Authority Council, whereas *Ìyálódes* in other areas did not receive pay from the government. When colonial officers asked the king to notify them of the women he wished to appoint, he provided names but emphasized that they had been chosen by the various "companies" or groups of trading women within the three sections of the town.[43] For the rest of the colonial period, Ìyálódes were appointed by the king and presented to the District Officer, receiving stipends that rose over time.

In the late 1940s, however, opposition to Ijebu Ode's Ìyálódes and their salaries mounted, linked to opposition to the taxes imposed upon women. A petition submitted to the king in 1949 from 12 societies of local market women objected to the appointment of Ìyálódes and the stipends paid to them, which were "not in accordance with our Native Law and custom."[44] The local branches of the Nigerian Women's Union and the Nigerian National Democratic Party likewise complained that the Ìyálódes did not represent the women of the town and "were not constitutionally appointed and elected." In 1953, when additional taxes on women were announced, male leaders joined the campaign: the Ijebu Ode District Council told the District Officer that it was no longer prepared to grant any money to the Ìyálódes.[45] The D. O. responded snippily that he thought the council was "adopting an extremely short-sighted attitude." The government was counting on women in the town to provide a substantial amount of new tax revenue. They would, he argued, be less likely to pay if the Ìyálódes were removed, since the latter were "the sole representatives of a section of the community which is expected this year to find by way of additional taxation a sum of approximately £3,200." Continuing opposition to Ìyálódes and taxation led to heated political protests by Ijebu Ode women.[46]

In many communities, Ìyálódes lost much of their political and economic power across the colonial period. Their official duties were taken over by men recognized by—and in some cases appointed by—colonial or urban authorities. Ìyálóde positions might be left vacant for long periods or became the subject of controversy. In Egbaland, no new woman chiefs were selected between 1898 and 1930 even though Madam Jojolola stressed the importance of maintaining those titles.[47] During the 1920s and early 1930s in Abeokuta, women's titles were one of the issues at dispute between the Egba king and the British Resident (both of whom opposed female public authority), women's economic organizations (which wanted women's chieftaincies to continue), and the Christian community (which wanted to create different titles).[48] When Madam Jojolola died in 1932, her own paramount title lapsed: no woman was named as Ìyálóde of all the Egba for the rest of the colonial period. Even when Ìyálódes were consulted by the governing council of their towns, they could not insist that action be taken. Abeokuta women complained in 1937 that Ìyálódes and their assistants now dealt with little more than petty matters of sanitation.[49]

Yet even in the late colonial years, women chieftaincies—including that of Ìyálóde—were eagerly sought in most towns for the honor they conveyed. The title might no longer convey political or judicial power, but becoming a chief conferred social status. A distinguished woman's titles would always be mentioned in the *oríkì* or praise song about her.[50] Further, in some communities after World War II, colonial authorities named female chiefs to local government bodies.

Women might extend their influence by combining chieftaincy positions with activity in political parties. In Lagos, the *Erelú* in the late 1940s was Madam Rabiatu, a Muslim woman in her mid-sixties.[51] The largest female exporter of textiles in the city and second only to the king in the sequence of customary chiefs, she was in charge of the markets and commercial sections of the city, and she participated in the appointment and installation of the king. But Madam Rabiatu gained additional visibility and new kinds of potential power through participation in the militant (Nigerian) Women's Party. In Ibadan, where the number of titled offices in the progression of *Ìyálóde* chieftaincies rose from four in 1893 to seven in 1951, wealthy and respected women involved in the emerging political parties vied for the titles.[52] Chief Abimbola, a prosperous female trader in beads, was the primary *Ìyálóde* between 1953 and 1961. Able to mobilize a large following for demonstrations, she gave her support to the Women's Movement of Nigeria, the National Council of Nigeria and the Cameroons (NCNC), and later the Action Group (Obafemi Awolowo's party). One of the secondary *Ìyálóde* chieftaincies was held in the 1950s by Wuraola Esan, the proprietress of a girls' school in Ibadan and a key figure in the women's wing of the Action Group. Hunmoani Alade, a successful businesswoman who headed several market associations and was at that time a key supporter of the Action Group, began her ascent through Ibadan's *Ìyálóde* chieftaincy positions in 1956.[53]

Traditional royal positions and chieftaincy titles likewise enhanced the status that elite women gained from formal educations and participation in Western institutions. Deborah Opeyemi Fasan (later Lady Jibowu), member of a well-connected family in Ekiti, received a science degree from the University of Manchester in England in 1947 and a diploma in education from the University of London in 1948 before returning to Nigeria, where she became an education officer for the government.[54] Married to an important barrister and later the principal of a college in Lagos, she was extremely active in civic and religious life. She served for 6 years as regent in the kingdom from which her family came and was honored with high chieftaincy titles in the towns of Ido Ajinare and Ido Ekiti.

Because the Yoruba were accustomed to accepting the authority of some women, even a person who held no formal title or office might be allowed to wield power when needed. A newspaper story from 1950 described an altercation on a bus in Ibadan between two local women, one of whom was trying to reserve a seat for a friend.[55] The women argued for some time, despite threats by the driver and conductor to put them both off the bus. At that point, "The stately figure and masculine comportment of Mrs. H. O. Soares of Anifara Street, Ibadan, in addition to the stern voice that rarely fails to convince, silenced the intercessors" and ordered the women to state their sides of the case. She then pronounced one of them "guilty even in her own statements." "Like a judge, stern and irrevocable, she declared, 'Nobody has any right to reserve seats in this bus, no law has provided for that'." It is interesting that although her authority was accepted by those on the bus, she was described in masculine and not altogether complimentary terms in the newspaper's account.

Economic Organizations and Protests

Women's organizations based upon economic activity were common in western and central Yorubaland during the nineteenth century and were found in most regions during the colonial period. The sellers of each commodity or group of goods within a market had their own ẹgbẹ́ or trade guilds, as did workers in the various crafts.[56] Ibadan, for instance, had separate women's societies (described by a British official as "small trades unions") for sellers of European cloth, native cloth, kola nuts, beads, livestock, palm wine, and other articles in 1937.[57] In Lagos, which had the most complex commercial system (with 26 markets in 1921, each divided into sections that handled particular kinds of items), the associations were usually based upon the physical structure of the market.

Market women's associations fixed prices for their goods, settled disputes between their own members, and dealt with other issues concerning supply and sales. Many of them provided informal credit to their members. These economically based ẹgbẹ́ had the right to make and enforce rules and bylaws, which they did through regular meetings, and each group had a recognized head. The organizations also spoke collectively on behalf of their members. In 1930, for example, a society of women poultry sellers in Ajegunle market wrote to the Lagos Executive Development Board asking that their part of the market be moved away from its present site in a swampy area beside the lagoon: the location was dangerous for their birds and for the young children they had to bring to market with them.[58]

In Lagos and some other large places, each market had a shared identity, one that transcended the individual commodity groups. The markets were headed by a female leader (called the alága in Lagos) elected by the market women on the basis of her personality and leadership.[59] Especially in communities that did not have a powerful Ìyálóde, the alágas were responsible for overall supervision and maintenance of the market, and they resolved disagreements between people in various sections of their market and acted as guardians of the women and their children. An example of a powerful market head is Bintu Balogun, who started selling pots and charcoal as a petty trader in Lagos early in the twentieth century.[60] In 1917 she was chosen as leader of the women at the Porto Novo Market in Marina Street. In that role she confronted "many leading men and women of the country," fearlessly arguing for the rights of her comrades. She was elected president of the Alakoro Women Dealers' Union in 1938, and during World War II, when salt was scarce, "it was through her agitation that the market women were allotted a quota and given permits to sell salt openly to people, thereby curbing what would have been the biggest black market dealings in salt."

The diversity of associations among Lagos market women is illustrated by the list of groups that attended the inaugural meeting of the Youths Section of the local branch of Ẹgbẹ́ Ọmọ Odùduwà, a Yoruba cultural group, in 1948.[61] Representatives of commodity-based organizations included dealers in imported cloth, African textiles, African dyed prints, black soap, gaàrí, poultry, fish, pepper, medicinal herbs, pots, pans and plates, and beads. Dyers and washer women spoke for craft and service workers. Central organizations from eight markets in the city plus a number of suburban ones also sent delegations, and the entire company was headed by the leader of all Lagos market women and the primary woman chief, Madam Alimotu Pelewura.

While in some settings the Ìyálóde, market women's groups, or alágas had exclusive authority over the markets, women's control was limited elsewhere by male officials.[62] In Ijebu Remo, the male Pampa Society had traditionally controlled the markets and sat with the Òṣùgbó to hear cases involving trading matters.[63] Palace officials in the Oyo kingdom appointed market attendants who arranged for housing of distant traders and regulated trade as well as collecting market fees in cash and kind. In Egba communities, a society of male "trade chiefs" called the Pàràkòyí originally dealt with all matters concerning trade. Meeting every 17 days, they promoted the commercial interests of their town, heard disputes, and passed regulations to ensure just prices and safeguard the quality of craft workmanship.[64] In the late 1930s they were expected to attend the markets, handling trivial quarrels and reporting more serious disputes to a policeman. Aiyetoro had Pàràkòyí too. In 1942, they sent men to see whether a woman was wrongly selling beans from her house; the next year a Pàràkòyí who was collecting foodstuffs from sellers, evidently as a market tax, arrested the daughter of one vendor when she grabbed back a melon he had taken from her.[65]

By the late 1920s, some town councils had started hiring male market masters to rent out stalls, collect rents, and represent urban authority on market days.[66] This practice challenged the rights of market women's own groups. In part as a response to that practice, many of the traders' associations in Lagos markets became more formal, developing committees and a constitution and applying for registration as official organizations.[67] The colonial Commissioner for Lagos Colony, supported by the Lagos Town Council, denied those applications, claiming that the market guilds were trying to take over powers that belonged to the urban government and its market masters. For instance, the sellers in Faji Market proposed the formation of a Women Vendors Guild in 1939.[68] Its aims were "to arrange and regulate market days, the sale of market wares, . . . to regulate and control native weights and measures, . . . and to fix and control prices of foodstuffs." The secretary of the town council objected to the plan, however, for it gave the women too much authority over the market; he said the idea "should be nipped in the bud."

As the colonial period advanced, some women's craft and market organizations mobilized public protests. To achieve greater power, these groups drew upon both traditional and Western modes of opposition, forged alliances with the emerging political parties, and occasionally made common cause with the associations of educated women that were being founded from the 1920s onward.[69] Here we see earlier Yoruba economic egbẹ́ re-working themselves and developing altered strategies to achieve new goals.

Several early instances of women's mass resistance occurred in Abeokuta, focused on economic issues. The head tax introduced there by Native Authorities in 1914, followed by a similar colonial tax in 1917, was to be imposed upon women as well as men.[70] Indeed, girls were to be taxed starting at age 15, whereas boys became responsible for the tax only at 17. Tax collectors were said to treat women roughly, sometimes invading their homes and even stripping them naked to see if they were old enough to pay tax. This was one of the factors that led to the rebellion of 1918, in which hundreds of people were killed and railway and telegraph lines destroyed. Though women evidently did not take direct part in that protest, they helped to organize it: it was later claimed that women dyers in Abeokuta had held a planning meeting at the home of Ìyálóde Jojolola, and she was called upon to testify at the inquiry that followed.

In the following decades, Abeokuta's craftswomen and traders mobilized more fully. They were activated by a bitter conflict between the female dyers of àdìrẹ cloth and the king of the Egba, the latter allied with the colonial Resident.[71] The dyers, of whom there were nearly 1,100 at work in 1926, had been hard hit by the global depression and competition with European-made goods, which damaged the export market for their cloths in West Africa. In an attempt to salvage their businesses, the women experimented with new dyeing techniques. In 1929, however, the king—at the urging of the Resident—banned the use of caustic soda. That was followed in 1933 by a ban on synthetic dyes. Many of the women continued to use the forbidden substances, and collectively they hired male lawyers to present their side of the case. In February 1936, the police began arresting dyers and confiscating any illegally dyed cloths, virtually shutting down the cloth market. The next morning, thousands of women traders marched to the royal palace, where they submitted a formal petition to the king and his council on behalf of the àdìrẹ workers to remove the bans. As part of their protest, the women sang abusive songs about the king. The colonial administration in London then set up a Commission of Inquiry, which eventually ruled that caustic soda and synthetic dyes might be used. The women's resistance and subsequent judgment from London weakened the authority of the king and Resident and revealed that local rulers—both African and British—were seriously out of touch with women's concerns.

It was, however, in Lagos—the center of Nigerian political developments during the colonial years—that working women's associations first demonstrated their full power. Organized protests by market women were usually triggered by economic concerns, and their leaders quickly learned that one of their most potent weapons was to shut down the city's markets. (Since most urban households bought food every few days, market closing would rapidly lead to hunger.) In November 1908, Lagos's chiefs called a mass meeting to object to a tax that raised money to provide public water.[72] The market sellers, who were strong supporters of the king and traditional chiefs, were worried that the profits made by female water carriers and traders were already so low that paying the tax would be a serious burden. On the day of the meeting, the market women closed all of Lagos's markets and shops, and some of them joined the 15,000 people who marched on Government House. In April 1909, 3,000 women attended another meeting, during which the markets were again shut. This time they agreed to collect 1 penny from each female trader to finance the campaign against the water tax.

Although the alágas of the individual markets had previously met on occasion to discuss matters of common concern, a central organization—the Lagos Market Women's Association—was created in the 1920s.[73] That project was initiated by Herbert Macaulay, the leader of the Nigerian National Democratic Party (NNDP), which represented the interests of the chiefs and market women, among others. Macaulay encouraged Madam Pelewura, the alága of the largest meat market in Lagos, to join together with women from the other markets.[74] The Lagos Market Women's Association grew rapidly, gaining a position as the semi-official representative of the city's female traders. Whereas in 1925 it had only 1,000 enrolled members, that number had grown to as many as 10,000 by the early 1940s.[75]

The Market Women's Association organized most of the protests in Lagos during the mid-colonial years. In the late 1920s it objected to the deposition of one of the traditional rulers, and it allied with the NNDP in campaigning against the introduction of male taxation in 1927. When rumors spread in 1932 that women in Lagos were going to be taxed, the market women sent a delegation to the administrator of the colony, who gave a reassuring reply. But two new war-time taxes were introduced in March 1940, whereupon the association—supported by the Lagos chiefs, the NNDP, and Macaulay's newspaper—decided to act.[76] In December 1940, it closed all the markets in Lagos, and several thousand women marched first to the commissioner for the colony and then to the governor. After additional mass meetings, the government made some concessions that led the association to abandon its campaign. During and shortly after World War II, when food was in short supply, the group organized resistance against price controls on foodstuffs, government confiscation of rice from sellers, and government distribution of food.[77] The association sent petitions to colonial officials, mounted mass rallies, threatened to shut the markets, and obtained legal assistance for women arrested for contravening the law.

Market women developed ties with the trade union movement in the early 1940s.[78] Some female traders were married to men who were wage earners and members of the early unions, and all urban wives were potentially threatened by the government's assumption that male wages could be kept low because women's earnings helped to support their families. When the unions called for a general strike in 1945, after failure to persuade the government to raise male wages, market women provided many kinds of support. During the strike, Olaniwun Adunni Oluwole, active before as a female preacher, emerged as a champion of workers' interests.[79]

Some observers in the late colonial period commented on market women's lack of interest in political issues (as opposed to their own economic concerns), especially their limited support for Nigerian independence. In their defense, Akin Mabogunje pointed out that market women's trade was not harmed by the white men, so "talks about driving the Europeans away for some abstract concept like political independence strikes no responsive chord amongst them."[80] Mba argued, however, that market women's protests were not confined to immediate economic issues but in some cases addressed matters of general importance to the community; they also showed innovative thinking about broader problems.[81]

In most communities, the ability of women's associations to function as effective pressure groups concerning economic or political issues was limited by lack of cohesion between women of contrasting socio-economic and educational backgrounds. In Lagos, for example, though many activists were

Yoruba women, they were divided into two groups: a large number of market sellers, the majority of whom were Muslim and had gone through no more than primary school; and a much smaller number of well-educated Christian women who were part of the traditional or new elites.[82] Market women had learned how to organize their own members on behalf of causes that mattered to them, but they were not joined by elite women in more encompassing organizations. The educated members of the Lagos Ladies (later Women's) League, for example, supported female traders: they backed market women's objections to higher rents for their stalls; they opposed the government's decision to impose taxes on women, on the grounds that most petty traders did not earn enough money to live decently even as it was; and they objected to the price regulations imposed by the government during World War II, which were harmful to female traders.[83] But the league did not enter into a joint association with market women. Similarly in Ibadan, though individual market leaders and elite women worked together, they did not form a common organization.[84] Not until the founding of the National Council of Women's Societies in 1957 did an association bring together women of all ranks from multiple places under a single institutional umbrella.

During the 1930s and 1940s, however, market women and educated women's organizations cooperated in the two places affected by ongoing female taxation, Ijebu Ode and Abeokuta. Ijebuland had a strong tradition that all elements in the community should be consulted before important decisions were made; educated men had been complaining about their own lack of representation in local government since the 1920s.[85] But it was women who actively protested in the early 1930s against the tax imposed on them, a levy made more burdensome by the depression of that period. (The tax rate was then 2.5s. per adult female and 5s. per adult male, but more women were taxed than men, presumably because they had more cash than their farmer husbands.[86]) In 1933 the king of Ijebu Ode wrote to colonial officials about "the intrigues and riots" caused by women who refused to pay the tax.[87] Further demonstrations were organized in July 1942, at a time when craftswomen and traders were suffering from the economic policies introduced by the government during World War II. These protests objected to the levying of taxes on women when they had no voice in town affairs. British officials then agreed "in principle" that "as women have paid tax in Ijebuland since its inception, they should have some voice in town affairs."[88] That agreement, which was approved by the king and "the people," stipulated that the town council would in future include the *Erelú* of the *Òṣùgbó* society and one female representative from each of the three wards in the town. The plan was apparently not implemented, however.

The situation became more heated in 1949, when women in Ijebu Ode were told that they would have to pay an additional 3.5s. each as an annual water tax. Already angry about the appointment and payment of Ìyálódes, twelve market women's associations in the town sent a collective protest to the king, saying that women traders would be ruined by the new tax.[89] Statements were also submitted by the local branches of the Nigerian Women's Union and the NNDP. The Ijebu Ode branch of the small but determined (Nigerian) Women's Party, which included both market women and educated women, used strategic rhetoric and displayed some knowledge of Western political thought in its petition to the colonial District Officer and Resident against the water tax.[90] "We are being told Your Honour, that taxation without representation is tyrany [sic], and since the Town Council does not represent our interests, we cannot be therefore affected by any unconstitutional decision taken." Whereas British officials representing His Majesty's Government claimed that they were sent to Nigeria "to protect the interests of the masses," the new tax violates that "contract," for the government has not listened to women's complaints and has only produced wailing. Warning that the water tax "may break the backs of the camels as women" and "run the women races down and reduce the population into nothing," the petitioners called upon the authorities to be "wise British Statesmen" and respond to the concerns of the people. But their written protests achieved nothing. In 1952, a third tax was imposed upon women, this one to support education, despite the fact that women were still not represented on local councils in Ijebuland.[91] The tax led to violent protests, and several of the women arrested for refusing to pay it died while in jail, together with the babies "on their backs." The following year, colonial officers announced that women would be allowed to compete for seats in Ijebu Ode in the next local government election.[92]

In Abeokuta shortly after World War II, a new organization joined market women and craftswomen with female members of the educated elite into an effective common unit.[93] Women traders and craft producers in Abeokuta felt that their economic interests had already been damaged by taxes and wartime food price controls, the government's requisitioning of foodstuffs from traders without remuneration, and the shrinking market for their cloth. To strengthen their political muscle in addressing their economic concerns, they decided in 1946 to merge with the Abeokuta Ladies' Club to form the Abeokuta Women's Union (AWU).

The Abeokuta Ladies' Club had been founded in the early 1940s by Mrs. Funmilayo Ransome-Kuti, a British-educated teacher who was head of the Abeokuta Girls' School. In 1925 she had married an Anglican minister and political activist who in 1932 became principal of the Abeokuta Grammar School for boys and was later a main organizer of the Nigerian Union of Teachers.[94] By the mid-1940s, Mrs. Ransome-Kuti, an instinctive politician, was becoming increasingly militant about women's issues and increasingly anti-colonial. She led the AWU in preparing a formal constitution and delighted in standing up to the police, judges, and District Officers. As part of her attempt to challenge European cultural dominance, she spoke Yoruba when meeting with British officials and always wore Yoruba clothing, encouraging the AWU's members to do the same.

In 1947 the AWU demanded abolition of the flat tax on women, criticized the system of government supported by the British, including the lack of representation and participation of women, and objected to the king of the Egba (Ademola II). After making little progress through letters to the press and public refusal to pay the flat tax, Mrs. Ransome-Kuti and the AWU moved to mass demonstrations.[95] On November 29, 1947, thousands of women sat on the grounds of the king's palace for 24 hours; the following week, they repeated their vigil for 48 hours. On both occasions, the city's markets were closed, and the AWU organized food, water, and sanitary facilities for the protesters. Pressure from the AWU continued in 1948. By this time it had become a very large movement, with 20,000 official members, most of them market women, and the support of 80,000–100,000 others. Despite the arrest and trial of 54 women for refusal to pay tax, Mrs. Ransome-Kuti was undeterred: she submitted a formal protest to the Colonial Office in London against the ill-treatment of women in Abeokuta and prepared a memorandum on the condition of women in Nigeria.[96] In April, the women carried out a 5-hour march through the streets and gained support from the leading men's organizations. King Ademola then agreed to submit to all demands except his own abdication. After further protests from the AWU and men's groups, Ademola went into temporary exile in July 1948, and the form of local government was modified. Pressure from the AWU led to a Commission of Inquiry into the taxation of Egba women, which recommended abolition of the new impositions.[97]

During those early "sit-ins" in Abeokuta, women utilized a variety of traditional Yoruba methods for signifying their dislike or scorn for someone above them.[98] They sang abusive songs about the king and his sexual abilities and carried out mock sacrifices and funeral rites for him. When senior men from the Ògbóni society tried to force the protesters to leave the palace compound, the women made up taunting parodies of the chant used to announce an Orò appearance, normally ordered by the Ògbóni, which would require their confinement indoors. They teased and insulted the British District Officer; when he ordered policemen to clear a way for him, the women turned angry, letting out "a continuous shout of derision."[99]

Clothing was used in symbolic ways. After a group of women leaders decided to mount their first protest at the king's palace, they "rose in a body. Hands flew to heads and off came the head-ties, unfurling in the air like hundreds of banners. The head-ties flew downwards, turned into sashes and arced round the waists to be secured with a grim decisiveness."[100] During the sit-in, women attacked the clothing of the *Ògbóni* who were attempting to restore order. Any *Ògbóni* they saw was "set upon. His shawl [which signified his office] was snatched, shredded, his wrapping cloth was stripped of him—fan, office staff, cap had all long disappeared." The *Ògbóni* were then beaten with their own ritual equipment, "left only with their undershorts when finally let through a gauntlet of abuse into the palace or back in the direction of their homes." The popular singer Fela, son of the Ransome-Kutis, later recalled that on the day the king returned to Abeokuta from his exile, his mother came storming into the house, emerging shortly thereafter dressed in men's clothing. "It was her way of saying, 'It takes a man to fight another man'."[101]

An even more powerful weapon in the hands of women was to bare themselves—or to threaten to do so—in a public protest. This was the strongest possible indicator of their displeasure, regarded as an almost spiritual act to humiliate a person who was failing to use appropriately the authority granted to him. In some communities it was considered taboo to view an elderly woman naked: anyone who did so might die.[102] It was thus a dramatic act when some of the older women in the Abeokuta protests stripped themselves entirely naked or wore only a small underskirt as they stood outside the royal palace, in full view of the king, calling for his abdication. As Judith Byfield noted, "By removing their clothes, the women symbolically removed their respect for Ademola and ultimately stripped him of his authority."[103] This practice was noted in colonial Gbongan too, where if the wishes of women were ignored, the king might find a crowd of chanting women in front of his palace, some of them naked.

Colonial Government and Political Parties

Women were largely excluded from colonial government and political activity until the 1940s and 1950s. Based upon the values brought with them from home, British officials believed that women were unsuited for "the rigors of public life."[104] Women were therefore not allowed to vote or contend for regional or national offices until the 1950s. But beginning in the 1930s and increasingly over the following decades, colonial administrators accepted the participation of women in local government bodies.[105] Though women could not elect their own spokespeople, one or two women were generally appointed to represent women's interests. In rural areas, chiefs from the traditional titled hierarchy were usually named, while in the towns, the choices were affected by pressure from newer kinds of women's organizations and early political parties. In Lagos, where women were allowed to vote in 1950, five women joined 51 men in contesting for seats on the town council (only one of whom was elected); in Ibadan, Wuraola Esan was elected to the Urban District Council in 1958.[106]

In Abeokuta, despite its economically active and politically organized women, female participation in local government was minimal. The Egba Council was enlarged several times during the colonial period, but no woman was invited to join it even though Ìyálóde Jojolola had commented repeatedly about their absence.[107] A petition sent to the king and council in 1920 by a large number of women and men asking for representation was likewise ignored. Nor were women consulted directly by the king on matters that concerned them, like the rules for marriage and divorce discussed in 1937. Female participation in other Egba institutions remained limited. The Central Council in 1950 consisted of 13 ex officio and 73 elected members, including four women; on the Egba Native Authority Executive Committee in 1955, two women joined 18 local men and various colonial officials.[108] It is because women had to operate largely outside the formal structure of colonial administration to make their concerns known that their organizations and protests were so significant.

Starting in the 1920s, but especially during the 1940s and 1950s, Western-style political parties began to develop in Nigeria. Both market women and female members of the educated elite tried to carve out places for themselves in these organizations, but their efforts were generally unsuccessful: men wanted to be sure that they themselves would dominate the government when Independence came. The NNDP had supported Lagos market women, and its constitution endorsed the principles of universal franchise and equal educational facilities for men and women.[109] But an editorial in the paper that served as the party's mouthpiece presented a strong statement in 1929 that women were to be wives, mothers, and thrifty housewives. The NNDP put forward no women as candidates for the Legislative Council or even for the Lagos Town Council.

Some women therefore turned to newer parties. In the late 1930s, the reformist Nigerian Union of Young Democrats was popular among market women; other traders and some elite women became members of the Nigerian Youth Movement.[110] Between 1944 and 1950, Madam Pelewura and many other market women supported the alliance between the NCNC, led by Dr. Azikiwe, and the older NNDP. After Pelewura's death in 1951, the political situation in Lagos became more complex, with unstable relationships between the various groups of market women, elite women, and the political parties, which were themselves increasingly defined along ethnic lines. During the 1950s the Action Group, headed by Obafemi Awolowo, won support from many women throughout Yorubaland.

Due largely to dissatisfaction with the leading parties' male domination and

weak commitment to women's concerns, women in Lagos, Abeokuta, and Ibadan founded several alternative parties during the 1940s and 1950s that dealt
explicitly—though not exclusively—with women's issues. In 1944, Oyinkan
Abayomi and several other educated women, mainly teachers, formed a new
association, the (Nigerian) Women's Party (NWP).[111] When Abayomi was
appointed to the Lagos Town Council, she gained a platform from which
to address the four issues highlighted by the NWP: education for girls and
adult women; employment of women in the Civil Service; the right of female
minors to trade freely in Lagos; and protection of market women's rights. The
NWP attempted to recruit market women to its ranks, but with limited success. In the later 1940s it had no more than 2,000 members, as compared with
five times that number in the Lagos Market Women's Association.

Pressure for change came also from the Nigerian Women's Union, a
national organization that succeeded the Abeokuta Women's Union in 1949.[112]
Led by Mrs. Ransome-Kuti, it emphasized the enfranchisement of women
and insisted that women be allowed to choose their own representatives. That
group was followed in 1953 by the Federation of Nigerian Women's Societies,
which campaigned against the payment of tax by women and tried to force
the colonial administration to name women to local councils and improve the
educational opportunities and social status of women. In 1954, a more conservative woman, Olaniwun Adunni Oluwole, founded the Nigeria Commoners'
Liberal Party.[113] Speaking on behalf of the rights of ordinary people and advo-
cating women's political involvement, the party opposed hasty independence
for Nigeria.

Some of the women's parties were influenced by the experience their leaders
had gained abroad. Yoruba women studying in Britain often joined political
organizations. Groups like the West African Students' Union and the Nigerian Union of Students of Great Britain and Ireland exposed Folayegbe Akintunde to critiques of colonialism and the concept of pan-Africanism, while
also showing how political parties operated in Britain.[114] Although foreign
student organizations were dominated by men, some women were named to
secondary leadership positions. In the 1950s, nationally or regionally defined
associations overseas were joined by ethnically specific groups, such as the
Ẹgbẹ́ Ọmọ Odùduwà run by and for Yoruba students. A few women's groups
within Nigeria developed international connections during the late colonial
years. Humuani Alaga, a Muslim leader of women traders in Ibadan, traveled to London and Dublin as a representative of the National Council of
Women's Societies, of which she was a founding member.[115] The Federation of
Nigerian Women's Societies became affiliated with the Women's International
Democratic Federation, of which Mrs. Ransome-Kuti was named world vice
president in 1953. (Her socialist beliefs and travel to communist China led to

problems with British officials and the United States.) None of the women's parties, however, had large enough memberships or sufficient political clout to force the mainstream parties to respond to their concerns.

By around 1950, as it became clear that Nigeria was going to sever its ties with Britain, the role of women in the post-colonial state came under discussion in the press. An editorial in the *West African Pilot* in 1950 headed "Reminder to Our Womenfolk" pointed to the limited presence of women in the nationalist movement.[116] Nigeria's political independence would necessarily require participation by women as well as men, but few currently took part in politics. "We therefore look forward to the formation of a Nigerian Women Congress which will crystallise the mental and ideological unity of Nigerian women." Women themselves began to demand the right to vote and to compete in elections. In 1952, Elizabeth Adekogbe asked in a fiery article in the *Nigerian Tribune* when Native Administrations that collected money from women in the form of taxes would decide to tolerate women on their councils.[117] Why, she asked, is there "not a single woman among the two hundred and fifty elected men in our Houses of Assembly," and why can women vote in only a few local elections rather than enjoying universal adult suffrage? She urged women to organize themselves into political parties and win seats in the next general elections, for women are "determined to press for and have our dues—no matter by what means."

Some women were indeed pressing for their dues. In the town of Gbongan, Mrs. Oyatade, who held one of the *Ìyálóde* chieftaincies, is credited with having pulled women into politics.[118] When she started attending political rallies in 1945 ("like a brave lioness," though with her husband's permission), she found few other women there, and they never spoke. She therefore formed the Gbongan Market Women Association as a way of "raising the political awareness of her fellow women." At first she merely reported to the market women about political issues, but later she began forcing them to attend rallies. If their husbands prohibited them from going, she refused to let the women sell in the market, whereupon the men backed down. Thus she helped Nigerian women "to gear up for the political race."

In the Western Region during the 1950s, that race was conducted largely between two major parties, the Action Group and the NCNC. Both parties realized that when women gained the franchise, female support would become essential.[119] They therefore tried to pull women into their organizations, setting up separate wings that helped with fund-raising, entertaining, and campaigning for votes. Those branches continued right up to Independence. But while women could hold leadership positions within their own wings, the actual power brokers at the center of the parties were almost exclusively male. In 1954, the NCNC's National Executive Committee included only two women out of 42 seats; at a meeting the following year, one of 22 members of the committee was a woman, as were two of 81 party members who attended as observers.[120] Nor did women gain the kind of rewards open to male politicians in thanks for service to their party, such as appointment to public boards.

Pre-Independence legislative bodies provided women with little hands-on experience in governance. No women were elected as regular members of the national or Western Region legislatures during the 1950s.[121] Mrs. Remi Aiyedun, a teacher from Abeokuta, was appointed to the latter in 1954 as "a special member representing women's interests"; she was joined the following year by Lady Oyinkan Abayomi.[122] In the 1959 legislative election, the NCNC refused to nominate Mrs. Ransome-Kuti as one of its candidates, even though she had for many years been a leader of its women. When she refused to step aside for a male candidate, she was expelled from the party.[123] In 1960, Wuraola Esan, the senior woman in the Action Group, was appointed (not elected) as the only female senator in Nigeria's first post-Independence national legislature.

In parallel fashion, when the parties laid out their agendas for an independent Nigeria, they offered no concrete plans for how women would contribute to the new nation or how matters of special importance to women would be addressed.[124] Male politicians in the 1950s were eager to take control of the governmental and administrative apparatuses that had been set up by the British and to expand programs such as education and health, but they did not give much thought to how those programs could be managed in a way that would benefit women.[125] (The Action Group's commitment to universal primary education forms an exception, for the party realized that free schooling would result in a larger increase in girls' enrollment than in boys'.) In campaigning for the 1960 elections, Wuraola Esan took a strongly partisan stance. She urged voters not to cast a single vote for NCNC candidates because "an NCNC government of the West would destroy the high institution of womanhood."[126] She did not, however, explain in any detail how her party would serve women. After its electoral victory in the Western Region, she said merely that she was confident that "the Action Group Government will continue its traditional policy of enhancing the position of women in the Region and providing for the welfare of their children."[127] Because the independent women's parties had failed to win widespread backing, due in part to ongoing divisions between market women and members of the educated elite, women had no vehicle for demanding that the issues that particularly concerned them be placed at the center of political debate and policy.

Women's lack of power in the parties that were to dominate the nascent state, and lack of attention to their concerns, had unfortunate consequences for Nigeria's future. When one compares women's earlier political roles as regents, advisors, chiefs, and authorized critics of official behavior with their virtual exclusion from leadership in the dominant parties of 1960, it becomes clear that women's ability to influence public policy had decreased considerably. In newly independent Nigeria, women no longer had recognized means for ensuring that their opinions were heard or for objecting effectively to bad governance. This was a loss for the nation. Further, it has been suggested that female leaders in the later 1940s and 1950s focused upon issues that affected the well-being of the whole community, rather than giving primary allegiance to a particular ethnic group or political party, as was true for most of the men who were trying to consolidate power at the time.[128] That observation echoes the comment made about female traders in the nineteenth century: they had learned to accommodate ethnic differences and generally advocated peace and harmony rather than war. The weak position of women in the government surely contributed to the problems faced by Nigeria during the first few generations of post-colonial rule.

The roles we have examined in the last two chapters complemented Yoruba women's other activities. Involvement in religious, cultural, and social activities reinforced women's desire to earn money of their own while at the same time demonstrating that they were essential to many aspects of their communities, not merely to the economy and their families. In the changing world of nineteenth-century and colonial Yorubaland, a limited number of women exercised formally acknowledged authority within religious, cultural, social, or governmental arenas. Their ability to do so meant that women could not be relegated to an ideological position inferior to that of men or deemed incapable of filling public roles. A much larger number of women participated in their religious congregations, extended families, economic units, and communities, often as members of *egbe* or other associations. Although indigenous forms of patriarchy could be deployed to control women during times of rapid economic and social change, the constraining features of Christianity, Islam, and colonialism were moderated by women's ability to work together. Women rarely held leadership positions in colonial government and the emerging political parties, though mass protests and women's associations gave some voice to their concerns. With the exception of the new forms of governance, Yoruba women enjoyed considerable agency, seen both in their decision-making ability as individuals or within organizations and in the positions of authority some of them filled.

12 | Patriarchy, Colonialism, and Women's Agency

HAVING EXAMINED YORUBA women's diverse roles during the nineteenth century and colonial era, we can now consolidate what we have learned about the three broader questions concerning gender and patriarchy, women and colonialism, and women's agency as decision makers.

Gender and Patriarchy

Yoruba culture already displayed certain patriarchal practices in the nineteenth century. The Yoruba worldview did not contain fixed gender definitions similar to those found in Western societies. Women were not regarded as a group with shared characteristics, nor were they assumed to be inferior to men. But in daily life, women were assigned extensive duties within the family and household that were not shared by men. Their domestic responsibilities made it difficult for women to focus time and energy on income-generating activities, even in western and central parts of Yorubaland, where they were more heavily involved in the market economy. They faced other gender-based handicaps as well. While some women were able to surmount those obstacles, especially during the unsettled conditions between around 1840 and the end of the century, ongoing disadvantages contributed to the concentration of women at the bottom of the trading system. Indigenous patriarchy was also enforced by controlling the behavior of women. In addition to the routine kinds of authority that men exercised over women within the family and community, religious and cultural practices that drew upon a belief in supernatural forces were occasionally used at times when women's increased economic prominence or social independence threatened to destabilize familiar gender relationships.

Christian missionaries, foreign merchants, and British colonial officials introduced a very different set of patriarchal attitudes and policies. Victorian middle-class ideology taught that women were weaker than men, both physically and emotionally, and that they should remain within the home. Although the most confining of British gender assumptions were loosened from the 1930s onward, those attitudes had already been built into many colonial institutions and policies. British expectations sometimes challenged Yoruba gendered beliefs and behaviors, but they might also reinforce them. When indigenous ideas about women coincided with British ones, the impact was particularly strong. Thus, the assumption that women's primary roles were as wives and mothers was almost never questioned: by Africans or Europeans, by men or women. But in areas where Yoruba attitudes and practices were dissimilar to foreign ones, women were often able to use the competing ideologies to their own benefit. They could, for example, gain strength from the economic patterns present in western Yorubaland from the mid-nineteenth century onward, while ignoring missionary and colonial objection to women who earned their own money.

Although the particular form of patriarchy present in colonial Yorubaland thus contained indigenous as well as foreign features, both types of male dominance were to some extent curtailed by women's own resistant or adaptive activities. When confronted with an economic policy that harmed their businesses, or when they were unhappy at being taxed when they could not vote or hold political office, women made their opinions known through their associations and sometimes through massive public protests. When women were prohibited from holding spiritual positions within the mainstream Christian churches and mosques, they extended their traditional *egbẹ́* into the religious realm, thereby gaining an alternative form of power within their congregations. Or they founded or joined independent Nigerian churches that gave them greater authority. The way patriarchy operated in practice, like the actual operation of colonialism, resulted from interaction between the attitudes and institutions of the dominant power and the values and strategies of those affected by its authority.

Women and Colonialism

Some of the colonial laws, policies, and institutions that implemented British gender assumptions weakened Yoruba women's previous position, while others provided unfamiliar—if unintended—opportunities. Here again, Yoruba women displayed great ingenuity in creating novel roles for themselves by syncretizing traditional patterns with elements introduced from outside. Particularly interesting is how they used their experience at working in groups to create new and influential organizations within the colonial context.

Yoruba women were disadvantaged by colonialism in some respects. In social and economic terms, the early missionaries introduced a model of a monogamous nuclear household (headed by a man with a stay-at-home wife) that had the potential to disrupt Yoruba women's traditional status within their families and their income-generating roles. Local craftspeople, including female weavers, dyers, potters, and soap makers, found it increasingly difficult to compete with inexpensive European manufactured goods. Colonial agricultural experts worked almost exclusively with male farmers, government loans were rarely extended to women, and women were effectively disqualified from the upper levels of the system that marketed export crops.

Christianity and Western education also had some negative consequences. Christianity eliminated the necessary roles that women had played within traditional Yoruba religion. Western schooling, initially and to some extent always associated with Christianity, offered more places to boys than to girls. The curriculum employed for girls stressed domestic training, impeding their entry into secondary schools and educated careers. Women's movement into the professions was delayed also by British reluctance (until after World War II) to hire African women in fields other than teaching and—eventually—nursing. Western education gave prestige to new types of learning and cultural transmission that were male dominated, and the burgeoning Yoruba cities were domains in which men had greater access to knowledge and employment.

Within the colonial system of government and law, women were largely excluded. The British did not recognize the advisory roles formerly played by some women chiefs, and women could not hold the offices that administered the system of indirect rule, including sitting as judges in the Native Courts. In some communities, the authority of town councils and their market masters gradually eroded the authority formerly held by market women's organizations and *Ìyálódes*. By the late colonial period, women were allowed to sit on some local bodies, but almost none were appointed to higher legislative assemblies. When Western-style political parties emerged in the decades before Independence, women rarely held leadership positions, and their concerns were poorly represented.

In other respects, however, Yoruba women benefited from colonialism. These gendered consequences were not necessarily foreseen by the British. The ending of the Yoruba civil wars and slave trading made life more secure and promoted peaceful trade, of particular value for women. The gradual disappearance of indigenous slavery and pawnship freed women and girls from involuntary labor, whether permanent or temporary. The growth of international commerce and construction of the railway and roads enabled female traders to expand their businesses. Colonial marriage legislation prohibited child betrothals, required a woman's consent to a union, made divorce far easier, and gave those women who entered monogamous marriages under the new ordinances improved inheritance rights for themselves and their children. Although colonial administrators were probably taken aback by the enthusiasm with which Yoruba women resorted to the courts to end their marriages, they did not step in to restrict divorce. Thanks to Western education, women moved into new occupations, some of which yielded a larger income and/or conveyed higher social status than traditional trading or craftwork.

Certain aspects of Yoruba life continued along familiar paths despite colonial efforts to introduce alternative patterns. In some cases the Yoruba simply ignored calls for change. The model of a domestic Christian wife, whose husband was the breadwinner and decision maker for his family, was generally dismissed by women and men alike as ridiculous (apart from a few households among the urban elite). Instead, most women continued to earn their own money, and respected senior women retained considerable authority within their extended families. In other instances, the Yoruba conformed nominally to the dictates of British rule while quietly continuing their own ways under the surface. Thus, the system of indirect rule, which allowed at least a modified form of traditional royal authority to continue, permitted women to maintain their importance in key rituals of kingship and in some settings to serve as regents.

Especially significant is how Yoruba women created niches for themselves in the interstices between indigenous patterns and the imported attitudes and practices of colonialism. During the mid-nineteenth century, as the production and sale of palm products boomed, women who had previously made oil for domestic consumption or traded only locally seized the chance to earn money within an evolving economic system that was still loosely structured and had no rigid gender definitions. As girls began to attend school, they converted the Western domestic arts they learned there, which were supposed to be used within the home, into ways of earning a good income. Educated women who entered service careers but found their jobs in schools and hospitals too poorly paid and too confining devised means of utilizing their training within private institutes or clinics, reflecting a traditional preference for running one's own business. Market women—occasionally in partnership with newly formed associations of elite women—used their organizational skills to form effective protest groups, mobilizing thousands of women and shutting down the economic life of their cities by closing the markets. Such movements, expressing opposition to financial or political policies that harmed women, were directed usually at colonial authorities, linked on occasion to unpopular kings supported by the British. When protesting, Yoruba women re-worked traditional forms of protest, such as insulting songs and special uses of clothing, to achieve new public goals. Colonialism thus had mixed consequences for Yoruba women, thanks in large part to their own ingenuity in spotting and developing opportunities within a system that was itself forced to accommodate to strong traditional beliefs and practices.

Women's Agency as Decision Makers

Women in all parts of Yorubaland who were neither slaves nor pawns made some decisions about their own lives, thereby exercising personal agency. A smaller number had authority over other people that enabled them to dictate what their followers or dependents should do. That agency or authority could be exercised either as individuals or as members of groups. Within the household, women commonly decided how domestic tasks should be carried out, and those with more seniority or status could direct the activities of people beneath them: mothers above children, senior wives above junior wives, and free women above slaves and pawns. During the colonial period, British marriage regulations, the availability of divorce, and expanded opportunities to earn money increased women's control over their own marriages. Some women held positions of recognized political, religious, or social authority in public domains. The system of Yoruba monarchy had included female rulers in earlier times, and throughout the nineteenth century and colonial era, female regents exercised royal power between the reigns of kings in some places. Women commonly displayed their authority in the rituals that occurred at particular stages of kingship, including the installation of the next ruler; royal women held designated roles within the palace system of some of the kingdoms. Priestesses in the òrìṣà cults gained respect as intermediaries between living people and the deities. Women who held a title within one of the churches or mosques exercised some influence over the decisions made by their congregations about practical and social—though not spiritual—matters. Women participated directly in some oral forms, while their attributes and powers were acknowledged by male artists and performers in other genres. Admired (and usually wealthy) women who had been awarded a chieftaincy position were expected to guide and control their followers. The Ìyálóde or other head of the hierarchy of female chiefs commanded considerable respect and obedience during the nineteenth century and in some towns during the twentieth as well.

Yoruba women were resourceful in carving out profitable niches for themselves within the public economy of the later nineteenth century and colonial era, thereby gaining new spheres in which to make decisions and acquiring new types of authority. Women utilized the labor of dependents, and sometimes of slaves, pawns, or employees, to produce marketable agricultural items or craft wares and to expand the volume and range of their trade. Women who acquired Western skills at school were creative in devising means of utilizing their education to generate an income. Teachers and nurses could shape the decisions of their students, patients, and families, their authority boosted by the high status that accompanied participation in British-linked careers even if they had chosen to set up their own establishments.

Women's decision-making ability was not, however, uniform between regions. Women had greater agency in western and central parts of Yorubaland. There, by the second half of the nineteenth century, many women generated some income to help support themselves and their children. They could choose which economic activities to pursue (though the range of options open to a woman with little capital and no specialized skills might be narrow), and their earnings remained their own. If they had money left after making essential purchases, they could decide how to invest the remainder: in education, religious rituals, civic ceremonies, or contributions to their natal or marital families or their egbẹ́. Older women held positions of authority within their own compounds and sometimes within the lineage, counted among the senior members who made decisions for the full group. When men were away, those women ran the households and farms. Women's egbẹ́ taught their members how to make group decisions, and their officers gained formal control. In the twentieth century, as egbẹ́ assumed new forms, some extended their impact beyond their own memberships. Organizations of educated women gave public voice to women's issues, while market women in the larger cities organized powerful mass protests. Because women as individuals seldom participated directly in the colonial system, group action constituted the best possible means of influencing government policy.

In eastern areas, which were less urbanized and had a less elaborate system of trade, men exercised greater authority within households during the nineteenth century and to some extent in the colonial era too. Women spent much of their time growing crops on family land, and if they sold some of that produce, the income went to their husbands. To generate an independent income through agriculture, women had to acquire farms of their own. Many eastern women engaged in some market trading, but usually on a part-time basis involving inexpensive goods. Their earnings were thus lower than among full-time businesswomen in the large western and central cities. Under those circumstances, the ability of even senior women in the family to make decisions might be constrained. Women's egbẹ́ were rare or absent in the nineteenth century, emerging only gradually during the colonial period and initially only for Christians. Eastern women were therefore less likely to benefit from group support or gain experience at functioning collectively.

The history of Yoruba women from 1820 to 1960 is a study of adaptability within a society affected by diverse patriarchal systems, negotiation between indigenous patterns and the forces of colonialism, and women's own agency. That history also helps to explain the puzzling contrast between the economic and social importance of many Yoruba women in Nigeria's post-colonial history and their limited political prominence. The system of governance created by the British when combined with the forms of rule developed by the political parties of the later 1940s and 1950s curtailed the participation of women in upper levels of power. In other aspects of family and public life, however, women continued to wield considerable influence, based upon the fundamental Yoruba belief that the community's well-being depended upon the involvement of both women and men in all spheres.

Glossary of Yoruba Words

àdìrẹ	A type of dyed cloth made by Yoruba women
àgìdí	A popular Yoruba food, usually served cold, made of corn (maize) that has been fermented, ground, and boiled
Ajé	An *òrìṣà* associated with money and wealth
alága	The chairperson of an occasion; the elected head of the women sellers in a particular market
baálẹ	The senior man and leader of a lineage; a head chief; the leading man in a village
dìpòmu	A ward at the king's palace in Abeokuta used to house women, especially those who had sued for divorce in the Native Courts
ẹgbẹ	An association or club
Ẹgbẹ Ọmọ Odùduwà	A Yoruba social organization
Egúngún	A masquerade that celebrated and appeased the ancestral spirits, usually performed by a secret society
ẹgúsí	Melon seeds
Erelú	A woman's chieftaincy title, often associated with membership in an *Òṣùgbó* society
ẹrú	A slave
Èṣù	An *òrìṣà*, a homeless, wandering trickster or troublemaker (sometimes associated with the devil) who was often propitiated at market places

èsúsú	A rotating savings and credit fund
gaàrí	Cassava grits (dried and coarsely ground tubers), used to make a thick porridge
Gẹ̀lẹ̀dẹ́	A type of masquerade in which costumed figures represented deities, powerful ancestors, and living people, often female, to honor and propitiate them
Ifá	A form of Yoruba divination (foretelling the future or revealing hidden causes) based upon contact between the human world and that of the spirits, coupled with a large body of poetry
ìwọ̀fà	A "pawn" or person who worked for another to repay a debt
ìyá	Mother, but more generally, an important woman
Ìyálóde	A high chieftaincy title given to the leading woman (literally "the mother") in the public sphere
Lísà Lóbùn	Title of the second main women's chieftaincy in Ondo
Lóbùn	Title of the highest woman chief in Ondo
Ọba	A paramount ruler, usually translated as "king" but could sometimes be a woman
Odùduwà	A semi-mythical, semi-historical figure from whom all Yoruba people are believed to have descended
Ògbóni	A secret society or council that exercises authority alongside the king; an archaic word meaning "a man"
Olódùmarè	The supreme being, God (literally, "owner of the universe")
oríkì	A praise chant, containing brief descriptions of an *òrìṣà*, person, or lineage history
òrìṣà	A deity, one of the lesser gods/goddesses under *Olódùmarè*
Orò	An *òrìṣà* worshipped especially by the Egba and Ijebu; the cult devoted to *Orò*, of which the *Ògbóni* or *Òṣùgbó* societies were an arm
Òṣùgbó	A society similar to *Ògbóni*, associated with *Orò*
Ọya	The Niger River; also the *òrìṣà* of that river, the wife of *Sàngó*
Pàràkòyí	A group of male chiefs who supervised the market and trade
Sàngó	The *òrìṣà* of thunder and lightning
Yẹmoja	The *òrìṣà* of rivers and streams, the mother of many other *òrìṣà*

Notes

Preface and Acknowledgments

1. Bantebya and McIntosh, *Women, Work, and Domestic Virtue in Uganda, 1900–2003* (Oxford: James Currey; Kampala, Uganda: Fountain Press; and Athens: Ohio University Press, all in 2006), recipient of the 2007 Aidoo-Snyder Prize awarded by the Women's Caucus of the African Studies Association. Prof. Bantebya was head of the Department of Women and Gender Studies at Makerere University when I taught there in 2002–2003.

Note on Language and Orthography

1. The acute accent ´ over a vowel indicates a high pitch; a vowel with no accent has a medium pitch; and the grave accent ` over a vowel indicates a low pitch.

1. Opening

1. All topics summarized in this introduction will be discussed more fully in succeeding chapters, with references.

2. This is the basic definition commonly used by Yoruba scholars. Yoruba is one of the Kwa languages, which are themselves part of the Niger-Congo family.

3. Peel, "Cultural Work"; his *Religious Encounter,* esp. ch. 10; Smith, *Kingdoms,* 6–9 and ch. 2; Lovejoy, "Yoruba Factor"; Falola, *Yoruba Gurus,* ch. 1; and Arifalo and Ogen, *The Yoruba,* 7–8, for this paragraph. The emergence of a shared Yoruba identity was assisted by the sense of cultural commonality that developed among Yoruba-speaking slaves who had been carried to the New World; when they returned to the region, they carried that feeling with them.

4. S. Johnson, *History,* xix.

5. Other Yoruba speakers living to the north and northeast of these provinces were included within the British province of Ilorin, which formed part of the North-ern Region. The Western Region also included Benin and Delta Provinces, on its eastern side, whose inhabitants were not Yoruba speakers.

6. Eltis, "Diaspora." For slavery, see pp. 46–53 amd 113–17, this volume.

7. Kuczynski, *Demographic Survey,* I, 576. For below, see *Population Census, 1963, Western Region,* I, i, and *Lagos,* I, i, which give figures for 1952 as well.

8. Both the western and the eastern Yoruba were divided into northern and southern clusters. Linguistic analysis suggests a far more complex set of relationships among the various Yoruba groups.

9. The northeastern Yoruba are sometimes called the "Okun" people from their form of greeting.

10. For examples of important new work, see Olukoju's "Introduction" and the essays in Olukoju, Apata, and Akinwumi, eds., *Northeast Yorubaland;* O. Akin-wumi, "Okun Yoruba"; Ogen, "Geography"; his "The Ikale"; O. Ojo, "More Than"; his "Slavery"; his "Warfare, Slavery"; his "Writing Yoruba Female Farmers"; and Olu-wakemi Adesina, "Gender Relations." For the early history of the various regions, see Obayemi, "The Yoruba."

2. Sources and Questions

1. For a discussion prepared in the early 1970s, see Biobaku, *Sources.*

2. NAI Epe District Officer's CrimRB, 1925–1926, 281–83. For below, see OAU Abeokuta MixC, CivRB, 1907–1909, 43–44.

3. Falola, *Yoruba Gurus,* 15. For below, see Arifalo and Ogen, *The Yoruba,* 1–3.

4. For examples of the many fine studies of African women in other settings, see Allman and Tashjian, "*I Will Not Eat Stone*"; Clark, *Onions;* Cooper, *Marriage;* Jeater, *Marriage, Perversion;* Schmidt, *Peasants, Traders;* Sheldon, *Pounders of Grain;* and those cited in notes 23 and 34 below.

5. These are standard academic definitions. The Yoruba themselves, however, commonly use the term "patriarchy" to refer to the power and influence that fathers have over their children, not to the relation between men and women.

6. Oluwole, *Womanhood,* esp. 9–11. Daramola showed that women are presented in some Yoruba proverbs as complex, strong, and powerful, as knowledgeable and superior to men, and as hardworking and productive ("Women").

7. Guyer, "Women's Farming," esp. 35.

8. Sudarkasa, "'Status of Women'," esp. 35–36. These scholars did not suggest that the Yoruba had a "dual-sex system" like that found among the Igbo people of southeastern Nigeria (e.g., Nzegwu, "Gender Equality," and cf. Amadiume, *Male Daughters*).

9. Oyewumi, "Making History."

10. For acceptance of some of her ideas, see, e.g., Okome, "African Women and Power," and cf. Bakare-Yusuf, "Beyond Determinism."

11. For this paragraph and the next, including quotations, see Bakare-Yusuf,

"Yoruba's Don't Do Gender," an on-line essay without page numbers. Peel objected to Oyewumi's distorted linguistic analysis and her excessive emphasis on seniority ("Gender"); members of a panel about Oyewumi's book chaired by Molara Ogundipe-Leslie at a meeting of the African Studies Association in Washington, D.C., 5–8 Dec. 2002, likewise expressed some strong reservations about the study.

12. For the continuation of Yoruba patterns among slaves in the western hemisphere, see, e.g., Falola and Childs, eds., *Yoruba Diaspora,* pts. 2 and 3.

13. See, e.g., an anonymous online submission posted 3 June 2005 to "The Nigerian Village Square Bookshelf."

14. H. and M. Drewal, *Gelede;* Abiodun, "Identity"; M. Drewal, *Yoruba Ritual;* and see pp. 190–205, this volume.

15. Sekoni, "Yoruba Market Dynamics."

16. Babatunde, *Critical Study,* ch. 6, for this paragraph. Post-menopausal women were seen as closely equivalent to men in terms of function and status.

17. See pp. 144–46, this volume.

18. See pp. 205–10, this volume.

19. A different set of expectations applied to working-class British women, who often had to work to help support their families and whose labor was needed in factories and by wealthier households.

20. The combination of indigenous Yoruba attitudes and practices with British ones has been described as "double patriarchy" (Ajayi-Soyinka, "Black Feminist Criticism," and her "Who Is Afraid").

21. Okome, "African Women and Power." For below, see Trager, *Yoruba Hometowns,* 268–72.

22. The technical term for a marriage in which the husband takes more than one wife is "polygyny," but in this study we will use the word "polygamy," which is commonly employed by Yoruba scholars.

23. See, e.g., Callaway, *Gender, Culture,* for European women in Nigeria; for women in other African settings, see Jeater, "British Empire"; Hanretta, "Women, Marginality"; Etienne, "Women and Men"; Hodgson and McCurdy, eds., *"Wicked" Women;* Allman, Geiger, and Musisi, eds., *Women in African Colonial Histories;* Levine, ed., *Gender and Empire;* and Burns, *Colonial Habits.*

24. Levine, "Preface" to *Gender and Empire,* vii.

25. E.g., Shields, "Palm Oil."

26. Mba, *Nigerian Women,* 54, but see also 67.

27. Byfield, "Women, Marriage," esp. 27–28. For below, see pp. 100–106, this volume.

28. Mba, *Nigerian Women,* 290–91.

29. Oyewumi, *Invention,* ch. 4, esp. 128.

30. Ibid., 152.

31. Denzer, "Yoruba Women," 36, for this paragraph, including the quotation below.

32. For historiographic summaries, see B. Awe, "Writing Women," and Okeke, "Reconfiguring Tradition."

33. E.g., Sidney Mintz wrote, "Probably no people on earth has institutionalized

women's rights to engage in trading activity so fully as have the Yoruba. Yoruba women not only have a wholly acknowledged right to trade and to use their capital as they see fit, but they also dominate the internal market system" ("Men, Women," esp. 260). Elizabeth Eames spoke of "the extraordinary economic and domestic roles of ordinary women in southwestern Nigeria" ("Why the Women," 260). Karin Barber, who lived and taught for many years in Nigeria and probably knew the Yoruba language as well as any outsider can, commented, "Yoruba women have been rightly noted in the scholarly literature for their success as traders and their unusual degree of economic and personal autonomy" ("Going Too Far," 76).

34. See, e.g., Mann, "Women, Landed Property," esp. 682, for this and below. Mann summarizes but disagrees with such works as Robertson, *Sharing the Same Bowl,* E. F. White, *Sierra Leone's Settler Women,* Ifeka-Moller, "Female Militancy," and Mba, *Nigerian Women.*

35. B. Awe, "Introduction," in B. Awe, ed., *Nigerian Women,* esp. x.

36. Afonja, "Changing Modes."

37. Belasco, *Entrepreneur,* 60.

38. Mann, "Women, Landed Property;" her "Owners, Slaves"; and her *Slavery.*

39. Barber, "Going Too Far." The quotation below is on 81–82.

40. Afonja offered more explicit and thoughtful definitions of the terms "power," "authority," and "control" with reference to Yoruba women, but they are too complex for our analysis ("Women," esp. 136–38).

3. Yorubaland, 1820–1893

1. Demography refers to the study of population patterns, both gross measures like the size of the total population and shaping factors like average age of marriage, number of births per woman, and levels of immigration and emigration.

2. Smith, *Kingdoms,* chs. 3 and 7–9; Atanda, *New Oyo Empire,* ch. 1; Law, *Oyo Empire;* and Ajayi, "Aftermath." The empire and city are called Old Oyo, to distinguish them from the new city called Oyo founded later by emigrants who moved farther south within Yorubaland.

3. Ajayi, "Aftermath," 136.

4. Smith, *Kingdoms,* ch. 10; Law, *Oyo Empire,* chs. 12–14; Atanda, *New Oyo Empire,* 28–42; and Ajayi, "Aftermath."

5. Law, *Oyo Empire,* 278.

6. Ajayi, "Aftermath."

7. Babayemi, "Oyo Palace," and, for this and below, Imoagene, *Social Mobility,* 3–17.

8. Ogen, "The Ikale," esp. 80–95.

9. Ajayi, "Aftermath," and Falola, *Political Economy,* ch. 2

10. Lloyd, *Political Development,* esp. preface, 23, and 47–48.

11. Peel, *Religious Encounter,* 64–65. For below, see Ayandele, "Yoruba Civil Wars."

12. Cowries are a type of shell from the Indian Ocean that were used as a trading currency throughout Africa (Adebayo, *"Kose-e-mani,"* esp. 147–52).

13. Ayandele, "Yoruba Civil Wars," 58–59. For below, see O. Ojo, "Warfare, Slavery," ch. 4.

14. Ajayi, "Aftermath," and Oguntomisin, "Refugees." For below, see Mabogunje, *Yoruba Towns,* 10.

15. Oguntomisin, "Refugees." Ibadan was established around 1830; by 1858 it already had nearly a hundred thousand dwellers (Falola, *Political Economy,* ch. 2, esp. 32).

16. Shields, "Palm Oil," 217–21.

17. Biobaku, *The Egba,* 38–44. For below, see Afolayan, "Women."

18. Watson, *Civil Disorder,* 46, and see pp. 134–41 and 221–22, this volume.

19. Matory, *Sex and the Empire,* 13–22.

20. Madam Tinubu and Efunsetan Aniwura: see pp. 134–40, this volume.

21. Mabogunje, *Urbanization,* 76–90, Ajayi, "Aftermath," and Ajayi and Smith, *Yoruba Warfare,* ch. 3.

22. Bascom, "Urbanization," and his "Early Historical Evidence."

23. Eades, *The Yoruba Today,* 43–45.

24. Law, *Oyo Empire,* 9. For below, see Ayandele, "Yoruba Civil Wars," and Ajayi, "Aftermath."

25. Ogen, "Geography," and his "The Ikale," esp. ch. 7. Ogen commented, "The Ikale simply did not feel any need for political centralisation and urbanisation basically because they were largely insulated against the destructive effects of the nineteenth century Yoruba inter-state wars which triggered off the rush for urbanisation by virtually all the belligerent Yoruba states" ("Geography," 219).

26. Biobaku, *The Egba,* 18.

27. *Church Missionary Intelligencer,* 6 (1855): 250.

28. Rev. J. Smith described the farm villages surrounding Ibadan as a cluster of farmers' huts "nestled in the bush": *Church Missionary Gleaner,* 18 (1868): 16.

29. Fadipe, *Sociology,* ch. 5.

30. Ajayi, "Aftermath," 149. For below, see *Church Missionary Intelligencer,* 6 (1855): 251.

31. Delany, "Official Report," 82–83.

32. Mabogunje, *Urbanization,* 91.

33. *Church Missionary Gleaner,* New Series, 8 (1858): 25–26. The author was probably Rev. H. Townsend.

34. Delany, "Official Report," 84, for this and below. Abeokuta's walls extended 27 miles in circumference, he said.

35. S. Johnson, *History,* 92, and Falola, *Political Economy,* 30. For below, see Mabogunje, *Urbanization,* 96–98.

36. Mabogunje, *Urbanization,* ch. 9.

37. Sudarkasa, *Where Women Work,* 57. For women's roles as traders, see pp. 127–34, this volume.

38. Callaway, "Spatial Domains," esp. 176.

39. Bowen, *Adventures,* 296–97, and cf. *Church Missionary Gleaner,* New Series, 8 (1858): 25–26.

40. *Church Missionary Gleaner,* 20 (1893): 101.

41. Ibid., 100.

42. Delany, "Official Report," 82–83, for this and the quotation below.

43. Bowen, *Adventures,* 297.

44. By the Yoruba method of reckoning, which counts both first and last days, these markets were held every five or nine days. For below, see Bowen, *Adventures,* 297.

45. Clarke, *Travels,* 267.

46. E.g., CMS, *Extracts from the Annual Letters of the Missionaries, 1888–1889,* 279.

47. CMS, *Extracts from the Annual Letters of the Missionaries, 1886–1887,* 308.

48. For nineteenth-century transport, see Ogunremi, *Counting the Camels,* esp. chs. 4, 5, and 7. In most parts of Yorubaland, animals larger than goats generally died from insect-borne diseases.

49. Bowen, *Adventures,* 307. For below, see Ogen, "Geography," and Kehinde, "Women."

50. Falola, "Yoruba Caravan System."

51. Eades, *The Yoruba Today,* 80–81.

52. Bowen, *Adventures,* 307–308. For below, see Clarke, *Travels,* 265.

53. Peel, *Religious Encounter,* ch. 4, and Morton-Williams, "Outline." For below, *Olódùmarè* means "owner of the universe"; *Olórun* means "owner of the heavens." For women's religious roles, see pp. 190–200, this volume.

54. Olajubu, *Women,* 2. For below, see Ilesanmi, "Significance of the Myths," who quotes a traditional saying: "God created the world in binary forms: day and night, hill and valley, male and female, the aged and the young, the house and the farm, the king and the chief, the sun and the moon, the resident and the visitor, the initiated and the uninitiated, the human and the brute, the husband and the wife, the slave and the son" (29).

55. Afonja, "Women," esp. 141.

56. Ogen, "The Ikale," 336. For below, see Olajubu, *Women,* 105–10.

57. Apter, *Black Critics,* 98. Barber suggests that this attitude paralleled the Yoruba belief that a human being could rise to power if he or she acquired a sufficient following of other people ("How Man Makes God").

58. For women's role in Yoruba religion and for witchcraft, see pp. 190–200 and 205–10, this volume.

59. Peel, "Gender," and his *Religious Encounter,* 88–92, for this paragraph.

60. See, e.g., Peel, *Religious Encounter,* 80–85 and 259–64, and Fadipe, *Sociology,* 292–300, for this paragraph. For women and the supernatural, see pp. 190–200 and 205–10, this volume.

61. Peel, *Religious Encounter,* 190–94, and Crowder, *Story of Nigeria,* 31–36 and 71–79, for this paragraph.

62. "*Ayé la báfá, ayé la bámàle, òsán gangan nìgbàgbó wolé dé.*"

63. Fadipe, *Sociology,* 290–92. Fadipe's was the first Ph.D. thesis written by an African (Arifalo and Ogen, *The Yoruba,* 20).

64. Gbadamosi, *Growth of Islam,* ch. 2. For below, see Adeleye, "Impacts."

65. Peel, *Religious Encounter,* ch. 7.

66. Ayandele, "Britain," and Ajayi, "Aftermath."

67. The account in this and the next four paragraphs unless otherwise noted is drawn from Ajayi, *Christian Missions,* esp. chs. 2–4 and 6–8; Ayandele, *Missionary Impact,* esp. chs. 2 and 5; and Crowder, *Story of Nigeria,* 111–18, 132–38, and 194–95.

68. Eades, *The Yoruba Today,* 28–29.

69. Ajayi, *Christian Missions,* ch. 8, and Ijagbemi, *Christian Missionary Activity,* esp. ch. 2. The Presbyterians worked mainly in eastern Nigeria (Johnson, *Of God and Maxim Guns*).

70. Groves, *Planting of Christianity,* vol. 2, 50–64, Denzer, "Abolition," and Olajubu, *Women,* 50–51.

71. E.g., of seven European recruits to the CMS Yoruba Mission in 1853, three died within the first 12 months and a fourth was sent home due to illness (Groves, *Planting of Christianity,* vol. 2, 54).

72. Peel, *Religious Encounter,* 249–50.

73. Ayandele, "Colonial Church." In 1868, Lagos's population of around 27,000 included 15,000 pagans, 8,000 Muslims, and 4,000 Christians; in 1891, the city contained around 54,000 pagans, 21,000 Muslims, and 10,000 Christians (Echeruo, *Victorian Lagos,* 82).

74. Gbadamosi, *Growth of Islam,* 127. For below, see Peel, *Religious Encounter,* 242.

75. Peel, *Aladura,* esp. ch. 3.

76. Ayandele, *Missionary Impact,* ch. 6; Ajayi, *Christian Missions,* chs. 7–8; and Peel, *Religious Encounter,* 142–44.

77. Ayandele, *Missionary Impact,* chs. 7–8, and his "Colonial Church."

78. Ajayi, *Christian Missions,* ch. 5; M. Crowder, *Story of Nigeria,* 118–19; and Gbadamosi, *Growth of Islam.* Western education and women's involvement in it are considered more fully on pp. 68–78, this volume.

79. CMS CA2 o 58 (Samuel Johnson), 28 Feb. 1876, and CA2 o 78 (Charles Phillips, Jr.), 7 Nov. 1877 and 11 Jan. 1878.

80. Eades, *The Yoruba Today,* 149–53, and Denzer, "Domestic Science Training," for this paragraph unless otherwise noted.

81. CMS, *Extracts from the Annual Letters of the Missionaries, 1886–1887,* 207, *1894–1895,* 204 and 215–16, *1897,* 11, and *1898,* 265.

82. As cited by Echeruo, *Victorian Lagos,* 50–51.

83. Mann, "Dangers," and her *Marrying Well,* ch. 4.

84. Echeruo, *Victorian Lagos,* 53 and ch. 4 for this and below. For music, see also pp. 202–203, this volume.

85. F. Coker, *A Lady,* 14–19, 24–25, and the photos on 2–3. After her marriage to Sir Kitoyi Ajasa, a lawyer and later politician from a returnee background in Dahomey who had moved to Lagos, she ran a hostel for children attending school in Lagos.

86. NAI Coker Papers 1/6/1. For below, see ibid., 3/7/61.

87. Ibid., 1/4/2.

88. Crowder, *Story of Nigeria,* ch. 10, for this paragraph.

89. O. Ojo, "Warfare, Slavery," esp. ch. 2.

90. Lovejoy, "Yoruba Factor," and Fage, "Slaves and Society," for this and below.

91. Hopkins, "Lagos Strike."

92. For a helpful introduction, see Childs and Falola, "Yoruba Diaspora." For below, see Biobaku, *The Egba*, 12–13.

93. O'Hear, "Enslavement."

94. Biobaku, *The Egba*, 34. For below, see *Church Missionary Intelligencer*, 6 (1855): 250–51.

95. Eltis, "Diaspora," for this and below.

96. Lovejoy, "Yoruba Factor," for this and below.

97. Of about 134,000 slaves arriving in the port of Havana, Cuba, between 1800 and 1820, most of whom came from the Bight of Benin, 52% were adult men or teen-aged boys; 22% were adult women or teen-aged girls; and 26% were children of no more than 10 years (Klein, "African Women"). Between 1811 and 1867, adult males constituted 46% of the slaves exported from the Bight of Benin, plus 21% adult women, 22% boys, and 12% girls (Eltis and Engerman, "Fluctuations").

98. Law, *Oyo Empire*, vii–viii.

99. Hodder and Ikwu, *Markets in West Africa*, 33–35.

100. Ajayi, "Ijaye War," for this and below. The quotation below is on 124.

101. For a broader discussion, see Denzer, "Abolition."

102. Oroge, "Institution of Slavery," esp. ch. 3, and see pp. 113–17, this volume, for women as slaves and mistresses.

103. A French traveler to Abeokuta noted in 1881 that he had encountered whole families of slaves who had been captured in war and put to work in the fields (Holley, *Voyage*, 36–37).

104. Oroge, "Institution of Slavery," chs. 1–3; Agiri, "Slavery"; and Fadipe, *Sociology*, 180–89.

105. Ogen, "The Ikale," chs. 5–6, esp. 330 and 348.

106. Falola, "Slavery."

107. Mabogunje, *Urbanization*, 93.

108. J. F. Ade Ajayi, "History and Society" (Univ. of Lagos Convocation Lecture, Lagos: Univ. of Lagos Press, 2004) 2–3, as cited by Ogen, "The Ikale," 345.

109. Aderibigbe, "Trade," 191, for this and below.

110. Biobaku, *The Egba*, 59, for this and the quotation below.

111. Ajayi, *Christian Missions*, 105–107.

112. Crowther to Venn, 4 Mar. 1857, as cited by ibid., 105.

113. White to H. Venn, 2 Feb. 1866, as cited by Peel, *Religious Encounters*, 69.

114. CMS, *Extracts from the Annual Letters of the Missionaries, 1888–1889*, 283–84.

115. For this and the next two paragraphs unless otherwise noted, see Oroge, "Institution of Slavery" (which highlights the contrast with chattel slavery, e.g., on iv–v); Falola, "Slavery"; Lovejoy, "Slavery"; and Ajisafe Moore, *Laws and Customs*, 11, 54–55, and 59–60.

116. Eades, *The Yoruba Today*, 148.

117. Campbell, "Pilgrimage," 191.

118. Falola, *Political Economy*, 63–64, and Hinderer, *Seventeen Years*, 61–62. One

of Ibadan's war chiefs in the 1830s had thousands of slaves, and in 1877 a missionary estimated that there were more slaves than freeborn people in Ibadan (Falola, "Slavery").

119. Fadipe, *Sociology*, 117.

120. See Shields, "Palm Oil," 272–75, and pp. 84–94 and 113–17, this volume, for examples involving female slaves. For below, see O. Ojo, "Slavery"; his "Warfare, Slavery," 181–98; and Ogen, "The Ikale," 331.

121. PRO CO 147/21, no. 49, encl., as cited by Shields, "Women and Slavery," 14.

122. Hopkins, "Lagos Strike," and CMS, *Extracts from the Annual Letters of the Missionaries, 1897*, 206–207, where a native minister in Abeokuta commented that times were hard because "we are passing through a state of transition from slave labour to free labour." Trade was at a standstill, in part due to bands of former slaves who were extorting money from travelers.

123. Adewoye, "Native Court," and NAAb E.C.R. 1/1, Egba Native Administration Rules and Bye-Laws, 1901–1933, 3. For later cases, see pp. 114–15, this volume.

124. Eltis, "Diaspora."

125. Fage, "Slavery and the Slave Trade," and his "Slaves and Society," for general discussions.

126. CMS CA2 o 61 (King), 7 April 1850.

127. For local people's involvement in slaving, see Ogen, "The Ikale," chs. 5–6.

128. See pp. 115–17, this volume.

129. Ofonagoro, *Trade and Imperialism*, chs. 2–3; Flint, "Economic Change"; and Eades, *The Yoruba Today*, 28, for this paragraph and the next.

130. Flint, "Economic Change," 391

131. Buchanan and Pugh, *Land and People*, 132, and Bascom, *The Yoruba*, 19, for this and below.

132. Delany, "Official Report," 72–73, for this and below.

133. Ekundare, *Economic History*, 50, and McPhee, *Economic Revolution*, 30–32. McPhee, who wrote in the mid-1920s, described the advertising gambit that suggested that by buying a particular company's candles (which were made from palm oil), a person would help to stop the slave trade as "a typical Victorian combination of good business and good morality" (31, note 2).

134. For women's roles in palm production, see pp. 133–35, this volume.

135. Ajayi, *Christian Missions*, 18–19.

136. McPhee, *Economic Revolution*, 30–31, and Buchanan and Pugh, *Land and People*, 132, for this and below.

137. Ekundare, *Economic History*, 51; McPhee, *Economic Revolution*, 33–36; Flint, "Economic Change"; Hopkins, *Economic History*, 131–34; and Lynn, "West African Palm Oil." Exports from West Africa to Britain, which in 1831 totaled only 163,000 hundredweight, had reached 500,000 hundredweight by 1845 and mounted to an even higher level in 1855 (Ekundare, 51, and McPhee, 33).

138. Hopkins, *Economic History*, 126.

139. Shields, "Palm Oil," 67–68, citing Clarke, *Travels*, 274; Campbell,

"Pilgrimage," 51; and R. H. Stone, *In Afric's Forest and Jungle; or Six Years among the Yorubans* (Edinburgh, 1900), 24.

140. Berry, *Cocoa,* ch. 2, and see convenient summaries in Eades, *The Yoruba Today,* 65–66, and Falola, "The Ijaye."

141. Berry, *Cocoa,* 41–43, and Babalola, "Colonialism."

142. Hopkins, *Economic History,* 127–28, for this paragraph.

143. Some scholars have argued that the transition had serious consequences for many states, creating instability that facilitated British imperial intervention. Others question whether there was any meaningful crisis, proposing that the transition may be better described as a gradual process of adaptation without revolution. See, e.g., Lynn, "West African Palm Oil," and Lovejoy and Richardson, "The Initial 'Crisis'."

144. Hopkins, *Economic History,* 125–26. Groundnuts (peanuts) were grown in other parts of West Africa.

4. Colonial Yorubaland, 1893–1960

1. Denzer, "Yoruba Women," 14.

2. Asiwaju, *Western Yorubaland,* chs. 3–6, and Crowder, *Story of Nigeria,* ch. 14.

3. Because Lagos was a Crown Colony, an African resident who wanted to make a request or submit a complaint to the government could petition the governor directly and, if unhappy with his decision, appeal to the Privy Council in London; people living in other parts of the Protectorate had to work through British administrative officers in their own regions.

4. Adewoye, *Judicial System,* esp. chs. 5–6. Native Courts were not introduced into some areas until the early 1920s, and further judicial reforms were implemented between 1933 and 1954 (ibid., ch. 7).

5. OAU Ilero NC CivRB, 1931–1935, 79. For *Ìyálódes,* see pp. 221–25, this volume. For below, see OAU Ife Itaogbolu Customary Court, Civil Record Book, 1958–1959, 76–86.

6. Rhodes House GB 0162 MSS.Afr.s.1836 (M. C. Atkinson), 36–37; also in Atkinson, *African Life,* 27–29.

7. E.g., Mamdani, *Citizen and Subject,* chs. 4 and 5, and his *Politics and Class Formation,* esp. 127. For below, see, e.g., Jeater, *Marriage, Perversion;* Chanock, *Law, Custom;* and Hawkins, *Writing and Colonialism.*

8. Mba, *Nigerian Women,* 52–58. For marriage and divorce, see pp. 96–106, this volume.

9. For women and property, see pp. 117–20, this volume.

10. Adewoye, "Native Court," for this and below.

11. Crowder, *Story of Nigeria,* ch. 15, for this and the next paragraph.

12. For women's roles, see pp. 226–34, this volume.

13. It would be interesting to trace these patterns by analyzing how people were sworn in local courts. Followers of traditional religion were sworn on iron or a cutlass; Christians on the Bible or occasionally a rosary; Muslims on the Koran. For women and religion, see pp. 190–200, this volume.

14. Blair, *Abeokuta,* 14.

15. Caldwell, Orubuloye, and Caldwell, "Destabilization," for this and below.

16. Peel, "Between Crowther and Ajayi," and Apata, "Women Cults." For the disparaging comments of a Sudan Interior Missionary working among the Yagba in northeastern Yorubaland in 1908, see Ademiluka, "Impact."

17. *Population Census, 1963, Western Region,* 2, 102. Of city dwellers, 44% were Christian and 51% Muslim (ibid.).

18. Matory, "Rival Empires." For below, see Ola, "Foundations."

19. Olusanya, "Charlotte Olajumoke Obasa."

20. Crowder, *Story of Nigeria,* 190–91.

21. Ofonagoro, *Trade and Imperialism,* chs. 5–6, for this and below. For railways, see also Omosini, "Railway Projects," and Oyemakinde, "Railway Construction."

22. Oyemakinde, "Impact"; his "Michael Imoudu"; his "Nigerian General Strike"; his "Railway Workers"; and Lindsay, *Working with Gender,* esp. chs. 2, 4, and 5.

23. Adebayo, "*Kose-e-mani.*"

24. Babalola, "Colonialism," and Asiwaju, *Western Yorubaland,* chs. 7–8.

25. Hodder and Ikwu, *Markets in West Africa,* 41–42; Ofonagoro, *Trade and Imperialism,* ch. 6; and Olutayo Adesina, "Adebisi Sanusi Giwa," for this and below.

26. For women's agricultural roles, see pp. 120–25, this volume.

27. Odunlami, "Women and Palm Oil"; Guyer, "Food, Cocoa"; Ogen, "Geography"; and his "The Ikale," ch. 6.

28. Neumark, *Foreign Trade,* 157, and Buchanan and Pugh, *Land and People,* 132–35.

29. Between 1931 and 1937, for example, the price for a ton of palm kernels ranged from just over £5 to more than £14.5 (Ojo, "More Than," Table 1).

30. Berry, *Cocoa,* 44–45. For below, see Bascom, *The Yoruba,* 23. For additional quantitative information, see Neumark, *Foreign Trade,* 157; McPhee, *Economic Revolution,* 40–44; Forde, "Rural Economies," 98–101; Galletti et al., *Nigerian Cocoa Farmers,* chs. 1–4 and 7–15; and Buchanan and Pugh, *Land and People,* 149–52.

31. Babalola, "Colonialism," 51–53. By the 1940s, the British-American Tobacco Company had persuaded a few farmers to raise tobacco for its cigarette factory in Ibadan.

32. Mba, *Nigerian Women,* 45. For women's protests against taxation, see pp. 226–34, this volume.

33. Babalola, "Colonialism," 51.

34. Sudarkasa, *Where Women Work,* 41. For additional snapshots of markets in small communities in Lagos's hinterland in 1927–1928, see RH GB 0162 MSS. Afr.s.1863 (I. F. W. Schofield), box 6, vol. 1, sheets 6 (Agege Market) and 8 (Ojo Market).

35. Hodder, "Rural Periodic."

36. For female traders, see pp. 148–64, this volume.

37. Hodder, "Yoruba Rural Market."

38. Schiltz, "Habitus."

39. Sudarkasa, *Where Women Work,* 63–64.

40. Hodder, "Yoruba Rural Market."

41. *Nigerian Chronicle,* 28 Jan. 1910, 5.

42. CMS, *Letters from the Front, 1912,* 93, and see pp. 205–208, this volume. For below, see *Nigerian Tribune,* 10 Mar. 1950, 8.

43. See pp. 127–33 and 148–64, this volume. For below, see Rouse, "Socio-Economic Position," 70–71.

44. Hodder, "Yoruba Rural Market."

45. *Daily Service,* 7 Sep. 1960, 11; Mba, *Nigerian Women,* 193–95; and Forde, *Yoruba-Speaking Peoples,* 8. In most seasons of the year it was rare for more than 5% of Akinyele's market traders to be male (Hodder, "Yoruba Rural Market").

46. See pp. 226–34, this volume.

47. Oyemakinde, "Pullen Marketing Scheme."

48. *Nigerian Tribune,* 3 Mar. 1950, 2. For below, see *Southern Nigeria Defender,* 14 May 1952, 1.

49. *Southern Nigeria Defender,* 15 April 1952, 1. For below, see NAI Epe District Officer's CrimRB, 1925–1926, 136, and *Daily Comet,* 16 August 1947, 4.

50. *Nigerian Tribune,* 3 Mar. 1953, 1.

51. Ekundare, *Economic History,* 351. For below, see *Population Census, 1963, Western Region,* I, i, and *Lagos,* I, i and 1 (figures for Western Nigeria, minus the Mid-West, plus Lagos). In 1963, 94% of the total Western Region population was Yoruba (*Western Region,* 2, 53).

52. *Population Census, 1963, Western Region,* 2, 8, and *Lagos,* I, i.

53. The term is *ará oko* (Lloyd, *Power and Independence,* 32–33).

54. Bascom, "Urbanization," for this and below. In 1963, Ibadan had 627,000 people and Lagos 665,000, in addition to the suburbs that were now growing up around them (*Population Census, 1963, Western Region,* I, 56, and *Lagos,* I, i).

55. Mabogunje, *Yoruba Towns,* for this paragraph.

56. Ibid., 10.

57. For problems with water, transport, and electricity in Lagos, see Olukoju, *Infrastructure Development.*

58. See, e.g., NAI Oyo Prof 2/1 OY 1188, a file from the 1920s about a new housing/market development near Ife designed as "a European reserve" in which the Africans could come to trade but not live.

59. Ekundare, *Economic History,* 356–59, for this paragraph.

60. Mba, *Nigerian Women,* 61–66, and Ajayi, *Christian Missions,* 138–39.

61. Lloyd, *Power and Independence,* 120.

62. *Nigerian Pioneer,* 21 May 1920, 9.

63. Denzer, "Yoruba Women," 19–20, and RH GB 0162 MSS.Lugard, part 2, 58/1, item 1, 21–24, for this and below.

64. Okeke-Ihejirika, *Negotiating Power,* 59.

65. Denzer, "Domestic Science Training," for this paragraph.

66. Ibid., 122.

67. Denzer, "Domestic Science Training," for this paragraph unless otherwise noted.

68. CMS, *Extracts from the Annual Letters of the Missionaries, 1903,* 197, and *1907,* 52.

69. *Egba Administrative Bulletin,* 2 (1927): 48–49. Boys received prizes in English

Composition, English Spelling and Dictation, Translation, Arithmetic, Handwriting, Hygiene and Sanitation, and Map Drawing.

70. Denzer, "Domestic Science Training."

71. Mann, "Dangers," 53, for this and the quotations below.

72. Archives, Dike Libr., Macaulay Collection, box 6, file 3, item 14.

73. For their work, see pp. 170–75, this volume.

74. Denzer, "Domestic Science Training." Denzer pointed out that the first British Lady Medical Officers in Nigeria had had military experience during World War I; Lady Ademola's educational choices were influenced by Dame Margery Perham, the distinguished British scholar of African administration; and Lady Clifford, who encouraged the founding of Queen's College, was a well-known writer of romance novels as well as the wife of the British governor (personal communication).

75. Denzer, "Domestic Science Training."

76. Denzer, "Yoruba Women," 22, and see pp. 170–75, this volume. For below, see, e.g., *West African Pilot*, 7 Apr. 1941, 2.

77. For a sample (male) apprenticeship contract, see Lloyd, "Craft Organization." For below, see C. Johnson, "Nigerian Women."

78. F. Coker, *A Lady*, 20–28. After her marriage to Moronfolu Abayomi, she taught music at Queen's College, Lagos, and was active in women's education, the Girl Guides, and women's political activity (ibid., chs. 5–7).

79. Archives, Gandhi Libr., Solanke Collection, e.g., box 11, file 7, item 20; box 11, file 8, item 31; and box 43, vol. 4, no. 6 of 1935, 1, and vol. 4, no. 7 of 1935, 32.

80. *Egba Administrative Bulletin*, 2 (1927): 46.

81. Denzer, "Domestic Science Training." Although Queen's College offered lip service to domestic science, to win support from the government, its principal and teachers always wanted to train future leaders (LaRay Denzer, personal communication).

82. *Annual Report of the Education Department, Nigeria, 1931*, 35–36.

83. *Nigerian Daily Times*, 30 Aug. 1948, 3. For below, see "Reminiscences Panel," Chief (Mrs.) Comfort Oredugba, the first Nigerian female mathematician.

84. Gbadamosi, "Establishment." For below, see C. Johnson, "Nigerian Women." Some hesitancy was expressed in the papers about the education of Muslim girls, for fear that after leaving school they would be sexually loose; a response pointed out that men are generally to blame for the seduction of girls (*Nigerian Daily Telegraph*, 6 June 1933, 7, and 15 June 1933, 4–5).

85. *The Comet*, 11 Oct. 1941, 11.

86. C. Johnson, "Nigerian Women," and see "Reminiscences Panel," Alhaja Humuani Alaga, merchant and women's leader. The Isabatudeen Girl's Grammar School in Ibadan opened its doors to 66 girls in 1963, accepting both Muslim and Christian girls; in 1967 it was approved to receive government grants-in-aid.

87. Female schooling progressed more slowly in some eastern areas, however. See, e.g., T. Ojo, "Impact," 26–31, which describes the low fraction of girls in Ondo schools during the 1930s.

88. Adewoye, "Native Court," 20.

89. NAAb E.C.R. 1/2/18, Complaints RB, 1945–1946, 27. For below, see Adedeji, *Metamorphosis*, ch. 2.

90. For their careers, see pp. 175–84, this volume.

91. *Annual Report of the Education Department, Nigeria, 1931*, 35–36.

92. *Nigerian Daily Times*, 16 Aug. 1948, 1 and 5.

93. *West African Pilot*, 19 Sep. 1955, 1. Of those, three married women and three unmarried ones were to study in Britain: two for professional teachers' certificates, two in courses for midwives or health visitors, one in the social sciences, and the last in an unspecified course.

94. K. A. Moore, "Story"; Ademola, "Impact"; Denzer, "Yoruba Women"; and Lipide, "Ode to Women," for this paragraph. She later married the first indigenous Chief Justice of the Nigerian Federation.

95. K. A. Moore, "Story," 324.

96. Her achievements were reported with pride in the local press: e.g., *Nigerian Daily Times*, 1 July 1935, 6, and 2 July, 2.

97. Denzer, *Folayegbe M. Akintunde-Ighodalo*, 25–103, and "Reminiscences Panel," Chief (Mrs.) F. M. Akintunde-Ighodalo, first Nigerian female Permanent Secretary, for this paragraph. For her later career, see pp. 177–78, this volume.

98. Denzer, "Yoruba Women," and M. Awe, "Women, Science."

99. LaRay Denzer, personal communication.

100. Ayandele, *Missionary Impact*, 283–85, for this and below.

101. Falola, *Yoruba Gurus*, 10–11. For below, see Arifalo and Ogen, *The Yoruba*, 10–14.

102. For women's recreational and cultural groups, see pp. 210–14, this volume.

103. Fadipe, *Sociology*, 323. For below, see ibid., 315–16.

104. Eades, *The Yoruba Today*, 151–53, and Lloyd, *Power and Independence*, 123–27.

105. For an example of how Western conceptions of gender were absorbed by educated Yoruba, see the review of *Tobias and the Angel*, a play performed in 1953 by the Dramatic Society of the University College at Ibadan and students at the university's Nursing School. British gender stereotypes were used in describing Wole Soyinka, later a Nobel Prize–winning Yoruba playwright, novelist, and poet, who played the leading role, and the young actresses: *Nigerian Tribune*, 21 Feb. 1953, 1.

106. Oyewumi, *Invention*, 154–55.

107. *Nigerian Daily Times*, 14 June 1930, 8, and *West African Pilot*, 5 Jan. 1950, 4.

108. *The Comet*, 11 Jan. 1941, 1. Nutritional supplements like Ovaltine and Marmite were also being promoted in Britain to alleviate the impact of wartime food shortages on children.

109. E.g., *Nigerian Pioneer*, 1920, passim. For below, see ibid., 1930, passim.

110. *Nigerian Daily Times*, 2 Feb. 1940, 7 and 6.

111. Ibid., 8 Feb. 1940, 6, and *West African Pilot*, 6 Jan. 1950, 3.

112. *Nigerian Daily Times*, 3 Feb. 1940, 3.

113. *West African Pilot*, 10 Apr. 1941, 2, and 9 Oct. 1946, 3; *Daily Comet*, 6 May 1946, 3, 7 May 1946, 3, and 9 May 1946, 3.

114. 3 July 1960, 2.

115. See pp. 170–75, this volume. For below, see pp. 175–84.

116. See pp. 226–34, this volume.

117. Oyewumi, *Invention,* 128–36.

5. Family and Marriage

1. Callaway, "Spatial Domains."

2. E.g., Little, *African Women,* and Sheldon, ed., *Courtyards, Markets,* for this and below.

3. Sudarkasa, "Status of Women"; Lloyd, *Power and Independence,* 33–36; Adigun, "Interplay"; and Falola, *Political Economy,* 43–50, for this and the next two paragraphs unless otherwise noted. For cognatic or bi-lineal descent, below, see Ogen, "The Ikale," 1.

4. It is interesting that Yoruba women's prominence in the economy and other aspects of the public world occurred within a largely patrilineal society, and one where married women moved to live with their husbands. The importance of Akan women in Ghana is often thought to be related to their matrilineal and matrilocal system (e.g., Clark, *Onions*).

5. Oguntomisin, "Refugees," and Falola, *Political Economy,* 44–45.

6. Denzer, "Yoruba Women."

7. Sudarkasa, "'Status of Women'," for this paragraph and the next.

8. Fadipe, *Sociology,* 132–33; Lloyd, *Power and Independence,* 37; and see p. 212, this volume.

9. E.g., Berry, *Fathers Work,* chs. 3 and 6, and Adeboye, "Changing Conception."

10. Fadipe, *Sociology,* 97–105, and Krapf-Askari, *Yoruba Towns,* ch. 4. For below, see OAU Ake Grade "A" NC, CrimRB, 1916–1918, 73–76.

11. In some compounds, each wife cooked separately for herself and her children, while in others, women joined together to cook collectively for everyone. That variation makes it difficult to apply Ekejiuba's conception of a "hearth-hold" as a family unit that shares a hearth and may be headed by a woman even if the larger family unit has a male head ("Down to Fundamentals").

12. Shields, "Palm Oil," 254–59. When Abel Kolawole of Shaki was charged by a policeman in the 1950s with assaulting Rachel Gjide, flogging her severely with a belt, he was merely cautioned when the court learned that Rachel was his younger sister and he was punishing her for bad conduct (OAU Shaki NC, CrimRB, 1957–1958, 56).

13. For that concept, as opposed to "wealth in things," see Guyer, "Wealth in People," and Guyer and Belinga, "Wealth in People."

14. Adedeji, *Metamorphosis,* 5.

15. But for "woman-to-woman" marriages, see pp. 85–86, this volume.

16. Fadipe, *Sociology,* 65. Because women commonly traded or pursued other income-generating activities before they wed, their age at first marriage was relatively high, especially in urban settings (Ogunsheye, "Les Femmes").

17. Adigun, "Interplay." For below, see Mann, "Dangers," 40.

18. S. Johnson, *History,* 113–17; Fadipe, *Sociology,* 65–87; and Ajisafe Moore, *Laws*

and Customs, 47–55. For later descriptions, see Babatunde, *Critical Study,* 201–207, and Boparai, "Woman in Family."

19. OAU JudicCo of Ibadan, CrimRB, 1934–1937, 149–50, and Byfield, "Pawns and Politics."

20. E.g., OAU Ake Grade "A" NC, CrimRB, 1916–1918, 234–35, NAI Iba Prof 3/2, 129, NAI Iba Div 1/1 2900, vol. 1, sheet 113; and NAAb E.C.R. 1/2/28, Complaints Comm RB, Book, 1952, R. No. 78496.

21. In Ado Ekiti in 1917, an *Ifá* priest arranged the marriage of a young girl whose father had died (OAU Ado Ekiti NC, CivRB, 1917–1918, 24–25). In a divorce case heard in Abeokuta in 1902, the woman said she disliked her husband, an old man she had married only because his *Ifá* fetish had chosen her while she was a child (NAAb E.C.R. 2/1/3, Civ. and CrimRB No. III, 1902–1903, 31 front).

22. Layonu, *Iyalode Hunmoani Alade,* 17–18 (in 1918); Adedeji, *Metamorphosis,* 105–106 (in 1936).

23. S. Johnson, *History,* 116–17.

24. NAAb E.C.R.2/1/3, Civ. and CrimRB No. III, 1902–1903, 12.

25. Ibid., 14.

26. Ibid., 16.

27. Ijagbemi, *Christian Missionary Activity,* 39–41, and Ademiluka, "Impact," for this paragraph.

28. E.g., OAU Abeokuta MixC, CivRB, 1907–1909, 93–94, and NAI Iba Prof 3/2, 182; Mba, *Nigerian Women,* 55.

29. Ogen, "The Ikale," chs. 5–6. For below, see T. Ojo, "Impact," 1.

30. E.g., in Idanre District in eastern Yorubaland, the future husband took firewood, yams, kola nuts, loaves of pounded yam, antelope legs, a rooster, oil, and pieces of cloth to the woman's father and mother and to the intended bride at various times between the arrangement of a marriage contract and the end of the marriage ceremonies; he was also expected to assist her father in building a house (NAI CSO 26/30052, 56, App. 14).

31. OAU JudicCo of Ibadan, CrimRB, 1934–1937, 29–30.

32. E.g., NAI Oshun Div 1/1 184/213, and Oshun Div 1/1 168, vol. 9, sheet 150.

33. E.g., *The Comet,* 4 Jan. 1941, 2; *Daily Times,* 3 Mar. 1955, 4; *Daily Service,* 7 Sep. 1960, 6; and below.

34. 15 April 1952, 3. That letter triggered many replies in later issues of the paper. For below, see 16 June 1952, 2.

35. 17 Sept. 1954, 4.

36. Adigun, "Interplay"; S. Johnson, *History,* 113–17; and Peel, *Religious Encounter,* 75.

37. Caldwell, Orubuloye, and Caldwell, "Destabilization," and Ayandele, *Missionary Impact,* ch. 11, for this paragraph and the next.

38. Shields, "Palm Oil," 291 and 293, for this and below.

39. Boserup, "Economics."

40. Shields, "Palm Oil," 91–92, and Fadipe, *Sociology,* 115.

41. Adedeji, *Metamorphosis,* 6.

42. OAU Ado Ekiti NC, CrimRB, 1922–1923, 4–7. The women, both of whom

were weavers, lived in the same compound but each had her own area and gate to the outside. For Odo bark and witchcraft in Akure District, see NAI CSO 26/4, 51 (pencil).

43. OAU Modakeke NC, CrimRB, 1941–1944, 93–95. For below, see NAAb E.C.R. 1/2/28, Complaints Comm. RB, 1952, case heard 29 April.

44. NAAb E.C.R. 1/2/28, Complaints Comm. RB, 1952, cases heard 6 May 1952, item 6.

45. For the latter, see, e.g., NAI CSO 26/4, 52 (pencil).

46. NAI CSO 30052, 58.

47. NAAb E.C.R. 1/2/18, Complaints RB, 1945–1946, 12.

48. Hinderer, *Seventeen Years,* 225.

49. OAU Ake Grade "A" NC, CrimRB, 1916–1918, 168–72.

50. OAU Modakeke NC, CrimRB, 1935–1936, 112; OAU JudicCo of Ibadan, CrimRB, 1934–1937, 62–63.

51. OAU Ado [Ekiti] NC, CrimRB, 1922–1923, 157–58.

52. Fadipe, *Sociology,* 90–92.

53. See, e.g., NAI CSO 26/30052, 57, App. 14, for Idanre.

54. E.g., NAAb E.C.R. 1/2/18, Complaints RB, 1945–1946, 1–11, passim.

55. Fadipe, *Sociology,* 90.

56. E.g., "*Òrìṣà bí ìyá kò sí, ìyá là bá máa bọ*" ("Mother is the only deity worthy of worship," literally, "a deity like that of mother is non-existent") and "*Ìyá ni wurà, baba ni dígí*" ("Mother is as precious as gold, while father is precious as glass").

57. Okome, "African Women and Power," and Isola, *Two Yoruba Historical Dramas,* P. Smith's Introduction, for this and below.

58. Sudarkasa, *Where Women Work,* 139.

59. For socialization, see Metiboba, "Changing Roles."

60. Adeniyi, *The Jewel,* 22.

61. See, e.g., F. Coker, *A Lady,* 13; Adeniyi, *The Jewel,* 15; Odebiyi, "Chief Kuforiji-Olubi"; Layonu, *Iyalode Hunmoani Alade,* 14–15; and Adedeji, *Metamorphosis,* 11.

62. Shields, "Palm Oil," 278–79.

63. See pp. 193–96 and 205–10, this volume.

64. S. Johnson, *History,* 115–16, and Ajisafe Moore, *Laws and Customs,* 75–76.

65. Ajisafe Moore, *Laws and Customs,* 11 and 75–76.

66. Peel, *Religious Encounter,* 62, from 1879–1880. For below, see ibid. and NAI Epe District Officer's CrimRB, 1925–1926, 428.

67. E.g., OAU Ado Ekiti NC, CivRB, 1917–1918, 19; NAI Oyo Prof 2/1 247/197 (from 1940); NAAb E.C.R. 1/2/28, Complaints Comm. RB, 1952, cases heard 8 May, item 1; *Nigerian Tribune,* 11 Aug. 1958, 2.

68. Gbadamosi, *Growth of Islam,* 201; Ajisafe Moore, *Laws and Customs,* 55–58; Boparai, "Woman in Family"; and Adeleye, "Impacts." Despite shared religious beliefs and acceptance of polygamy, however, Muslim Yoruba women in Ibadan rarely married Hausa immigrants (Cohen, *Custom and Politics,* 53–54).

69. For court cases involving the conflict between betrothal under native custom vs. marriage under the Marriage Ordinance and questions about what constituted a valid Christian marriage, see *NLR,* XVII, 59, and XVIII, 63.

70. Adigun, "Interplay."

71. Mann, "Dangers"; her *Marrying Well,* ch. 4; and her "Historical Roots," for this paragraph.

72. E.g., Herbert Macaulay had a long-standing affair with Stella Davies during the 1920s (LaRay Denzer, personal communication).

73. Mann, "Historical Roots."

74. The same pattern was true in Britain at the time: middle-class and aristocratic women generally ignored the existence of their husbands' mistresses. For below, see Ogunsheye, "Les Femmes."

75. For a parallel shift among elite Igbo women in eastern Nigeria, see Okeke-Ihejirika, *Negotiating Power,* ch. 2.

76. CMS CA2 o 45 (Dr. Arthur Aylett Harrison), 11 April 1861, and, without mentioning her by name, CA2 o 49 (David Hinderer), 2 Jan. 1860.

77. CMS CA2 o 56 (James Johnson), 18 Sep. 1879, as cited by Byfield, *Bluest Hands,* 23. For below, see Mann, *Marrying Well,* 79.

78. Denzer, "Yoruba Women," and see pp. 170–84, this volume.

79. For a broader discussion of colonialism's affect on female sexuality and marriage, see Jeater, "British Empire."

80. Mba, *Nigerian Women,* 52–58, and Fapohunda, "Nuclear Household," 283. For inheritance under the new ordinances, see pp. 118–19, this volume.

81. Adigun, "Interplay," and Denzer, "Yoruba Women."

82. Adewoye, *Judicial System,* 269–70.

83. Peel, *Religious Encounter,* 244–45.

84. Fadipe, *Sociology,* 90–93. For below, see Byfield, "Women, Marriage."

85. Lindsay, "Domesticity," and her *Working with Gender,* esp. ch. 5.

86. Oyemakinde, "Nigerian General Strike," and Lindsay, "Domesticity"

87. Lindsay, *Working with Gender,* chs. 5–6.

88. Lloyd, *Power and Independence,* 124–27, and Krapf-Askari, *Yoruba Towns,* 147–51.

89. Oyewumi, *Invention,* 132.

90. Lloyd, *Power and Independence,* 126.

91. Galetti et al., *Nigerian Cocoa Farmers,* 71–72.

92. Ayandele, *Missionary Impact,* ch. 11.

93. Adigun, "Interplay," and Eades, "Authority."

94. Laitin, "Conversion."

95. *Colonial Reports—Annual, Nigeria, 1922,* 9, and RH GB 0162 MSS.Afr s.2216 (Barbara Akinyemi), 46–47. Akinyemi, a Scottish nurse who had recently taken a government job in Lagos, commented in 1947 that "from the maternity and child welfare point of view, it seems the second wife idea is a very good thing. It relieves the mother of a young baby (provided they don't both have babies at the same time) to nurse her baby instead of chasing round marketing, cooking, cleaning and looking after older children as our Western mothers have to do. Perhaps that explains why the mothers here breast feed their babies so excellently and without any bother."

96. Fadipe, *Sociology,* 315.

97. Boserup, *Woman's Role,* 38–41 and 47–48, and LaRay Denzer, personal communication.

98. *Lagos Weekly Record,* 31 July 1920, editorial, and *Lagos Daily News,* 20 Jan. 1932, 8, 23 Jan. 1932, 3, and 19 Jan. 1932, 2.

99. *The Comet,* 3 May 1941, 5, and cf. ibid., 8 Nov. 1941, 1, continued on 15 Nov.

100. *The Comet,* 29 May 1943, 14–15.

101. E.g., the distinguished demographer Prof. Akin L. Mabogunje sang the praises of polygamy in 1961. Commenting that "the European mind" finds it impossible to understand the kind of mature, selfless love that leads an established wife to encourage her husband to take a younger one, he concluded, "If polygamy disappears from Africa, it will not be because of any inherent superiority of monogamy" but rather because men cannot afford to support the many children that result from it ("The Market-Woman," 16).

102. E.g., Sudarkasa, *Where Women Work,* 97–116.

103. *Daily Times,* 25 Sep. 1950, 5.

104. Adeleye, "Impacts," Laitin, "Conversion," and Boparai, "Woman in Family."

105. Mba, *Nigerian Women,* 52–58, and Cornwall, "Wayward Women."

106. Ademiluka, "Impact," and Caldwell, Orubuloye, and Caldwell, "Destabilization."

107. NAAb E.C.R. 1/1, Egba Native Administration Rules and Bye-Laws, 1901–33, 37 and 44–45.

108. Such a study is well advanced for the Ikale people of southeastern Yorubaland: Oluwakemi Adesina, "Gender Relations."

109. Adewoye, "Native Court."

110. In the 1960s the rate of legal divorce in Yorubaland was high by African standards (Matory, *Sex and the Empire,* 111).

111. NAAb E.C.R. 1/1, Egba Native Administration Rules and Bye-Laws, 1901–1933, 62.

112. NAI CSO 26/30052, 57, from Idanre.

113. Cornwall, "Wayward Women." For below, see OAU Ilero NC, CivRB, 1931–1935, 36–37.

114. NAAb E.C.R. 1/2/18, Complaints RB, 1945–1946, 2.

115. Levine, "Sexuality, Gender," 141.

116. OAU Ado Ekiti NC, CivRB, 1917–1918, 89. For below, see *Nigerian Tribune,* 3 Mar. 1950, 2.

117. NAAb E.C.R. 2/1/3, Civ. and CrimRB No. III, 1902–1903, 6. For below, see *NLR,* XVII, 108.

118. The Supreme Court of Nigeria heard several cases during the 1930s and early 1940s that defined adultery more precisely (*NLR,* X, 92; XII, 4; and XVI, 103).

119. Oluwakemi Adesina, personal communication. For below, see NAI CSO 26/30052, 59.

120. NAI Oyo Prof 2/1 247/158, concerning a decision in the Bere court.

121. NAI Oshun Div 1/1 184/78.

122. For another example of dramatic language, see NAI Oyo Prof 2/1 247/298, in

which a woman asking for review of an earlier judgment in a divorce suit claimed in 1941 that her husband had "displayed a great deal of bigmanship, having bribed the big-guns of the community who advised him to engage false witnesses against me. . . . Fancy!!" She closed by asking the British Resident in Oyo "to have mercy upon me, to set me free from the jaws of the two footed lion who is trying very hard to swallow me up alive."

123. See, e.g., NAI CSO 26/30052, 57.

124. E.g., OAU JudicCo of Ibadan, CrimRB, 1934–1937, 55–56, and NAAb E.C.R. 1/2/28, Complaints Comm. RB 1952, cases heard 6 May 1952, item 6. For the different criteria laid out by the Nigerian Supreme Court in 1940, see *NLR*, XVI, 9.

125. NAI Iba Div 1/1 16, vol. 6, 1952–1957, sheet 972.

126. NAI Epe District Officer's CrimRB, 1925–1926, 362.

127. NAI Iba Prof 3/2, 6.

128. Fadipe, *Sociology*, 92; *Nigerian Daily Telegraph*, 6 July 1933, 5; and *West African Pilot*, 25 Jan.–10 Feb. 1938, passim. See also *NLR*, XVI, 83, and XVII, 94.

129. Oluwakemi Adesina, personal communication.

130. Byfield, "Pawns and Politics."

131. Ibid.

132. Blair, *Abeokuta*, 28, pars. 154–55.

133. NAAb E.C.R. 1/2/18, Complaints RB, 1–12, passim.

134. Hawkins, "Woman in Question," argued that litigation in the colonial courts concerning relationships between women and men was almost always decided to the advantage of the latter.

135. Shields, "Palm Oil," 260–71.

136. Byfield, *Bluest Hands*, 64–67.

137. See, e.g., Hawkins, "Woman in Question," and Tashjian and Allman, "Marrying." For below, see Jeater, "British Empire."

6. Labor, Property, and Agriculture

1. The term "trading" as used in Nigeria encompasses all kinds of buying and selling: offering goods in a local market or selling them on the streets as a hawker; running a shop; or acting as a dealer or wholesaler. Women's work—much of it informal and self-employed—has been grossly under-recorded in statistical surveys of employment in Nigeria as in many countries (Pittin, "Documentation," and Afonja, "Changing Modes").

2. Fadipe, *Sociology*, 87–89, 147–51, and 194, and Lloyd, *Power and Independence*, 37–38. The claim of weak gender division of labor is, however, based heavily on patterns in the western and central parts of Yorubaland.

3. See pp. 120–25, this volume.

4. See pp. 126–68, this volume.

5. See pp. 169–84, this volume.

6. See pp. 30–38, this volume.

7. Sudarkasa, *Where Women Work*, 99–103 and 109–16, and Eades, *The Yoruba Today*, 68–69.

8. Denzer, "Domestic Science Training," for this paragraph.

9. In the pattern of "woman-to-woman" marriage found in some eastern Yoruba communities, however, the main incentive for taking a younger wife was to produce children, not to obtain immediate labor (see pp. 85–86, this volume).

10. Mann, *Slavery*, 285–95.

11. E.g., slaves formed an essential part of the economic system in Ikaleland and Ekiti, just as they did in better-studied areas like Egbaland and Ibadan that form the basis for standard accounts (Ogen, "The Ikale," ch. 6, and O. Ojo, "Warfare, Slavery," chs. 3 and 8). See pp. 46–53, this volume.

12. Robertson and Klein, "Women's Importance."

13. Shields, "Women and Slavery." For below, see O. Ojo, "Warfare, Slavery," 262–63.

14. CMS CA2 098/13 (Young), 6 Mar. 1876, and CA2 098/26 (Young), 4 Aug. 1879, both as cited by Shields, "Palm Oil," 96.

15. For this and below, see CMS CA2 056/28, Johnson to Wright, 2 Aug. 1879, as cited by Oroge, "Institution of Slavery," 208, and Shields, "Palm Oil," 96.

16. PRO CO 147/46, no. 124, enc. 3, Scott to Hethersett, Aug. 1881, as cited by Shields, "Palm Oil," 96.

17. Shields, "Women and Slavery." After a year in Robbin's household, Awa was taken by his principal wife to a nearby slave market, where she was sold to two other women and later to a man before escaping.

18. Shields, "Palm Oil," 131–33, for this and below.

19. Mann, *Slavery*, 214.

20. Shields, "Palm Oil," 131–34. For below, see Fadipe, *Sociology*, 182.

21. Shields, "Palm Oil," 271–76.

22. E.g., the sale of a slave woman for 50 bags (of cowries) and her child for 70 bags in the late 1880s after the death of their master and their inheritance by a younger relative (OAU Abeokuta NC of Appeals, CrimRB, 1911–1920, 46–50). In another case, Sadatu, who described herself as a slave in 1920, said that after her original owner died, his brother took her but immediately turned her and her children out of the house (NAI Iba Prof 3/2, 32). For sacrifices, see O. Ojo, "Slavery," and his "Warfare, Slavery," 181–98.

23. E.g., NAAb E.C.R. 2/1/3, Civil and CrimRB No. III, 1902–1903, 1 front. For below, see ibid., 12.

24. Ibid., 44 back–50 front. For below, see OAU Abeokuta NC of Appeals, CrimRB, 1911–1920, 46–50, and NAI Iba Prof 3/2, 32.

25. E.g., NAAb E.C.R. 2/1, CivC RB, 1931–1938, 37.

26. S. Johnson, *History*, 126–30 (written in the 1890s) and Ajisafe Moore, *Laws and Customs*, 63–66 (information gathered between 1906 and 1924); Oroge, "*Iwofa*"; Lovejoy and Richardson, "Business of Slaving"; Falola, "Slavery"; Falola and Lovejoy, "Pawnship"; and Law, "On Pawning."

27. Oroge, "*Iwofa*," and Byfield, "Pawns and Politics."

28. Oroge, "Institution of Slavery," 180 and ch. 6.

29. OAU Ife NC, CivRB, 1934, 3–4.

30. Falola and Lovejoy, "Pawnship."

31. OAU Abeokuta MixC, CivRB, 1907–1909, 43–44.

32. Ibid., 82. For below, see NAI Oshun Div. 1/1 168, vol. 3, Ede NC, 1930s, 292–93.

33. Denzer, "Nigerian Women," citing an unpublished paper by Judith Byfield.

34. S. Johnson, *History,* 129.

35. Ibid., 128, and Ajisafe Moore, *Laws and Customs,* 63–66.

36. Oroge, "*Iwofa*"; *Egba Administrative Bulletin,* 2 (1927): 125; and NAAb E.C.R. 1/1, Egba Native Administration Rules and Bye-Laws, 1901–1933, 66. For below, see NAI Iba Prof 3/2, 77.

37. NAI Oyo Prof 2/1 247/197.

38. Falola, "Pawnship." Among those interviewed by Falola in 1989 were a woman who had became a pawn in the 1940s when her father died and the family needed money for his funeral; a woman who had two pawns of her own in the 1940s; a woman who for 12 years during the 1940s and 1950s was one of several pawns used to make soap; a woman who had 16 pawns around 1950; a woman who was widowed in 1953 and became a pawn a year later; and a woman who was a pawn until the early 1960s (note 3).

39. *Nigerian Daily Telegraph,* 18 Nov. 1933, 1; *Egbaland Echo,* 15 Oct. 1954, 3; and Adedeji, *Metamorphosis,* 10.

40. Denzer, "Yoruba Women."

41. Ajisafe Moore, *Laws and Customs,* 10–11; Adigun, "Interplay"; Oyewumi, *Invention,* 142–46; and Mba, *Nigerian Women,* 52–58, for this paragraph and the next unless otherwise noted.

42. G. Coker, *Family Property,* 126–27 and 158. But for variations in local practice, see Afonja, "Land Control."

43. E.g., *NLR,* V, 50; X, 82; and XII, 67; and Adewoye, *Judicial System,* 270–74. For below, see Fadipe, *Sociology,* 140–46, and Lloyd, *Power and Independence,* 37–38.

44. Adewoye, "Native Court." For below, see, e.g., OAU Ake Grade "A" NC, CivRB, 1918, 106.

45. Mann, "Women, Landed Property."

46. Ibid., for this paragraph. Of 72 land grants in the 1850s, for example, only four went to women.

47. Ajisafe Moore, *Laws and Customs,* 11.

48. Mann, "Dangers," and her "Historical Roots," for this and below. For outside wives, see p. 95, this volume.

49. Barnes, "Women."

50. OAU Modakeke NC, CrimRB, 1935–1936, 117. For below, see NAAb E.C.R. 2/1, 45 and 59–60.

51. NAI Oshun Div 6/7 A 22/57.

52. Comhaire-Sylvain, "Le Travail," 169–87.

53. NAI Comcol 1 197/S.178. For shops in Lagos owned by women in the 1950s, see *NLR,* XIX, 94, and XXI, 8.

54. Larger animals could survive in some drier regions. Horses were sometimes purchased by wealthy people in rainforest zones as status symbols, but they generally did not live long.

55. Oroge, "Institution of Slavery," 153–55, and Ogen, "The Ikale," 328–29.

56. Clarke, *Travels,* 260.

57. Bowen, *Adventures,* 308; Delany, "Official Report," 85; and *Church Missionary Gleaner,* 18 (1868): 18. When Hugh Clapperton traveled in the Oyo area in 1825–1826, he commented that "all the labor of the land" was performed by women (*Journal,* 58). It is not clear whether his observation was correct, suggesting a change in gendered labor patterns by mid-century, or whether he generalized wrongly from what he saw during a harvest season.

58. Law, "Legitimate Trade," and Afonja, "Changing Modes."

59. CMS CA2 o 98/11, 11 July 1875, as cited by Shields, "Palm Oil," 58. For below, see CA2 o 98/22, 9 Aug. and 12 Sep. 1878, as cited by Shields.

60. Oluwakemi Adesina, personal communication, and Ogen, "The Ikale," 331–33, for this and below.

61. Ogen, "The Ikale," 334.

62. Women's role should not, however, be exaggerated. Scholars have often been misled by how processing and trading in agricultural products were classified in the 1952–1953 Nigerian Census. In Lagos township, 92% of working women were found by the census to be engaged in "trading and clerical," as one might expect, with only 8% reporting "agriculture and fishing" as their primary occupation. In the Western Region, however, 73% of women were listed as working primarily in agriculture, with only 27% in trade. The problem is that census enumerators were told to count any kind of food processing and any kind of trade that involved agricultural produce under the heading of agriculture, not trade. Since many women who did not work in the fields processed or traded foodstuffs, the apparent numbers for agriculture are distorted (Ekundare, *Economic History,* 361; for instructions to enumerators, O. Ojo, "More Than").

63. Forde, "Rural Economies," 82. For below, see ibid., 85.

64. Bascom, *The Yoruba,* 20–23. For below, see Guyer, *African Niche Economy,* 58.

65. Kehinde, "Women," 10–11, for this and below.

66. Bascom, *The Yoruba,* 20.

67. Denzer, "Nigerian Women."

68. O. Ojo, "Writing Yoruba Female Farmers."

69. Babalola, "Colonialism," summarizes the relevant evidence.

70. See Berry, *Cocoa,* esp. ch. 6, and Afonja, "Land Control," for Ondo, Ife, and Abeokuta.

71. Guyer, "Food, Cocoa." This pattern modifies Grier's argument for Ghana that women's labor power for cocoa growing was deliberately exploited by British capitalists and local patriarchal men: women's work enriched someone other than themselves ("Pawns, Porters").

72. Guyer, "Food, Cocoa," Figures 1 and 2, based on numbers in Galletti et al., *Nigerian Cocoa Farmers,* 294, 298, and 347.

73. T. Ojo, "Impact," 42–47, and O. Ojo, "More Than," for this paragraph.

74. O. Ojo, "More Than." Some women quietly held back agricultural proceeds, investing them in other ventures (T. Ojo, "Impact," 15).

75. Idowu and Guyer, *Commercialization,* 7–11.

76. NAAb E.C.R. CivRB, 1920–1922, 24, and E.C.R. 1/2/18, Complaints RB, 1945–1946, 18.

77. NAI MinJust (W) 8/2, Ibadan, CivRB, 1947–1949, appeal no. 294; ibid., no. 241. For below, see OAU Ife NC, CivRB, 1934, 6–8.

78. Denzer, *Folayegbe M. Akintunde-Ighodalo,* 8–9.

79. O. Ojo, "More Than."

80. See pp. 134–41, this volume, for this and below.

81. Timothy-Asobele, *Dance and Theatre,* 5.

82. OAU Ife NC, CrimRB No. 22, 1938, 122–23. For below, see Berry, *Cocoa,* 165.

83. Olawoye, "Impact," and T. Ojo, "Impact," 46–48.

7. Income-Generating Activities in the Nineteenth Century

1. For real estate and agriculture, see pp. 117–25, this volume.

2. Wright, "Narrative," 325–26. For *Orò,* see pp. 205–208, this volume.

3. *Church Missionary Gleaner,* New Series, 1 (1850–1851): 138.

4. Clapperton, *Journal,* 12, and Lander and Lander, *Niger Journal* (ed. Hallett), 70–71.

5. Ajayi, Introduction to "Samuel Ajayi Crowther."

6. Clapperton, *Journal,* 28, and a similar statement in Lander and Lander, *Niger Journal,* 70. For below, see Clapperton, *Journal,* 21. Oroge suggested, however, that since Oyo royal women were supposed to be secluded, these may have been trader-slaves of the king, not actual wives ("Institution of Slavery," 205–206).

7. Lander and Lander, *Niger Journal,* 71.

8. Clarke, *Travels,* 245.

9. Bowen, *Adventures,* 296–97, for this and below.

10. Burton, *Abeokuta,* vol. 1, 131.

11. Bowen, *Adventures,* 307. Women were not common in trans-Saharan caravans, however (Falola, "Yoruba Caravan System").

12. S. Johnson, *History,* 245.

13. CMS CA2 o 76 (Samuel Pearse), Jan. 1866.

14. Bowen, *Adventures,* 301. For beer, see also *Church Missionary Intelligencer,* 6 (1855): 250.

15. *Church Missionary Gleaner,* New Series, 1 (1850–1851): 188. For below, see *Church Missionary Intelligencer,* 6 (1855): 250.

16. Delany, "Official Report," 120. For below, see Hodder and Ukwu, *Markets in West Africa,* Pt. I, 29.

17. Clapperton, *Journal,* 64. For below, see ibid., 68.

18. Lander and Lander, *Niger Journal,* 71. For below, see Burton, *Abeokuta,* vol. 1, 130.

19. CMS CA2 o 61 (Thomas King), March 1850. For below, see ibid., 21 Feb. 1852.

20. CMS CA2 o 77 (Charles Phillips, Sr.), 25 July 1853, and CA2 o 57 (Nathaniel Johnson), 28 Oct. 1876. For below, see CA2 o 76 (Samuel Pearse), Annual Letter, 1874.

21. Hodder, "Yoruba Rural Market," and Marshall, "Women, Trade."

22. In those societies, including the Akan of Ghana and the Igbo of southeastern Nigeria, many women who traded continued to cultivate as well (Sudarkasa, *Where Women Work,* 1).

23. Afonja, "Changing Modes," esp. 308–309.

24. Peel, *Religious Encounter,* 287–88. For a corrective to descriptions of the Ikale as lazy and undeveloped, see Ogen, "The Ikale," ch. 5, and his "Geography."

25. Oguntuyi, *History of Ekiti* (Ibadan: Bisi Books, 1979), 140–41, as cited by Caldwell, Orubuloye, and Caldwell, "Destabilization," 231.

26. Ogen, "The Ikale," 91; Saba, "Inter-Group Relations"; and T. Ojo, "Impact," 12–14, for this and below.

27. Falola, "Gender, Business."

28. The wives of a chief in Abeokuta were trading far north of their home in 1856 (*Church Missionary Intelligencer,* Jan. 1856: 20 [Mr. and Mrs. Townsend], as cited by Falola, "Place of Women," note 21). The round-trip journey from Abeokuta to Ilorin during the nineteenth century took 40 days, an absence from husband and children that would have been prohibitive for a younger woman (Falola, "Yoruba Caravan System").

29. Shields, "Palm Oil," 122–23.

30. Lander and Lander, *Niger Journal,* 71. For below, see Richard and John Lander, *Journal of an Expedition,* vol. 1, 148, a passage not included in the abridged edition by Hallett. Since many of the king's wives would have been inherited from his predecessors or received as unwelcome gifts, he may have sent older women out to trade while keeping younger ones at the palace.

31. Fadipe, *Sociology,* 156–57, for this and below.

32. For *egbẹ́,* see pp. 210–214, this volume; Bascom, "*Esusu*"; Falola, "Money and Informal Credit"; and Adebayo, "Pre-Colonial."

33. Campbell, "Pilgrimage," 200. For below, see CMS CA2 o 43/68 (C. A. Gollmer), 4 June 1861, as cited by Shields, "Palm Oil," 126.

34. For pawning, see pp. 115–17, this volume.

35. Shields, "Palm Oil," 134–41 and 174–77, for this and below. For *òrìṣà* and *Ifá,* see pp. 190–96, this volume.

36. Ilesanmi, "Yoruba Worldview." The quotation below is on 91. That assessment is similar to women's stance with respect to warfare in the nineteenth century and their approach to political activities during the late colonial period: see pp. 133, 141, and 238–39, this volume.

37. Delany, "Official Report," 72–73, and Campbell, "Pilgrimage," 187.

38. E.g., Mann, *Slavery,* 134–35.

39. S. Johnson, *History,* 124, and Odunlami, "Women and Palm Oil," who suggested that the prohibition may have been introduced by women to keep men from taking over these profitable activities.

40. Ogen, "Geography," and his "The Ikale," esp. 357–65. Local Ikale people found that they gained higher net profits by renting out their palm groves and using their remaining land to grow food crops that they sold to the Urhobo and others.

41. CMS CA2 o 61 (King), 13 Oct. 1850, and Parliamentary Papers, vol. 45, no.

11, Campbell to Clarendon, 28 March 1858, as cited by Shields, "Palm Oil," 74. For below, see Whitford, *Trading Life,* 105.

42. Shields, "Palm Oil," 128–31. For below, see ibid., 106–108.

43. Mann, "Owners, Slaves," for this and below, and Shields, "Palm Oil," 97–98.

44. Burton, *Abeokuta,* vol. 1, 129.

45. Parliamentary Papers, vol. 63, no. 8, enc. 1, Rowe to Derby, 1887, as cited by Shields, "Palm Oil," 129.

46. The following account integrates material from Yemitan, *Madame Tinubu;* Biobaku, "Madame Tinubu"; his *The Egba,* 55–57; Mba, *Nigerian Women,* 9–11; Afigbo, "Women"; and Falola, "Gender, Business."

47. S. Johnson, *History,* 393.

48. Biobaku, *The Egba,* 57.

49. Parliamentary Papers, Consular, Bight of Benin, vol. 43, no. 16, Campbell to Clarendon, 26 May 1856, as cited by Shields, "Palm Oil," 161.

50. Delany, "Official Report," 78–80.

51. Biobaku, "Madame Tinubu," 38.

52. Ibid., 37–38.

53. Mba, *Nigerian Women,* 11, citing an unidentified source published in 1931.

54. Ibid.

55. The following account integrates material from B. Awe, "Iyalode Efunsetan Aniwura"; Mba, *Nigerian Women,* 8–9; and Falola, "Gender, Business."

56. For her role as *Ìyálóde,* see p. 222, this volume.

57. B. Awe, "Iyalode Efunsetan Aniwura," 57. The Ààre was the male political head of the city-state; "conjuring" meant minting her own money (Falola, "Gender, Business"). For *oríkì,* see p. 200, this volume.

58. CMS CA2 o 58 (Johnson), 1 May 1874, for her deposition; ibid., 30 June 1874, for her assassination. A popular play about her life written by Akinwumi Isola in 1966 presented her death as a suicide ("Efunsetan Aniwura," in Isola, *Two Yoruba Historical Dramas*). Barber pointed out that in Isola's play, "The ideological opposition to the idea of a woman building up productive 'wealth in people' for her own socio-political advancement" was powerfully represented, including portrayal of Efunsetan as a witch ("Going Too Far," 79–80).

59. Mba, *Nigerian Women,* 9.

60. Afolayan, "Women," and Denzer, "Yoruba Women," for this paragraph.

61. Afolayan, "Women," 80.

62. Denzer, *Iyalode,* 8–13; her "Women Chiefs"; Mba, *Nigerian Women,* 7–13; and B. Awe, "Iyalode Efunsetan Aniwura."

63. Awoyele, "Women."

64. Mba, *Nigerian Women,* 11; Byfield, "Dress and Politics"; and her "Women, Marriage."

65. Sudarkasa, *Where Women Work,* 83; O'Hear, "Craft Industries"; and Delany, "Official Report," 120.

66. See, e.g., Renne, *Cloth;* Renne and Agbaje-Williams, eds., *Yoruba Religious Textiles;* and T. Akinwumi, "Taboos."

67. Flint, "Economic Change," 388, for this and below.

68. John Adams, *Remarks on the Country Extending from Cape Palmas to the River Congo* (London, 1823), 96–98, as cited by Lloyd, Introduction to "Osifekunde of Ijebu," 232, and Adams, *Remarks,* 108, as cited by Shields, "Palm Oil," 79.

69. Osifekunde, "Land and People," 263.

70. T. E. Bowdich, *Mission from Cape Coast Castle to Ashantee* (London, 1819), 226, and G. Robertson, *Notes on Africa, Particularly those Parts which are Situated between Cape Verde and the River Congo* (London, 1819), 287 and 290, both as cited by Lloyd, Introduction to "Osifekunde of Ijebu," 233. For below, see Clapperton, *Journal,* 136.

71. Lander and Lander, *Niger Journal,* 71, and S. Johnson, *History,* 123–24.

72. S. Johnson, *History,* 123–24.

73. Campbell, "Pilgrimage," 184.

74. Saba, "Inter-Group Relations."

75. Clapperton, *Journal,* 16.

76. Campbell, "Pilgrimage," 186. For below, see S. Johnson, *History,* 119 and 124.

77. Clapperton, *Journal,* 14–16, for this and below.

78. Shields, "Palm Oil," 83–84, and Delany, "Official Report," 120.

79. Campbell, "Pilgrimage," 186.

80. Shields, "Palm Oil," 130, for this and below.

81. Parliamentary Papers, vol. 63, no. 8, enc. 1, Rowe to Derby, 1887, as cited by Shields, "Palm Oil," 130.

82. CMS CA2 o 70/48 (Moore), 12 May 1862, as cited by Shields, "Palm Oil," 82.

83. Flint, "Economic Change," 389. For below, see PRO CO 879/33, pt. 1, no. 399, no. 23, enc. 1, Millson to Colonial Secretary, 1890, as cited by Shields, "Palm Oil," 83.

84. An advertisement from 1910 for journeymen tailors and apprentices makes clear that "the art of Tailoring" was reserved for men: *Lagos Standard,* 2 Feb. 1910, 2.

85. Denzer, "Stitches."

86. O'Hear, "Pottery Making," and Cardew, *Pioneer Pottery,* esp. ch. 7.

87. Shields, "Palm Oil," 74–77, and Byfield, *Bluest Hands,* 15.

88. See pp. 208–209, this volume.

8. New Approaches to Familiar Roles during the Colonial Period

1. For the very different situation of women in British colonial Uganda, see Bantebya and McIntosh, *Women, Work,* chs. 3–5.

2. Denzer, "Yoruba Women," 23.

3. T. Ojo, "Impact," 12.

4. Marshall, "Marketing"; Sudarkasa, *Where Women Work,* ch. 4; O. Akinwumi, "Women Entrepreneurs"; Hodder, "Yoruba Rural Market"; Watts, "Rural Women"; Trager, "Customers and Creditors"; her "Market Women"; and her "Yoruba Markets," ch. 3. Information about Lagos in the later 1940s comes from Comhaire-Sylvain, "Le Travail," 169–87. Though the latter account is not broken down by ethnic

group, the author noted that most of the women who sold textiles in the city were Yoruba, as were nearly all the larger dealers in *gàrí.*

5. Thus, in the Awe area in the early 1960s, hundreds of women traded between the nearby farm lands (including rural markets) and the town, but fewer than a dozen regularly traded farm products between Awe and Lagos or Ibadan (Sudarkasa, *Where Women Work,* 76).

6. One trader in textiles, a mother of six children, went twice each month from Lagos to Abeokuta to make purchases. In 1947, she made a total of 30 such trips (Comhaire-Sylvain, "Le Travail," 169–87).

7. Schiltz, "Habitus," 740.

8. Galletti et al., *Nigerian Cocoa Farmers,* 557–59.

9. Sudarkasa, *Where Women Work,* 119–20; Schiltz, "Habitus"; Watts, "Rural Women"; and Hodder, "Yoruba Rural Market," for this and below.

10. Ogen said that non-commercial production of palm oil in Ikaleland was left in the hands of old women, servants, and slaves ("The Ikale," 359). For snapshots of women preparing oil near Otta and Ifo in 1953, see RH GB 0162 MSS.Afr.s.1863 (I. F. W. Schofield), box 8, vol. 7, sheet 8, front.

11. Pim, *Financial and Economic History,* 76–77. For below, see Forde, "Rural Economies," 85.

12. Omoleye, "Palm Produce," 8–22.

13. For wine, see, e.g., OAU JudicCo of Ibadan, CrimRB, 1934–1937, 86, and Aiyetoro NC, CrimRB, 1942, 103.

14. OAU Abeokuta NC of Appeals, CrimRB, 1911–1920, 117–19. For below, see NAI Epe District Officer's CrimRB, 1925–1926, 239–41.

15. Forde, "Rural Economies," 83.

16. Ibid., 83–84. For below, see O. Ojo, "More Than."

17. They may have stayed in touch through a hometown association: see pp. 212–13, this volume.

18. NAI Oyo Prof 2/1 247/205.

19. Berry, *Cocoa,* 164–65, 172, and 175.

20. OAU JudicCo of Ibadan, CrimRB, 1934–1937, 62–63. For below, see OAU Ife NC, CivRB, 1934, 32–33 and 36–37.

21. OAU Ife NC, CrimRB, 1938, 115–18.

22. E.g., OAU Ado Ekiti NC, CivRB, 1917–1918, 12–13, and NAI Epe District Officer's CrimRB, 1925–1926, 25; OAU Ado Ekiti NC, CivRB, 1917–1918, 38 and 43–44.

23. Idowu and Guyer, *Commercialization,* 23–30 and 7–11.

24. NAI Epe District Officer's CrimRB, 1925–1926, 251–53 and 398. For below, see NAI MinJust (W) 8/1/1, 95–98.

25. NAI Epe District Officer's CrimRB, 1925–1926, 263–65.

26. OAU Modakeke NC, CrimRB, 1941–1944, 73–76, and OAU Itaogbolu CustC, CivRB, 1958–1959, 107–108. For below, see NAI Epe District Officer's CrimRB, 1925–1926, 239–41.

27. Comhaire-Sylvain, "Le Travail," 475–502. For below, see NAI Oyo Prof 2/1 247/195.

28. NAI Epe District Officer's CrimRB, 1920–1923, 16.

29. NAI Epe District Officer's CrimRB, 1925–1926, 23. For below, see OAU JudicCo of Ibadan, CrimRB, 1934–1937, 62–63.

30. Archives, Dike Libr., Herbert Macaulay Collection, box 6, file 3, item 14. For below, see Comhaire-Sylvain, "Le Travail," 475–502.

31. Ogunsheye, "Les Femmes."

32. NAI Epe District Officer's CrimRB, 1925–1926, 80. For below, see OAU Ife NC, CrimRB, 1938, 1–2.

33. NAI Oyo Prof 2/1 247/205.

34. *Nigerian Daily Telegraph,* 22 Apr. 1933, 1. For below, see OAU Shaki NC, CrimRB, 1957–1958, 70–72.

35. OAU Ado Ekiti NC, CivRB, 1917–1918, 58, and OAU Modakeke NC, CrimRB, 1935–1936, 5–13. For below, see *Daily Times,* Sat. Supp., 24 Jan. 1953, 1 ("Women Who Matter").

36. *Nigerian Daily Telegraph,* 8 Feb. 1933, 1.

37. Rouse, "Socio-Economic Position," 71. For below, see OAU Aiyetoro NC, CrimRB, 1942, 7–8 and 24–29, and OAU Aiyetoro Grade "D" NC, CrimRB, 1954, 28.

38. *Southern Nigeria Defender,* 1 July 1952, 1 and 4.

39. Adedeji, *Metamorphosis,* 1–2. For below, see T. Ojo, "Impact," 52.

40. Comhaire-Sylvain, "Le Travail," 169.

41. Sudarkasa, *Where Women Work,* 2. For below, see T. Ojo, "Impact," 49–52, and Ogen, "The Ikale," ch. 6.

42. Comhaire-Sylvain, "Le Travail," 169–87.

43. Mabogunje, "Evolution."

44. Comhaire-Sylvain, "Le Travail," 500–501.

45. Ibid., 169–87, for the rest of this paragraph.

46. Ibid., 475–502.

47. Mabogunje, "The Market-Woman," 14–15, for this and below.

48. Hodder, "Yoruba Rural Market." But cf. Sudarkasa, *Where Women Work,* 157.

49. Boserup, *Woman's Role,* 42.

50. Sudarkasa, *Where Women Work,* 128.

51. NAI Iba Div 1/1 1651. The Syrians were from what is now Lebanon.

52. Sudarkasa, *Where Women Work,* 2.

53. Trager, "Market Women."

54. Mabogunje, "The Market-Woman," 16. For the demands placed upon educated Igbo working women by their natal families, see Okeke-Ihejirika, *Negotiating Power,* 161–64.

55. Falola, "Gender, Business."

56. See pp. 205–10, this volume.

57. See pp. 219–26, this volume.

58. In Hodder and Ukwu, *Markets in West Africa,* 50–51, for this and the quotation below.

59. Hodder, "Yoruba Rural Market."

60. Mabogunje, "The Market-Woman," 15.

61. Ibid., 16.

62. Trager, "Customers and Creditors," and her "Yoruba Markets," 209–44.

63. *Nigerian Daily Times,* 7 Feb. 1940, 6.

64. Falola, "Gender, Business."

65. E.g., *Daily Service,* 7 Sep. 1960, 2 (theft) and 1 (fraud).

66. Sudarkasa, *Where Women Work,* 117.

67. Mabogunje, "The Market-Woman," 16.

68. Caldwell, Orubuloye, and Caldwell, "Destabilization," and Sudarkasa, *Where Women Work,* 76 and appendix.

69. Sudarkasa, *Where Women Work,* 139. See also Hoffman, *Frauen,* 110–14.

70. Mabogunje, "The Market-Woman," for this paragraph. The quotations below are on 15.

71. Frobenius, *Voice,* vol. 1, 157–58.

72. Denzer, *Folayegbe M. Akintunde-Ighodalo,* 10 and 17. For below, see NAI Epe District Officer's CrimRB, 1925–1926, 158.

73. Adedeji, *Metamorphosis,* 9–10 and 47–50.

74. Adeniyi, *The Jewel,* 21–22.

75. NAI Iba Div 1/1 2900, vol. 1, sheet 215. The girl was later abducted and raped.

76. NAI Oyo Prof 1 3662.

77. *West African Pilot,* 9 Oct. 1946, 1.

78. Fadipe, *Sociology,* 155–56.

79. Mabogunje, "The Market-Woman," 16.

80. E.g., OAU Ife CustC, Grade C, CivRB, 1940, 31, and NAI Osun Div 1/1 184/144. For below, see OAU Itaogbolu CustC, CivRB, 1958–1959, 21–26.

81. NAI Oshun Div 1/1 184/78.

82. Comhaire-Sylvain, "Le Travail," 169–87.

83. Sudarkasa, *Where Women Work,* 117–18.

84. In the Awe area in the early 1960s, most market traders had working capital of £1–£15 (Sudarkasa, *Where Women Work,* 85–86). For below, see Marshall, "Marketing."

85. In the type generally found in the colonial period, contributors paid in a fixed sum of money at stipulated intervals for a stated length of time, after which they received the amount they contributed minus a small sum claimed as a fee by the organizer of the *èsúsú* (Sudarkasa, *Where Women Work,* 94–95).

86. OAU Abeokuta MixC, CivRB, 1907–1909, 4–7.

87. *NLR,* V, 33–37. For below, see Archives, Dike Libr., Obisesan Collection, box D, file 6, letter dated 11 Sept. 1930.

88. *Nigerian Daily Telegraph,* 4 Aug. 1933, 1. For below, see *NLR,* XVII, 24–26.

89. Hodder, "Yoruba Rural Market." Women were still used as porters in the late 1950s, when they commonly head loaded up to 80 lbs. over rough bush paths for several miles (ibid.).

90. NAI MinJust (W) 8/1/1, 95–98 and 69–70.

91. Lipede, "An Ode to Women," and Denzer, "When Wealth Kills," for this

paragraph. The title of *Ìyálóde* of the Egba had lapsed for several decades before being awarded to her.

92. Barber, *I Could Speak,* 231–34, for this paragraph. The quotation below is on 234. By the late colonial period, women rarely dealt in meat.

93. O. Ojo, "More Than."

94. NAI Oshun Div 1/1 1146/8, her loan application in 1952. Her 1955 application was postponed until sufficient electricity and water had become available in Oshogbo (NAI Oshun Div 1/1 1146/59).

95. *Daily Times,* 2 May 1953, 7 ("Women Who Matter"), and Denzer, "Alhaja Humuani Alaga." See also pp. 73 and 236, this volume.

96. That chieftaincy was charged with overseeing women's welfare and the economic well-being of all traders, both women and men.

97. Sudarkasa, *Where Women Work,* 83–84, and Denzer, "Yoruba Women."

98. Byfield, "Innovation," and her *Bluest Hands,* chs. 1–3 and 6, for this paragraph.

99. See pp. 228–29, this volume.

100. OAU Ado Ekiti NC, CivRB, 1917–1918, 24–100, passim.

101. OAU Ado [Ekiti] NC, CrimRB, 1922–1923, 4–7 and 13–17; 39–42 and 47. For below, see OAU Ado Ekiti NC, CivRB, 1917–1918, 93, and OAU Ado [Ekiti] NC, CrimRB, 1922–1923, 56–57.

102. T. Ojo, "Impact," 51. Potters and mat makers also suffered. For below, see O. Ojo, "Ekiti Women," 79.

103. See Forde, "Yoruba-Speaking Peoples," 8–9, and references to female dyers in Ibadan (*Nigerian Daily Times,* 28 Aug. 1948, 2), near Ife (OAU Modakeke NC, CrimRB, 1941–1944, 1–2), and in Ondo (OAU Itaogbolu CustC, CivRB, 1958–1959, 107–108). For below, see Comhaire-Sylvain, "Le Travail," 475–502.

104. T. Akinwumi, "Taboos." For below, see Forde, "Yoruba-Speaking Peoples," 9.

105. Renne, "Decline," and her *Cloth,* 141. For below, see Galletti et al., *Nigerian Cocoa Farmers,* 557–59.

106. T. Ojo, "Impact," 55–56. For below, see Comhaire-Sylvain, "Le Travail," 475–502.

107. Comhaire-Sylvain, "Le Travail," 475–502, for this paragraph.

108. *Daily Times,* 2 Mar. 1955, 10; *Daily Times,* 1 Jan. 1960, 12.

109. *West African Pilot,* 19 Oct. 1950, 5.

110. *West African Pilot,* 14 July 1960, 2.

111. Fakunle, "Looking Good," and Comhaire-Sylvain, "Le Travail," 475–502.

112. *Daily Times,* 2 Jan. 1960, 8. For below, see Comhaire-Sylvain, "Le Travail," 475–502.

113. By contrast, a study of Hausa immigrants living in one section of Ibadan in the early 1960s found that around a fifth of all women earned money from sex work and that such work carried little stigma. Prostitutes might later marry, and some wives sought independence through divorce and prostitution (Cohen, *Custom and Politics,* 55–57).

114. NAI Epe District Officer's CrimRB, 1925–1926, 398.

115. NAI Oyo Prof 2/1 247/159.

116. For sex work in other African contexts, see, e.g., L. White, *Comforts of Home* (for colonial Nairobi, Kenya); Bakwesegha, *Profiles* (for Kampala, Uganda, in the mid-1970s); and Songue, "Prostitution" (for Cameroon in the early 1990s).

117. NAI Epe District Officer's CrimRB, 1925–1926, 46–48.

118. See, e.g., Okeke-Ihejirika, *Negotiating Power,* esp. 131–36.

119. Comhaire-Sylvain, "Le Travail," 169–87, for this and below.

120. *Daily Times,* 7 Jan. 1953, 8, and Olusanya, "Charlotte Olajumoke Obasa."

121. *Daily Service,* 15 May 1958, 5.

9. Western Skills and Service Careers

1. See pp. 68–71, this volume. For the different impact of missionaries on young women and their work in Uganda, see Bantebya and McIntosh, *Women, Work,* 52–62.

2. *Nigerian Pioneer,* 5 Mar. 1920, 7. For below, see Mann, "Dangers."

3. Sewing machines, operated by foot treadles, were advertised from the turn of the century onward (e.g., *Lagos Standard,* 6 June 1900, 4).

4. Bray, "Craft Structure," and *Nigerian Tribune,* 13 Mar. 1950, 7.

5. Stella Davies Coker had an English school friend's mother buy clothes for her trousseau and ship them from Liverpool in 1898 (NAI Coker Papers 1/4/2, letter from Lucy Hutchinson, 24 Feb.); Diana Bridges, wife of a British colonial officer, recalled that when she was preparing to go to Nigeria in 1927, she was warned to take all her clothes with her, as she would be able to buy nothing there (RH GB 0162 MSS.Afr.s.1634, 2). As early as 1907, however, Augusta George, whose name suggests she may have been from a returnee background, was working as a seamstress in Lagos and Abeokuta (OAU Abeokuta MixC, CivRB, 1907–1909, 43–44).

6. Denzer, "Domestic Science Training," and her "Stitches."

7. *Nigerian Daily Telegraph,* Christmas edition, 1933, 45. For below, see Comhaire-Sylvain, "Le Travail," 475–502.

8. By the 1940s and 1950s, seamstresses earned two to three times more than teachers or nurses (Denzer, "Stitches").

9. Denzer, *Folayegbe M. Akintunde-Ighodalo,* 21–24.

10. T. Ojo, "Impact," 54–55 and see 26–31.

11. Aronson, *City,* 127–28.

12. OAU Ife NC, CivRB, 1934, 68.

13. See pp. 71–72, this volume, for educational programs. For below, see NAAb E.C.R. 1/1/32, 1 and 6.

14. *Nigerian Daily Times,* 2 June 1930, 11. For below, see Denzer, "Domestic Science Training."

15. Denzer, "Stitches."

16. Denzer, "Domestic Science Training." For below, see her "Stitches."

17. *Daily Times,* 2 Oct. 1950, 9. For below, see *Daily Times,* 7 Oct. 1950, 6. The men who escorted Durosinmi to the ceremony had all made the pilgrimage to

Mecca, and she was presented with extensive gifts by her *ẹgbẹ́*, the Young Women Muslim Association.

18. *Daily Times,* Saturday Supplement, 17 Jan. 1953, 1. A barrister was a lawyer qualified to plead cases in the courts. For below, see *Sunday Times,* 20 June 1954, 7.

19. Archives, Gandhi Library, Solanke Collection, box 43, vol. 4, no. 2 of 1935, 26–28. For below, see ibid., box 58, file 1.

20. Adeniyi, *The Jewel,* 36–44.

21. Denzer, "Nigerian Women," and *The Comet,* 27 Aug. 1938, 16.

22. *Colonial Reports—Annual, Nigeria, 1934,* 61; RH GB 0162 MSS.Afr.s.2216 (Barbara Akinyemi), 25; *Nigerian Tribune,* 10 Mar. 1953, 4; *Daily Times,* 7 Jan. 1960, 6 and 11.

23. Editorial cited by Denzer, "Women in Government Service," 17.

24. *West African Pilot,* 23 Sep. 1955, 2.

25. RH GB 0162 MSS.Afr.s.1836, 126. She later became secretary to Premier Awolowo.

26. *Nigerian Tribune,* 15 Sep. 1960, 3.

27. *Nigerian Daily Times,* 5 June 1930, 2. Herbert Macaulay grumbled in an essay written probably in the early 1930s that women who had been to school now wanted to be saleswomen or clerks, rather than doing manual work or engaging in trade (Archives, Dike Libr., Herbert Macaulay Collection, box 6, file 3, item 14). For below, see Comhaire-Sylvain, "Le Travail," 169–87.

28. *West African Pilot,* 14 July 1960, 6. For below, see *Daily Times,* 7 Jan. 1960, 12.

29. NAI CSO 26/2 13554; Denzer, "Women in Government Service"; *Daily Comet,* 11 May 1946, 4; *The Comet,* 22 May 1943, 1; and *Daily Comet,* 2 Aug. 1947, 3. For below, see *The Comet,* 31 Oct. 1936, 10.

30. E.g., *Daily Times,* 1 Jan. 1953, 2, and 31 Jan., 1. For below, see *Daily Service,* 10 May 1958, 4.

31. PRO CO 763/36, #30327/26; Comhaire-Sylvain, "Le Travail," 475–502; and Denzer, "Women in Government Service."

32. Trager, *Yoruba Hometowns,* 78.

33. *Nigerian Daily Telegraph,* Christmas edition, 1933, 19. For below, see *West African Pilot,* 2 July, 1.

34. Denzer, "Nigerian Women"; her *Folayegbe M. Akintunde-Ighodalo,* 108; her "Women in Government Service"; and *Sunday Times,* 5 May 1957, 9. For below, see *West African Pilot,* 18 July 1960, 5.

35. Comhaire-Sylvain, "Le Travail," 475–502, for this and below.

36. Ibid., 171. For below, see pp. 214 and 231, this volume.

37. CMS, *Letters from the Front, 1912,* 89.

38. *Nigerian Pioneer,* 28 May 1920, 9.

39. *Lagos Daily News,* 21 Jan. 1932, 3.

40. NAI Oyo Prof 1 399, vol. 2, and Denzer, "Domestic Science Training," who argues that these numbers show that women were making inroads into the teaching profession. For below, see Comhaire-Sylvain, "Le Travail," 475–502.

41. Denzer, "Domestic Science Training."

42. *Nigerian Daily Times,* 8 Jan. 1946, 4; *Nigerian Tribune,* 30 Mar. 1950, 3; and

Daily Times, 2 Oct. 1950, 9. For below, see, e.g., *Daily Times,* 1 Jan. 1960, 12, and *Nigerian Tribune,* 1 Aug. 1960, 1.

43. Comhaire-Sylvain, "Le Travail," 475–502.

44. PRO CO 763/18, 713/30, nos. 26 and 28, and CO 763/36, 30316/15.

45. E.g., *Lagos Weekly Record,* 26 June 1920, 3. For below, see Comhaire-Sylvain, "Le Travail," 475–502.

46. Odebiyi, "Chief Kuforiji-Olubi." For another example, see Mrs. Kofoworola Pratt under nursing, p. 181, this volume.

47. PRO CO 763/36, 30316/15, 17–18, and 24. Denzer points out that the colonial government had been slow to start appointing British women too: "governing the empire was clearly regarded as men's work" ("Women in Government Service," 6).

48. Denzer, *Folayegbe M. Akintunde-Ighodalo,* 105–35, for this and below. For her education, see pp. 74–75, this volume.

49. *Lagos Weekly Record,* 17 July 1920, 8.

50. *Nigerian Pioneer,* 21 Feb. 1930, 7. For below, see PRO CO 763/18, 997/30, #1.

51. *Nigerian Daily Times,* 2 Jan. 1946, 4, and, for this and below, *West African Pilot,* 20 July 1960, 8.

52. *West African Pilot,* 5 Jan. 1950, 1.

53. For accounts of her life, see, e.g., RH GB 0162 MSS.Afr.s.1862 (M. C. Atkinson), 9–13; ibid., MSS.Afr.s.1863 (I. F. W. Schofield), box 2, file 2, item 1; and Denzer, "Women in Government Service"; cf. PRO CO 763/28, #30447. She clashed with Mrs. Ransome-Kuti, the other extremely powerful woman in Abeokuta.

54. *Egba Bulletin,* issue for Oct./Nov. 1955, as included in the Schofield papers cited above.

55. NAI CSO 26/2 15834, 14b, and see also NAI Oyo Prof 1 1766. For below, see Comhaire-Sylvain, "Le Travail," 475–502.

56. *The Comet,* 11 Oct. 1941, 9.

57. *Nigerian Daily Times,* 3 Jan. 1946, 2. For below, see *Nigerian Tribune,* 13 Mar. 1950, 6.

58. Denzer, "Women in Government Service."

59. *Colonial Reports—Annual, Nigeria, 1931.* By 1938 the numbers had risen to 63 European nursing sisters plus 572 African midwives and nurses (*Colonial Reports—Annual, Nigeria, 1938,* and cf. PRO CO 763/18, 1007/30, #1).

60. Denzer, "Women in Government Service." Men still worked as nurses at the African Hospital in Lagos in 1946 and at Lagos General Hospital in 1950 (*West African Pilot,* 15 Oct. 1946, and *Daily Times,* 6 Oct. 1950, 5).

61. Bush, "Gender and Empire," and Denzer, "Yoruba Women."

62. Comhaire-Sylvain, "Le Travail," 475–502.

63. As cited by Denzer, "Women in Government Service," 11.

64. *Evening Times,* 5 Jan., 2. For below, see *West African Pilot,* 6 Jan. 1950, 3, and *Daily Times,* 4 Jan. 1960, 16.

65. T. Ojo, "Impact," 58.

66. Archives, Gandhi Libr., Solanke Collection, box 43, vol. 4, no. 3 of 1935, 16–17, and box 59, file 6, letter to Matron, Prince of Wales Hospital, Tottenham, 12 Sept. 1948.

67. *West African Pilot,* 12 Jan. 1950, 3; Akinsanya, *An African,* esp. 6–15 and 21–22; and Denzer, "Yoruba Women," for this and below. Her husband, formerly a pharmacist in government service in Nigeria, was then a medical student at Edinburgh University.

68. Denzer, "Yoruba Women," 27.

69. For formal complaints by the Nigeria Nurses Association against British nursing sisters, see *West African Pilot,* 20 Oct. 1950, 5, and *Nigerian Tribune,* 1 Mar. 1950, 6. Barbara Akinyemi likewise objected in the late 1940s to the high-handed actions of European nursing sisters when dealing with African medical workers (RH GB 0162 MSS.Afr.s.2216, 17–18).

70. *Annual Report, Nigeria, 1948,* 66.

71. Adedeji, *Metamorphosis,* chs. 4–5.

72. NAI CSO 26/2 15834, 1–2.

73. NAAb E.D.C. 3/1/70, 1 Nov. 1928. For below, see Comhaire-Sylvain, "Le Travail," 475–502.

74. RH GB 0162 MSS.Afr.s.2216, 17–18. For below, see ibid., 36.

75. E.g., RH GB 0162 MSS.Afr.s.1680 (Revd. R. A. Wright), box 2, letter to his mother, 4 Sept. 1931; PRO CO 763/18, 789/30; and CO 850/168/9.

76. Denzer, "Intersections." For below, see her "Nigerian Women," and personal communication.

77. Comhaire-Sylvain, "Le Travail," 475–502.

78. E.g., in 1955, the Egba Native Authority Executive Committee awarded a scholarship to Miss V. O. Coker to support her study of mathematics, physics, and chemistry at the College of Arts and Technology, Ibadan, so that she would be qualified to study medicine (NAAb E.C.R. 1/1, Minutes, 1955, 29, 44, 50, and 100).

79. Archives, Dike Libr., Herbert Macaulay Collection, box 6, file 3, item 27.

80. Comhaire-Sylvain, "Le Travail," 475–502, for this and below.

81. Denzer, "Women in the Lagos Press." For below, see 30 Nov., 2 and 5, and 1 Dec., 2 and 6.

82. *Nigerian Daily Telegraph,* Christmas edition, 1933, 37–38 and 44.

83. See, e.g., *West African Pilot,* 25 Nov. 1937, 2, and 31 Jan. 1938, 2. For below, see *Nigerian Daily Times,* 13 July, 4.

84. Denzer, "Intersections."

85. Comhaire-Sylvain, "Le Travail," 475–502, and Sat. Supp., 10 Jan., 1. See also Olatoregun, "History of Women," ch. 2.

86. NAI Oyo Prof 2/3 C.215.

87. For the government's previous position that "continuance of a woman's employment after marriage would be undesirable," expressed in 1924 and continued for another decade, see NAI CSO 26/2 13554.

88. NAAb E.D.C. 3/1/414, 52 and 70. For below, see, e.g., NAI MH(Fed) 1/1 6675/7.

89. Alege, "History," ch. 2; Denzer, "Nigerian Women"; and *Nigerian Daily Telegraph,* 16 Jan. 1933, 1 and 5 (about Stella Thomas, who was of Sierra Leonean parentage but practiced initially in Lagos).

90. Comhaire-Sylvain, "Le Travail," 475–502. For below, see *Daily Times,* 2 Oct. 1950, 9.

91. Denzer, "Intersections." For below, see *Nigerian Daily Times,* 16 Aug. 1948, 1 and 5.

10. Religion, Cultural Forms, and Associations

1. Ogen, "The Ikale," 333. For below, see J. Ojo, "Orisa Oko."

2. Ogboja, "Historical Account."

3. Opefeyitimi, "Myths and Women," and Babatunde, "Ketu Myths." For below, see Lucas, *Religion,* 93–95; Lawal said that *Odùduwà* had two identities, with his/her primary sex varying by region (*Gelede Spectacle,* 24).

4. Barber, "Going Too Far."

5. CMS CA2 o 58, July 1874. For below, see Babayemi, "Oyo Palace."

6. McKenzie, *Hail Orisha!,* 394–98, 400–420, and 438–40, and Olajubu, *Women,* 110–13.

7. Peel, "Gender," and his *Religious Encounters,* 88–92. For below, see CMS CA2 o 58 (Samuel Johnson), 20 June 1875, and CA2 o 61 (Thomas King), 10 Oct. 1850.

8. Okome, "African Women and Power." *Sàngó,* although commonly described in "male" terms, had many "female" characteristics (Matory, "King's Mail-Order Bride," and Oyewumi, "Making History").

9. This practice has been described by some Western academics as "cross-dressing" or transvestitism, a position attacked by Yoruba scholars as displaying ignorance of Yoruba ideas about gender (e.g., Matory, *Sex and the Empire,* and M. Drewal, *Yoruba Ritual,* as critiqued by Okome, "African Women and Power," and Oyewumi, "Making History").

10. Olajubu, *Women,* 16–17 and 78–79, and Ogunniyi, "Socio-Cultural Impact."

11. Apata, "Women Cults," and Ademiluka, "Impact."

12. Afonja, "Women." For below, see OAU Ake Grade "A" NC, CrimRB, 1916–1918, 153–57.

13. Belasco, *Entrepreneur,* chs. 4 and 6, for this paragraph.

14. Ogunyemi, *Africa Wo/Man Palava,* 29–35. Mammywata was found all along the West African coast, not just in Yoruba areas.

15. Olupona, *Kingship, Religion,* ch. 6.

16. Falola, "Gender, Business."

17. Joan Wescott, "The Sculpture and Myths of Eshu-Elegba, the Yoruba Trickster," *Africa,* 32 (1962): 336–54," as cited by Sudarkasa, *Where Women Work,* 57. For an *òrìṣà* that made peace after *Èṣù* had caused a disruption, see Figure 10.1, this volume.

18. Babayemi, "Oyo Palace."

19. Some highly educated and thoughtful Yoruba continued to argue for the existence of supernatural forces right through the twentieth century: see, e.g., Obafemi Awolowo's call for a study of the positive potential of juju (Arifalo and Ogen, *The Yoruba,* 31–37) and Oluwole, *Witchcraft,* ch. 1.

20. OAU Ake Grade "A" NC, CrimRB, 1916–1918, 123. For below, see ibid., 30–34.

21. Ibid., 168–72

22. E.g., NAAb E.C.R. 2/1/3, 27, 31–32, and 33–34, and E.C.R. 2/1/5, 1–51, passim. For below, see OAU Ado Ekiti NC, CivRB, 1917–1918, 34–35, and NAI Iba Prof 3/2, 234.

23. OAU Ake Grade "A" NC, CrimRB, 1916–1918, 5–6. For below, see NAI Iba Prof 3/2, 237.

24. Peel, "Gender," for this and below. For the use of witchcraft accusations to control women, see pp. 205–10, this volume.

25. Ilesanmi, "Significance of the Myths." For below, see Afonja, "Changing Patterns" and cf. Layiwola, "Womanism."

26. Shields, "Palm Oil," 276–89.

27. Apter, *Black Critics*, 98–116.

28. Olajubu, *Women*, 41.

29. Gbadamosi, *Growth of Islam*, 199. For *Orò*, see pp. 205–208, this volume.

30. NAI Epe District Officer's CrimRB, 1925–1926, 151–52. For Epe and its heavily Muslim population, see Oguntomisin, *Transformation*.

31. Laitin, "Conversion," and his *Hegemony,* 70–74. Muslim law prohibited menstruating women or those carrying "dirty" children (who had urinated or defecated) to come into the mosque.

32. In Hausa areas of northern Nigeria, which generally enforced a stricter view of Islam than did the Yoruba, peasant women and poor urban women left their households to work (Coles and Mack, "Women"). Hausa women in Yorubaland traded even if they were secluded (Hill, "Hidden Trade," and Cohen, *Custom and Politics,* esp. ch. 2).

33. Ogungbile, "Religious Experience," for this paragraph. For other kinds of *egbé*, see pp. 210–15, this volume.

34. Madam Pelewura, a wealthy market woman active in Lagos politics in the 1930s, was a devout Muslim but never made the pilgrimage. It was not lack of money that kept her from Mecca, but lack of time (C. Johnson, "Nigerian Women," 135). For Pelewura, see pp. 229–30 and 235, this volume.

35. Denzer, "Yoruba Women."

36. E.g., *West African Pilot*, 7 Apr. 1941, 4.

37. *The Comet*, 5 June 1943, 16.

38. *Daily Times*, 2 May 1953, 7.

39. C. Johnson, "Nigerian Woman," 246–49; Denzer, "Yoruba Women"; and her "Alhaja Humuani Alaga," for this and below.

40. For the debate over polygamy, see pp. 98–99, this volume. For below, see Peel, *Religious Encounter,* 54 and 232–33.

41. Peel, *Religious Encounter,* 234. For the rest of this paragraph, see ibid., 233–42, and his "Gender."

42. Modupe Oduyoye, "Planting of Christianity."

43. *Nigerian Tribune*, 15 Mar. 1950, 7.

44. Ayegboyin, "Women in Missions," 50–58 and 68, for this and below.

45. Peel, *Aladura*, 183, and Ayandele, "Aladura." For below, see Callaway, "Women," and Olajubu, *Women*, 56–61.

46. In Ekiti North, these included the use of drums, dancing, prophesying, and "fetishism" (T. Ojo, "Impact," 19). For below, see Denzer, "Yoruba Women."

47. Olajubu, *Women*, 53.

48. *Southern Nigeria Defender*, 7 June 1952, 1. For below, see T. Ojo, "Impact," 20–21.

49. Lawal, *Gelede Spectacle*, 26–30.

50. Kolawole, "Women's Oral Literature"; Barber, "*Oriki*"; her *I Could Speak;* and Olajubu, *Women*, 34–38, for this paragraph. *Oríkì* were joined by an adjunct form (the *ìtàn*) that offered narratives or myths about the *òrìṣà*. For an *oríkì* about Efunsetan, see p. 139, this volume.

51. Barber, "*Oriki*," esp. 314, for this and below.

52. Afolayan, "Women."

53. OAU Modekeke NC, CrimRB, 1935–1936, 115, and Aiyetoro NC, CrimRB, 1942, 105–10. For below, see Denzer, "Fela," 116, and pp. 232–34, this volume.

54. Apter, "Discourse"; the quotations below are on 69. For ritualized complaints in Ondo, see p. 219, this volume.

55. Timothy-Asobele, *Dance and Theatre*, 4.

56. Drummers were usually male, but women played the drums in some royal festivals and musical groups (e.g., B. Awe, "Antiquities," and Timothy-Asobele, *Dance and Theatre*, photo facing p. 8).

57. *Lagos Standard*, 9 Feb. 1910, 4 and 6.

58. Olusanya, "Charlotte Olajumoke Obasa." For below, see *Nigerian Pioneer*, 23 Jan. 1920, 6.

59. *Nigerian Pioneer*, 26 Mar. 1920, 8.

60. *Nigerian Daily Telegraph*, Christmas edition, 1933, 37–38 and 44.

61. Oyelola, "Image of Woman"; Witte, "Invisible Mothers"; and Abiodun, "Woman," for this paragraph.

62. Layiwola, "Womanism." In a few places, women were admitted into *Egúngún* cults, but they did not perform and might not even handle the costumes and masks.

63. Babatunde, *Critical Study*, ch. 6; M. Drewal, *Yoruba Ritual;* and Lawal, *Gelede Spectacle*, for this paragraph.

64. E.g., H. and M. Drewal, *Gelede*, as challenged by Ibitokun, *Dance as Ritual Drama*.

65. Mann, *Slavery*, 289. For below, see Afonja, "Women," 154.

66. Although the *Orò* societies were male dominated, each had a female elder called *Ìyá Orò* who had to sanction the group's actions (Henry J. Drewal, personal communication). *Orò* societies were often an arm of *Ògbóni* councils: see p. 221, this volume.

67. As late as 1958, women in Ibadan were told to stay indoors for a day because a masquerade that they were not allowed to see would finish up the annual *Egúngún* festival (*Nigerian Tribune*, 31 July 1958, 1).

68. CMS CA2 o 61, 12 April 1850.

69. Ibid., 24 Feb. 1852.

70. Bowen, *Adventures,* 138–39.

71. CMS CA2 o 61/37, 12 April 1850, and Bowen, *Adventures,* 139–40.

72. Shields, "Palm Oil," 179–80.

73. Law, "'Legitimate' Trade." For below, see Shields, "Palm Oil," chs. 3–4 and pp. 248–54.

74. *Nigerian Daily Times,* 3 July 1935, 9, reporting on an event in Ajegunle, on the edge of Lagos. Bascom noted in the 1930s that whereas the authority of these cults had formerly rested upon secrets that were concealed from women, their position was now maintained only through female complicity: most women realized that local men wore *Egúngún* costumes and that the voice of *Orò* was produced by a bullroarer, but they were not punished so long as they kept their knowledge quiet ("Sociological Role," section 3).

75. Shields, "Palm Oil," 276–89.

76. Belasco, *Entrepreneur,* 102–103.

77. Barber, *I Could Speak,* 231–36, for this paragraph. The quotations below are on 235.

78. Barber, "Going Too Far," 77–78. Ayantayo also seized palm groves from other compounds so as to have direct access to the oil she traded.

79. Matory, "Rival Empires," and Peel, *Aladura,* 96–98.

80. NAI Ije Prof 1/4011, sheet 26.

81. Schiltz, "Habitus." For below, see Apter, "Atinga Revisited."

82. Matory, "Rival Empires," 504.

83. NAI Oyo Prof 2/3 C 226.

84. Fadipe noted in the 1930s the Yoruba tendency to form organizations (*Sociology,* 243).

85. E.g., the many women who attended the first anniversary of the king of Lagos's installation in 1950 came not with their families but rather in their "groups and societies" (*Daily Times,* 1 Oct. 1950, 1).

86. Fadipe, *Sociology,* 257.

87. See pp. 226–34, this volume.

88. Oluwakemi Adesina, personal communication; NAI CSO 26/31014, par 40.

89. Fadipe, *Sociology,* 257–58.

90. Oyewumi, "Ties."

91. Fadipe, *Sociology,* 258.

92. Ibid., 257–58.

93. A man in Ondo Division gave his wife £3 "to make feast for her Company" in the 1950s (OAU Itaogbolu CustC, CivRB, 1958–1959, 50–54).

94. *The Comet,* 9 Aug. 1941, 16.

95. See p. 132, this volume.

96. For religious *egbẹ́,* see pp. 196–99, this volume.

97. Hoffman, *Frauen,* 177–85.

98. Raji, "Women."

99. See pp. 226–34, this volume.

100. *Evening Times,* 13 Feb. 1956, 2.

101. *Nigerian Daily Times,* 5 Jan. 1946, 2. For below, see Osiruemu, "Women in

the Trade Union Movement"; *West African Pilot,* 20 Oct. 1950, 5; *Nigerian Tribune,* 1 Mar. 1950, 6; and T. Ojo, "Impact," 60.

102. Rhodes House GB 0162 MSS.Afr.s.1863 (I. F. W. Schofield), box 7, vol. 1. For below, see *Daily Times,* 7 Jan. 1949, 9.

103. NAI Abe Prof 8/2, 21, par. 111. For below, see Afonja, "Women," 149.

104. Ogen, "The Ikale," 90; NAI CSO 26/30052, 50, App. 10.

105. *NLR,* I, 81–106. For below, see *Lagos Standard,* 2 Mar., 2. Princess Grace "told them of their family tradition of three generations before her as a thing of yesterday," and her decision "was of unanimous satisfaction to all concerned."

106. Comhaire-Sylvain, "Associations." For below, see O. Ojo, "More Than."

107. Trager, *Yoruba Hometowns,* esp. 49–53.

108. Denzer and Mbanefoh, "Women's Participation."

109. Comhaire-Sylvain, "Associations." For below, see *Lagos Daily News,* 16 Jan. 1932, 1.

110. Honey, "Structure, Agency," and Okafor and Honey, "Nature." For below, see Trager, *Yoruba Hometowns,* 92–95.

111. *Lagos Daily News,* 4 Jan. 1932, 3.

112. *West African Pilot,* 16 July 1950, 1; *Daily Times,* 2 Oct. 1950, 8. For below, see *Nigerian Daily Times,* 4 Jan. 1946, 8.

113. E.g., *The Magic Flute, Oedipus Rex,* and *Dido and Aeneas*: Rhodes House GB 0162 MSS.Afr.s.1836 (M. C. Atkinson), 113–14; *Daily Times,* 1 Mar. 1955, 11; and *Nigerian Tribune,* 11 Mar. 1953, 3–4.

114. *Nigerian Pioneer,* 9 Apr. 1920, 4. LaRay Denzer pointed out, however, that the domestic rhetoric was designed to win colonial government support (personal communication). For below, see *Daily Times,* 7 Oct. 1950, 10.

115. *Nigerian Daily Times,* 4 Jan. 1946, 3.

116. *Daily Times,* 4 Oct. 1950, 12; *Nigerian Tribune,* 4 Mar. 1953, 4; and *Evening Times,* 23 Feb. 1956, 4.

117. Segun, *Ping Pong,* esp. ch. 1. At University College she was the co-editor of the student paper with Chinua Achebe and later became a popular author, described in 2003 as "the matriarch of Nigerian women writers" (Segun, "Interviews with/ accounts of"). The latter references were kindly given to me by LaRay Denzer.

118. Denzer, "Yoruba Women," and Olusanya, "Charlotte Olajumoke Obasa."

119. Johnson-Odim, "Lady Oyinkan Abayomi," and F. Coker, *A Lady,* chs. 6–7. She was later active in the YWCA and Ladies Progressive Club, worked with the Market Women's Unions, and was a leading figure in the Lagos Youth Movement and the (Nigerian) Women's Party.

120. Hoffman, *Frauen,* 179–83. For below, see *Daily Times,* 17 Jan. 1953, 1 ('Women Who Matter").

121. NAI Oyo Prof 1 3662. For below, see Denzer, *Folayegbe M. Akintunde-Ighodalo,* 106–108. For her education, see pp. 74–75, this volume; for her employment, see pp. 177–78.

122. E.g., *The Comet,* 4 Oct. 1941, 19–20, 11 Oct., 2 and 20, 19 Oct., 14–15, and 25 Oct., 1 and 17.

123. Afonja, "Women," and see pp. 226–34, this volume.

11. Regents and Chiefs, Economic Organizations, and Politics

1. Okonjo, "Women's Political Participation," 82.

2. Mba, *Nigerian Women,* 13.

3. Pearce, "Women."

4. Oyewumi, "Making History."

5. Mba, *Nigerian Women,* pp. 2–3. Female rulers were mentioned in Oyo, Ondo, Akure, Ile-Ife, and Ekiti (Akande, "Impact," and Falola, "Place of Women"). For below, see Afonja and Aina, "Introduction," 12.

6. Afonja, "Women," esp. 142.

7. Olajubu, *Women,* 90–92, for this and the quotations below.

8. Afonja, "Women"; Mba, *Nigerian Women,* 5–6; and Lipede, "An Ode to Women."

9. Olupona, "Women's Rituals." Oral history says that the first <O.>ba (usually translated as "king," but more accurately "ruler") was a woman, Pupupa. The first male ruler was said to have been put in office by his mother, which may reflect a transition from a matricentered to a patricentered society. Ondo and some of the other eastern Yoruba kingdoms had a bilateral kinship system, in which people traced their descent through both male and female lines.

10. Olupona, "Women's Rituals," 321.

11. Afonja, "Women," and Mba, *Nigerian Women,* 5–6.

12. Lipede, "An Ode to Women," and B. Awe, "Antiquities." For below, see T. Ojo, "Impact," 9, and Awoyele, "Women."

13. S. Johnson, *History,* 63; Babayemi, "Oyo Palace"; Mba, *Nigerian Women,* 3–6; Okonjo, "Women's Political Participation"; and Afonja, "Women," for this and below.

14. Matory, *Sex and the Empire,* 9.

15. Ibid. For other ritualized complaints, see pp. 200–202, this volume.

16. Denzer, "Yoruba Women."

17. Denzer, *Iyalode,* 1–5; Mba, *Nigerian Women,* 7–13; B. Awe, "Iyalode"; and Oyewumi, "Making History."

18. Denzer, "Yoruba Women," 10.

19. Akande, "Impact." The *Erelú* was a member of the *Ògbóni* and the only person outside the king's family who had direct access to him.

20. At the NAI and summarized by Denzer, "Yoruba Women." The quotation below is on 29.

21. NAI CSO 26/4/30014, par. 45; CSO 26/30052, 50, App. 10a–b; CSO 26/29734, vol. 1, 43–44; T. Ojo, "Impact," 8–9; and Ogen, "The Ikale," 91–92.

22. RH GB 0162 MSS.Afr.s.1881 (A. F. B. Bridges), 143–44.

23. *Nigerian Daily Times,* 8 Feb. 1940, 4.

24. Morton-Williams, "Yoruba Ogboni Cult"; Atanda, "Yoruba Ogboni Cult": Weisser, *Frauen,* chs. 4–6; Mba, *Nigerian Women,* 5; and Okome, "African Women and Power," for this and below. These societies were most common among the Egba and Ijebu.

25. Afonja, "Women."

26. NAI Oyo Prof 1 1512, 1–4.

27. E.g., NAI CSO 26/30274, 9 and 11, and CSO 26/31216, 2–3, par. 8 (and version 2, 12, par. 42). For below, see NAI CSO 26/29813, 3–4.

28. NAI Ije Prof 2 C55/1, 4–5, par. 14, 75, par. 124, and 83–84 (53 in pencil), par. 157.

29. Fadipe, *Sociology,* 253, and Afigbo, "Women." Ife had traditionally used different titles for the "head of the women in the town" and another for the "mother of the market." Those women sat in the court of justice, were in charge of market women, and settled disagreements between them.

30. Mba, *Nigerian Women,* 7–13. For below, see Denzer, *Iyalode,* 1.

31. Denzer, *Iyalode,* 2; Mba, *Nigerian Women,* 7–13; and Okonjo, "Women's Political Participation."

32. See pp. 135–37, this volume. For below, see Afolayan, "Women." Ondo did not use the title of *Ìyálóde.*

33. Denzer, *Iyalode,* 5–13; her "Women Chiefs"; Mba, *Nigerian Women,* 7–13; and B. Awe, "Iyalode Efunsetan Aniwura," for this paragraph. See also p. 140, this volume.

34. Hinderer, *Seventeen Years,* 110–11, for this and below.

35. For Efunsetan, see pp. 137–40, this volume; Shields, "Palm Oil," 220; and Denzer, *Iyalode,* 13–15. Ibadan's *Ìyálóde* also acted as regent for a few months after the death of the ruler in 1912 (B. Awe, "The Iyalode").

36. NAI CSO 26/31014. For below, see Awoyele, "Women," 4–6.

37. Byfield, "Dress and Politics," and her "Women, Marriage."

38. *Nigerian Pioneer,* 9 Apr., 6b; ibid., 19 Mar. 1920, 7. For below, see 18 July 1935, 9.

39. Denzer, "Yoruba Women."

40. NAI Iba Prof 3/2, 4, and OAU JudicCo of Ibadan, CrimRB, 1934–1937, 97–98. For below, see NAI Iba Prof 3/2, 128.

41. In accordance with British usage, local taxes in Nigeria were called "rates."

42. NAI Ije Prof 1 574, Awujale to District Office, 28 Dec. 1933, and Ije Prof 2 C55/1.

43. NAI Ije Prof 1 574, District Officer to Awujale, 2 Jan. 1934, Awujale to District Officer, 30 Jan. 1934, and sheets 6–7. For below, see ibid., sheets 8–18.

44. NAI Ije Prof 1 574, sheet 48. For below, see ibid., sheets 51–53. The NWU had recently been founded by Mrs. Ransome-Kuti; the NNDP was Macaulay's old party, allied at this time with the NCNC and supported by both educated women and market traders (see pp. 229–30 and 235–36, this volume).

45. Ibid., sheet 60. For below, see ibid., sheet 62. The District Officer provided detailed figures on taxation, showing that 67,000 women in Ijebu Division were liable for the new rate of 5s.; in the town itself, 12,776 women were expected to pay (ibid., sheet 69).

46. See pp. 231–32, this volume.

47. Mba, *Nigerian Women,* 40; Byfield, "Dress and Politics"; and her "Women, Marriage."

48. Byfield, *Bluest Hands,* 173–74.

49. NAI Abe Prof 8/2, 20–21, par. 110.

50. Barber, *I Could Speak,* 272.

51. Comhaire-Sylvain, "Le Travail," 169–87. For below, see *Daily Comet,* 27 May 1946, 1.

52. Denzer, "Women Chiefs"; her *Iyalode,* 13–41; and her "Gender." At the installation of the fifth *Ìyálóde* in 1935, 16,000 people gathered to witness the ceremony (Denzer, *Iyalode,* 17). By 1990 there were 25 chiefs in Ibadan's *Ìyálóde* line. For below, see Denzer, *Iyalode,* 23–27; for the Women's Movement of Nigeria, see Zdunnek, *Marktfrauen,* 47–51.

53. Layonu, *Iyalode Hunmoani Alade,* esp. 25.

54. Denzer, *Folayegbe M. Akintunde-Ighodalo,* 16, note 15, for this paragraph. Fasan served as chair of a number of educational and other boards, was a founding member of the National Council of Women's Societies and the Nigerian Association of University Women, and participated in many Christian religious and charitable organizations.

55. *Nigerian Tribune,* 10 Mar. 1950, 3.

56. Hoffman, *Frauen,* 163–69. Ajisafe Moore, writing in the 1920s, said that in Yoruba customary law, before a person could enter into trade or a craft, she or he had to inform the body of people who were carrying on that type of work. After payment of a fee, the new entrant would be taught the regulations of the guild (*Laws and Customs,* 46–47). See also p. 211, this volume.

57. NAI Iba Prof 3/4, 30, par 62. For below, see Mba, *Nigerian Women,* 193–96.

58. Archives, Dike Libr., Herbert Macaulay Collection, box 6, file 3, item 22.

59. In some communities, supervision of the individual markets had traditionally been assigned to a woman chief titled *Ìyálójà* (the mother or leading woman in the market) or *Ìyálájé.* For those titles in the nineteenth century, see S. Johnson, *History,* 66; for Ekiti North, see T. Ojo, "Impact," 13; for Dugbe market in Ibadan, see Mercy Oduyoye, *Daughters,* 97.

60. *Daily Times,* 24 Jan. 1953, 1 ("Women Who Matter"), for this and below.

61. *Nigerian Daily Times,* 24 Aug. 1948, 8.

62. In Oyo even in the early 1960s, the market women ran their own affairs. The city council played no part at all: no outside officials were present in the market, and no one collected fees (Sudarkasa, *Where Women Work,* 60–61).

63. NAI CSO 26/31216, 3, par. 10. For below, see Babayemi, "Oyo Palace."

64. Biobaku, *The Egba,* 6. For below, see Blair, *Abeokuta,* 16, par. 90, and 17, par. 92.

65. OAU Aiyetoro NC, CrimRB, 1942, 32–33; ibid., 105–10.

66. See, e.g., RH GB 0162 MSS.Afr.s.1863 (papers of I. F. W. Schofield), box 6, vol. 1, sheet 6, top left, a snapshot from 1928 of Agege Market north of Lagos with its Market Master standing in front center, and Figure 4.1, this volume.

67. Mba, *Nigerian Women,* 193–96, and, e.g., NAI ComCol 1 248/61 and 248/70.

68. NAI ComCol 1 248/24, esp. 2–3 and 7, for this and below.

69. Denzer, "Yoruba Women." For elite women's groups, see p. 214, this volume.

70. Mba, *Nigerian Women,* 44–45 and 135–39, and her "Olufunmilayo Ransome-Kuti."

71. Byfield, *Bluest Hands,* chs. 4 and 5, for this paragraph.

72. Mba, *Nigerian Women,* 196–97.

73. C. Johnson, "Grass Roots"; Mba, *Nigerian Women,* 197–201 and 205–206; and Falola, "Gender, Business."

74. Pelewura, an uneducated Muslim who started as a fish seller, had gradually expanded her trade until she was able to purchase her own canoes, hire fishermen, and build storage facilities. By the early 1920s she was using her considerable organizational skills to run what was considered one of the most efficient markets in the city.

75. C. Johnson, "Grass Roots," and Johnson-Odim, "Lady Oyinkan Abayomi."

76. Mba, *Nigerian Women,* 201–204; NAI ComCol 1/2401; and NAI CSO 26/23610/S.988.

77. Oyemakinde, "Pullen Marketing Scheme," and C. Johnson, "Grass Roots."

78. Lindsay, "Domesticity," and her *Working with Gender,* ch. 4.

79. Olusanya, "Olaniwun Adunni Oluwole."

80. Mabogunje, "The Market-Woman," 16.

81. Mba, *Nigerian Women,* 296–99.

82. Ibid., 193–96.

83. Olusanya, "Charlotte Olajumoke Obasa," and NAI ComCol 1 248/121.

84. Denzer, "Alhaja Humuani Alaga."

85. Ayandele, "Ideological Ferment." In 1928, a more radical group, led by Rev. Ransome-Kuti, called for a democratic form of government in Ijebu Ode, in which the traditional rulers/chiefs would be deprived of power and replaced by an elective County Council (ibid.).

86. NAI CSO 26/30274, 20. In Ago town in Ijebu Province, for example, about 4,100 women paid a total of £510 in tax in 1933; 3,300 men paid £834 (NAI CSO 26/29813, App. A).

87. NAI Ije Prof 1 574, letter from Awujale to District Officer, 28 Dec. 1933. For below, see NAI Ije Prof 2 C55/1, 83–84 (53 in pencil), par. 157.

88. NAI Ije Prof 2 C55/1, 83–84 (53 in pencil), par. 157.

89. NAI Ije Prof 1 574, sheet 48. For below, see ibid, sheets 51–53. For *Ìyálódes,* see pp. 223–24, this volume.

90. NAI Ije Prof 1 574, unnumbered sheets, dated 12 July 1949.

91. *Southern Nigerian Defender,* 15 April 1952, 1 (for this and below), and *Nigerian Tribune,* 5 May 1952, 2. At some point during this conflict, to the annoyance of local colonial officials, Ijebu Ode was visited by Mrs. Ransome-Kuti and Mrs. Adekogbe, each of whom claimed to represent "women's interests in the Region" (NAI Ije Prof 1 574, sheet 67).

92. NAI Ije Prof 1 574, sheet 60.

93. For this and the next two paragraphs, see Byfield, "Dress and Politics"; her "Taxation, Women"; C. Johnson, "Grass Roots"; Mba, "Olufunmilayo Ransome-Kuti"; her *Nigerian Women,* 138–40; Johnson-Odim and Mba, *For Women,* ch. 4;

and Thomas, "Egbaland." Byfield is currently working on a detailed study of the Abeokuta tax revolt.

94. *Lagos Daily News,* 23 Jan. 1932, 2, and *Daily Times,* 31 Jan. 1953, 1 ("Women Who Matter").

95. *Nigerian Daily Times,* 23 Sept. 1947, 2

96. NAAb E.D.C. 3/1/264, item 15, and PRO CO 763/37, #30658/5.

97. PRO CO 763/37, #30658/5.

98. Byfield, "Dress and Politics"; Soyinka, *Ake,* 196–213; and Denzer, "Fela." Soyinka, a nephew of the Ransome-Kutis, was present at these events as a boy.

99. Soyinka, *Ake,* 210–11.

100. Ibid., 202. For below, see ibid., 213.

101. As quoted by Denzer, "Fela," 116.

102. Byfield, "Dress and Politics," for this and below.

103. Ibid., 43. For below, see Awoyele, "Women." Even in 2007, some of the pre-election protests in Ondo town were carried out by "half-clad women"; USAAfrica Dialogue@googlegroups.com (accessed 17 April 2007). I am grateful to Fehintola Mosadomi for the latter reference.

104. Mba, *Nigerian Women,* 39.

105. Denzer, "Yoruba Women."

106. *Daily Times,* 2 Oct. 1950, 9; Denzer, "Gender."

107. Mba, *Nigerian Women,* 40; Byfield, "Dress and Politics"; and her "Women, Marriage." For below, see NAAb E.C.R. 2/1/30, 48–53.

108. NAAb E.D.C. 3/1/264, item 28; NAAb E.C.R. 1/1, Minutes, Egba Native Authority Exec. Comm., 1955, 23.

109. Mba, *Nigerian Women,* 204–207. For below, see *Lagos Daily News,* 19 April 1929, as cited by Denzer, *Women in Government Service,* 5–6.

110. Mba, *Nigerian Women,* 206–13 and 231–33, and Johnson-Odim, "Lady Oyinkan Abayomi," for this and below. Lady Abayomi headed the Ladies' Section of the NYM and helped to recruit other women to it.

111. F. Coker, *A Lady,* 80 and 88; Johnson-Odim, "Lady Oyinkan Abayomi"; C. Johnson, "Grass Roots"; Denzer, "Yoruba Women"; and *Daily Times,* 10 Jan. 1953, 1 ("Women Who Matter"), for this paragraph. The organization was initially called the Women's Party, later the Nigerian Women's Party.

112. Mba, "Olufunmilayo Ransome-Kuti"; Johnson-Odim and Mba, *For Women,* chs. 5–6; and Simola, "Construction."

113. Olusanya, "Olaniwun Adunni Oluwole."

114. Denzer, *Folayegbe M. Akintunde-Ighodalo,* 79–84.

115. C. Johnson, "Nigerian Women," 242–43 (where the first name is spelled Humani). For below, see Johnson-Odim and Mba, *For Women,* ch. 6.

116. *West African Pilot,* 18 Jan. 1950, 2.

117. *Nigerian Tribune,* 5 May 1952, 2. Ironically, the only women allowed to vote in the Western Region between 1954 and 1958 were those who paid taxes, the other side of the coin from the protests against female taxation (Denzer, "Gender").

118. Awoyele, "Women," for this and below.

119. E.g., *Nigerian Tribune,* 21 Feb. 1953, 1; RH GB 0162 Micr.Afr.608 (microfilm copy of Papers of the NCNC, 1952–1957), meeting of NCNC Western Women Association's Executive Comm. held 9 Sept. 1956 at Mrs. Ransome-Kuti's home in Abeokuta; and RH GB 0162 MSS.Afr.s.1863 (I. F. W. Schofield), box 8, vol. 7, sheet 21, back, a photograph of a women's Action Group meeting in 1954.

120. RH GB 0162 Micr.Afr.608 (NCNC papers, 1952–1957), meeting held Jan. 1954; ibid., meeting held 22–23 Dec. 1955.

121. Okonjo, "Women's Political Participation."

122. *Daily Times,* 2 Mar. 1955, 6, and F. Coker, *A Lady,* 90. For below, see Denzer, "Yoruba Women."

123. The new party she then formed, the Commoners People's Party, enjoyed no success (Chuku, "Breaking Ethnic Barriers"). Mrs. Esan, below, had been named by the Action Group as a female advisor to discussions about the Nigerian constitution in London, and in 1960 she was the only woman to serve on the federal executive committee of the party (Denzer, "Gender").

124. E.g., *Nigerian Tribune,* 21 Feb. 1953, 1, and RH GB 0162 Micr.Afr.608 (NCNC papers, 1952–1957), passim.

125. Pearce, "Women."

126. *Nigerian Tribune,* 1 Aug. 1960, 1.

127. *Nigerian Tribune,* 11 Aug. 1960, 1.

128. Chauduri, "Book Review." For below, see pp. 133 and 141, this volume.

List of References

Manuscript Sources

Church Missionary Society Archive, Birmingham University Library (used through the Adam Matthew microfilm edition). Letters/Reports of:

Harrison, Dr. Arthur Aylett	CMS CA2 o 45
Hinderer, David	CMS CA2 o 49
Johnson, Nathaniel	CMS CA2 o 57
Johnson, Samuel	CMS CA2 o 58
King, Thomas	CMS CA2 o 61
Maser, J. A.	CMS CA2 o 68
Pearse, Samuel	CMS CA2 o 76
Phillips, Charles, Jr.	CMS CA2 o 78
Phillips, Charles, Sr.	CMS CA2 o 77
Read, James	CMS CA2 o 79

Because many of the document numbers were either absent or illegible on the microfilmed copy used, all references to the CMS manuscripts provide the CA2 o call number, with the name of the missionary in parentheses, followed by the date of the letter or report cited.

Gandhi Library, University of Lagos: Ladipo Solanke Collection

Kenneth Dike Library, University of Ibadan, Archives: Herbert Macaulay Collection and Akinpelu Obisesan Collection

National Archives in Abeokuta. Documents from the following classes (in addition to the Native Court Records listed separately below): Ake Palace documents, Egba Council Records, Egba Divisional Council, and *Egba Administration Bulletins*

National Archives in Ibadan. Documents from the following classes (in addition to the Native Court Records listed below): Abeokuta Province, Coker Papers, Commissioner of Colony Office (Lagos), Chief Secretary's Office, Dept. of Commerce and Industry, Ekiti Division, Federal Ministry of Health (Lagos), Ibadan Division, Ibadan Province, Ijebu Province, Ilesha Division, Iwo District, Ondo Province, Oshun Division, and Oyo Province

Native Court Records (including appeals):

Abeokuta:
    Ake Native Court: Civil Record Book, 1911 (OAU)
    Ake Grade "A" Native Court
        Civil Record Books: 1918 (OAU); 1922 (OAU)
        Criminal Record Book, 1916–1918 (OAU)
    Mixed Court
        Civil Record Book, 1907–1909 (OAU)
        Criminal Record Book, 1914 (OAU)
    Native Court of Appeals, Criminal Record Book, 1911–1920 (OAU)
Ado Ekiti:
    Civil Record Book, 1917–1918 (OAU)
    Criminal Record Book, 1922–1923 (OAU)
Aiyetoro Native Court: Criminal Record Books: 1942 (OAU); Grade "D," 1954 (OAU)
Aka Native Court (near Tede, Oyo District): Criminal Record Book, 1934–1952 (OAU)
Bere Native Courts, Nos. 1 and 2: appeals against, 1952–1957 (NAI)
Ede Native Court: appeals against: 1930s (NAI); 1951–1953 (NAI)
Egba Council:
    Civil and Criminal Record Book, 1902–1903 (NAAb)
    Civil Record Books: 1920–1922 (NAAb); 1931–1938 (NAAb)
    Complaints to: 1945–1946 (NAAb); 1952 (NAAb)
    Criminal Record Book, 1902 (NAAb)
Epe District Court: Criminal Record Books: 1911–1912 (NAI); 1920–1923 (NAI); 1925–1926 (NAI)
Ibadan:
    Civil Record Book, 1901–1902 (NAI); appeals to: 1933–1939 (NAI); 1947–1949 (NAI)
    District, Criminal Record Book, 1905–1907 (NAI)
    Judicial Council, Criminal Record Book, 1934–1937 (OAU)
    Magistrate's Court, 1945–1951 (NAI)
    Province, Civil Record Book, 1920–1923 (NAI)
Ife Native/Customary Court:
    Civil Record Books: 1934 (OAU); 1940 (OAU)
    Criminal Record Book, 1938 (OAU)
Ilero Native Court: Civil Record Book, 1931–1935 (OAU)
Itaogbolu Customary Court: Civil Record Book, 1958–1959 (OAU)
Modakeke Native Court: Criminal Record Books: 1935–1936 (OAU); 1941–1944 (OAU)

Ojaba Native Courts, Nos. 1 and 2:
    Appeals against: 1950–1953 (NAI); 1953–1957 (NAI)
    Transfers from: 1951–1952 (NAI); 1953–1956 (NAI)
    Oshogbo Magistrate's Court: Criminal Cases, 1938–1943 (NAI)
    Shaki Native Court: Criminal Record Book, 1957–1958 (OAU)

Obafemi Awolowo University, Ife-Ife, Hezekiah Oluwasanmi Library, basement room. Native Court records, as listed separately above.

Public Record Office (The National Archives, Kew):

CO 763/18, Register of correspondence, 1930
CO 763/28, Register of correspondence, 1940
CO 763/36 and 37, Registers of correspondence, 1948
CO 763/41, Register of correspondence, 1950
CO 850/168/9, Conditions of women in service, 1940

Rhodes House, Bodleian Library, University of Oxford. GB 1062:

Micr.Afr.608 (microfilm copy of papers of the National Council of Nigeria and the Cameroons, 1952–1957)
MSS.Afr.s.1634 (Diana Bridges)
MSS.Afr.s.1680 (Revd. Ruthven A. Wright)
MSS.Afr.s.1836 (Michael C. Atkinson)
MSS.Afr.s.1863 (Ivor F. W. Schofield)
MSS.Afr.s.1881 (Albert F. B. Bridges)
MSS.Afr s.2216 (Barbara Akinyemi)
MSS.Lugard, Part II, 58/1 (Lord Lugard)

Newspapers

These papers were used for some or all months in the years listed.
Comet, The (Saturday edition), 1936, 1938, 1940–1941, 1943
Daily Comet, 1946–1947
Daily Service, 1955, 1958, 1960
Daily Times, 1950, 1953, 1955, 1957, 1960
Egbaland Echo, 1954
Evening Times, 1956
Lagos Daily News, 1932, 1934
Lagos Standard, 1900, 1910, 1919
Lagos Weekly Record, 1920
Nigerian Chronicle, 1910
Nigerian Daily Telegraph, 1933
Nigerian Daily Times, 1930, 1935, 1940, 1943, 1946–1948
Nigerian Pioneer, 1920, 1930
Nigerian Times, 1910
Nigerian Tribune (Ibadan), 1950, 1952–1953, 1958, 1960
Southern Nigerian Defender, 1952
Sunday Times, 1954, 1957

West African Pilot, 1937–1938, 1941, 1946–1947, 1950, 1955, 1960
Yoruba News, 1936, 1938, 1942–1944

British Colonial Government Reports

Annual Report of the Education Department, Nigeria, 1931. Lagos: Government Printer, 1932.

Blue Book, Colony and Protectorate of Nigeria, 1936. Lagos: Government Printer, 1937.

Colonial Reports—Annual, Nigeria, 1921 and *1922.* London: HMSO, 1922 and 1923.

Colonial Reports—Annual, Nigeria, 1926. Lagos: Government Printer, 1927.

Colonial Reports—Annual, Nigeria, 1931. London: HMSO, 1932.

Colonial Reports—Annual, Nigeria, 1934. London: HMSO, 1935.

Colonial Reports—Annual, Nigeria, 1938. London: HMSO, 1939.

Colonial Reports—Annual, Nigeria, 1948. London: HMSO, 1949.

Church Missionary Society Publications
(used through the Adam Matthew microfilm edition)

Church Missionary Gleaner, New Series, 1 (1850–1851).

Church Missionary Gleaner, 8–11 (1858–1861).

Church Missionary Gleaner, 18 (1868).

Church Missionary Gleaner, 20–22 (1893–1895).

Church Missionary Gleaner, 24 (1897).

Church Missionary Intelligencer, 6 (1855).

Church Missionary Outlook, 57–58 (1930–1931).

Church Missionary Outlook, 61 (1934).

Extracts from the Annual Letters of the Missionaries, 1886–7, 1887–8, and *1888–9.* London, [1888, 1889, and 1890].

Extracts from the Annual Letters of the Missionaries, 1893–4 and *1894–5.* London, 1895 and 1896.

Extracts from the Annual Letters of the Missionaries, 1897 and *1898.* London, 1898 and 1899.

Extracts from the Annual Letters of the Missionaries, 1903 and *1904.* London, 1904 and 1905.

Extracts from the Annual Letters of the Missionaries, 1907 and *1908.* London, 1908 and 1909.

Letters from the Front, [1911–12]. London, 1912.

Other Nineteenth- and Twentieth-Century Printed Primary Sources

Adedeji, Sulia. *Metamorphosis of a Kid Trader.* Ibadan: GLJ General Services, 1995.

Ajisafe Moore, E. A. *The Laws and Customs of the Yoruba People.* Abeokuta: M. A. Ola, 1924.

Atkinson, Michael C. *An African Life: Tales of a Colonial Officer.* London: Radcliffe Press, 1992.

Blair, J. H. *Abeokuta Intelligence Report* [written in 1937]. Ibadan: Caxton Press, [c. 1980], a printed version of NAI Abe Prof 8/2.

Bowen, T. J. *Adventures and Missionary Labors in Several Countries in the Interior of Africa from 1849 to 1856.* Charleston, S.C.: Southern Baptist Publication Soc., 1857.

Burton, Richard F. *Abeokuta and the Camaroons Mountains,* vol. 1. London: Tinsley Brothers, 1863.

Campbell, Robert. "A Pilgrimage to My Motherland: An Account of a Journey among the Egbas and Yorubas of Central Africa, in 1859–60." In M. R. Delany and Robert Campbell, *Search for a Place: Black Separatism and Africa, 1860,* ed. Howard H. Bell. Ann Arbor: University of Michigan Press, 1969, 149–250.

Clapperton, Hugh. *Journal of a Second Expedition into the Interior of Africa from the Bight of Benin to Soccatoo.* London: John Murray, 1829.

Clarke, William H. *Travels and Explorations in Yorubaland 1854–1858,* ed. J. A. Atanda. Ibadan: Ibadan University Press, 1972.

Crowther, Samuel Ajayi. "Narrative." In Philip D. Curtin, ed., *Africa Remembered: Narratives by West Africans from the Era of the Slave Trade.* Madison: University of Wisconsin Press, 1967, 298–316.

Delany, M. R. "Official Report of The Niger Valley Exploring Party." In M. R. Delany and Robert Campbell, *Search for a Place: Black Separatism and Africa, 1860,* ed. Howard H. Bell. Ann Arbor: University of Michigan Press, 1969, 23–148.

Fadipe, N. A. *The Sociology of the Yoruba,* ed. F. O. Okediji and O. O. Okediji. Ibadan: Ibadan University Press, 1970.

Frobenius, Leo. *The Voice of Africa,* vol. 1. London: Hutchinson & Co., 1913.

Hinderer, Anna. *Seventeen Years in the Yoruba Country,* 2nd ed. London: Seeley, Jackson, and Halliday, 1873.

Holley, M. *Voyage à Abéokouta.* Lyon, France: Mougin-Rusand, 1881.

Johnson, Samuel. *The History of the Yorubas from the Earliest Times to the Beginning of the British Protectorate.* Lagos: Church Missionary Society, 1921.

Lander, Richard, and John Lander. *Journal of an Expedition to Explore the Course and Termination of the Niger,* vol. 1, 2nd ed. London: Thomas Tegg, 1838.

———. *The Niger Journal of Richard and John Lander,* ed. and abridged by Robin Hallett. London: Routledge and Kegan Paul, 1965.

Moore, E. A. Ajisafe. *See under* Ajisafe.

Moore, Kofoworola Aina. "The Story of Kofoworola Aina Moore, of the Yoruba Tribe, Nigeria." In Margery Perham, ed., *Ten Africans.* London: Faber and Faber, 1936, 323–43.

Nigeria Law Reports, 21 vols., covering 1881–1955. Lagos: Government Printer, 1915–1957.

Osifekunde of Ijebu (recorded by M. A. P. d'Avezac-Macaya). "The Land and People of Ijebu." In Philip D. Curtin, ed., *Africa Remembered: Narratives by West Africans from the Era of the Slave Trade.* Madison: University of Wisconsin Press, 1967, 223–88.

Population Census of Nigeria, 1963, Western Region, vols. 1 and 2, and *Lagos,* vol. 1. Lagos: Federal Census Office, n.d.

Whitford, John. *Trading Life in Western and Central Africa* [orig. publ. 1877], 2nd ed., ed. A. G. Hopkins. London: Frank Cass, 1967.

Wright, Joseph. "Narrative." In Philip D. Curtin, ed., *Africa Remembered: Narratives by West Africans from the Era of the Slave Trade.* Madison: University of Wisconsin Press, 1967, 322–33.

Secondary Studies (including unpublished works)

Abiodun, Rowland. "Woman in Yoruba Religious Images." *African Languages and Cultures,* 2 (1989): 1–18.

Adebayo, A. G. *"Kose-e-mani:* Idealism and Contradiction in the Yoruba View of Money." In Endre Stiansen and J. I. Guyer, eds., *Credit, Currencies and Culture: African Financial Institutions in Historical Perspective.* Uppsala, Sweden: Nordiska Afrikainstitutet, 1999, 146–75.

———. "Pre-Colonial Institutional Frameworks for Moneylending and Loan Repayment among the Yoruba." *Paideuma,* 38 (1992): 163–76.

Adeboye, Olufunke. "The Changing Conception of Elderhood in Ibadan, 1830–2000." *Nordic Journal of African Studies,* 16 (2007): 261–78.

Adeleye, M. O. "Impacts of Islam on Some Social Features of Ijesa People of Nigeria." *Islamic Quarterly,* 37 (1993): 63–72.

Ademiluka, S. S. "The Impact of Christian Missionary Activity on the Socio-Cultural Heritage of the O-Kun Yoruba." In Ayodeji Olukoju, Z. O. Apata, and O. Akinwumi, eds., *Northeast Yorubaland: Studies in the History and Culture of a Frontier Zone.* Ibadan: Rex Charles, 2003, 134–42.

Ademola, Lady Kofoworola. "The Impact of Colonialism on Women's Education." Unpublished paper, Symposium on Impact of Colonialism on Nigerian Women, WORDOC, University of Ibadan, Oct. 1989.

Adeniyi, Tola. *The Jewel: The Biography of Chief (Mrs.) H. I. D. Awolowo.* Ibadan: Gemini Press, 1993.

Aderibigbe, A. B. "Trade and British Expansion in the Lagos Area in the Second Half of the Nineteenth Century." *Nigerian Journal of Economic and Social Studies,* 4 (1962): 188–95.

Adesina, Olutayo C. "Adebisi Sanusi Giwa (?–1938): The Life and Career of an Ibadan Entrepreneur and Community Leader." *Lagos Notes and Records,* 12 (2006): 28–42.

Adesina, Oluwakemi A. "Gender Relations in Ikaleland in Historical Perspective." Ph.D. thesis, History, University of Ibadan. In progress.

Adewoye, Omoniyi. *The Judicial System in Southern Nigeria, 1854–1954.* Atlantic Highlands, N.J.: Humanities Press, 1977.

———. "The Native Court as Mediator of Social Change in Ibadan, 1893–1957." Unpublished paper.

Adigun, Olayide. "The Interplay of Conflicting Rules: A Survey of the Customs of the Yorubas and the Effect of Modern Legislation." *Law and Anthropology,* 4 (1989): 281–305.

Afigbo, A. E. "Women in Nigerian History." In Martin O. Ijere, ed., *Women in Nigerian Economy*. Enugu: Acena Publishers, 1991, 22–40.

Afolayan, Funso. "Women and Warfare in Yorubaland during the Nineteenth Century." In Toyin Falola and R. Law, eds., *Warfare and Diplomacy in Precolonial Nigeria*. Madison: African Studies Program, University of Wisconsin, 1992, 78–86.

Afonja, Simi. "Changing Modes of Production and the Sexual Division of Labor among the Yoruba." *Signs*, 7 (1981): 299–313.

———. "Changing Patterns of Gender Stratification in West Africa." In Irene Tinker, ed., *Persistent Inequalities: Women and World Development*. New York: Oxford University Press, 1990, 198–209.

———. "Land Control: A Critical Factor in Yoruba Gender Stratification." In Claire Robertson and I. Berger, eds., *Women and Class in Africa*. New York: Africana Publishing Co., 1986, 78–91.

———. "Women, Power and Authority in Traditional Yoruba Society." In Leela Dube, E. Leacock, and S. Ardener, eds., *Visibility and Power: Essays on Women in Society and Development*. Delhi: Oxford University Press, 1986, 136–57.

Afonja, Simi, and Bisi Aina. Introduction to Simi Afonja and B. Aina, eds., *Nigerian Women in Social Change*. Ile-Ife: Obafemi Awolowo University Press, 1995, 1–46.

Agiri, Babatunde. "Slavery in Yoruba Society in the 19th Century." In Paul E. Lovejoy, ed., *The Ideology of Slavery in Africa*. Beverly Hills, Calif.: Sage Publications., 1981, 123–48.

Ajayi, J. F. Ade. "The Aftermath of the Fall of Old Oyo." In J. F. A. Ajayi and M. Crowder, eds., *History of West Africa*, vol. 2. New York: Columbia University Press, 1973, 129–66.

———. *Christian Missions in Nigeria, 1841–1891: The Making of a New Elite*. Evanston, Ill.: Northwestern University Press, 1965.

———. "The Ijaye War, 1860–5." In J. F. Ade Ajayi and R. Smith, *Yoruba Warfare in the Nineteenth Century*. Cambridge: Cambridge University Press, 1964, 59–128.

———. Introduction to "Samuel Ajayi Crowther of Oyo." In Philip D. Curtin, ed., *Africa Remembered: Narratives by West Africans from the Era of the Slave Trade*. Madison: University of Wisconsin Press, 1967, 289–98.

Ajayi, J. F. Ade, and Robert Smith. *Yoruba Warfare in the Nineteenth Century*. Cambridge: Cambridge University Press, 1964.

Ajayi-Soyinka, Omofolabo. "Black Feminist Criticism and Drama: Thoughts on Double Patriarchy." *Journal of Dramatic Theory and Criticism*, 7 (1993): 161–76.

———. "Who Is Afraid of Agency? Theorizing African Women Out of the Victim Syndrome." In Jepkorir R. Chepyator-Thomson, ed., *African Women and Globalization*. Trenton, N.J.: Africa World Press, 2005, 67–94.

Akande, J. O. "Impact of Colonialism on Nigerian Women and Legal System." Unpublished paper, Symposium on Impact of Colonialism on Nigerian Women, WORDOC, University of Ibadan, Oct. 1989.

Akinsanya, Justus A. *An African 'Florence Nightingale': A Biography of Chief (Dr) Mrs Kofoworola Abeni Pratt.* Ibadan: Vantage, 1987.

Akinwumi, Olayemi. "The Okun Yoruba and the Nineteenth Century Crisis in Nigeria." *Ife Journal of History,* 4 (2007): 81–97.

———. "Women Entrepreneurs in Nigeria." *Africa Update,* 7 (2000), an online journal, www.ccsu.edu/afastudy/upd7-3.htm, accessed 11/29/2005.

Akinwumi, Tunde M. "Taboos and the Control of Social Roles and Quality of Owo Ritual Textiles." *Lagos Notes and Records,* 11 (2005): 26–43.

Alege, Kehinde T. "A History of Women in the Legal Profession in Nigeria." B.A. Long Paper, History, University of Lagos, 1994.

Allman, Jean, Susan Geiger, and Nakanyike Musisi, eds. *Women in African Colonial Histories.* Bloomington: Indiana University Press, 2002.

Allman, Jean, and Victoria Tashjian. *"I Will Not Eat Stone": A Women's History of Colonial Asante.* Portsmouth, N.H.: Heinemann, 2000.

Amadiume, Ifi. *Male Daughters, Female Husbands: Gender and Sex in an African Society.* London: Zed Books, 1987.

Apata, Z. O. "Women Cults and Colonial Responses, 1897–1960: The Case of Okun-Yoruba People." Unpublished paper, Symposium on Impact of Colonialism on Nigerian Women, WORDOC, University of Ibadan, Oct. 1989.

Apter, Andrew. "Atinga Revisited: Yoruba Witchcraft and the Cocoa Economy, 1950–1951." In Jean and John Comaroff, eds., *Modernity and Its Malcontents: Ritual and Power in Postcolonial Africa.* Chicago: University of Chicago Press, 1993, 111–28.

———. *Black Critics and Kings: The Hermeneutics of Power in Yoruba Society.* Chicago: University of Chicago Press, 1992.

———. "Discourse and Its Disclosures: Yoruba Women and the Sanctity of Abuse." *Africa,* 68 (1998): 68–97.

Arifalo, S. O., and Olukoya Ogen. *The Yoruba in History up to 1987.* Lagos: First Academic Publishers, 2003.

Aronson, Dan R. *The City Is Our Farm: Seven Migrant Ijebu Yoruba Families.* Boston: G. K. Hall, 1978.

Asiwaju, A. I. *Western Yorubaland under European Rule, 1889–1945.* Atlantic Highlands, N.J.: Humanities Press, 1976.

Atanda, J. A. *The New Oyo Empire: Indirect Rule and Change in Western Nigeria, 1894–1934.* London: Longman, 1973.

———. "The Yoruba Ogboni Cult: Did It Exist in Old Oyo?" *Journal of the Historical Society of Nigeria,* 6 (1973): 365–72.

Awe, Bolanle. "Antiquities in Ibadan and the Ijesa Kingdom." *African Notes,* Special Number on African Antiquities, papers from Symposium at the Institute of African Studies, University of Ibadan, April, 1972, 71–76.

———. Introduction to Bolanle Awe, ed., *Nigerian Women in Historical Perspective.* Lagos: Sankore, 1992, v–xi.

———. "Iyalode Efunsetan Aniwura (Owner of Gold)." In B. Awe, ed., *Nigerian Women in Historical Perspective.* Lagos: Sankore, 1992, 55–71.

———. "The Iyalode in the Traditional Yoruba Political System." In Alice Schlegel, ed., *Sexual Stratification: A Cross-Cultural View.* New York: Columbia University Press, 1977, 144–60.

————. "Writing Women into History: The Nigerian Experience." In Karen Offen, R. R. Pierson, and J. Rendall, eds., *Writing Women's History: International Perspectives.* Bloomington: Indiana University Press, 1991, 211–20.

Awe, Bolanle, ed. *Nigerian Women in Historical Perspective.* Lagos: Sankore, 1992.

Awe, Muyiwa. "Women, Science and Technology in the Colonial Era." Unpublished paper, Symposium on Impact of Colonialism on Nigerian Women, WORDOC, University of Ibadan, Oct. 1989.

Awoyele, Matthew O. "Women in Gbongan Politics (1900–1990)." B.A. Long Essay, History, University of Ibadan, 1999.

Ayandele, E. A. "The Aladura among the Yoruba: A Challenge to the 'Orthodox' Churches." In Ogbu Kalu, ed., *Christianity in West Africa: The Nigerian Story.* Ibadan: Daystar Press, 1978, 384–90.

————. "Britain and Yorubaland in the Nineteenth Century." In E. A. Ayandele, *Nigerian Historical Studies.* London: Frank Cass, 1979, 19–42.

————. "The Colonial Church Question in Lagos Politics, 1905–11." In E. A. Ayandele, *Nigerian Historical Studies.* London: Frank Cass, 1979, 227–47.

————. "The Ideological Ferment in Ijebuland, 1892–1943." *African Notes,* 5 (1970): 17–41.

————. *The Missionary Impact on Modern Nigeria, 1842–1914.* London: Longmans, 1966.

————. "The Yoruba Civil Wars and the Dahomian Confrontation." In E. A. Ayandele, *Nigerian Historical Studies.* London: Frank Cass, 1979, 43–64.

Ayegboyin, Deji Isaac. "Women in Missions: A Case Study of the Baptist Women's Missionary Union in Nigeria." Ph.D. diss., University of Ibadan, 1991.

Babalola, Ademola. "Colonialism and Yoruba Women in Agriculture." In Simi Afonja and B. Aina, eds., *Nigerian Women in Social Change.* Ile-Ife: Obafemi Awolowo University Press, 1995, 47–55.

Babatunde, Emmanuel D. *A Critical Study of Bini and Yoruba Value Systems of Nigeria in Change,* Lewiston, Maine: Edwin Mellen Press, 1992.

————. "Ketu Myths and the Status of Women: A Structural Interpretation of Some Yoruba Myths." *African Notes,* 12 (1988): 29–34.

Babayemi, S. O. "Oyo Palace Organization: Past and Present." *African Notes,* 10 (1986): 4–24.

Bakare-Yusuf, Bibi. "Beyond Determinism: The Phenomenology of African Female Existence." *Feminist Africa,* 2 (2003), an online journal: www.feministafrica.org/fa%202/02-2003/bibi.html, accessed 10/26/2005.

————. "'Yoruba's Don't Do Gender': A Critical Review of Oyeronke Oyewumi's *The Invention of Women: Making an African Sense of Western Gender Discourses.*" Online: www.codesria.org/Links/conferences/gender/BAKARE-YUSUF.pdf, accessed 10/26/05. Published in slightly different form in Signe Anfred et al., eds., *African Gender Scholarship.* Dakar, Senegal: Council for the Development of Social Science Research in Africa, 2004, 61–81.

Bakwesegha, Christopher J. *Profiles of Urban Prostitution: A Case Study from Uganda.* Nairobi: Kenya Literature Bureau, 1982.

Bantebya Kyomuhendo, Grace, and Marjorie Keniston McIntosh. *Women, Work, and Domestic Virtue in Uganda, 1900–2003.* Oxford: James Currey Press; Kampala, Uganda: Fountain Press; and Athens: Ohio University Press, all 2006.

Barber, Karin. "Going Too Far in Okuku: Some Ideas about Gender, Excess, and Political Power." In Mechthild Reh and G. Ludwar-Ene, eds., *Gender and Identity in Africa*. Münster, Germany: Lit, 1995, 71–83.

———. "How Man Makes God in West Africa: Yoruba Attitudes towards the Orisa." In Roy R. Grinker and C. B. Steiner, eds., *Perspectives on Africa*. Oxford: Blackwell, 1997, 392–411.

———. *I Could Speak until Tomorrow: Oriki, Women, and the Past in a Yoruba Town*. Washington, D.C.: Smithsonian Institution Press, 1991.

———. "*Oriki*, Women and the Proliferation and Merging of *Orisa*." *Africa*, 60 (1990): 313–37.

Barnes, Sandra T. "Women, Property, and Power." In Peggy R. Sanday and R. G. Goodenough, eds., *Beyond the Second Sex: New Directions in the Anthropology of Gender*. Philadelphia: University of Pennsylvania Press, 1990, 255–80.

Bascom, William. "The Early Historical Evidence of Yoruba Urbanism." In Ukandi G. Damachi and H. D. Seibel, eds., *Social Change and Economic Development in Nigeria*. New York: Praeger, 1973, 11–39.

———. "The *Esusu:* A Credit Institution of the Yoruba." *Journal of the Royal Anthropological Institute*, 82 (1952): 63–69.

———. "The Sociological Role of the Yoruba Cult-Group." *American Anthropologist*, New Ser. 46 (1944): 3–75.

———. "Urbanization among the Yoruba." *American Journal of Sociology*, 60 (1955): 446–54.

———. *The Yoruba of Southwestern Nigeria*. New York: Holt, Rinehart and Winston, 1969.

Belasco, Bernard I. *The Entrepreneur as Culture Hero: Preadaptations in Nigerian Economic Development*. New York: Praeger, 1980.

Berry, Sara S. *Cocoa, Custom, and Socio-Economic Change in Rural Western Nigeria*. Oxford: Clarendon Press, 1975.

———. *Fathers Work for Their Sons: Accumulation, Mobility and Class Formation in an Extended Yoruba Community*. Berkeley: University of California Press, 1985.

Biobaku, Saburi O. *The Egba and Their Neighbours, 1842–1872*. Oxford: Clarendon Press, 1957.

———. "Madame Tinubu." In [Nigerian Broadcasting Corporation], *Eminent Nigerians of the Nineteenth Century*. Cambridge: Cambridge University Press, 1960, 33–41.

Biobaku, Saburi O., ed. *Sources of Yoruba History*. Oxford: Clarendon Press, 1973.

Boparai, Harindar. "Woman in Family: Law and Attitudes—The Nigerian Experience." In Simi Afonja and B. Aina, eds., *Nigerian Women in Social Change*. Ile-Ife: Obafemi Awolowo University Press, 1995, 164–77.

Boserup, Ester. "The Economics of Polygamy." In Roy R. Grinker and C. B. Steiner, eds., *Perspectives on Africa*. Oxford: Blackwell, 1997, 506–17.

———. *Woman's Role in Economic Development*. New York: St. Martin's Press, 1970.

Bray, J. M. "The Craft Structure of a Traditional Yoruba Town." *Transactions of the Institute of British Geographers*, 46 (1969): 179–93.

Buchanan, K. M., and J. C. Pugh. *Land and People in Nigeria: The Human Geography of Nigeria and Its Environmental Background*. London: University of London Press, 1955.

Burns, Kathryn. *Colonial Habits: Convents and the Spiritual Economy of Cuzco, Peru*. Durham, N.C.: Duke University Press, 1999.

Bush, Barbara. "Gender and Empire: The Twentieth Century." In Philippa Levine, ed., *Gender and Empire*. Oxford: Oxford University Press, 2004, 77–111.

Byfield, Judith A. *The Bluest Hands: A Social and Economic History of Women Dyers in Abeokuta (Nigeria), 1890–1940*. Portsmouth, N.H.: Heinemann, 2002.

———. "Dress and Politics in Post-World War II Abeokuta (Western Nigeria)." In Jean Allman, ed., *Fashioning Africa: Power and the Politics of Dress*. Bloomington: Indiana University Press, 2004, 31–49.

———. "Innovation and Conflict: Cloth Dyers and the Interwar Depression in Abeokuta, Nigeria." *Journal of African History*, 38 (1997): 77–99.

———. "Pawns and Politics: The Pawnship Debate in Western Nigeria." In Paul E. Lovejoy and T. Falola, eds., *Pawnship, Slavery, and Colonialism in Africa*. Trenton, N.J.: Africa World Press, 2003, 357–85.

———. "Taxation, Women, and the Colonial State: Egba Women's Tax Revolt." *Meridians: Feminism, Race, Transnationalism*, 3 (2003): 250–77.

———. "Women, Marriage, Divorce and the Emerging Colonial State in Abeokuta (Nigeria) 1892–1904." In Dorothy L. Hodgson and S. A. McCurdy, eds., *"Wicked Women" and the Reconfiguration of Gender in Africa*. Portsmouth, N.H.: Heinemann, 2001, 27–46.

Caldwell, John C. *Theory of Fertility Decline*. London: Academic Press, 1982.

Caldwell, John C., I. O. Orubuloye, and P. Caldwell, "The Destabilization of the Traditional Yoruba Sexual System." *Population and Development Review*, 17 (1991): 229–62.

Callaway, Helen. *Gender, Culture, Empire: European Women in Colonial Nigeria*. Basingstoke, England: MacMillan, 1987.

———. "Spatial Domains and Women's Mobility in Yorubaland, Nigeria." In Shirley Ardener, ed., *Women and Space: Ground Rules and Social Maps*. New York: St. Martin's Press, 1981, 168–86.

———. "Women in Yoruba Tradition and in the Cherubim and Seraphim Society." In Ogbu U. Kalu, ed., *The History of Christianity in West Africa*. London: Longman, 1980, 321–32.

Cardew, Michael. *Pioneer Pottery*. New York: St. Martin's, 1969.

Chanock, Martin. *Law, Custom and Social Order: The Colonial Experience in Malawi and Zambia*. Cambridge: Cambridge University Press, 1985.

Chaudhuri, Nupur. "Book Review." *National Women's Studies Association Journal*, 13 (2001): 172–76.

Childs, Matt D., and Toyin Falola. "The Yoruba Diaspora in the Atlantic World: Methodology and Research." In Toyin Falola and M. D. Childs, eds., *The Yoruba Diaspora in the Atlantic World*. Bloomington: Indiana University Press, 2004, 1–14.

Chuku, Gloria I. "Breaking Ethnic Barriers and Urban Interethnic Conflicts: The

Gender Imperative." In Adebayo Oyebade, ed., *The Transformation of Nigeria: Essays in Honor of Toyin Falola*. Trenton, N.J.: Africa World Press, 2002, 359–82.

Clark, Gracia. *Onions Are My Husband: Survival and Accumulation by West African Market Women*. Chicago: University of Chicago Press, 1994.

Cohen, Abner. *Custom and Politics in Urban Africa: A Study of Hausa Migrants in Yoruba Towns*. Berkeley: University of California Press, 1969.

Coker, (Chief) Folarin. *A Lady: A Biography of Lady Oyinkan Abayomi*. Ibadan: Evans Brothers, 1987.

Coker, G. B. A. *Family Property among the Yorubas*. London: Sweet & Maxwell, 1958.

Coles, Catherine, and Beverly Mack. "Women in Twentieth-Century Hausa Society." In Catherine Coles and B. Mack, eds., *Hausa Women in the Twentieth Century*. Madison: University of Wisconsin Press, 1991, 3–26.

Comhaire-Sylvain, Suzanne. "Associations on the Basis of Origin in Lagos, Nigeria." *American Catholic Sociological Review*, 11 (1950): 234–36.

———. "Le Travail des Femmes à Lagos, Nigeria." *Zaïre*, 5 (1951): 169–87 and 475–502.

Cooper, Barbara M. *Marriage in Maradi: Gender and Culture in a Hausa Society in Niger, 1900–1989*. Portsmouth, N.H.: Heinemann, 1997.

Cornwall, Andrea. "Wayward Women and Useless Men: Contest and Change in Gender Relations in Ado-Odo, S.W. Nigeria." In Dorothy L. Hodgson and S. A. McCurdy, eds., *"Wicked" Women and the Reconfiguration of Gender in Africa*. Portsmouth, N.H.: Heinemann, 2001, 67–84.

Crowder, Michael. *The Story of Nigeria*, 4th ed. London: Faber and Faber, 1978.

Curtin, Philip D. Introduction to "Joseph Wright of the Egba." In Philip D. Curtin, ed., *Africa Remembered: Narratives by West Africans from the Era of the Slave Trade*. Madison: University of Wisconsin Press, 1967, 317–22.

Daramola, Adeyemi. "Women and Political Leadership in Nigeria: A Discourse Analysis of Yoruba Proverbs." *Lagos Notes and Records*, 11 (2005): 13–25.

Denzer, LaRay. "Abolition and Reform in West Africa." In J. F. A. Ajayi and M. Crowder, eds., *History of West Africa*, vol. 2, 2nd ed. London: Longman, 1987, 48–85.

———. "Alhaja Humuani Alaga: A Tribute." WORDOC Newsletter 1 (1997): 8–10.

———. "Domestic Science Training in Colonial Yorubaland, Nigeria." In Karen T. Hansen, ed., *African Encounters with Domesticity*. New Brunswick, N.J.: Rutgers University Press, 1992, 116–39.

———. "Fela, Women, Wives." In Trevor Schoonmaker, ed., *Fela: From West Africa to West Broadway*. New York: Palgrave MacMillan, 2003, 111–34.

———. *Folayegbe M. Akintunde-Ighodalo: A Public Life*. Ibadan: Sam Bookman, 2001.

———. "Gender and Decolonization: A Study of Three Women in West African Public Life." In J. F. A. Ajayi and J. D. Y. Peel, eds., *People and Empires in African History*. London: Longman, 1992, 217–36.

———. "Intersections: Nigerian Episodes in the Careers of Three West Indian Women." Forthcoming.

———. *The Iyalode in Ibadan Politics and Society, c. 1850–1997.* Ibadan: Sam Bookman, 1998.

———. "Nigerian Women under Colonial Rule: A Bibliographic Essay." In Bolanle Awe and L. Denzer, eds., *Nigerian Women and Colonialism.* Forthcoming.

———. "Stitches Make Money: The Evolution of the Seamstress Trade in Southern Nigeria." In N. Wolff, M. Litrell, and B. Wahab, eds., *Proceedings of the Textiles and Clothing Research Workshop, the Polytechnic, Ibadan, Nigeria, July 13–15, 1995.* Ibadan: USAID Iowa-Nigeria University Development Linkages Project, 1995, 28–31.

———. "When Wealth Kills: The Assassinations of Three Yoruba Businesswomen, 1996." In Adigun A. B. Agbaje, L. Diamond, and E. Onwudiwe, eds., *Nigeria's Struggle for Democracy and Good Governance.* Ibadan: Ibadan University Press, 2004, 303–24.

———. "Women Chiefs in Ibadan Public Life, 1893–1997." In Olufemi Vaughan, ed., *Indigenous Political Structures and Governance in Nigeria.* Ibadan: Bookcraft, 2004, 101–30.

———. "Women in Government Service in Colonial Nigeria, 1862–1945." Working Papers in African Studies No. 136, African Studies Center, Boston University, 1989.

———. "Women in the Lagos Press in the 1930s." Unpublished paper given at the African Studies Association meeting, Washington, D.C., Nov. 2005.

———. "Yoruba Women: A Historiographical Study." *International Journal of African Historical Studies,* 27 (1994): 1–39.

Denzer, LaRay, and Nkechi Mbanefoh. "Women's Participation in Hometown Associations." In Rex Honey and S. I. Okafor, eds., *Hometown Associations: Indigenous Knowledge and Development in Nigeria.* London: Intermediate Technology Publications, 1998, 123–34.

Drewal, Henry J., and Margaret T. Drewal. *Gelede: Art and Female Power among the Yoruba.* Bloomington: Indiana University Press, 1983.

Drewal, Margaret T. *Yoruba Ritual: Performers, Play, Agency.* Bloomington: Indiana University Press, 1992.

Eades, J. S. "Authority and Religious Ideology among the Yoruba." *Studies in Third World Societies,* 26 (1985): 139–66.

———. *The Yoruba Today.* Cambridge: Cambridge University Press, 1980.

Eames, Elizabeth A. "Why the Women Went to War: Women and Wealth in Ondo Town, Southwestern Nigeria." In Gracia Clark, ed., *Traders Versus the State: Anthropological Approaches to Unofficial Economies.* Boulder, Colo.: Westview Press, 1988, 81–97.

Echeruo, Michael J. C. *Victorian Lagos: Aspects of Nineteenth Century Lagos Life.* London: MacMillan, 1977.

Ekejiuba, Felicia I. "Down to Fundamentals: Women-Centred Hearth-Holds in Rural West Africa." In Deborah F. Bryceson, ed., *Women Wielding the Hoe.* Oxford: Berg, 1995, 47–61.

Ekundare, R. Olufemi. *An Economic History of Nigeria 1860–1960*. New York: Africana, 1973.

Eltis, David. "The Diaspora of Yoruba-Speakers, 1650–1865: Dimensions and Implications." In Toyin Falola and M. D. Childs, eds., *The Yoruba Diaspora in the Atlantic World*. Bloomington: Indiana University Press, 2004, 17–39.

Eltis, David, and Stanley L. Engerman. "Fluctuations in Sex and Age Ratios in the Transatlantic Slave Trade, 1663–1864." *Economic History Review*, 46 (1993): 308–23.

Etienne, Mona. "Women and Men, Cloth and Colonization: The Transformation of Production-Distribution Relations among the Baule (Ivory Coast)." In Roy R. Grinker and C. B. Steiner, eds., *Perspectives on Africa*. Oxford: Blackwell, 1997, 518–35.

Fage, J. D. "Slavery and the Slave Trade in the Context of West African History." *Journal of African History*, 10 (1969): 393–404.

———. "Slaves and Society in Western Africa, c. 1445-c. 1700." *Journal of African History*, 21 (1980): 289–310.

Fakunle, Oluseun O. "Looking Good: A Study of the Nigerian Hair Care Industry with Special Reference to Ibadan, 1900–1997." B.A. Long Essay, History, University of Ibadan, 1999.

Falola, Toyin. "Gender, Business, and Space Control: Yoruba Market Women and Power." In Bessie House-Midamba and F. K. Ekechi, eds., *African Market Women and Economic Power*. Westport, Conn.: Greenwood Press, 1995, 23–40.

———. "The Ijaye in Diaspora, 1862–1895." *Journal of Asian and African Studies*, 22 (1987): 67–79.

———. "Money and Informal Credit Institutions in Colonial Western Nigeria." In Jane I. Guyer, ed., *Money Matters: Instability, Values and Social Payments in the Modern History of West African Communities* (Portsmouth, N.H.: Heinemann, 1995, 162–87.

———. "Pawnship in Colonial Southwestern Nigeria." In Paul E. Lovejoy and T. Falola, eds., *Pawnship, Slavery, and Colonialism in Africa*. Trenton, N.J.: Africa World Press, 2003, 387–408.

———. "The Place of Women in Pre-Colonial Yoruba Economy." In *Seminar Papers, 1978–79, Department of History, University of Ife*. Ile-Ife: Kosalabaro Press, n.d., 139–59.

———. *The Political Economy of a Pre-Colonial African State: Ibadan, 1830–1900*. Ile-Ife: University of Ife Press, 1984.

———. "Slavery and Pawnship in the Yoruba Economy of the Nineteenth Century." In Paul E. Lovejoy and T. Falola, eds., *Pawnship, Slavery, and Colonialism in Africa*. Trenton, N.J.: Africa World Press, 2003, 109–35.

———. "The Yoruba Caravan System of the Nineteenth Century." *International Journal of African Historical Studies*, 24 (1991): 111–32.

———. *Yoruba Gurus: Indigenous Production of Knowledge in Africa*. Trenton, N.J.: Africa World Press, 1999.

Falola, Toyin, and M. D. Childs, eds. *The Yoruba Diaspora in the Atlantic World*. Bloomington: Indiana University Press, 2004.

Falola, Toyin, and Paul E. Lovejoy. "Pawnship in Historical Perspective." In Paul E. Lovejoy and T. Falola, eds., *Pawnship, Slavery, and Colonialism in Africa.* Trenton, N.J.: Africa World Press, 2003, 1–26.

Fapohunda, Eleanor R. "The Nuclear Household Model in Nigerian Public and Private Sector Policy: Colonial Legacy and Socio-Political Implications." *Development and Change,* 18 (1987): 281–94.

Flint, J. E. "Economic Change in West Africa in the Nineteenth Century." In J. F. Ade Ajayi and M. Crowder, eds., *History of West Africa,* vol. 2. New York: Columbia University Press, 1973, 380–401.

Forde, Daryll. "The Rural Economies." In Daryll Forde and Richenda Scott, *The Native Economies of Nigeria,* vol. 1, ed. Margery Perham. London: Faber and Faber, 1946, 29–215.

———. *The Yoruba-Speaking Peoples of South-Western Nigeria* (Ethnographic Survey of Africa). London: International African Institute, 1951.

Galletti, R., K. D. S. Baldwin, and I. O. Dina. *Nigerian Cocoa Farmers: An Economic Survey of Yoruba Cocoa Farming Families.* Oxford: Oxford University Press, 1956.

Gbadamosi, G. O. "The Establishment of Western Education among Muslims in Nigeria, 1896–1926." *Journal of the Historical Society of Nigeria,* 4 (1967): 89–115.

———. *The Growth of Islam among the Yoruba, 1841–1908.* Atlantic Highlands, N.J.: Humanities Press, 1978.

Grier, Beverly. "Pawns, Porters, and Petty Traders: Women in the Transition to Cash-Crop Agriculture in Colonial Ghana." In Paul E. Lovejoy and T. Falola, eds., *Pawnship, Slavery, and Colonialism in Africa.* Trenton, N.J.: Africa World Press, 2003, 299–323.

Groves, C. P. *The Planting of Christianity in Africa,* vol. 2, 1840–1878. London: Lutterworth, 1954.

Guyer, Jane I. *An African Niche Economy: Farming to Feed Ibadan, 1968–88.* Edinburgh: Edinburgh University Press, 1997.

———. "Food, Cocoa, and the Division of Labour by Sex in Two West African Countries." *Comparative Studies in Society and History,* 22 (1980): 355–73.

———. "Wealth in People and Self-Realization in Equatorial Africa." *Man,* New Ser. 28 (1993): 243–65.

———. "Women's Farming and Present Ethnography: Perspectives on a Nigerian Restudy." In Deborah F. Bryceson, ed., *Women Wielding the Hoe.* Oxford: Berg Publishers, 1995, 25–46.

Guyer, Jane I., and S. M. E. Belinga. "Wealth in People as Wealth in Knowledge: Accumulation and Composition in Equatorial Africa." *Journal of African History,* 36 (1995): 91–120.

Hanretta, Sean. "Women, Marginality and the Zulu State: Women's Institutions and Power in the Early Nineteenth Century." *Journal of African History,* 39 (1998): 389–415.

Hawkins, Sean. "'The Woman in Question': Marriage and Identity in the Colonial Courts of Northern Ghana, 1907–1954." In Jean Allman, S. Geiger, and

N. Musisi, eds., *Women in African Colonial Histories*. Bloomington: Indiana University Press, 2002, 116–43.

———. *Writing and Colonialism in Northern Ghana*. Toronto: University of Toronto Press, 2002.

Hill, Polly. "Hidden Trade in Hausaland." *Man*, 4 (1969): 392–409.

Hodder, B. W. "Rural Periodic Day Markets in Part of Yorubaland." *Transactions and Papers of the Institute of British Geographers*, 29 (1961): 149–59.

———. "The Yoruba Rural Market." In Paul Bohannan and George Dalton, eds., *Markets in Africa*. Evanston, Ill.: Northwestern University Press, 1962, 103–17.

Hodder, B. W., and U. I. Ukwu. *Markets in West Africa: Studies of Markets and Trade among the Yoruba and Ibo*. Ibadan: Ibadan University Press, 1969.

Hodgson, Dorothy L., and Sheryl A. McCurdy, eds. *"Wicked" Women and the Reconfiguration of Gender in Africa*. Portsmouth, N.H.: Heinemann, 2001.

Hoffman, Hortense. *Frauen in der Wirtschaft eines Entwicklungslandes: Yoruba-Händlerinnen in Nigeria*. Saarbrücken, Germany: Breitenbach, 1983.

Honey, Rex. "Structure, Agency and the Modification of Indigenous Institutions." In Rex Honey and S. I. Okafor, *Hometown Associations: Indigenous Knowledge and Development in Nigeria*. London: Intermediate Technology Publications, 1998, 142–53.

Hopkins, A. G. *An Economic History of West Africa*. New York: Columbia University Press, 1973.

———. "The Lagos Strike of 1897: An Exploration in Nigerian Labour History." *Past and Present*, 35 (1966): 133–55.

Ibitokun, Benedict M. *Dance as Ritual Drama and Entertainment in the Gelede of the Ketu-Yoruba Subgroup in West Africa*. Ile-Ife: Obafemi Awolowo University Press, 1993.

Idowu, Olukemi, and Jane Guyer. *Commercialization and the Harvest Work of Women, Ibarapa, Oyo State, Nigeria*. Ibadan: Institute of African Studies, University of Ibadan, WORDOC Occasional Paper No. 2, 1991.

Ifeka-Moller, Caroline. "Female Militancy and Colonial Revolt: The Women's War of 1929, Eastern Nigeria." In Shirley Ardener, ed., *Perceiving Women*. New York: Wiley, 1975, 127–57.

Ijagbemi, Adeleye. *Christian Missionary Activity in Colonial Nigeria: The Work of the Sudan Interior Mission Among the Yoruba, 1908–1967*. Lagos: Nigeria Magazine, 1986.

Ilesanmi, T. M. "The Significance of the Myths of Women in Socio-Political Role Sharing among Yoruba People." In Mary E. M. Kolawole, ed., *Gender Perceptions and Development in Africa*. Lagos: Arrabon Academic Publishers, 1998, 29–43.

———. "The Yoruba Worldview on Women and Warfare." In Toyin Falola and R. Law, eds., *Warfare and Diplomacy in Precolonial Nigeria*. Madison: African Studies Program, University of Wisconsin, 1992, 87–92.

Imoagene, Oshomha. *Social Mobility in Emergent Society*. Canberra: Australian National University Press, 1976.

Isola, Akinwumi. *Two Yoruba Historical Dramas: Efunsetan Aniwura, Iyalode*

Ibadan, and Tinuubu, Iyalode Egba (trans. P. J. O. Smith). Trenton, N.J.: Africa World Press, 2005.

Jeater, Diana, "The British Empire and African Women in the Twentieth Century." In Philip D. Morgan and S. Hawkins, eds., *Black Experience and the Empire.* Oxford: Oxford University Press, 2004, 228–56.

———. *Marriage, Perversion, and Power: The Construction of Moral Discourse in Southern Rhodesia, 1894–1930.* Oxford: Clarendon Press, 1993.

Johnson, Cheryl. "Grass Roots Organizing: Women in Anticolonial Activity in Southwestern Nigeria." *African Studies Review,* 25 (1982): 137–57.

———. "Nigerian Women and British Colonialism: The Yoruba Example." Ph.D. dissertation, Northwestern University, 1978.

Johnson-Odim, Cheryl. "Lady Oyinkan Abayomi." In Bolanle Awe, ed., *Nigerian Women in Historical Perspective.* Lagos: Sankore, 1992, 149–62.

Johnson-Odim, Cheryl, and Nina E. Mba. *For Women and the Nation: Funmilayo Ransome-Kuti of Nigeria.* Urbana: University of Illinois Press, 1997.

Johnston, Geoffrey. *Of God and Maxim Guns: Presbyterianism in Nigeria, 1846–1966.* Waterloo, Ontario: Wilfrid Laurier University Press, 1988.

Kehinde, Odole. "Women in the Socio-Economic Development of Yorubaland: The Ondo Example." B.A. Long Essay, History, Obafemi Awolowo University, Ife, 1991–1992.

Klein, Herbert S. "African Women in the Atlantic Slave Trade." In Claire C. Robertson and M. A. Klein, eds., *Women and Slavery in Africa.* Madison: University of Wisconsin Press, 1983, 29–38.

Kolawole, Mary E. M. "Women's Oral Literature as Site for Dynamic Self-Expression." In Mary E. M. Kolawole, ed., *Gender Perceptions and Development in Africa.* Lagos: Arrabon Academic Publishers, 1998, 15–28.

Krapf-Askari, Eva. *Yoruba Towns and Cities: An Enquiry into the Nature of Urban Social Phenomena,* Oxford: Clarendon Press, 1969.

Kuczynski, R. R. *Demographic Survey of the British Colonial Empire,* vol. 1: West Africa. Oxford: Oxford University Press, 1948.

Laitin, David D. "Conversion and Political Change: A Study of (Anglican) Christianity and Islam among the Yorubas in Ile-Ife." In Myron J. Aronoff, ed., *Culture and Political Change.* New Brunswick, N.J.: Transaction Books, 1983, 155–88.

———. *Hegemony and Culture: Politics and Religious Change among the Yoruba.* Chicago: University of Chicago Press, 1986.

Law, Robin. "'Legitimate' Trade and Gender Relations in Yorubaland and Dahomey." In Robin Law, ed., *From Slave Trade to 'Legitimate' Commerce.* Cambridge: Cambridge University Press, 1995, 195–214.

———. "On Pawning and Enslavement for Debt in the Precolonial Slave Coast." In Paul E. Lovejoy and T. Falola, eds., *Pawnship, Slavery, and Colonialism in Africa.* Trenton, N.J.: Africa World Press, 2003, 55–69.

———. *The Oyo Empire c. 1600–c. 1836.* Oxford: Clarendon Press, 1977.

Lawal, Babatunde. *The Gelede Spectacle: Art, Gender, and Social Harmony in an African Culture.* Seattle: University of Washington Press, 1996.

Layiwola, Dele. "Womanism in Nigerian Folklore and Drama." *African Notes,* 11 (1987): 27–33.

Layonu, Taslim A. *Iyalode Hunmoani Alade (The Embodiment of Truth).* Ibadan: Famlod, 1990.

Levine, Philippa. "Sexuality, Gender, and Empire." In Philippa Levine, ed., *Gender and Empire.* Oxford: Oxford University Press, 2004, 134–55.

Levine, Philippa, ed. *Gender and Empire.* Oxford: Oxford University Press, 2004.

Lindsay, Lisa A. "Domesticity and Difference: Male Breadwinners, Working Women, and Colonial Citizenship in the 1945 Nigerian General Strike." *American Historical Review,* 104 (1999): 783–812.

———. *Working with Gender: Wage Labor and Social Change in Southwestern Nigeria.* Portsmouth, N.H.: Heinemann, 2003.

Lipede, (Princess) Abiola. "An Ode to Women of Egbaland." In Oladapo Odebiyi, ed., *Abeokuta 1985.* N.p., n.d., 109–17.

Little, Kenneth. *African Women in Towns: An Aspect of Africa's Social Revolution.* Cambridge: Cambridge University Press, 1973.

Lloyd, Peter C. "Craft Organization in Yoruba Towns." *Africa,* 23 (1953): 30–44.

———. Introduction to "Osifekunde of Ijebu." In Philip D. Curtin, ed., *Africa Remembered: Narratives by West Africans from the Era of the Slave Trade.* Madison: University of Wisconsin Press, 1967, 217–23.

———. *The Political Development of Yoruba Kingdoms in the Eighteenth and Nineteenth Centuries.* London: Royal Anthropological Institute of Great Britain and Ireland, 1971.

———. *Power and Independence: Urban Africans' Perception of Social Inequality.* London: Routledge & Kegan Paul, 1974.

Lovejoy, Paul E. "Slavery in the Context of Ideology." In Paul E. Lovejoy, ed., *The Ideology of Slavery in Africa.* Beverly Hills, Calif.: Sage Publications, 1981, 11–38.

———. "The Yoruba Factor in the Trans-Atlantic Slave Trade." In Toyin Falola and M. D. Childs, eds., *The Yoruba Diaspora in the Atlantic World.* Bloomington: Indiana University Press, 2004, 40–55.

Lovejoy, Paul E., and David Richardson. "The Business of Slaving: Pawnship in Western Africa, c. 1600–1810." In Paul E. Lovejoy and T. Falola, eds., *Pawnship, Slavery, and Colonialism in Africa.* Trenton, N.J.: Africa World Press, 2003, 27–54.

———. "The Initial 'Crisis of Adaptation': The Impact of British Abolition on the Atlantic Slave Trade in West Africa, 1808–1820." In Robin Law, ed., *From Slave Trade to 'Legitimate' Commerce.* Cambridge: Cambridge University Press, 1995, 32–56.

Lucas, J. Olumide. *The Religion of the Yorubas.* Lagos: C.M.S. Bookshop, 1948.

Lynn, Martin. "The West African Palm Oil Trade in the Nineteenth Century and the 'Crisis of Adaptation'." In Robin Law, ed., *From Slave Trade to 'Legitimate' Commerce.* Cambridge: Cambridge University Press, 1995, 57–77.

Mabogunje, Akin L. "The Evolution and Analysis of the Retail Structure of Lagos, Nigeria." *Economic Geography,* 40 (1964): 304–23.

———. "The Market-Woman." *Ibadan,* 11 (1961): 14–17.

————. *Urbanization in Nigeria.* New York: Africana Publishing Corp., 1968.

————. *Yoruba Towns.* Ibadan: Ibadan University Press, 1962.

Mamdani, Mahmood. *Citizen and Subject: Contemporary Africa and the Legacy of Late Colonialism.* Princeton, N.J.: Princeton University Press, 1996.

————. *Politics and Class Formation in Uganda.* New York: Monthly Review, 1976.

Mann, Kristin. "The Dangers of Dependence: Christian Marriage among Elite Women in Lagos Colony, 1880–1915." *Journal of African History,* 24 (1983): 37–56.

————. "The Historical Roots and Cultural Logic of Outside Marriage in Colonial Lagos." In Caroline Bledsoe and G. Pison, eds., *Nuptiality in Sub-Saharan Africa: Contemporary Anthropological and Demographic Perspectives.* Oxford: Clarendon Press, 1994, 167–93.

————. *Marrying Well: Marriage, Status and Social Change among the Educated Elite in Colonial Lagos.* Cambridge: Cambridge University Press, 1985.

————. "Owners, Slaves and the Struggle for Labour in the Commercial Transition at Lagos." In Robin Law, ed., *From Slave Trade to 'Legitimate' Commerce.* Cambridge: Cambridge University Press, 1995, 144–71.

————. *Slavery and the Birth of an African City: Lagos, 1760–1900.* Bloomington: Indiana University Press, 2007.

————. "Women, Landed Property, and the Accumulation of Wealth in Early Colonial Lagos." *Signs,* 16 (1991): 682–706.

Marshall, Gloria A. "The Marketing of Farm Produce: Some Patterns of Trade among Women in Western Nigeria." In *Conference Proceedings, March 1962.* Ibadan: Nigerian Institute of Social and Economic Research, 1963, 88–99. *See also* Niara Sudarkasa.

————. "Women, Trade, and the Yoruba Family." Ph.D. thesis, Columbia University, 1964.

Matory, J. Lorand. "The King's Mail-Order Bride: The Modern Making of a Yoruba Priest." In Flora E. S. Kaplan, ed., *Queens, Queen Mothers, Priestesses, and Power: Case Studies in African Gender.* New York: New York Academy of Sciences, 1997, 381–400.

————. "Rival Empires: Islam and the Religions of Spirit Possession among the Oyo-Yoruba." *American Ethnologist,* 21 (1994): 495–515.

————. *Sex and the Empire That Is No More: Gender and the Politics of Metaphor in Oyo Yoruba Religion.* Minneapolis: University of Minnesota Press, 1994.

Mba, Nina E. *Nigerian Women Mobilized: Women's Political Activity in Southern Nigeria, 1900–1965.* Berkeley: Institute of International Studies, University of California, 1982.

————. "Olufunmilayo Ransome-Kuti." In Bolanle Awe, ed., *Nigerian Women in Historical Perspective.* Lagos: Sankore, 1992, 133–48.

McKenzie, Peter. *Hail Orisha! A Phenomenology of a West African Religion in the Mid-Nineteenth Century.* Leiden, the Netherlands: Brill, 1997.

McPhee, Allan. *The Economic Revolution in British West Africa.* London: George Routledge & Sons, 1926.

Metiboba, S. O. "The Changing Roles of the Family in Socialization Process: The Case of the O-Kun Yoruba." In Ayodeji Olukoju, Z. O. Apata, and O. Akinwumi, eds., *Northeast Yorubaland: Studies in the History and Culture of a Frontier Zone.* Ibadan: Rex Charles, 2003, 124–33.

Mintz, Sidney W. "Men, Women, and Trade." *Comparative Studies in Society and History,* 13 (1971): 247–69.

Morton-Williams, Peter. "An Outline of the Cosmology and Cult Organization of the Oyo Yoruba." *Africa,* 34 (1964): 243–61.

———. "The Yoruba Ogboni Cult in Oyo." *Africa,* 30 (1960): 362–74.

Neumark, S. Daniel. *Foreign Trade and Economic Development in Africa: A Historical Perspective.* Stanford, Calif.: Food Research Institute, Stanford University, 1964.

"The Nigerian Village Square Bookshelf, Ideas Exchange, Bookshelf," anonymous online submission posted 6/3/2005, www.nigeriavillagesquare.com/board/showthread.php?=51670#post51670, accessed 10/26/2005.

Nzegwu, Nkiru. "Gender Equality in a Dual-Sex System: The Case of Onitsha." *Jenda,* 1 (2001), an online journal: www.jendajournal.com/vol1.1/nzegwu.html, accessed 10/26/2005. This is a revised and extended version of a paper originally published in *Canadian Journal of Law and Jurisprudence,* 7 (1994): 73–95.

Obayemi, Ade. "The Yoruba and Edo-speaking Peoples and Their Neighbours before 1600." In J. F. A. Ajayi and M. Crowder, eds., *History of West Africa,* vol. 1. New York: Columbia University Press, 1976, 196–263.

Odebiyi, Oladapo. "Chief (Mrs.) D. B. A. Kuforiji-Olubi (MON): Stainless Steel Woman of Nigeria." In Oladapo Odebiyi, *Builders of Modern Nigeria,* vol. 2. Lagos: V. B. O. International, 1985, 769–87.

Odunlami, B. A. "Women and Palm Oil Production in Ijebuland in the Colonial Times." Unpublished paper, Symposium on Impact of Colonialism on Nigerian Women, WORDOC, University of Ibadan, Oct. 1989.

Oduyoye, Mercy Amba. *Daughters of Anowa: African Women and Patriarchy.* Maryknoll, N.Y.: Orbis Books, 1995.

Oduyoye, Modupe. "The Planting of Christianity in Yorubaland." In Ogbu Kalu, ed., *Christianity in West Africa: The Nigerian Story.* Ibadan: Daystar Press, 1978, 239–302.

Ofonagoro, W. Ibekwe. *Trade and Imperialism in Southern Nigeria 1881–1929.* New York: NOK Publishers International, 1979.

Ogboja, Abimbola A. "A Historical Account of the Olua Festival in Osi Ekiti." B.A. Long Essay, History, Obafemi Awolowo University, Ife, 1983–1984.

Ogen, Olukoya. "Geography and Economy in Southwestern Nigeria: A Critique of Colonial Anthropology on the Pre-colonial Economy Geography of Ikaleland." *Ife Journal of History,* 4 (2007): 205–25.

———. "The Ikale of South-eastern Yorubaland, 1500–1900: A Study in Ethnic Identity and Traditional Economy." Ph.D. thesis, University of Lagos, 2006.

Ogungbile, David O. "Religious Experience and Women Leadership in Nigerian Islam." *Jenda,* 6 (2004), an online journal: www. jendajournal.com/issue6/ogungbile.html, accessed 10/26/2005.

Ogunniyi, Olatunde. "The Socio-Cultural Impact of Osun Worship on the People of Esa-Odo." B.A. Long Essay, History, Obafemi Awolowo University, Ife, 1985–1986.

Ogunremi, Gabriel O. *Counting the Camels: The Economics of Transportation in Pre-Industrial Nigeria*. New York: NOK Publishers International, 1982.

Ogunsheye, F. Adetowun. "Les Femmes du Nigeria." *Presence Africaine*, New Ser. 32–3 (1960): 121–38.

Oguntomisin, G. O. "Refugees and the Evolution of New Forms of Government in Yorubaland in the First Half of the Nineteenth Century." *Essays in History*, 2 (1982): 40–46.

———. *The Transformation of a Nigerian Lagoon Town: Epe, 1852–1942*. Ibadan: John Archers, 1999.

Ogunyemi, Chikwenye O. *Africa Wo/Man Palava: The Nigerian Novel by Women*. Chicago: University of Chicago Press, 1996.

O'Hear, Ann. "Craft Industries in Ilorin: Dependency or Independence?" *African Affairs*, 86, 345 (Oct., 1987): 505–21.

———. "The Enslavement of Yoruba." In Toyin Falola and M. D. Childs, eds., *The Yoruba Diaspora in the Atlantic World*. Bloomington: Indiana University Press, 2004, 56–73.

———. "Pottery Making in Ilorin: A Study of the Decorated Water Cooler." *Africa*, 56 (1986): 175–92.

Ojo, J. R. O. "Orisa Oko, The Deity of the 'Farm and Agriculture' among the Ekiti." *African Notes*, 7 (1972–3): 25–61.

Ojo, Olatunji. "Ekiti Women in Agricultural Production 1890–1960." M.A. thesis, History, University of Ibadan, 1997.

———. "More Than Farmers' Wives: Yoruba Women and Cash Crop Production, c. 1920–1957." In Adebayo Oyebade, ed., *The Transformation of Nigeria: Essays in Honor of Toyin Falola*. Trenton, N.J.: Africa World Press, 2002, 383–404.

———. "Slavery and Human Sacrifice in Yorubaland: Ondo, c. 1870–94." *Journal of African History*, 46 (2005): 379–404.

———. "Warfare, Slavery and the Transformation of Eastern Yorubaland c. 1820–1900." Ph.D. thesis, York University, Toronto, 2003.

———. "Writing Yoruba Female Farmers into History: A Study of the Food Production Sector." In Toyin Falola and C. Jennings, eds., *Africanizing Knowledge: African Studies across the Disciplines*. New Brunswick, N.J.: Transaction Publishers, 2002, 387–404.

Ojo, Tunji. "The Impact of Colonialism on Women in Ekiti North, 1895–1960." B.A. Long Essay, History, University of Ibadan, 1992.

Okafor, Stanley I., and Rex Honey. "The Nature of Hometown Voluntary Associations in Nigeria." In Rex Honey and S. I. Okafor, eds., *Hometown Associations: Indigenous Knowledge and Development in Africa*. London: Intermediate Technology Publications, 1998, 9–16.

Okeke, Phil E. "Reconfiguring Tradition: Women's Rights and Social Status in Contemporary Nigeria." *Africa Today*, 47 (2000): 49–63.

Okeke-Ihejirika, Philomina E. *Negotiating Power and Privilege: Igbo Career Women in Contemporary Nigeria*. Athens: Ohio University Press, 2004.

Okome, Mojubaolu Olufunke. "African Women: Reflections on Their Social, Economic and Political Power." Unpublished paper, available online through www.africanphilosophy.com/scholar/women3.htm, accessed 6/29/2004.

———. "African Women and Power: Reflections on the Perils of Unwarranted Cosmopolitanism." *Jenda,* 1 (2001), an online journal: www.jendajournal.com/vol1.1/okome.html, accessed 10/26/2005.

———. "Listening to Africa, Misunderstanding and Misinterpreting Africa: Reformist Western Feminist Evangelism on African Women." Unpublished paper given at the African Studies Association meeting, Philadelphia, Nov. 1999, online at www.africaresource.com/scholar/women4.htm, accessed 10/26/2005.

Okonjo, Kamene. "Women's Political Participation in Nigeria." In Filomina C. Steady, ed., *The Black Woman Cross-Culturally.* Cambridge, Mass.: Schenkman, 1981, 79–106.

Ola, C. S. "Foundations of the African Church in Nigeria." In Ogbu Kalu, ed., *Christianity in West Africa: The Nigerian Story.* Ibadan: Daystar Press, 1978, 337–42.

Olajubu, Oyeronke. *Women in the Yoruba Religious Sphere.* Albany: State University of New York Press, 2003.

Olatoregun, Damilola O. "The History of Women in the Print Media." B.A. Long Paper, History, University of Lagos, 1992.

Olawoye, Janice E. "The Impact of Colonialism on Nigerian Women: The Case of Women in Agriculture." Unpublished paper, Symposium on Impact of Colonialism on Nigerian Women WORDOC, University of Ibadan, Oct. 1989.

Olukoju, Ayodeji. *Infrastructure Development and Urban Facilities in Lagos, 1861–2000* (Ibadan: Institut Français de Recherche en Afrique, Occasional Publication No. 15, 2003).

———. "Introduction." In Ayodeji Olukoju, Z. O. Apata, and O. Akinwumi, eds., *Northeast Yorubaland: Studies in the History and Culture of a Frontier Zone.* Ibadan: Rex Charles, 2003, 1–5.

Olukoju, Ayodeji, Z. O. Apata, and Olayemi Akinwumi, eds. *Northeast Yorubaland: Studies in the History and Culture of a Frontier Zone.* Ibadan: Rex Charles, 2003.

Olupona, Jacob K. *Kingship, Religion, and Rituals in a Nigerian Community: A Phenomenological Study of Ondo Yoruba Festivals.* Stockholm: Almqvist & Wiksell, 1991.

———. "Women's Rituals, Kingship and Power among the Ondo-Yoruba of Nigeria." In Flora E. S. Kaplan, ed., *Queens, Queen Mothers, Priestesses, and Power: Case Studies in African Gender.* New York: New York Academy of Sciences, 1997, 315–36.

Olusanya, G. O. "Charlotte Olajumoke Obasa." In Bolanle Awe, ed., *Nigerian Women in Historical Perspective.* Lagos: Sankore, 1992, 105–20.

———. "Olaniwun Adunni Oluwole." In Bolanle Awe, ed., *Nigerian Women in Historical Perspective.* Lagos: Sankore, 1992, 121–31.

Oluwole, Sophie B. *Witchcraft, Reincarnation and the God-Head.* Lagos: Excel, 1992.

———. *Womanhood in Yoruba Traditional Thought.* [Bayreuth?]: Iwalewa-Haus, 1993.

Omoleye, Abiodun F. "Palm Produce Economy in Ondo State, 1900–1980." B.A. Long Essay, History, Obafemi Awolowo University, Ife, 1985–1986.

Omosini, Olufemi. "Railway Projects and British Attitude towards the Development of West Africa, 1872–1903." *Journal of the Historical Society of Nigeria,* 4 (1971): 491–507.

Opefeyitimi, Ayo. "Myths and Women of Power in Yoruba Orature." In Mary E. M. Kolawole, ed., *Gender Perceptions and Development in Africa.* Lagos: Arrabon Academic Publishers, 1998, 45–61.

Oroge, E. Adeniyi. "The Institution of Slavery in Yorubaland with Particular Reference to the Nineteenth Century." Ph.D. thesis, University of Birmingham, 1971.

———. "*Iwofa:* An Historical Survey of the Yoruba Institution of Indenture." In Paul E. Lovejoy and T. Falola, eds., *Pawnship, Slavery, and Colonialism in Africa.* Trenton, N.J.: Africa World Press, 2003, 325–56.

Osiruemu, Edith. "Women in the Trade Union Movement in Nigeria: The Constraints." *Jenda,* 6 (2004), an online journal: www.jendajournal.com/issue6/osiruemu.html, accessed 10/26/2005.

Oyelola, Pat. "The Image of Woman in the Yoruba Art of the Twentieth Century." *Nigeria Magazine,* 57 (1989): 100–114.

Oyemakinde, Wale. "The Impact of the Great Depression on the Nigerian Railway and Its Workers." *Journal of the Historical Society of Nigeria,* 7 (1977): 143–60.

———. "Michael Imoudu and the Emergence of Militant Trade Unionism in Nigeria, 1940–1942." *Journal of the Historical Society of Nigeria,* 7 (1974): 541–61.

———. "The Nigerian General Strike of 1945." *Journal of the Historical Society of Nigeria,* 7 (1975): 693–710.

———. "The Pullen Marketing Scheme: A Trial in Food Price Control in Nigeria, 1941–1947." *Journal of the Historical Society of Nigeria,* 6 (1973): 413–23.

———. "Railway Construction and Operation in Nigeria, 1895–1911." *Journal of the Historical Society of Nigeria,* 7 (1974): 303–24.

———. "The Railway Workers and Modernization in Colonial Nigeria." *Journal of the Historical Society of Nigeria,* 10 (1979): 113–24.

Oyewumi, Oyeronke. "Conceptualizing Gender: The Eurocentric Foundations of Feminist Concepts and the Challenge of African Epistemologies." *Jenda,* 2 (2002), an online journal: www.jendajournal.com/vol2.1/oyewumi.html, accessed 10/26/2005.

———. *The Invention of Women: Making an African Sense of Western Gender Discourses.* Minneapolis: University of Minnesota Press, 1997.

———. "Making History, Creating Gender: Some Methodological and Interpretive Questions in the Writing of Oyo Oral Traditions." *History in Africa,* 25 (1998): 263–305.

———. "Ties that (Un)Bind: Feminism, Sisterhood and Other Foreign Relations." *Jenda,* 1 (2001), an online journal: www.jendajournal.com/vol1.1/oyewumi.html, accessed 10/26/2005.

Pearce, Tola Olu. "Women, The State and Reproductive Health Issues in Nigeria."

Jenda, 1 (2001), an online journal: www.jendajournal.com/vol1.1/pearce.html, accessed 10/26/2005.

Peel, J. D. Y. *Aladura: A Religious Movement among the Yoruba.* Oxford: Oxford University Press, 1968.

——. "Between Crowther and Ajayi: The Religious Origins of the Modern Yoruba Intelligentsia." In Toyin Falola, ed., *African Historiography: Essays in Honour of Jacob Ade Ajayi.* Harlow, England: Longman, 1993, 64–79.

——. "The Cultural Work of Yoruba Ethnogenesis." In Elizabeth Tonkin, M. McDonald, and M. Chapman, eds., *History and Ethnicity.* London: Routledge, 1989, 198–215.

——. "Gender in Yoruba Religious Change." *Journal of Religion in Africa,* 32 (2002): 136–66.

——. *Religious Encounter and the Making of the Yoruba.* Bloomington: Indiana University Press, 2000.

Pim, Alan. *The Financial and Economic History of the African Tropical Territories.* Orig. publ. 1940; New York: Argosy-Antiquarian, 1970.

Pittin, Renée. "Documentation of Women's Work in Nigeria: Problems and Solutions." In Christine Oppong, ed., *Sex Roles, Population and Development in West Africa.* Portsmouth, N.H.: Heinemann, 1987, 25–44.

Raji, Adesina Yusuf. "Women in Pre-colonial Yorubaland, West Africa." *Africa Update,* 5 (1998), an online journal: www.ccsu.edu/afastudy/upd5–2.htm, accessed 10/26/2005.

"Reminiscences Panel." Unpublished transcription from Symposium on Impact of Colonialism on Nigerian Women, WORDOC, University of Ibadan, Oct. 1989, including statements by Lady Ademola as Chair, Alhaja Humuani Alaga, Chief (Mrs.) Folayegbe M. Akintunde-Ighodalo, Chief (Mrs.) Grace Ogundipe, Chief (Mrs.) Comfort Oredugba, and Mrs. Titilola Sodeinde.

Renne, Elisha P. *Cloth That Does Not Die: The Meaning of Cloth in Bunu Social Life.* Seattle: University of Washington Press, 1995.

——. "The Decline of Women's Weaving among the North-east Yoruba." *Textile History,* 23 (1992): 87–96.

Renne, Elisha P., and Babatunde Agbaje-Williams, eds. *Yoruba Religious Textiles.* Ibadan: BookBuilders, 2005.

Robertson, Claire C. *Sharing the Same Bowl: A Socioeconomic History of Women and Class in Accra, Ghana.* Bloomington: Indiana University Press, 1984.

Robertson, Claire C., and Martin A. Klein. "Women's Importance in African Slave Systems." In Claire C. Robertson and M. A. Klein, eds., *Women and Slavery in Africa.* Madison: University of Wisconsin Press, 1983, 3–25.

Rouse, Terri S. "The Socio-Economic Position of Yoruba Women from 1915 to 1925 with Emphasis on the Market Women." M.P.S. thesis, Cornell University, 1977.

Saba, Folashade O. "Inter-Group Relations among Akoko Communities in the Pre-colonial Times." In Ayodeji Olukoju, Z. O. Apata, and O. Akinwumi, eds., *Northeast Yorubaland: Studies in the History and Culture of a Frontier Zone.* Ibadan: Rex Charles, 2003, 6–15.

Schiltz, Marc. "Habitus and Peasantisation in Nigeria: A Yoruba Case Study." *Man,* New Ser. 17 (1982): 728–46.

Schmidt, Elizabeth. *Peasants, Traders, and Wives: Shona Women in the History of Zimbabwe, 1870–1939.* Portsmouth, N.H.: Heinemann, 1992.

Segun, Mabel. "Interviews with/accounts of": (1) *Daily Sun,* Nov. 27, 2005, online: www.sunnewsonline.com/webpages/features/literari/2005/nov/27/literari-27 -11-2005-002.htm, accessed 25 Oct 2006; and (2) PEN Nigeria Center: The Nigerian Writers' Archive and Documentation Series, online: www.nigeria-pen.org/dialoga/html, accessed 25 Oct. 2006.

———. *Ping Pong: Twenty-five Years of Table Tennis.* Ibadan: Daystar Press, 1989.

Sekoni, Ropo. "Yoruba Market Dynamics and the Aesthetics of Negotiation in Female Precolonial Narrative Tradition." *Research in African Literatures,* 25 (1994): 33–46.

Sheldon, Kathleen. *Pounders of Grain: A History of Women, Work, and Politics in Mozambique.* Portsmouth, N.H.: Heinemann, 2002.

Sheldon, Kathleen, ed. *Courtyards, Markets, City Streets: Urban Women in Africa.* Boulder, Colo.: Westview Press, 1996.

Shields, Francine. "Palm Oil and Power: Women in an Era of Economic and Social Transition in 19th Century Yorubaland (South-western Nigeria)." Ph.D. thesis, University of Stirling, 1997.

———. "Women and Slavery in Historical Context: The Yoruba Area in the Nineteenth Century." Unpublished paper given at the UNESCO/SSHRC Summer Institute on Identifying Enslaved Africans, York University, Toronto, July–August 1997.

Simola, Raisa. "The Construction of a Nigerian Nationalist and Feminist, Funmilayo Ransome-Kuti." *Nordic Journal of African Studies,* 81 (1999): 94–116.

Smith, Robert. *Kingdoms of the Yoruba,* 3rd ed. Madison: University of Wisconsin Press, 1988.

Songue, Paulette Beat. "Prostitution, a *Petit-métier* during Economic Crisis: A Road to Women's Liberation? The Case of Cameroon." In Kathleen Sheldon, ed., *Courtyards, Markets, City Streets.* Boulder, Colo.: Westview Press, 1996, 241–55.

Soyinka, Wole. *Ake: The Years of Childhood.* New York: Random House, 1981.

Stiansen, Endre, and Jane I. Guyer, eds. *Credit, Currencies and Culture: African Financial Institutions in Historical Perspective.* Uppsala, Sweden: Nordiska Afrikainstitutet, 1999.

Sudarkasa, Niara. "The 'Status of Women' in Indigenous African Societies." In Rosalyn Terborg-Penn, S. Harley, and A. B. Rushing, eds., *Women in Africa and the African Diaspora.* Washington, D.C.: Howard University Press, 1987, 25–41.

———. *Where Women Work: A Study of Yoruba Women in the Marketplace and in the Home.* Ann Arbor: Museum of Anthropology, University of Michigan, 1973, a revised version of "Women, Trade, and the Yoruba Family," written as Gloria Marshall.

Tashjian, Victoria B., and Jean Allman. "Marrying and Marriage on a Shifting

Terrain: Reconfigurations of Power and Authority in Early Colonial Asanate." In Jean Allman, S. Geiger, and N. Musisi, eds., *Women in African Colonial Histories*. Bloomington: Indiana University Press, 2002, 237–59.

Thomas, Dapo. "Egbaland and the Crisis of 1948: A Critical Assessment." *Ife Journal of History,* 4 (2007): 23–53.

Timothy-Asobele, S. J. *Dance and Theatre: A Pictorial Illustration of Kabba All Women Woro Musical Ensemble.* Lagos: Upper Standard, n.d.

Trager, Lillian. "Customers and Creditors: Variations in Economic Personalism in a Nigerian Marketing System." *Ethnology,* 20 (1981): 133–46.

———. "Market Women in the Urban Economy: The Role of Yoruba Intermediaries in a Medium-Sized City." *African Urban Notes,* Series B, 2 (1975/6): 1–9.

———. "Yoruba Markets and Trade: Analysis of Spatial Structure and Social Organization in the Ijesaland Marketing System." Ph.D. dissertation, University of Washington, 1976.

———. *Yoruba Hometowns: Community, Identity, and Development in Nigeria.* Boulder, Colo.: Lynne Rienner, 2001.

Watson, Ruth. *"Civil Disorder is the Disease of Ibadan": Chieftaincy and Civic Culture in a Yoruba City.* Athens: Ohio University Press, 2003.

Watts, Susan J. "Rural Women as Food Processors and Traders: *Eko* Making in the Ilorin Area of Nigeria." *Journal of Developing Areas,* 19 (1984): 71–82.

Weisser, Gabriele. *Frauen in Männerbünden: Zur Bedeutung der Frauen in den Bünden der Yoruba.* Sozialwissenschafliche Studien zu internationalen Problemen, Band 178. Saarbrücken, Germany: Breitenbach, 1992.

White, E. Frances. *Sierra Leone's Settler Women Traders: Women on the Afro-European Frontier.* Ann Arbor: University of Michigan Press, 1987.

White, Luise. *The Comforts of Home: Prostitution in Colonial Nairobi.* Chicago: University of Chicago Press, 1990.

Witte, Hans. "The Invisible Mothers: Female Power in Yoruba Iconography." *Visible Religion,* 4 (1985): 301–25.

Yemitan, Oladipo. *Madame Tinubu: Merchant and King-Maker.* Ibadan: University Press Ltd., 1987.

Zdunnek, Gabriele. *Marktfrauen in Nigeria: Ökonomie und Politik im Leben der Yoruba-Händlerinnen.* Hamburg: Institut für Afrika-Kunde, 1987.

Index

MARJORIE KENISTON McINTOSH is Distinguished Professor of History Emerita at the University of Colorado, Boulder. Her African studies include *Women, Work, and Domestic Virtue in Uganda, 1900–2003*, written with Grace Bantebya Kyomuhendo, which received the 2007 Aidoo-Snyder Prize awarded by the Women's Caucus of the African Studies Association. She is also author of *Working Women in English Society, 1300–1620* and *Controlling Misbehavior in England, 1370–1600*.